THE COSMOLOGY OF
GIORDANO BRUNO

PAUL HENRI MICHEL

The Cosmology of
Giordano Bruno

Translated by
Dr R. E. W. Maddison, F.S.A.
Librarian of the Royal Astronomical Society

HERMANN: PARIS
METHUEN: LONDON
CORNELL UNIVERSITY PRESS: ITHACA, NEW YORK

Translated from the original French text *La cosmologie de Giordano Bruno*, published by Hermann, Paris, in 1962 in their series *Histoire de la Pensée*

English translation © 1973 by Hermann, Paris
Published in France by Hermann
293 rue Lecourbe 75015 Paris
Published in Great Britain by Methuen & Co Ltd
11 New Fetter Lane, London EC4
Published in the USA, Canada and Mexico by Cornell University Press
124 Roberts Place, Ithaca, New York 14850

ISBN (Hermann) 2 7056 5674 X
ISBN (Methuen) 0 416 76990 X
ISBN (Cornell)   0–8014–0509–2

Library of Congress Catalog Card Number 72–13062

Contents

Giordano Bruno in Legend and History

One of the privileges, if indeed it can be regarded as such, that Bruno shares with many great men, but which he possesses to an unusual degree, is to be at once famous and unknown, renowned and obscure. Much has been written about him. A bibliography of articles relating to him, published in 1926 by Virgilio Salvestrini of Pisa, and then continued down to 1950 by Luigi Firpo, contains about two thousand items. Nevertheless, most people at the present time who have heard his name know nothing about him except that he was burnt at the stake.

During his lifetime he was far from being unnoticed; his reputation, sometimes, but not always, based on scandal, reached the highest ranks of society. Popes and kings interested themselves in his works, particularly his mnemotechnic secrets—a dubious and precarious glory that was soon clouded by his trial and extinguished by his condemnation. The new physics and the new astronomy, scared by his death, refrained from paying him tribute. His name is not mentioned by Galileo in the *Nuncius sidereus*. True, Kepler expressed surprise at this omission; and Martin Hasdale in a letter dated 15 April 1610 informed Galileo to that effect, but Galileo remained deaf to such diffident protests: he never even evoked the memory of Bruno. The silence of Descartes, even though broken two or three times by a fleeting allusion, is no less significant. Beneath the veil of almost total oblivion, often voluntary and long maintained, the elements of a legend, itself the prelude to passionate exegesis, have been developed.

The legend first of all appears as a pious fiction, for only those who approved of the severity of the Holy Office, or who, at least, were bent on justifying it, dared to raise their voices. Thus, an enlightened person such as Marin Mersenne, an avowed anti-Aristotelian and open to all scientific innovations, saw Bruno as 'the most dangerous thinker . . . of deists, atheists or free-thinkers'. This opinion pre-

9

vailed without any counterbalance throughout the whole of the seventeenth century; it is expressed with surprising brutality in the first edition (1696) of Bayle's *Dictionnaire*, where a short notice, which is moreover full of inaccuracies, makes Bruno an 'abominable' character. The eighteenth century scarcely modified a portrait already painted in the darkest colours. Subsequent editions (1701–1715) of the *Dictionnaire* made no change. Quétif and Echard, in their bibliography of the preaching-friars,[1] avoid giving a list of Bruno's writings simply by refusing to acknowledge him to be a Dominican: 'There is no document, (they say), to prove that he ever wore the habit of St Dominic!' Therefore, there was no need to mention his writings. In the nineteenth century the myth of a diabolical Bruno persisted, but the literature to which it gave rise was smaller in quantity, and being less virulent was half stifled by the lively growth of another literature, the expression of another myth that suddenly arose and soon triumphed.

It is remarkable that the new legend bases its authority on the same facts as the first one, as well as on the same errors. As for the facts, (by which we mean those relating to biography), the new legend confines itself to presenting them in a fresh light and giving them another meaning: that which was only sound justice becomes martyrdom. Moreover, it claims to restore truth to the facts; it strives to do so, and on occasion corrects certain flagrant inaccuracies, which had been long accepted without verification. As for the errors (those relating to the interpretation of Bruno's thought and betraying inadequate knowledge, when it is not complete ignorance of his writings), they are not corrected; on the contrary, they have been piously collected together in order to be used for other purposes: the accusations of innate godlessness, atheism and materialism are retained, but to the glory of the accused and not to his shame. In this way the elements of a new portrait, lacking fidelity just as much as the former, notwithstanding the good intentions of those who inspired it, have been assembled. A character is established in conventional imagery, and becomes familiar to a fresh public of devotees, just as incapable as the former one of judging its authenticity. Finally, after 1870, statues were erected to him in Italy: at Rome, where, mighty and saturnine, he dominates the *Campo dei Fiori*, the very site of his execution; at Naples, in one of the courtyards of the University; and elsewhere, too. Numerous political and partisan manifestations provide the pretext for exalting his genius as much as his character, and, naturally, seeing that he was the victim of obscurantism and ignorance, his profound learning. He has been credited with attainments to which he never made any claim, nor ever possessed. Certain apologists even go so far as to make him a mathematician, whereas he himself on every possible occasion proclaimed himself to be an enemy of mathematics and any mathematization of physics.

The work carried out in the field of Brunonian studies during the nineteenth century is none the less admirable. Parallel with and independently of the two legends, one of which suddenly springs into life whilst the other stubbornly survives, history comes into action and gradually supplants them both. In this connection particular importance must be given to the decade 1840–1850, a decisive turning point, or rather starting point, for historical research. In 1846–1847, Christian Bartholmess published his *Jordano Bruno*, in two volumes, at Paris; it was immediately followed by Moritz Carrière's *Die philosophische Weltanschauung der Reformationszeit in ihren Beziehungen zur Gegenwart*,[2] a large part of which is devoted to Giordano Bruno. These two authors certainly have a sympathetic approach to their subject, and the impartiality with which they treat it is instructive besides being noteworthy. At a much later date, Spampanato wrote of Bartholmess, 'he did not allow himself to succumb to the temptation to exaggerate the merits of his hero, nor to minimize or suppress his faults'.

It is perhaps surprising that these first attempts at biography and criticism without passion should have seen the light of day in France and Germany rather than in Italy. The political conditions in the peninsula—especially in the Kingdom of Naples up to 1860—suffice to explain a delay which would otherwise have been made good, before completion of Italian unity, by the analysis of Roberto Spaventa[3] and by the documented biography of Domenico Berti.[4]

After 1870, the amount of bibliographic material relating to Bruno defies description. We can only refer the reader to Salvestrini's compilation, which is most detailed and carefully assembled; it has the sole defect, arising from its completeness, that works of real value are rather lost amongst a mass of occasional articles or pamphlets, which have not always been inspired by a regard for truth.

In 1880, Berti published his *Documenti*, an indispensable accompaniment to his *Vita*; that work provides the starting point for all subsequent biographical study. Berti's works were revised, annotated and corrected in various places by Vincenzo Spampanato, whose *Vita di Giordano Bruno*[5] is authoritative. The Latin works of Bruno (*Opera latine conscripta*) appeared over the years 1879–1891 under the direction of Francesco Fiorentino; they are in eight volumes, the last of which contains previously unpublished manuscripts from Moscow, Augsburg and Erlangen. Until these volumes were published, the Latin works had been available to the public only through the incomplete edition of Gfrörer.[6] The slightly better known works in the vernacular, the texts of which had been established by Paul de Lagarde,[7] were reissued under the editorship of Giovanni Gentile, first in 1907, and again in 1925.

Amongst the historians, philologists and philosophers who have studied the life and teachings of Bruno, and whose writings we have on many occasions had need to consult, we must mention Felice Tocco, Erminio Troilo, Émile Namer, Léonard Olschki, Augusto Guzzo, Antonio Corsano, Rodolfo Mondolfo, Luigi Cicuttini, Frances A. Yates, Dorothea W. Singer, Giovanni Aquilecchia, and especially Mgr Angelo Mercati who published *Il Sommario del processo di G. Bruno* preserved in the archives of the Vatican. This list of acknowledgements is by no means exhaustive.

It is only to be expected that these authors, according to their own convictions, should have different opinions on the character of Bruno, his thought and even the circumstances of his death; but not one of them has failed to observe the scrupulous discipline of history, and all of them through their writings have contributed to restore the authentic character of a great historical figure whom we in our turn are now able, thanks to them, to describe without running too much risk of departing from the truth.

The life of Giordano Bruno—his outward life, the chain of events that interest a biographer—may be divided into three periods; they are so distinct that one is tempted to call them three acts, or even three epochs. The first and longest covers his childhood at his birthplace and his youth at Naples until he left the monastery (1548–1576); the second covers his travels and adventures across Europe (1576–1591); the last starts with his return to Italy, continues with his imprisonment, and ends with his being condemned to death (1591–1600).

Nola, a small town situated to the east of Naples and episcopal see of which St Paulinus (*d.* 431) had been bishop, derived its glory from its great Samnite antiquity and from the siege which it withstood against Hannibal as much as from a sermon by St Peter and the records of its religious history. Bruno was born there in 1548; his father was a soldier, 'man at arms', in the Spanish service; he was given the baptismal name of Filippo. Very little is known about his earliest years. However, his works sometimes reveal echoes of the musings inspired by the horizons of his little universe, bounded on one side by Monte Cicala, close and verdant, and on the other by Vesuvius, distant and gloomy. They were horizons of childhood destined to be crossed over; bounds which gave promise of boundlessness; and above all they were, as Filippo noted in his youth and as Giordano said later, illusory differences likely to disappear and then reappear reversed, because they are merely the effect of distance: thus, Vesuvius when seen close to appears verdant whilst Monte Cicala becomes gloomy and indistinct.

In 1565, when he was seventeen years old, Filippo Bruno entered the monastery of S. Domenico at Naples; he took the habit of the Preaching Friars and received the name of Giordano, which he retained from that time onwards and to which he gave lustre. One year later, in 1566, he took his first vows; he was ordained priest in 1572; and became doctor of theology in 1575. His training was therefore that of a theologian; and, as a philosopher, it was that of an Aristotelian: 'I was nurtured, (he wrote), in peripatetic disciplines. . . .' That was obvious, even without the admission and in spite of the violence of his polemics, for he remained always more or less attached to the language of the Schoolmen and their methods of argument, even in the account of deliberately anti-Aristotelian physics and cosmology. On the other hand, he never denied his profound admiration for him whom he designated as 'the light and honour of peripateticism'—St Thomas Aquinas.

Up to 1575, there was nothing to give any warning of his revolt and flight. We do not know what took place within him; but the little that is known of the circumstances of his life allows us to guess that his intellectual gifts were noticed by his superiors and secured him favours that were not limited to the narrow circle of the monastery. In 1571, Pius V called him to Rome in order to receive instruction in the *ars memoriae*—mnemotechny, a subject that Bruno never ceased to cultivate with great assiduity. In 1572, the same pope accepted dedication of his first work, a moral and allegorical account of Noah's ark: the work has not survived.

In 1576, he fled. The immediate reasons for this sudden flight are obscure. We know that two legal proceedings had been instituted against him, for his name appears twice in the *Index processatorum, 1527–1621*, on pages 29 and 30, but no details are given. The files relating to the two cases, presumably requisitioned by the Holy Office, must have disappeared at the same time as the other documents connected with the trial at Rome. There is no doubt but that Giordano showed himself to be intractable, stubborn and rather unsociable; he openly derided his brothers in religion, and certain outward forms of catholic devotion inspired him with a scorn which he hardly troubled to disguise. A certain passage in the *Spaccio della bestia trionfante* (3rd Dialogue) dealing with the tail of the she-ass that carried Jesus to Jerusalem reveals what he thought about relics; and by his statements from Venice we know that he removed the pictures of saints from his cell in the monastery at Naples, but allowed the crucifix to remain. Such facts betray the intellectual character of his personal religion and possibly also a veiled hostility to paintings—and to any work of art.

His departure from Naples, assigned by Berti to the close of 1576, took place, as shown by Spampanato, in February of that year: Bruno was still at the monastery on 30 January, but already at Rome in March. He did not remain there for long; it was hardly safer for him to stay in Rome than in Naples. He took the road once more northward; he passed through Siena, Lucca, and stayed for four months in the small town of Noli in Liguria, where he gave instruction in the sphere (*i.e.* astronomy) to a group of gentlemen and taught grammar to the children. Noli was only a halting place, where he remained a little longer than in others, in a travel across northern Italy that lasted for another two years. At Milan, in 1578, he resumed the religious habit that he had abandoned on leaving Naples. Dressed in this way, he crossed the Alps and arrived at Chambéry before winter.

There, as Montaigne discovered on his return from Italy, 'On parle français'. Bruno, being really out of his element for the first time, sought refuge in the Dominican monastery, one of the twenty-seven monasteries of the Order maintained by the Gallican Congregation in the province of France. The bad season being over, he thought of setting off again, but an Italian priest advised him not to go further in that way (meaning thereby, France), 'where he would find little sympathy'. Bruno, therefore, set out for Geneva, which town (he was assured) welcomed heretics, the unorthodox, exiles from all countries and of all religious persuasions. His disappointment was matched by his first enthusiasm: he was to learn to his cost that the Venerable

Consistory, where Antoine de La Faye held sway after Calvin and Théodore de Bèze, was no less intolerant than the Holy Office at Rome. Having registered himself as a student at the University, he was soon in disagreement with his teachers. Being unable to reply on the spot by word of mouth, he caused a pamphlet to be printed in which the opinions of La Faye were bluntly contradicted. Punishment for such audacity was not delayed: he was arrested together with his printer, imprisoned, and threatened with the direst punishment (August 1579). He secured his release from prison only by acknowledging his guilt and on condition that the scandalous libel should be destroyed—as was done, unfortunately, down to the last copy. Finally, Bruno had to present himself before the Consistory and solemnly acknowledge his errors for a second time.

After this misadventure, he fled Geneva as he had fled Naples three years before. He stayed at Lyons for several weeks (September–October, 1579); and thence, after passing through Avignon and Montpellier, he reached Toulouse, where he was attracted by the fame of an ancient, flourishing university.

Toulouse was the place in which he made by far the longest stay during these first years of exile. He remained there about twenty months; and if the troubles caused by the civil wars made him decide to remove, at least he was never troubled personally whilst he was there. He was honourably received, as is attested by the account of his life preserved amongst the documents relating to his trial at Venice; a chair at the University was bestowed upon him; he gave instruction there, as at Noli, in astronomy, and gave a commentary on Aristotle's *De Anima*. These lectures were written and probably printed, but nothing remains of them. Seeing that the registers of the University earlier than 1682 no longer exist, there is no surviving record of Bruno's career at Toulouse. The exact date of his departure is unknown. We know that he was still at Toulouse in the middle of 1581, and that he was at Paris before the end of summer.

Contrary to the discouraging warnings of the Italian priests at Chambéry, he found friends and followers at Paris as he had done at Toulouse. He taught mnemotechny and theology; and was presented to Henri III, who was just as curious about the *ars memoriae* as Pius V had been. His thirty lectures on the divine attributes have not been printed and the text is unknown, though it may still be hidden in some collection of manuscripts in the form of notes. On the other hand, in 1582, he published *De umbris idearum* and three

15

treatises on mnemotechny. These are the earliest works of his that have survived.

In the spring of 1573, being furnished with royal letters of introduction to Michel de Castelnau, ambassador of Henri III to Queen Elizabeth, he left Paris for London. His newly acquired celebrity drew suspicion on him. Cobham, the English ambassador at Paris, thought it necessary to inform Walsingham, secretary of state, that 'doctor Giordano Bruno of Nola, professor of philosophy, whose religion I cannot commend intends to pass into England'.

From 1583 to 1585, he divided his time between Oxford, where he taught, and London, where he lived as a gentleman at the French embassy, and where he published in the vernacular his six treatises in the form of dialogues, using false imprints of Venice and Paris. Three of them were dedicated to Michel de Castelnau, the other three to Sir Philip Sidney, the poet. It was in England, too, that he undertook the drafting of his Latin cosmological poems, which were completed in Germany and printed at Frankfurt in 1591.

He retained happy memories of the two years spent 'in the temperate climate of Great Britain'. Nevertheless, there, as everywhere else, the violence of his controversy raised hostility about him, especially at Oxford, a stronghold of Aristotelianism, amongst those doctors 'whose pedantic pig-headedness (he said), would tire the patience of Job', which he was far from possessing.

At the end of 1585, Castelnau was recalled from London. Bruno returned to France with him, but left his service. At Paris, midst all kinds of material difficulties and disputes, he found time to publish an account of Aristotle's physics (*Figuratio aristotelici Physici auditus*, 1586). He made an attempt at reconciliation with ecclesiastical authority: he begged the Nuncio to ask the Pope to annul his excommunication, but without requiring him to resume the monk's habit. The Nuncio, however, judged it impossible to make the request involving, as it did, a condition.

After returning from England, Bruno was without employment; he lived 'at his own expense', that is to say, no doubt, from what he gained by giving lessons. After his setback with the Nuncio, there was nothing to keep him in Paris more than elsewhere; so, he did not delay setting out on his travels again. He then went to seek his fortune in Germany. After having crossed the Rhineland and Hesse, he came to Wittenberg on the Elbe, south of Magdeburg (summer, 1586). After twenty months of comparative tranquillity, he was again in conflict with the local religious authorities, the Calvinists—who had never forgiven him—having put the Lutherans in the background. In March 1588, he left Wittenberg for Prague, where he did not stay long, because he was unable to find adequate means of subsistence. Turning northwards, he reached Helmstedt, where he was excommunicated (once more!) by the Consistory of which Gisbert Voët was the chief pastor. However, thanks to the protection of Heinrich Julius, Herzog von Braunschweig, he held his own against his adversaries, and worked relentlessly on his cosmological poems. Finally, after a year and a half—the normal duration for him of a lengthy stay anywhere—he decided to leave (20 August 1590).

The final stages of his wanderings embraced Frankfurt, Zürich and then Frankfurt again, where his three Latin poems appeared in 1591: the *De Minimo* for the Spring Fair, the *De Monade* and the *De Immenso* for the Autumn Fair. He was able to supervise complete production of the first item only, for he left Frankfurt during the summer.

In response to a call from, and relying on the promises of, Giovanni Mocenigo, patrician of Venice, who wished to be initiated into the secrets of mnemotechny, Bruno returned to Italy, passing through Bavaria and the Tyrol; before the end of August, he was at Venice. To his misfortune, that was the end of the journey and the beginning of the tragedy that ended at the stake.

In addition to mnemotechny, Bruno gave instruction in geometry to his pupil. The lessons must have started in October, seeing that during his preliminary interrogations in May 1592 he stated that they were continued for seven or eight months. He was lodged first at Padua, then at Venice in the Mocenigo palace. Up to the end of April there was nothing to foreshadow the denunciation that was to destroy him, and which Spampanato calls 'the foulest of betrayals'. In May, Bruno expressed a wish to go to Frankfurt for the purpose of superintending the printing of his latest works which he had left with Johann Wechel. He promised to return to Venice as soon as possible. Mocenigo, being distrustful, opposed the journey; he feared that his teacher would lavish everywhere the famous 'secrets' that he wanted to reserve to himself. Bruno insisted and made ready to depart. It was then that Mocenigo denounced him as an enemy of religion and the founder of a sect. Arrested, pulled from his bed that very night, Bruno was taken the next day (23 May 1592) to the prison of the

Holy Office. Three days later he appeared before his judges who demanded an account of all his doings and of all his philosophical opinions. Interrogation followed interrogation. Put on record and fortunately preserved, they constitute the chief biographical source of Bruno. They provided him, in effect, with the opportunity of giving a very circumstantial account of his life, besides a justification of his teaching.

According to the Venetian documents published by Berti, and afterwards by Spampanato, it appears that this first trial could have ended without too much harm to the accused. On the one hand, the judges seemed inclined to leniency; on the other, the 'delinquent' admitted his errors—a proceeding that must have awakened memories of his misfortune at Geneva—and declared his intention of offering to the Pope his latest work which was due to be published. The affair became complicated in September, when Rome demanded extradition of the fugitive Dominican. It was at first refused, but in January 1593, the Venetian senate, being desirous for political results to give satisfaction to Clement VIII, yielded to the insistence of Rome, and by a large majority agreed to the extradition that was so imperiously demanded. Bruno left Venice in February; he was at Rome, and in prison, on the 27th of the same month.

Concerning the much longer, and unfortunately more obscure, trial at Rome, we are certain only of its outcome. The documents had been stored at the Vatican until the beginning of the nineteenth century without ever being studied by historians, either because they were indifferent or too prudent. Curiosity was eventually awakened, but too late. In 1810, part of the Roman archives were taken to Paris on the orders of Napoleon whose intention was to centralize the secret archives of all Europe in the capital of the Empire. The treaties of 1815 stipulated that the documents so removed should be restored to their countries of origin; and it was whilst they were on their return journey, between 1815 and 1817, that the documents relating to Bruno's trial disappeared. Mgr Mercati assumes that they were mixed up with a lot of valueless files and, presumably, burnt. Fortunately, the erudite chief of the Vatican archives discovered a *Summary* of the trial in 1940, and published it in 1942.[8] Whatever interest these extracts may have, they do not console us for the loss of the original documents, particularly as they were drawn up at the end of 1597 and throw no light on the final stages of the trial, which are covered only by some later additions. Nevertheless, thanks to the information contained in the *Summary*, coupled with the evidence of contemporaries, certain facts may be considered to be adequately established.

1. The main charges.—Some are of a purely religious nature: denial of Christ's divinity; mythical character of the Holy Writ; belief in universal salvation at the end of time, and particularly salvation of the fallen angels. Others concern the philosophical and scientific opinions set forth in the Latin and the vernacular cosmological treatises, especially in the *Cena de le Ceneri*, in the treatise *De l'Infinito Universo et Mondi*, and in *De Immenso*: eternity of the universe, plurality of worlds, rejection of geocentrism, etc.

2. The change in attitude of Giordano in the course of his trial.—The documents surviving from the two trials, Venetian and Roman, pose a psychological problem from which it is impossible to escape, even though we are not in a position to resolve it.

In the course of his numerous interrogations Bruno gave an account of his life, as was required of him, and gave a summary of his teachings. His answers were always to the point; he argued, but without asperity; he smiled, and occasionally joked; he knew when to appear conciliating, either by accommodating his own ideas to catholic dogma, or, when the disagreement was insurmountable, by simply complying and admitting that he had not conformed in his thought 'to that which one should believe'. With the passage of years, he seemed to have trod more and more the path of repentance, and to such a point that in December 1598 he was considered worthy of having use again of the breviary of the Preaching Friars (*Provideatur ei de breviario, quo utuntur fratres ordinis praedicatorum*). In April 1599, he acknowledged his guilt. He remained (or seemed to remain), in this frame of mind for several months longer, as is attested for the last time by a document dated 24 August. Now, there is another document, dated 16 September, which notes the fact of his obstinacy and continued persistence in error. He never wavered from this final stiffening of opinion. We know the famous reply he made to his judges on the day he was condemned: 'Perhaps you have greater fear in passing sentence on me than I have in hearing it' (*Majori forsitan cum timore sententiam in me fertis quam ego accipiam*). He surrendered to his doom with the same steadfastness, whereas he could have avoided it by making retraction and submission. They were asked of him right to the end. He refused to make them.

There we have the terms of the problem. Francesco Olgiati in a work[9] published in 1924 under the auspices of the Università Cattolica del Sacro Cuore pays tribute to this lofty attitude in a man who, throughout his life, gave proof of many kindnesses and great versatility. After having recalled that Bruno, a catholic at Rome when he was counting on the Pope's protection, was very close to becoming a Calvinist on arriving at Geneva; that he made an enthusiastic panegyric on Martin Luther, 'a new Alcides has risen on the banks of the Elbe', when at Wittenberg; and that he had done the same for Queen Elizabeth, when at London, Olgiati then deals with the changes in Bruno during his trial. However, he limits himself to stating the facts, and takes care not to draw any conclusions.

In the light of the fresh documents that he published in 1942, Mgr Mercati has tried, for the first time, to explain the sudden, belated and final intransigence of Bruno which cost him his life. 'This fresh attitude (he wrote), the indubitable sign of a troubled mind and perhaps even of a psychic change, was interpreted by his judges as stubbornness and obstinacy.' The writer of those lines admits the mistake of the judges, but the unduly medical nature of his diagnosis has caused surprise and, sometimes, offence.[10] It might have been more generous and, we hope, truer to admit, that this surge of energy, far from betraying a clouding of the mind, was, on the contrary, evidence of a supreme and lucid effort of the 'heroic frenzy'.

3. The execution 17 February 1600.—According to the usual practice for autos-da-fé at Rome, those condemned to the stake were executed in prison and burnt in effigy. Consequently, various authors, such as Haym, Quadrio, Moreri and Bayle, have believed it possible to deny the atrocious exception to this rule in the case of Bruno. Unfortunately, there is no doubt whatever, seeing that the execution was public and was mentioned by several witnesses (Letter from Gaspard Schopp, written on the very day; *Relations de la Compagnie de San Giovanni decollato*); Bruno died at the stake.

The above notes are no more than an incomplete recital of a sequence of events. They give no more than a preliminary idea of the character of a man whose tormented life consisted not only of fortuitous vicissitudes, but also was to a very considerable extent subjected to innate law or will-power which expressed itself, depending on the circumstances, through sudden impulses or mature decisions. We should like to know him better, and first of all to *see him* as he was. Unfortunately, his statues are not very helpful. They are tributes to a martyr and exhibit only too clearly their polemical intent; they set before us a kind of robust giant, massive and muffled; the size of his limbs and the ampleness of his clothing symbolize to the best advantage the twofold dignity of heroism and character.

Fortunately, a portrait of Bruno survives: it is somewhat suspect, although it does have the advantage of going back to its subject indirectly. It was engraved at Paris by C. Meyer in the first quarter of the nineteenth century and was based on an old engraving belonging to a collector at Munich that had possibly been taken from a lost work of Bruno's to which it might have been the frontispiece. This portrait was reproduced for the first time by T. A. Rixner and T. Siber in their work *Leben und Lehrmeinungen berühmter Physiker am Ende des 16. und Anfang des 17. Jahrhunderts* (Sulzbach, 1819–1826); it was published again by Francesco Flora in his edition of the *Eroici furori* (Turin, 1928), by Luigi Firpo in his revised edition of Salvestrini's *Bibliography*, as well as by other writers. The original engraving has not survived, so there is nothing to guarantee the fidelity of the copy made by Meyer. However, presumption is favourable: we have before us a lively man, rather thin, with an abundant head of hair, a slight moustache, and dreamy eyes. He is young; he still wears the white robe of the Dominicans.

Young? Was he not ever thus? When could he have had the time to grow old? We must not forget he died at the age of fifty-two, after eight years of seclusion. His career as a man of letters and as a philosopher was of the shortest: it started late and ended soon. All his works that have come down to us were written between 1582 and 1592, between his thirty-fifth and forty-fifth years.

His character is revealed on every page of his books, especially in the dedications, prefaces and forewords where he readily unburdens himself. His friendships were passionate, his enmities fierce. He was violent in controversy; his anti-Aristotelianism could not be expressed only in articulate, reasoned arguments, but needed vehement sarcasm and invective against the Master, his followers, whether heathen, christian or arab, and even against his opponents when he considered them incapable of carrying on a good battle. He had no mercy on Pierre de la Ramée (Ramus) and Francesco Patrizi (Patricius). As for

Aristotle himself, a burlesque dialogue displays him reincarnated as an ass, who having acquired better principles admits and deplores his former errors.

The out-spokenness of the writer (and his courage, too, for the satire on Aristotle was not without its danger at a time when the Schools imposed their law everywhere) was only one aspect of his impetuous nature, impatient of all restraint. There are others: the vow of chastity seemed to him no less irksome than the vow of obedience. In the letter to Sir Philip Sidney, which prefaces the dialogues of the *Eroici furori*, he proclaims without any cloak of false modesty—even quite unblushingly—what he thinks of sexual appetite and unreasonable demand. Having first of all contrasted 'heroic' or 'sacred' love (*i.e.*, that which has the First Principle for its object) with 'profane' love, he expresses the opinion that man should not on any account become a slave to the latter: 'In so far as women are concerned, there is one thing that I am safe in holding in abomination; it is that love based on passionate and inordinate sensual pleasure which certain individuals entertain for them, surrendering themselves thereto to such a degree that their whole being is enslaved thereby, and the powers and noblest acts of their intellectual life become subjected to it.' Nevertheless man should make use of the faculties he has received from his Creator: 'Is it for me to oppose the sacred order of nature? . . . God forbid that such a thought should ever enter my head.' In fact, it never had, and he bluntly says: '. . . I have never had a desire to become a eunuch. On the contrary, I should be ashamed if I agreed to yield on that score were it only a hair to any man worth his salt in order to serve nature and God . . . I do not believe in being tied, for I am certain that all the laces and tags that all present and future dealers in laces and tags have ever been able, or will be able, to plait or knot, even though they were aided by death itself, would not suffice for that purpose.' He admitted later (see the documents in Mercati, p. 102) that if, as regards the number of women, he had not rivalled King Solomon, at least he had done his best.

With regard to the intellectual portrait of Giordano Bruno, which is of even more interest to us than his physical and moral portrait, an outline of his teachings will disclose the essential features. However, it will perhaps be convenient as a preliminary to outline some revealing details, not of elaborated thoughts, but of the background and climate from which they sprang.

Hasty in enthusiasm, Bruno never forgave those who disappointed him: his expressions of admiration, forthwith repudiated, gave place to ironic repentance, or to vengeful anger. Fabrizio Mordente, a mathematician of Naples, had designed a compass which made it possible 'to divide any line in to as many equal or unequal parts as one wished'; Bruno, after having declared this invention to be 'almost divine', withdrew his most flattering opinion, and, in a dialogue entitled *The Idiot Triumphant*, derided him whom he had erstwhile treated as the greatest mathematical genius of all time.

Susceptible to the effect of surprise, Bruno himself experienced the desire to give surprise—a desire which sometimes took precedence of persuasion. Nothing pleased him more than to reveal to some impatient and admiring listener the secrets of mnemotechny, which consisted only in the association of ideas with symbolic figures and in exercising the memory by requiring an extra effort on its part. His liking for paradox was so great that he never rid himself of it even under the severities of prison life. The Capuchin friar, Celestino, one of his companions in captivity at Venice, reports that when speaking of Cain and Abel he maintained that he was an upright man, a Pythagorean before Pythagoras, not allowing the murder of animals, and that he was right to kill that wretched person who was his brother. This utterance was repeated to his judges, who, with a certain warmth of feeling, demanded an explanation of it. Giordano maintained that he had said it jokingly, and that if it were wrong to kill animals, then it was certainly more so to kill one's brother.

Behaviour of that kind betrays care-free capriciousness; at first it was regarded only as insolence, but it is ascribable to a long misunderstood form of expression. At the beginning of the century, Bruno was still, or almost, excluded from handbooks of literature: some few lines barely recalled that he was the author of a comedy, *Candelaio*, lost amongst a confused mass of didactic and philosophical work. The writer was neglected; the poet was ignored; following the fashion of the time, it was forgotten that, like Lucretius, he had given a poetic form to his Latin cosmological work; and that though his vernacular treatises are in prose, a prose moreover admirable for its liveliness and vigour, yet they are interspersed with sonnets and songs recited or improvised by the speakers of the dialogue.

That is especially true of the *Eroici furori*, in which Bruno reveals himself not only as a poet, but also as a theoretician of poetry. The first dialogue starts in effect with an invocation to the Muses, which is not a simple exercise in rhetoric but promises a debate in which the author finds occasion to express through his characters (particularly Tansillo) the outcome of his meditations on the value of the rules, which 'are derived from poetry', and would in no wise be able 'to give birth to it'; on the true rule, identified with the hidden methodical arrangement of internal necessity, so that there are 'as many true rules as there are true poets'; on the liberty and spontaneity of the mind. In this dispute in which, in short, *rule* is opposed by *frenzy*—in other words Aristotle and Plato—the author rallies to the side of Plato and the platonists, as one would expect from the title of the work itself.

One could say that such poetics had their inspiration in Seneca's *Phaedra*, but it would be fairer to say they find confirmation there, seeing that there is no textual confirmation of their source. They agree well with their author's impetuous temperament, or rather, they enable us to understand the nature of this impetuosity; they illuminate their profundity; and finally they prepare us for reading the poems whose main purpose is to put the themes of profane love on to a spiritual plane, where ecstasy, anguish, despair or exaltation of the soul in search of the divine are expressed in a generous profusion of myths and symbols. Bruno's poetry leads us straight to his religion, and it is here that we must, above all, take care to avoid the snare of legend. Bruno was undeniably rebel and heterodox; his refusal of any positive *credo*, and the freedom with which he derided the most venerable rites have caused him to be refused, and not without reason, the character of a christian; quite wrongly, however, he has been denied the character of 'friend of God', whereas in his metaphysical dialogues he entrusts the task of setting forth his teaching to characters who are not called Philotheus or Theophilus by accident.

On this matter which has been discussed for so long and with so much passion, certain facts should be remembered:

As a Doctor of Theology he was fully aware of the dogmas of his religion. He knew them so well, that in his defence (the Venetian documents confirm this) he makes them agree with his principles with such subtlety that it is best not to be deceived thereby. On the other hand, there can be no question as to his candour, for when his judges demanded an account of certain passages in his works to which exception was taken, he answered that even if he were familiar with the opinions of great reformers, he was neither convinced nor blinded by them: 'I have read the works of Melanchthon, Luther,

Calvin and other tramontane heretics, not for the purpose of learning their doctrine nor to avail myself of it, *for I consider them more ignorant than myself,* but out of curiosity. . . .'

The defence was clever, but specious in view of the fact that the speaker regarded the orthodoxy of the Roman Church with the same detachment as he did the heresies, and was not afraid to subject it to the same criticism and to rate it as being in need of the same purging. In fact, on the one hand, he rejects that which seems to him to belong to superstitious practice; and on the other hand, he gives a philosophical interpretation to that which he believes he can rescue. His attitude towards the Church recalls that of the Pythagoreans of the first century towards classical paganism. This comparison is suggested, notwithstanding the obvious difference between the historical circumstances, by Giordano Bruno himself, who on so many occasions betrays his preference for the adepts of Pythagoreanism, especially for Virgil whose authority he is fond of quoting, not failing to describe him by the expression *il pitagorico poeta*.

With regard to Bruno's religious opinions, the greatest mistake would therefore be to seek proof of profound impiety in his attacks on established religions, whereas on the contrary he never ceased to be prey to obsession with the divine, attracted by the darkness of the unknowable in the same way that a butterfly (he said so himself, using an image, the sad prophetic nature of which he was unaware) is attracted by light and the flame which consumes it.

NOTES

1. *Scriptores Ordinis Praedicatorum*, Paris, 1719.
2. Stuttgart and Tübingen, 1847. See pages 365 to 494 for Bruno.
3. Roberto Spaventa, *Saggi di critica filosofica, politica e religiosa*, Napoli, 1867, pp. 137–267.
4. Domenico Berti, *La vita di Giordano da Nola*, Torino, 1868.
5. *Vita di Giordano Bruno, con documenti editi e inediti*, Messina, 1921.
6. Friedrich Gfrörer, *Jordani Bruni Nolani Scripta, quae latine confecit, omnia . . .*, Stuttgart, 1836, 2 vols.
7. *Le Opere italiane di Giordano Bruno*, Göttingen, 1888, 2 vols.
8. Angelo Mercati, *Il Sommario del processo di G. Bruno . . .*, Città del Vaticano, 1942, Studi e testi, vol. 101.
9. *L'Anima dell' Umanesimo e del Rinascimento*, Milan, 1924.
10. Benedetto Croce has given an account of Mgr Mercati's work in an article entitled 'Insultes à Giordano Bruno', (*La Critica*, 1942, pp. 283–284), in which he insinuates that the documents relating to the trial at Rome, missing since 1817, were deliberately destroyed.

The Cosmology of Giordano Bruno

Introduction

If cosmology be worthy of the name of a science, it is undoubtedly, of all sciences, the one that bristles most with inaccessible heights, and nevertheless the one that is most generally open to enquiries of the mind, for the questions raised by the subject are not only insoluble but also directed to everyone in a compelling manner. The man does not exist to whom at some time in his life these questions have not occurred, and who has not then experienced, in a manner most suitable to his character, the attraction of the unfathomable: vaguely formulated misgivings or the glow of faith, bewilderment or mental strain. Few, however, adventure beyond the field of enquiry, and their answers, however wide the knowledge on which they are based, are never more than temporary hypotheses or decisions of the mind. Furthermore, they do not differ greatly, or at least, they can be separated into a small number of groups. The universe is either finite or infinite, continuous or discontinuous, created or uncreated, eternal or limited in time, etc. Combinations of Yes and No to these possibilities provide a short list of solutions, and seeing that all of them have been proposed and defended, it seems that we should have the greatest difficulty, in respect of a given system, in revealing its true elements. It is a fact, however, that the reading of certain texts—even when superabounding in quotations and reminiscences as do those left by Giordano Bruno—impresses us with a feeling of unimpeachable originality; a feeling, moreover, which will be verified by a fuller examination, provided that this originality be sought not so much in the solutions as in the conditions of the problems, and not so much in the substance of the arguments as in the method and style of the argument. If the dilemmas in which all logical thought easily wraps itself yield so few end-points in such a domain, nevertheless, the starting-points and possible routes are innumerable; consequently, the writings of a philosopher who has meditated on the problem of the universe will always have, whether he wants it or not, the character of a testimony, a personal confidence, all the more precious and moving the more the 'frenzies' of his intellect are inseparable from those of poetry and love.

If we intend to pick out the irreducible originality contained in a system of the universe, we shall look at it from this point of view; but that will not make it unnecessary to isolate the conclusions for the purpose of considering them independently of the way in which they are expressed and the vicissitudes of their genesis, for it is in this way that the system will no longer appear unique but in relation to other systems; in this way it will become possible to classify it and place it in historical perspective. We have there two ways or methods of approach which must be followed; and they are particularly applicable to our present study from the fact of the remarkable personality of Giordano Bruno, and the importance of the time when his work was developed, which time coincides with the extreme decadence of geocentrism, and, as regards cosmology, with a turning point in history.

I. THE HISTORICAL CONTEXT

In the twelfth century, Aristotle's *Physica* and *De Coelo* were incorporated in the scientific inheritance of the West through the efforts of Domenico Gonzalez, Gerard of Cremona and Michael Scot, who made Latin translations of those works from Arabic versions. Almost simultaneously Ptolemy's *Almagest* was translated.[1] From that time onwards, in spite of stubborn resistance,[2] a system of the universe came into its own, and for long after remained a subject of recognized education. Two talented men, Albertus Magnus and St Thomas Aquinas,[3] were responsible for this revolution in human thought, which at the time was 'adaptation of peripateticism to Christian dogma'.

From a technical point of view, the Ptolemaic system is much superior to the Aristotelian. Although the Ptolemaic tables were better adapted to the prediction of celestial motions, they nevertheless contained small errors, which being cumulative finally became obvious. A correction was imperative; so a group of astronomers at Toledo, assembled by Alfonso X (*El Sabio*), of Castile, carried out a series of calculations which culminated in the *Alphonsine Tables, ca.* 1272. With this improvement, the geocentric system seemed to be capable of continuing; and it remained virtually unshaken until the Copernican revolution.

If we restrict ourselves to the broadest outlines, that was the destiny from the twelfth to the sixteenth century of what we shall call for the sake of simplicity the 'Aristotelian scheme'. Naturally, if we go into details, then its history is more tortuous and more complicated. The heliocentric hypothesis of Copernicus, though it was far from being greeted with unanimous favour, had none the less been prepared through a slow erosion of the Aristotelico-Ptolemaic system. In this connection, we may recall the boldness of Nicole Oresme in accepting, in the fourteenth century, the notion of the revolution of the Earth round the Sun. However, heliocentrism itself had already been transcended. Some theologians in the thirteenth century accepted the plurality of worlds, at least as a theoretical possibility by adducing the infinite power of God; others went so far as to maintain the possibility of an infinite universe.[4]

This concept of an infinite universe, setting itself against the Aristotelian and scholastic concept of a closed, geocentric universe, asserted itself more and more vigorously during the fifteenth century. One fact which cannot be overemphasized in this connection was the sudden divulgement of the long-forgotten poem by Lucretius. Modern editors of *De rerum natura* have two groups of manuscripts at their disposal which are separated by a gap of more than five centuries. The manuscripts of the first group go back to a Carolingian period. The others all belong to fifteenth-century Italy and all derive from the same prototype 'brought to Italy by Poggio in 1414'.[5] D. W. Singer (who places Poggio's discovery in 1417)[6] is of the opinion that there is no doubt whatever that this discovery—which, in any case, coincides with the adolescence of Nicolas of Cusa—must have influenced his thought, especially his concept of an infinite universe, without limit or centre—a bold, heterodox concept, and even scandalous in the view of the universities, but apt to seduce minds freed from scholastic tradition. The concept spread during the sixteenth century, as is proved by the *Notebooks* of Leonardo da Vinci. The renaissance of Greco-Latin letters rendered the hegemony of Aristotle even more precarious. The authority of other Greek philosophers, especially the pre-Socratic, encouraged all kinds of boldness.

During the sixteenth century, scientific progress was so rapid, the movement of ideas was so intensive and the surviving documents are so numerous that it is very difficult for an historian of world systems to arrange such rich and complex material. With regard to the question, we might even say quarrel, concerning geocentrism (which most certainly is not what astronomy comes down to, though its scientific and religious interest are of prime importance), we are fortunate in having an excellent point of reference—the *De revolutionibus orbium coelestium* published by Copernicus in the very year of his death, 1543. In this work, Copernicus sets forth the rotation of the Earth on its axis and its revolution round the Sun as an hypothesis and by mathematical demonstration. Being still faithful to the dogma of circular motion, he was obliged to retain the expedient of eccentrics and epicycles in order to take account of the appearances. In spite of his caution he set astronomy upon a new path. Heliocentrism imagined by Antiquity was finally reborn, being based on calculation as a plausible mathematical hypothesis.

The great figure of Copernicus dominated during his lifetime a whole host of men of science. Giovanni Battista Riccioli, a Jesuit of Ferrara, born in 1598, published his *Almagestum novum* at Bologna in 1651. This large work in two folio volumes is preceded by a *Chronicon duplex astronomorum vel astrologorum*, which is a chronological catalogue followed by an alphabetical one of astronomers who have distinguished themselves by their works from Antiquity down to the middle of the seventeenth century. It contains more than one hundred names for the sixteenth century alone. It must be admitted that this long list contains the names of many unimportant men. Still, it is not complete. We note the absence of Giordano Bruno, who should have been worthy of admission, considering some of the names that are included.

In this vast range we shall restrict our inquiry to authors who died after 1543. The earliest of them, although they survived Copernicus, had lived and written before publication of *De revolutionibus orbium. coelestium* and had not repudiated their works. For the most part they remained adherents to the system of concentric spheres which seemed to them a satisfactory picture of reality. The more or less numerous modifications introduced by them into a cosmic scheme whose general features they accepted are a measure of their knowledge and their qualms of conscience; the modifications comply with their care for a better explanation of the phenomena to 'save the appearances'. Several names may be mentioned in this group of *savants*; they were all contemporaries of Copernicus, but younger than he.

Girolamo Fracastoro (or Fracastorius) (1478–1553), of Verona, physician and astronomer, a student with Copernicus at Padua. His *Homocentria* (Venice, 1538), introduces some modifications to the Ptolemaic system of epicycles. Bruno, rather careless of chronological accuracy, as he not infrequently was, makes him appear in his dialogues *De l'infinito universo et mondi*.

Oronce Fine (1494–1555), of Briançon, astronomer and mathematician, son of François Fine, himself an astronomer, published his *Théorique des cielz*, Paris, 1528; it describes the universe in accordance with the data in the *Almagest*, and as consisting of eight concentric spheres. The work was reprinted in 1558 and as late as 1607.

Petrus Apianus (the Latinized form of Peter Bienewitz) (1495–1552), of Leisnig, another adherent to classical astronomy, published an *Astronomicum Caesareum* (Ingolstadt, 1540) which contains a description of various instruments intended for the reproduction of celestial motions. He wrote also the *Instrumentum primi mobilis* (Nürnberg, 1534).

Jean Fernel (1497–1558), of Clermont in Beauvaisis, was sometimes called Ambianus, because his father came from Amiens. He was noted for his geodetic works, and was particularly famous as a physician. In his youth he was interested in astronomy and published *Monalosphaerium* (Paris, 1526). After 1534 he devoted himself entirely to medicine.

Alessandro Piccolomini (1508–1578), of Siena. Although younger than those we have already mentioned, nevertheless he had published his two treatises *De la sfera del mondo libri quattro* and *Delle stelle fisse libro uno* before 1543. The interest of these works, like that of the *Théorique des cielz* by Oronce Fine, lies in the fact that they were written in the vernacular, and not in Latin. Proof of the success of *La Sfera* is provided by the number of editions that were published. The cosmic architecture is based on that of Ptolemy and Aristotle, but to the eight spheres of Oronce Fine, Piccolomini adds another two, which are interposed between the seventh (that of Saturn) and the last (that of the fixed stars). Additions of this kind became more and more frequent. In the work of Riccioli mentioned above, there is a classification of astronomers according to the number of spheres they ascribed to the structure of the universe. Bruno ridiculed these precise statements and their differences one from the other; he refused to reduce the universe, which he regarded as infinite, to seven, eight or nine spheres rather than to ten or more. The *Sfera* was translated into Latin (Bâle, 1568), and into French by Jacques Goupyl (Paris, 1550). The latter version was reprinted in 1608. With regard to the Italian reprints, we have been able to consult five, all later than 1543, being published in 1548, 1559, 1561, 1566 and 1595. Very likely there are others. The number of these subsequent editions coupled with their late appearance reveals the persistent vogue of traditional geocentrism.

However, this persistence is revealed not only by the republication of works that appeared before *De revolutionibus orbium coelestium*: the second half of the sixteenth century provided a profusion of fresh works conceived in the same spirit. Some of them are noteworthy; most of them are only curiosities.

James Bassantin, a Scot, born in the reign of James II (1486–1513), died in 1568, published his *Astronomique discours* (Lyon, Jean de Tournes, 1557), in French. A Latin version appeared two years later at Geneva. This work, in which the author limits himself to explaining the Ptolemaic planetary system, is not greatly valued by astronomers. We quote it as being one of the earliest of the innumerable post-Copernican manuals on geocentric astronomy, a list of which would extend not only to the end of the sixteenth century but over into the seventeenth century as well.

Nicodemus Frischlin (1547–1590), of Balingen, adhered to the Aristotelian scheme, but with a full knowledge of the case, for he was fully aware of the Copernican doctrine and explained the reasons why he considered it to be erroneous in his book *De astronomicae artis cum doctrina coelesti et naturali philosophia congruentia*.[6b]

With Tycho Brahe (1546–1601), we are confronted with a more complicated hypothesis. The great Danish astronomer put forward a theory that takes account of the work of Copernicus whilst retaining one at least of the fundamental facts of ancient astronomy, for he leaves the Earth stationary at the centre of the universe, the Sun revolves round the Earth, and the planets revolve round the Sun. These views are explained in a work entitled *Astronomiae instauratae progymnasmata* which certain bibliographers claim to have been printed for the first time at Copenhagen in 1589. I have never seen a copy of this edition. The earliest ones available at the present time are those of 1602 (Uraniborg), 1603 and 1610 (Prague).[7]

These supporters of geocentrism, who were by far in the majority, were opposed by several pioneers of the new astronomy, the defenders of heliocentrism revived by Copernicus.

Taking them in chronological order, we shall mention first of all, Georgius Ioachimus de Porris, called Rhaeticus (1514–1576), of Feldkirchen in the canton of the Grisons, one of the earliest and most fervent followers of Copernicus. He was not content to follow his teacher; he preceded him, in a manner of speaking; for, without waiting for the publication of *De revolutionibus orbium coelestium*, he published his own summary of it under the title *De libris Revolutionum eruditissimi Nic. Copernici narratio*. This work was published at Danzig in 1540, again in 1541, then in 1566, on this occasion together with the text of *De revolutionibus*. Being even bolder than Copernicus, Rhaeticus put forward the new system as a statement of physical reality, and not as a mathematical hypothesis.

Michael Maestlin (or Moestlin) (1550–1631), of Göppingen, was another fervent adept of the new doctrine which he popularized in his teaching, and for which he never ceased to fight. In his *Judicium M. Moestlini de opere astronomico D. Frischlini*, he defends Copernicus against the criticisms of Frischlin. When he was teaching in Italy he converted the young Galileo, then an adherent of Ptolemaic astronomy, to Copernicanism. Furthermore, he had the glory of counting Johannes Kepler amongst his pupils.

David Origanus, a Silesian, lived at the end of the sixteenth and the beginning of the seventeenth century. He was already active scientifically in 1589. He accepted terrestrial motion. He was the author of *Novae motuum coelestium ephemerides* (*1595–1655*) . . . *cum Introductione in qua chronologica, astronomica et astrologica ex fundamentis ipsis tractantur* (Frankfurt, 1609).

Thomas Digges, born in Kent, matriculated in the University of Cambridge in May 1546, died in 1595, was the first professional astronomer to maintain the thesis of an infinite universe. Copernicus, although he placed the Sun, assumed to be stationary, at the centre of the planetary system, nevertheless set the limit of the universe at the sphere of fixed stars. Thomas Digges, in an *Appendix* to *Prognostication Everlastinge*, (London, 1576), written by his father Leonard Digges, describes a heliocentric and boundless universe in which the stars are dispersed 'in sphaericall altitude without ende'.[8] The diurnal revolution of distant, yet non-uniformly distant, stars is only an illusion caused by the rotation of the Earth on its axis.

In the closing years of the sixteenth century the hypothesis of an infinite universe acquired more and more supporters. Mention may be made of Patricius and Gilbert.

Francesco Patrizi (or Patricius) (1529–1597), of Cherso, published his *Nova de universis philosophia*, Ferrara, 1591; reprinted, Venice, 1593. The infinite nature of the universe is asserted in the fourth and last part of this work, which is entitled *Pancosmia*; it is decidedly anti-Aristotelian in tone. It is quite possible that Bruno saw the first edition of the *Nova philosophia* before he was imprisoned in May 1592.

William Gilbert (1540–1603), of Colchester, set forth his views in a work entitled *De magnete magnetisque corporibus et de magno magnete tellure philosophia nova plurimis argumentis demonstrata*,[8b] London, 1600. The apparent diurnal motion of the celestial vault is explained by Gilbert by the rotation of the Earth upon its axis. The Sun is the centre of the planetary system. To this Copernican outlook the author added the concept of an infinite universe. The *De magnete* was published too late for Bruno to have had any knowledge of it. On the contrary, it is Gilbert who quotes Bruno; but it is possible that his views on an infinite universe were known before 1591.

The purpose of the above account is to emphasize the diversity of doctrines and tendencies that were current at the time Bruno wrote and published his cosmological works between 1582 and 1591. Controversy centred chiefly on the following matters: geocentrism or heliocentrism, immobility or motion of the Earth, motion of the planets, closed universe or infinite universe. The answer to any one of these questions has no influence at all on the answers that will be provided to the others. Assertion of terrestrial motion, for example, does not necessarily imply heliocentrism or an infinite universe. Copernicus made the Sun the centre of a cosmos which is cognate with that of Ptolemy and whose extreme limit is the sphere of fixed stars; Tycho Brahe believed in the Earth's immobility whilst admitting revolution of the other planets round the Sun. On the other hand, the debate ranged far beyond astronomical technique, and the arguments put forward differed according to the scientific, philosophic or religious viewpoint with which the problems to be resolved were regarded.

Professional astronomers, having some idea of the difficulties inherent in the mathematical interpretation of apparent motions in the heavens, maintained an attitude of extreme prudence on the subject of heliocentrism, after the time of Copernicus. Their justifiable hesitation resulted from the difficulty of incorporating in a new system certain factual data which seemed incompatible with it, or from the obligation of accepting certain consequences of the system which seemed incompatible with common sense, for example, putting the fixed stars of no observable parallax at an inconceivable distance from the Earth. We shall consider this particular point later on; for the present it will suffice to note that this caution on the part of *savants* partly explains the long survival of traditional astronomy even in the seventeenth century.

With regard to the infiniteness of the universe, philosophers were bolder in their thinking, being less burdened by any scruple to reconcile their cosmic vision with the mass of accumulated knowledge and to incorporate it in the system in a perfectly coherent manner. Francis Bacon, in his *Historia naturalis et experimentalis*,[9] London, 1622, mentions certain authors who were interested in cosmology and who based their doctrines 'on imagination rather than on experience'. In the list of names given by him, we find that of Bruno, together with those of Telesius, Gilbert and Patricius. All four believed in an infinite universe.

There now remains the religious point of view. Aristotelianism tended to become an article of faith, seeing that it was sanctioned by the highest ecclesiastical authorities and by a large part of the enlightened clergy. A system that set the firmament above the Earth, making thereby two substantially distinct worlds, balancing each other as it were and amenable to a superior natural philosophy, was not such a system most conformable literally to the Holy Scriptures, to which it brought the precious support of human knowledge? Having been secured at the price of long conflicts, the memory of which was still vivid, conciliation between Aristotelianism and the Christian faith had to be stabilized. Above all, it was necessary to guard against leaving the problem open, and at all cost to defend, if need be by violence, a synthesis harmonized with dogma against every attack by new theories. Aristotle reigned supreme in the great protestant and catholic universities, at Oxford just as much as at Paris and Padua. The Oxonians went so far as to impose a fine on any proposition found to be contrary to the opinion of the Master.[10] In catholic countries, the attitude of the Church stiffened towards the end of the sixteenth century and beginning of the seventeenth, and culminated in the tragedies with which we are familiar. A measure of this change in attitude is provided by the frequency of the condemnations as well as by the number of them applied to older works that had been published in times of greater freedom: the *De revolutionibus orbium coelestium*, dedicated by Copernicus to Pope Paul III, was not put on the Index until 1616.[11]

Étienne Gilson, in 1628, wrote: 'In the opinion of all the minds that count, Aristotelianism is no longer more than a dismantled fortress.' No doubt! but the minds that count are not in the majority and do not make the laws.

Aristotle was never more blindly followed than in the first decades of the seventeenth century;[12] and if it be true that deeply religious men at that time were not insensible of the attraction of heliocentrism, nevertheless many of them acquiesced in the decisions of the hierarchy, and, especially perhaps, bowed before proofs which they believed to be irrefutable. Bérulle regretted that human knowledge had established the truth of geocentrism at a time when the Sun, the centre of the universe and source of its light, would have been a symbol better suited to the divine majesty.[13] It was not the founder of the French Oratory that Gilson had in mind, but Mersenne who, in the preface to *Quaestiones in Genesim* (1623) protested against the opinion of those *savants* who were too much inclined to think that all catholic theologians swear only by Aristotle—and in evidence thereof cited Telesius, Bruno, Campanella, Kepler and Galileo.[14]

Although they reflect two quite different tendencies, Mersenne's protest and Bérulle's resignedness are symptoms that portend abandonment by the Church in a more or less distant future of a cosmology henceforth out-of-date.

II. THE ATTITUDE OF GIORDANO BRUNO TOWARDS HIS PROBLEM

If it be indispensable for a perfect understanding of the work of a philosopher to recall the historical circumstances under which it was conceived, written and published, then care must be taken to avoid regarding this work as a consequence or effect of external causes. Whatever his attitude of submissiveness or of revolt, a man reflects his environment; he forms part of it, too, and modifies it to some extent. If he be a writer, he depends on his authors; but first of all he selects them, and even if the reading of some of them be imposed on him by custom or pressure of any kind, he will not give them all the same attention; many will be forgotten, whilst others, being improperly understood, will be retained in a distorted manner in his memory; some will influence his thought, but most of them will only corroborate unconsciously the certainties whose sources were in him.

Husserl said that an arithmetician has only number in mind 'being preoccupied with numerical operations, but not with the phenomenological problems posed by the relation between number and the consciousness of number';[15] and we may add that the reader of a mathematical work has the same indifference to the origin of the text before him as to its development in the consciousness of the author: except in the case where the psychology of the consciousness is the purpose of the study, the reader goes straightway to the results, which alone are of interest to him. Now, it is quite different in the case of the cosmologist and his reader, for the universe is a subject of thought which contains everything, with the result that the thinker is less tempted to disregard his actual thought whose paths as much as their objectives constitute part of the subject that he proposes to study.

The condemnations, vindications and passionate discussions to which the work of Giordano Bruno has given rise lead us to conclude, without any investigation, that the author is present in this work, which can be penetrated only through him, with his connivance; and that the picture of the universe to which it leads us appears to us only in the perspectives where he has placed himself. That is to say, we shall reach it only by taking into account his character, his inclinations, his loves and his hates, and, naturally, his intellectual make-up, his knowledge and lack of knowledge, as well as what he remembered and wished to remember, forgot and wished to forget of the lessons to be learned from the period in which he lived.

Mathematics and physics

With the Dominicans at Naples, where, on his own admission, he was 'nurtured in the doctrines of the Peripatetics',[16] Bruno did not receive in his youth that mathematical instruction which would have facilitated his approach to problems in astronomy; and it would seem that he made no great effort subsequently to rectify this omission. He was obviously repelled by mathematics, and if his disdain for the subject betrays some resentment, his opinion is none the less sincere and the result of reflection. In the classification of human knowledge, the subject ought to be placed, in his opinion, on the level of preliminary learning, As a result we find him becoming angry at those who extol Archimedes for ignoring everything, whilst his home-town was falling, his house in flames and his life in danger, 'in order to persist in discovering some relationship between a curve and a straight line—the diameter and the circumference—or to resolve some other problem, all excellent occupations for youth, but ill becoming a man of his ability, who ought to have devoted his old age to matters more worthy of elucidation by mental activity'.[17]

The answer to this expression of opinion, far from contradicting or even introducing some reservation, only clarifies the severe judgement that is stated there: it reveals complete agreement between the two speakers of the dialogue—and its author. Euclid and Archimedes are reproached, for the same reason as the grammarians Priscian and Donatus, for having dallied even into old age over tasks suitable for those 'of still tender years', but not for adult minds 'relieved of all fetters, and therefore qualified and prepared for greater things'.[18] Frequently, in other places, mathematics is compared with physics and treated like an almost futile game compared with the study of realities. Seeing that we are speaking as natural philosophers, says a character in the dialogues *De l'infinito*, 'we have no need to resort to mathematical phantasies';[19] and in *Cena de le ceneri*, 'To toy with geometry is one thing, to verify according to nature is another.'[20]

When Bruno comes to make allusion to the virtues of number, it is then that he enters the paths of highly questionable arithmology, and, moreover, without conviction. The best example of this is provided by the Latin poem *De monade*, which is entirely devoted to the symbolism of the first ten numbers. One has only to open the book anywhere to find passages like the following: 'the pentad, which springs from the first even and odd numbers, will be sometimes good and sometimes evil, like the five senses, or like the five fingers of the hand, which are the vehicles and instruments of good and evil'.[21]

Nevertheless, it is only right to acknowledge that Bruno did not abide by the reveries of *De monade*. On several occasions, in connection with physical or cosmological questions, such as infinite divisibility, he attempted to plunge into, what was for him, the dangerous and hostile territory of positive mathematics. There are three texts in question: the dialogues relating to the compass of Fabrizio Mordente; *Centum et sexaginta articuli adversus huius temporis mathematicos atque philosophos*, and certain parts of *De minimo*.

Fabrizio Mordente, of Salerno, had invented and with the help of his brother Gasparo had constructed a compass with eight limbs, a description of which was given by Bruno in the dialogue *De Mordentii Salernitani circino* (Paris, 1586), and the use of which even forty years later is proved by a pamphlet in French entitled: *La géométrie réduite en une facile et briefve praticque par deux excellens instruments, dont l'un(e) est le pentatomère ou compas de proportion de Michel Connette . . . L'autre est l'usage du compas à huit poinctes inventé par Fabrice Mordente* (A Paris, chez Charles Hulpeau, 1626). As indicated by the title, Mordente's compass was intended to reduce the work of designers and computators; it enabled certain problems in geometry to be solved, and to construct, for example, two figures having a given proportion to each other; or to carry out certain operations, such as the extraction of square roots and cube roots, the answers being read off on graduated scales, as on a slide-rule. It was, therefore, a practical instrument, which made it possible to obviate the tedious work in finding an approximate value in certain cases. Mordente, unfortunately, seemed not to realize that his compass gave only approximations, and flattered himself that he had solved problems hitherto insoluble. Consequently, Bruno has been criticized for his enthusiasm for Mordente who, by his genius, would have resuscitated the fallen arts, revived the dead sciences, and opened up unexplored paths;[22] his enthusiasm has been judged all the more surprising seeing that Bruno elsewhere deplores the inaccuracy of trigonometrical tables and blames the mathematicians for being satisfied with approximations.[23] In the *Spaccio* we find him ascribing to himself through Minerva the credit of having squared the circle; and, yet, in *De minimo*, he denies the possibility of solving this problem in Book II, whereas he admits it in Book III.[24] As Felice Tocco has remarked, 'Bruno speaks two languages when he criticises contemporary mathematics', now demanding faultless, rigorous reasoning, then accepting solutions based on the elimination of negligible differences.[25]

There are not only two languages, but also two lines of thought; and the accent is put on the first or the second according as the philosopher has in mind the abstract science of mathematics or the concrete science of nature. That is the reason, acceptable or not, why his attitude towards mathematics becomes understandable only in the light of his physical conceptions. Bruno believed, with Plato, that nothing is perfect in reality; and, for him, that is the basis of the problem, for, as we shall see later, according to him everything that is possible exists, and conversely that which does not exist is impossible. There is nothing possible that has not been brought into being, hence there is no infinite divisibility, and every division, if we were required to take it far enough, would lead to the insuperable obstacle of a minimum. To remove this physical theory on to the mathematical plane and to ask, for example, a geometer to fix a limit to the division of any quantity would be to revert to a singularly archaic period of knowledge, and to step even further back in time than to the Pythagorean discovery of irrational quantities. Bruno recognizes the mathematician's right (and on occasion his duty) to pursue his investigations beyond what is physically possible and beyond the rational; subject always to the requirement that it is freely admitted that the mathematical entities are henceforth no more than enquiries of the mind and the reasonings relating thereto are phantasies, reveries and pastimes (*fantasticherie e trastulli*).

Rational solutions in many cases are only approximate solutions, but these approximations are suggested and put forward by nature. Contrary to a Leonardo, Bruno does not think that every science should be subject to mathematical investigation. Very often it should even be avoided. His field of study being the tangible universe, the physicist is justified in challenging any construction making use of material foreign to solid reality, and to refrain from an excess of rigorousness that would direct him to useless exercises and would divert him from contemplation and knowledge of the cosmos.

In this perspective we shall be less surprised to discover that astronomy, being removed from the realm of mathematics, becomes a branch of physics. When Bruno proudly declares that he does not wish to see 'with the eyes of Copernicus or Ptolemy, but with his own',[26] he means that he will restrict himself 'to the contemplation of nature'. In his view, computational astronomy is an interpretation or translation of reality. No doubt, those who pursue it make their contribution to knowledge, but they do not always understand the true significance of the facts which they have reduced to formulae. They resemble those peasants who gave a circumstantial account of a battle: being ignorant of military affairs, they misunderstood the reasons for the victory, whereas the experienced military man listening to them understood what they were saying.[27] So, Copernicus, loaded with praise but tied willy-nilly to 'the ancient and true philosophy' (*i.e.*, to Greek heliocentrism and certain pre-Socratic physiologers), is deprived of his chief title to fame, namely, his mathematical demonstration of heliocentrism. 'He freed himself from Ptolemy, Hipparchos and Eudoxos', but 'he hardly deviated from them,' for, 'being more in love with mathematics than with nature,' he was unable to penetrate and get sufficiently to the core of reality so as to cut off vain principles at their root and thereby triumph over the contradictions and difficulties that he encountered.[28] Later on we shall deal with the conclusions to be derived from these comments.

Philosophical conformation

It is already clear that Bruno's cosmology will not be that of a mathematician, an astronomer, nor even that of a physicist in the modern sense of the word; it will be rather that of a man of letters and a philosopher. In spite of his travels during a wandering and adventurous life, he remained a studious individual, with a preference for meditation and reading; and in spite of his declared independence of his most admired authors, to say nothing of those he rejected, the recollection of one or the other of them is revealed throughout his writings. Praise and criticism, quotations, commentaries, furtive borrowings or simple allusions, all shed their light.

One name in particular is noticeable—that of Aristotle. At a time when such an attitude was audacious and not without danger, Bruno never ceased from professing his anti-Aristotelianism, but this opposition itself reveals expropriation. He retained very little from the physical theories of the Stagyrite, to whom he usually adopts the contrary view; but he kept the Master's vocabulary, the outlines of his thought, his manner of presenting problems, as well as certain fundamental theses such as the indissolubility of matter and of form in the world of experience. Finally, his claim to propose a cosmological system in agreement with objective reality and not simply stated as a coherent hypothesis is eminently Aristotelian. The besetting desire to free himself from Aristotle, to destroy him in himself, leads Bruno to interminable refutations, such as that of *De coelo* in the dialogues *De l'infinito*, or that of the *Physica* in *Figuratio Aristotelici Physici auditus*; it leads him to vehement invective and farcical satire, excellent in its way, the best example of which is provided by *Cabala del cavallo Pegaseo*. This pamphlet, published at

41

London in 1585, stages an ass which, under the name of Onorio,[29] confides his worldly experiences. Subjected to metempsychosis, but having succeeded in not drinking the waters of Lethe, he recalls his former lives as an animal and a human being, in the course of which his soul had the strange fortune to occupy the body of Aristotle. 'I declared myself', said he, 'prince of the Peripatetics. I taught at Athens, under the portico of the Lyceum, according to the light or more truly according to the darkness that prevailed within me; I disseminated a perverse teaching on the principles and substance of things; I raved in an excess of ecstasy on the essence of the soul and showed myself incapable of correctly understanding the nature of the motion of the universe; in a word I was the man through whose fault the wheel of natural and divine knowledge, which was in an exalted state in the time of the Chaldeans and Pythagoreans, became clouded and fell to its lowest state.'[30]

The religious experience of his years at Naples left an indelible recollection of the Holy Scriptures on Bruno's memory. If we may judge from the number of quotations he makes from them, then his preference seems to have been for *The Song of Solomon, The Wisdom of Solomon, The Book of Job, The Book of Psalms*, and in the *New Testament, The Epistles of St Paul*.

Among the philosophers of Antiquity, the pre-Socratics held first place: their effort to reduce the diversity of things to a single principle is approved with enthusiasm rarely contradicted. In this connection, Tocco notes that Bruno's admiration extends to thinkers whose doctrines show profound differences, and that it would be convenient to separate them into at least two groups: those who accept the cosmogony, and those who reject it in the name of unity; on the one hand he puts the Ionians, the Pythagoreans down to Heraclitos, and on the other the School of Eleatic philosophers.[31] Bruno has been taxed with not having made this distinction.[32] We shall see how he justifies an apparently haphazard eclecticism and to what extent his conception of the universe reconciles the vicissitudes of a cosmogony with Parmenidian immobility. His references are not limited to borrowings from the pre-Socratics; he finds what he needs equally well in later schools; whenever he finds it useful to do so, he calls upon Democritos, Epicuros, Lucretius, the neo-Platonists and on hermetic writings.

A stranger to philological discipline, he never disguised his aversion from grammarian humanism. So, we shall not be surprised to find that in the field of textual criticism he was not in advance of his times. The currently received attributions were accepted without examination; he cites Dionysios the Areopagite as a writer of the first century, and attributes to Archytas of Tarentum the καθολικοὶ λόγοι δέκα of the pseudo-Archytas, a late imposture of neo-Pythagorism, made for the purpose of proving that the Aristotelian categories were known before Aristotle was born.[33]

With regard to combined quotations from authors separated in time or by doctrine, it should be noted that in most cases, but not always, they are made in reference to a specific question to which the authors quoted have given the same reply. Thus, Bruno will say that Heraclitos, Democritos, Epicuros, Pythagoras, Parmenides and Melissos were aware of infinite space, as is manifested by the surviving fragments of their works, and on this score they are to be set against the Aristotelians who maintained and still maintain the finiteness of the universe.[34] In another place, on the subject of substantial unity, we read: 'If we reflect deeply with the *natural* philosophers, leaving the logicians to their phantasies, we shall find everything that constitutes difference and number is pure accident. . . .'[35] The 'natural' philosophers in this instance are the pre-Socratic physiologers and all those who, subsequently, have reduced the manifold to unity, in contrast with those who, with Aristotle, either following his example or before him, have introduced distinctions and categories into reality.

Certain comparisons may appear arbitrary; nevertheless, as an attentive reader, Bruno seizes the character peculiar to each of his authors and shrewdly sets it off as occasion requires, as for example in that passage of *Eroici furori* where he shows by what methods and by what routes each of them has gone in pursuit of truth: 'There went the Pythagorean seeking truth by following the traces and impressions she has left in nature, and they are numbers which, in a certain way, cause its progress, reasons and methods to become apparent; for, number, manifoldly applied, to measurement, time and weight, translates all things into the truth of existence. . . . Then there went Plato working round the subject, pruning it, as it were, placing barriers so that inconsistent and fugitive aspects should remain as though caught in a net, being retained by an entanglement of definitions; for he considered that superior things exist by participation, similitude and reflection in inferior things, and *vice-versa*, where they assume more dignity and excellence; and that truth is in one or the other according to a certain law of analogy, order and gradation which always causes the lowest degree of the superior order to meet the highest degree of the lower order. Consequently, by means of intermediate steps, he was able to raise himself in nature from the lowest to the highest, as from evil to good, from darkness to light, from sheer power to pure action.'[36]

Neither Pythagoras nor Plato is admired without reservations, for Bruno was unable to accept that number is the principle of things, nor the existence of ideas as separate substances. Yet he defends these thinkers against the warped criticism and 'pedantic censure of Aristotle'.[37] He did not make Plato into a god, or even a saint, as did the earliest Platonists of Florence. He discusses him, but refuses him the first rank which he would more willingly accord to a Pythagoras or a Plotinos.[38]

These different and emphatic appraisals reflect confidence in the attitude of the moment and the arbitrariness attached to complete liberty of free enquiry. Both were certain to displease a host of mediocrities, and Bruno implies that he was not unaware of the possibility when, at the close of the third dialogue in *De l'infinito*, he introduces a discussion between two characters, the theme of which is precisely the principle of authority. Fracastor, a Veronese astronomer (here expressing the views of the author), asserts that no one is obliged to fall in with the opinions of others any more than with their tastes: 'It is not right to deprive a donkey of his cabbage and expect his tastes to be the same as ours. The diversity of minds and intelligences is just as great as that of [vital] spirits and stomachs.'[39] Burchio, an imaginary character of limited common sense, and respecter of recognized authorities, expresses surprise on hearing this contradiction of the opinions of philosophers and *savants* who had been revered everywhere for ages: 'Do you mean, then, that Plato is ignorant, that Aristotle is an ass, and that their followers are senseless, stupid and fanatic?' Fracastoro protests that he said no such thing; on the contrary, he regards these great men as 'heroes of the Earth', but he hastens to add, 'I do not wish to believe them without reason, nor to accept propositions when the contradictory propositions are distinctly true . . . and you would have understood that had you not been completely deaf and blind.' The dispute continues in this tone until Burchio, roused to indignation and at a loss for argument, cries: 'Go to the deuce! wiser than Aristotle, more divine than Plato, more profound than Averroes, more discerning than the large number of philosophers and theologians who have been explained, admired and praised to the skies by so many nations throughout the ages.'

The independence of mind incomprehensible to the common people is allied in Bruno with the haughtiest opinion of himself. Theophilus in the *Cena de le ceneri*—he is both spokesman and panegyrist for Bruno—enumerates on a page, intended to surprise the reader, but which inclines to make him smile, the ancient and modern philosophers who have accepted terrestrial motion: Nicetas of Syracuse, Philolaos, Heraclides of Pontos, Ecphantos, Plato in the *Timaeus*,[40] Copernicus and others down to the 'divine Cusa, in the second book of *De docta ignorantia*'; but, he adds, Bruno was indebted to them for very little, 'for he deduced that truth from other principles, his very own, and more solid; thanks to which, not by authority but by sense and reason, he considers it to be as certain as anything can be'.[41]

The mention of Nicholas of Cusa and Copernicus shows that Bruno appraises recent authors with the same freedom as the old ones.[42] Furthermore, he makes frequent use of them without acknowledgement, so that a straight-forward statement of his quotations would provide an incomplete picture of the extent of his reading. Marsilio Ficino, for example, is not mentioned once in the vernacular dialogues, whereas he is one of the obvious sources of the *Eroici furori*, and he is rarely mentioned (though admittedly with honour) in the Latin poems.[43] The authors to whom Bruno makes most frequent reference, and for whom he shows the most consistent admiration, even though he may on occasion contradict them, are Ramon Lull and the Cardinal da Cusa. The influence of Ramon Lull is undeniable, but hardly affects cosmology. On the other hand, the essential themes of infinite space and the plurality of worlds found in da Cusa and others are retained.

The case of St Thomas Aquinas is rather special. Bruno speaks little of him, but always with the greatest respect and spares him the sarcasms that he heaps on the Aristotelians, or at least most of them, for an exception has to be made in the case of Averroes also.

As for other philosophers and theologians of the Middle Ages, his sympathy and hostility towards them, like his enthusiasm and change of mood, depend on the agreement of their systems with his own. He did not forgive Duns Scotus for having conceived the idea of divine liberty as pure contingency, whereas David of Dinant (known to him only through the discussions of Albertus Magnus and St Thomas Aquinas on his doctrines) is quoted twice in the treatise *De la causa*, where he is praised for having raised matter to the dignity of 'divine thing'.[44] Avicebron is approved for the same reason in *De vinculis*, but censured for having maintained that forms are only accidents of matter.[45]

One part of the speculations on the first ten numbers contained in *De monade* has been borrowed from Cornelius Agrippa, and quoted word for word elsewhere in the *Theses de magia* (a pamphlet written at Helmstedt in 1590). Paracelsus is placed above all other physicians, but his theory of the three hypostatical principles—sulphur, mercury and salt—was rejected as being incompatible with the hypothesis (which meant certainty for Bruno) of a unique material substratum for all composite bodies.[46]

He was familiar with Lefèvre d'Étaples and Charles de Bovelles. With regard to the former, he says that his philosophical work, which agrees with the doctrines of the peripatetics (*juxta peripateticorum dogmata*), is one of the glories of France; he considered the latter as being perhaps inferior to Lefèvre in style, but superior in genius, judgement and breadth of knowledge,[47] if they are referred to the Aristarchians.

On the other hand, he heaps graphic invectives on Pierre de la Ramée and Francesco Patrizi, calling one an arch-pedant, and the other *sterco di pedante*.[48]

Finally, we may mention the names of some astronomers who have not been noticed above, but whose works are quoted either in the poetical text or the glosses of *De immenso* and *De monade*: Albumasar (*De immenso*, IV, ix), Christoph Rothmann (*De immenso*, VI, xx), Olaus Cimber (*De immenso*, VI, xx), Cecco d'Ascoli, whose death at the stake is recalled by Bruno, *in campo Florae*, on that *Campo dei Fiori* which was to be the place of his own execution (*De monade*, IX) Cornelius Gemma and Elyseus (*De immenso*, VI, xx).

Throughout the works of Bruno we find evidence of his wide reading, which either stimulated his critical vein, or served as a starting point for his own investigations, or gave support to his own theses. It has been claimed that his remarks on perceptible minima are undoubtedy an echo of Lucretius, rather than the conclusion from experiment.[49] Nevertheless, the development of a cosmological theme is introduced by recalling some personal observation: a remote childhood impression, such as a flight of birds or the view of distant mountains; the sight of water flowing between the banks of a river, of the Thames returning to its source at high tide, of an object falling from the top of a mast to the deck of a ship.

Whether it be the page he has read or a more direct approach to reality, it is the subsequent reflection and meditation that are decisive, the moment when a system is developed through an inner discourse of reason. As soon as a question arises, how does this development take place? We should be very far from the truth in assuming here a judicious assembly and quiet collation of material provided by reading and experience. By crediting him with methodical and orderly work, we should run too much risk in altering the picture of a mind whose impulse, ever pathetic and affected by a kind of intoxication, has no other direction but to go from one full certainty to another certainty that endeavours to make itself more persuasive, though it is not so well founded.

The effort of discursive thought seems to tend particularly to verification of intuition; it leads to the discovery of a presentient universe. Even when the sytem is apparently based on external evidence (proven facts, results of accumulated knowledge), observations and proofs are never brought in except to give further verification of a truth that every mind tuned to the universe is qualified to grasp, and which contains in itself its own proof. As for the teachings given in the Schools or transmitted through books, they are never calmly received, but are embraced with enthusiasm or rejected with fury according as they agree or do not agree with the expectations of the philosopher.

He sought the universe first of all within himself, and it was there that he found it; the receding horizons of an inner abyss having offered him the first view of that which is boundless and formless. Reflection and meditation on tangible data (and on the opinions of others) find their use, but the path that leads to all knowledge of the principles is, in the first instance, that of introversion.

Bruno claimed to be only slightly indebted to his most admired authors—Nicholas of Cusa and Copernicus, and this vainglorious claim sometimes raises a smile. However, it has also been said of him, and we believe with some justification, that Bruno threw out the first notions of the cosmological concept among the moderns, and that his originality consists less in his 'pantheism' than in his explanation of this 'cosmological concept'—'in other words, of a metaphysics reduced to its proper function which is to interpret in its entirety the world of experience';[50] and, may we add, of an experience, both inward and outward, which is itself complete.

III. THE TEXTS

The works in which Bruno set forth and defended his cosmological opinions fall into two groups:

1. Dialogues in the vernacular. These comprise six treatises whose wide range may be considered as a single work.[51] The first three, which are the only ones of direct interest to us, have been collected together by Gentile under the general title of *Dialoghi metafisici* (Metaphysical dialogues). 'Cosmological' would be, perhaps, a better qualifying adjective. The next three treatises, the *Dialoghi morali* (Moral dialogues), deal with man and human destiny. They were all written and published at London between the years 1584 and 1585.

The three metaphysical treatises are, in order of publication:

a) *La cena de le ceneri* (The Communion of ashes) in which Copernican heliocentrism is both exalted and transcended in opposition to the Aristotelian and Ptolemaic systems.

b) *De la causa, principio et uno* (Cause, principle and unity). This title, being more explicit, gives more indication of the subject. It deals with an investigation and examination of the first principle, relation of God to the universe, structure of matter and the material universe.

c) *De l'infinito universo et mondi* (The infinite universe and worlds),[52] in which the thesis of infinitude is maintained. It refutes Aristotle's *De coelo* point by point.

The first and third treatises deal with the same problems and come to similar conclusions, but differ profoundly in style and arrangement of the argument.

The original editions of these texts have become extremely rare, but they are available in several modern editions, particularly that of Giovanni Gentile (Bari, 1925); and, as regards the *Cena de le ceneri*, there is the excellent critical edition of Giovanni Aquilecchia (Turin, 1955).

The treatise *De la causa* has been translated into French by Émile Namer (Paris, 1930), with an introduction and very informative notes on sources relating to Brunonian thought. There is an English translation by Dorothea Waley Singer of the dialogues *De l'infinito universo et mondi* (New York and London, 1950), which is prefaced by an important study of Giordano Bruno's life and philosophical work.

2. Latin poems. With regard to these three poems, which are divided into numerous chapters mostly followed by a prose commentary, it may be said with even more justification than in the case of the vernacular dialogues that they constitute a single work. They were published twice during 1591, though the author intended to have them printed in a single volume prefaced by a dedicatory letter to the Duke of Brunswick, which would indicate the scope and plan. They are usually referred to by their abbreviated titles *De minimo, De monade* and *De immenso*. The full titles are as follows:

De triplici minimo et mensura ad trium speculativarum scientiarum et multarum activarum artium principia libri V.

De monade, numero et figura liber consequens quinque de minimo magno et mensura. (It will be noted that the order of the two works is precisely stated.)

De innumerabilibus, immenso et infigurabili, seu de universo et mundis libri octo.

At the beginning of 1591 Bruno was at Frankfurt, but he had to leave hastily when he received the final printed sheets of *De minimo*. The dedication had not yet been written. *De minimo* appeared by itself, at the time of the Spring Fair, with the imprint *Francofurti, apud J. Wechelum et P. Fischerum consortes*. The printing went on, and the following two poems (together with the Letter of Dedication, which ought to have been placed at the beginning of volume one) were published together, with the same imprint, in time for the Autumn Fair.[53]

These original printings are no less rare than the vernacular dialogues. Fortunately, the edition of Fiorentino and the analyses of Felice Tocco are available.

The first and third poems resume in a new guise, but with variations that it is essential to note, the arguments put forward in the metaphysical dialogues. *De minimo* deals more particularly with the structure of matter and its ultimate elements; *De monade* is a digression on the virtues of numbers and the way of constructing elementary figures; *De immenso* describes the result of these constructions, namely, the innumerable worlds constituting the universe. On the author's own admission, only this last poem puts forward a principle based upon facts. The first poem conveys rather the activity of an intellect anxious to penetrate the secrets of nature; and the second is an uncertain investigation—misgivings, too easily appeased by verbal explanations:

'*In primo volumine studiose cupimus, in secundo incerti quaerimus, in tertio clarissime invenimus. In primo plus valet sensus, in secundo verba, in tertio res.*'[54]

It goes without saying that in examining the fundamental works of Bruno, which have been listed above, we cannot neglect making reference to his other writings, especially the *Eroici furori* and to the following Latin works:

Figuratio Aristotelici Physici auditus (Paris, 1586);

Camoeracensis acrotismus seu rationes articulorum physicorum adversus peripateticos Parisiis propositorum (Wittenberg, 1588);[55] and

Summa terminorum metaphysicorum ad capessandum logicae et philosophiae studium (Zürich, 1595; written in 1591).

Is there such a thing as, and can we speak of, Giordano Bruno's 'system of the universe'? The purpose of the present work being to give an affirmative answer to this question, there is no need to linger over the matter at this stage; but there is another more immediately urgent question which can be formulated as follows: Has Bruno left a systematic exposition of his tenets?[56] In this connection, a first appraisal of the texts leads to two findings which incline the reader to contradictory conclusions according as he considers the literary types to which they belong or the manner in which they are put together. In fact, Brunonian cosmology is expressed in works which are either familiar dialogues or poems—at least if we restrict ourselves to the chief of them; on the other hand, these dialogues and poems have in common a scholarly, careful and almost meticulous method of utterance which relates them rather to the orderly writings of theologians than to the notebooks of a Leonardo. On opening these books, one is struck by the abundance of subdivisions into chapters and paragraphs (obligingly announced in the foreword), and by the profusion of sub-titles and numbered arguments.

This rigid framework gives a finished design which ought not to make us prejudge the picture in whose interior freedom of expression asserts its rights. The form given by Bruno to his description of the universe—it has frequently been said, but will bear repetition—is characterized by three tokens: it is poetic, polemic and aphoristic.

It is poetic not only on account of the translation of astronomical theorems into hexameters: 'Copernicus versified', wrote Erminio Troilo with regard to certain passages in *De immenso*;[57] and not only by the introduction of poetic texts into the *Cena de le ceneri* and *De l'infinito*, but also by the ever present underlying lyricism, sometimes bursting forth even from the prose. A picture of the universe impressed on the mind like the souvenir of an obsessive dream looms on every page under the torn veil of appearances.

We have no need to revert to the polemical strain in Bruno's treatises: criticism of adverse arguments is usually accompanied by violent and sarcastic expressions, and even praise is interrupted by the least disagreement in order to make room for sudden severe judgement.

The 'aphoristic'[58] character of our texts is equally noteworthy, though it is not so readily apparent. In fact, it is very often concealed under the apparatus of a prolix argumentation. The arguments themselves, however, based on pre-suppositions, implied axioms, or postulates stated as evidence lead the reader to positive assertions rather than to proved conclusions. In this respect, Bruno has been compared with the pre-Socratics, and it is true that his judgements concerning the principles of things, the structure of matter, the infinite, continuity and discontinuity are reminiscent of fragments from the earliest physiologers of Ionia rather than from treatises of Aristotle.[59]

The universe as it appears through the dialogues, poems and glosses of Bruno results less from a logical construction or methodical reflection on tangible data than from response to a vision antecedent to all experience and into which the thinking individual transfers his most intimate secret. Consequently, there is nothing surprising in the propensity for aphorism; neither in polemical violence, for the whole man is in action; if the discussion becomes exacerbated, it is because it no longer turns on a subject that can be calmly and almost impartially considered in such and such perspective, but on the perspective itself, which can no longer be selected.

As for the irruptions of poetry, it is too easy to see in them the consequence of the same causes. Bruno uses and abuses images: they flourish spontaneously in him, and he has recourse to them in a stereotyped manner. His treatises on mnemotechny with the promising titles *Triginta sigillorum explicatio, De imaginum compositione* offer a vast repertoire of subjects or allegorical attributes each of which should evoke a moral entity by association. This rather too simple mechanical procedure may undoubtedly be criticized and its efficacy may be doubted, apart from its utility, for the mental effort needed to retain the figures is just as great as that which would have to be made in order to retain the entities they represent;[60] we are obliged to remember the excesses of baroque allegory and the codified iconology of Cesare Ripa. With emblems in *Eroici furori*, Bruno is more fortunate and rises from allegory to symbol and shows a remarkable sense of myth. The fable, the poetic image, and metaphor are no longer vain ornaments, but become vehicles of thought. Finally, in the cosmological treatises the profusion of mythological figures and fictions serves not only the desire to flatter the reader's taste, but also the concern for unfolding a passage from semblance to essence, from shadow to substance. Being a reflection of ineffable truth, symbol is suited to a description of a universe which is itself a reflection of God.

It is suited also (and the author was possibly not fully conscious of the fact) to the declaration of a doctrine which, in spite of its pretension of setting up a system, is in the first place the transposed recital of a personal adventure, a kind of journey of the soul towards a mental picture predicted and desired even before it became recognized and designated as the *Brunonian Philosophy*. In the 'noble dwelling', where the 'heart' that 'knoweth beyond knowledge' was preceded by the waft of a wing, there the mind is nurtured in exile, as we are told by the legend of the solitary sparrow, that is to say, where the realm of reason no longer stretches.[61] Having returned to its own domain, the mind will seek in vain, from the truths by which it has been overwhelmed, the full and soothing confirmation that will always be refused to it in that state—*in questo stato*—in which we exist.

NOTES

1. See George Sarton, *Introduction to the history of science*, II, pp. 172, 340, 579. There are two independent translations of the *Almagest*; one was made from the Greek by an anonymous translator in Sicily in 1160; the other from the Arabic by Gerard of Cremona in 1175. See Sarton, *ibid.*, p. 403.

2. Evidence is provided by the numerous condemnations pronounced by the ecclesiastical authorities.

3. Étienne Gilson, *La philosophie au moyen âge*, Paris, 1922, vol. II, 4.

4. See H. De Wulf, *Histoire de la philosophie médiévale*, Louvain and Paris, 1947, Vol. III.

5. Alfred Ernout, *Introduction à Lucrèce, De la Nature*, Paris, coll. Guillaume Budé, 1920, Vol. I, p. xxi.

6. D. W. Singer, *Giordano Bruno*, London and New York, 1950, p. 52, n. 14.

6b. *On the conformity of astronomy with celestial theory and natural philosophy.*

7. Only the second part of *Astronomiae instauratae progymnasmata* appeared at Oranienburg in 1588 under the title *De mundi aetherii recentioribus phaenomenis liber secundus*, and not at Copenhagen in 1589 (as Brunet says when mentioning this edition without describing it). The first part was published for the first time at Prague after Tycho Brahe's death and under the supervision of Kepler; its title is *Tychonis Brahe Dani Astronomiae instauratae progymnasmata quorum haec prima pars de restitutione motuum solis & lunae, stellarumque inerrantium tractat . . .* Typis inchoata Uraniburgi Daniae, absoluta Pragae Bohemiae MDCII. Some copies with the same imprint bear the date 1603. John Allyne Gade (*The life and times of Tycho Brahe*, Princeton and New York, 1947) does not take it into account. A new edition appeared at Frankfurt in 1610.

8. *A Prognostication everlasting of ryght good effect . . .* published by L. Digges . . . corrected and augmented by T. Digges, London, 1576. The appendix is entitled: *A perfit description of the caelestiall orbes according to the most aunciente doctrines of the Pythagoreans, latelye revived by Copernicus and by geometricall demonstrations approved.*

8b. *On the magnet and magnetic bodies and the great Earth magnet, a new philosophy demonstrated by numerous arguments.*

9. Pp. 3–4.

10. See V. Spampanato, *Vita di Giordano Bruno, con documenti editi e inediti*, Messina, 1921, Vol. I, p. 338.

11. Under the pontificate of Paul V, Redento Baran-Zano, a Barnabite of Serravalle Sesia, still affirmed terrestrial motion in his *Uranoscopia*, Geneva, 1617 (Cap. X, quaest. 3a), but the following year in *Nova de motu terrae copernicaeo juxta Summi Pontificis mentem disputatio*, Geneva, 1618, he retracted, consequent upon condemnation of the Copernican system by Paul V. See Aldo Mieli, *Gli scienzati italiani*, Rome, 1921–1923, Vol. I, p. 211.

12. Numerous works in support of geocentrism were still being published in the second half of the seventeenth century; for example, Orazio Maria Bonfioli, *De immobilitate Terrae tractatus*, Bologna, 1667.

13. See Jean Dagens, *Bérulle et les origines de la restauration catholique (1575–1611)*, Bruges, Desclée De Brouwer, 1952, p. 22.

14. E. Gilson, *Étude sur le rôle de la pensée médiévale dans la formation du système cartésien*, Paris, 1951, p. 271; see *ibid.*, p. 41, n. 1.

15. Edmund Husserl, *Idées directrices pour une phénoménologie* (trans. P. Ricœur), p. 327, n. a.

16. '. . . *gli Peripatetici nella dottrina de quali siamo allievati, et nodriti in gioventú . . .*' *Eroici Furori*, p. 109; see also Spampanato, *Vita di Giordano Bruno*, chap. V, *Studi e sacerdozio*.

17. *Eroici Furori*, pp. 366–367.

18. *Ibid.*

19. '*Tanto che, dove naturalmente* [*i.e.*, according to a knowledge of nature] *possiamo parlare, non è mestiero di far ricorso alle matematiche fantasie.*' *Infinito*, p. 345.

20. *Cena*, p. 209.

21. '*Ac totidem sensus animae putat esse fenestras,*
     Externos vulgus, qui tum bona tum mala menti
     Insinuant, operam veluti distinctio quinis
     Aptata est digitis, unde et fas omne nefasque est.'
          De monade, VI, verses 67–70. (*Opera*, I, ii, p. 405.)

22. '. . . *ubi tandem Fabritius Mordens Salernitanus inventionum mechanicarum*

53

parens non modo hujusce generis artes collapsas instaurat, emortuas revocat, mutilas perficit: sed et quasdam pro impossibiltatis specie nunquam intentas exsuscitat.' *Due dialoghi sconosciuti e due dialoghi noti* ... edited by Giovanni Aquilecchia, p. 31. Bruno's excessive admiration for Mordente was noted particularly by Tocco, *Opere di Giordano Bruno*, p. 119, and more critically by Olschki, *Giordano Bruno*, chap. xiv. With regard to the relationships between Bruno and Mordente, which were far from being always cordial, see the note by G Aquilecchia on pp. vii–xxiii of the work mentioned.

23. *De minimo*, III, ix (*Opera*, I, iii, pp. 258–261).

24. *Spaccio*, p. 171; *De minimo*, II, vii and viii (*Opera*, I, iii, pp. 212 ff); and III, xii (pp. 266–267); in this last mentioned chapter the possibility of quadrature is said to result from equivalence of the smallest arc with the least chord; see the prose commentary, p. 267: '*Ut minimum primamque partem licet invenisse, ita et ex indifferentia suppositi minimi arcus et* minimae chordae via est ad possibilem circuli quadraturam. . . .'

25. Tocco, *Opere de Giordano Bruno*, p. 164.

26. *Cena*, p. 90.

27. *Cena*, pp. 90–91.

28. *Cena*, pp. 92–93: '*Uomo che quanto al giudizio naturale è stato molto superiore a Tolomeo, Ipparco, Eudoxo, et tutti gli altri, ch'han camminato appo i vestigii di questi: al che è divenuto per essersi liberato da alcuni presuppositi falsi de la commune e volgar filosofia, non voglio dir cecità. Ma però non se n'è molto allontanato: perche lui più studioso de la matematica che de la natura, non ha possuto profondar, e penetrar sin tanto che potesse a fatto toglier via le radici d' inconvenienti e vani principii, onde perfettamente sciogliesse tutte le contrarie difficultà, e venesse a liberar e sé, ed altri da tante vane inquisizioni, e fermar la contemplazione ne le cose costante e certe.*'

29. On the choice of this name, see *Cabala*, p. 271, n. 1. According to Bartholmess and Spampanato, Gentile assumes that 'Onorio' (from ὄνος and *rio*) could mean 'wicked donkey' (*asino malvagio*).

30. '*Mi dissi principe de' peripatetici; insegnai in Atene nel sottoportico Liceo: dove, secondo il lume, e per dir il vero, secondo le tenebre che regnavano in me, intesi ed insegnai perversamente circa la natura de li principi e sustanza delle cose, delirai più che l'istessa delirazione circa l'essenza de l'anima, nulla possevo comprendere per dritto circa la natura del moto e de l'universo; ed in conclusione son fatto quello per cui la scienza naturale e divina è stinta nel bassissimo de la ruota, come in tempo de gli Caldei e Pitagorici è stata in esaltazione.*' *Cabala*, p. 281.

31. *Opere latine di Giordano Bruno*, pp. 327 ff.

32. This criticism is made by Tocco, but particularly by L. Olschki, *Giordano Bruno*, Bari, 1927, p. 62; and less severely by V. Di Giovanni, *Giordano Bruno e le fonti della suo dottrina*, Palermo, 1888, p. 147.

33. '. . . *quindi i Peripatetici e Platonici* ... *innumerabili specie comprendono sotto determinati geni, quali Archita primo volse fussero diece.*' *Causa*, p. 259. G. Gentile has the following note on this passage: '*Il Bruno, attenendosi manifestamente a Simplicio, crede autentico lo scritto sulle categorie* ... *dello Pseudo Archita* ... *Non è punto verisimile, come pare al Lasson* ... *che il Bruno abbia avuto sott'occhio i* Καθολικοὶ λόγοι δέκα, *pubblicati dal Camerario la prima volta a Venezia nel 1561. . . .*' Gentile has confused two editions here: that of the Greek text by Camerarius, Leipzig, [n.d., 1564], and the Greek-Latin edition of Domenico Pizzimenti, Venice, 1561.

34. *Cena*, p. 207.

35. '. . . *profondamente considerando con gli filosofi naturali, lasciando i logici ne le lor fantasie, troviamo che tutto lo che fa differenza e numero è puro accidente. . . .*' *Causa*, p. 251.

36. *Eroici furori*, II, ii, pp. 371–373.

37. '*Onde Pitagora, Parmenide, Platone non denno essere si sciocamente interpretati, secondo la pedantesca censure di Aristotele.*' *Causa*, p. 144.

38. *Causa*, p. 257; *Eroici furori*, p. 420 and n. 13.

39. *Infinito*, pp. 364–366.

40. *Timaeus*, 40 *b–c*. With regard to this passage, the meaning of which is dis-

puted, see the note and account by Albert Rivaud, pp. 155 and 59–63 of the edition published by Guillaume Budé, Paris, 1925.

41. '*Ma certamente al Nolano poco si aggiunge che il Copernico, Niceta Siracusano Pitagorico, Filolao, Eraclide di Ponto, Ecfanto Pitagorico, Platone nel Timeo (ben che timida, ed incostantemente perchè l'avea più per fede che per scienza) ed il divino Cusano nel secondo suo libro De la dotta ignoranza, ed altri in ogni modo rari soggetti, l'abbino detto insegnato ed confirmato prima: perchè lui lo tiene per altri proprii e più saldi principii, per i quali non per autoritate, ma per vivo senso e raggione, ha così certo questo, come ogn'altra cosa che possa aver per certa.' Cena*, pp. 149–150.

42. F. Tocco gives several examples in *Le fonti più recenti della filosofia del Bruno (Rendiconti della R. Accad. dei Lincei, classe di scienze morali, storiche e filologiche*, Ser. V, Vol. I, fasc. 7 and 8, pp. 503–538 and 585–622).

43. For example, *De monade*, V (*Opera*, I, ii, p. 408): '*Unus e principibus Platonicis, Ficinus.*'

44. *Causa*, pp. 139 and 245; and see Tocc, *Fonti*, p. 505.

45. *De Vinculis* (*Opera*, III, p. 696); *Causa*, pp. 203 and 213.

46. *Oratio valedictoria* (*Opera*, I, i, p. 17).

47. Lefèvre and Bovelles are mentioned by Giordano Bruno among the authors who have praised Raymond Lull or are recommended by him: '*Mitto quantum Lullio tribuat mille in propositis Stapulensis ille Faber, in cuius unica philosophia iuxta Peripateticorum dogmata Gallia gloriatur; mitto Carolum Bovillum, non tam (si Aristarchorum ferulae subiiciantur) orationis stilo Fabro ipso humilior, quam (si e cathedra philosophiae examinentur) ingenio illustrior iudicioque in multiplici disciplinarum genera maturior et excultior, qui de Lullii vita scripsit, Lullianae doctrinae edit ubique specimen et ubique pro summo habet honore, ut Lullianus appareat.' De lampada combinatoria*, Dedicatory letter (*Opera*, II, ii, p. 235).

48. 'Pedant's excrement.' *Causa*, p. 202.

49. D. W. Singer, *Giordano Bruno*, London and New York, 1950, p. 62.

50. Armando Carlini, '*La metafisica del Rinascimento*' in *Giornale critico della filosofia italiana*, 1948, p. 31.

51. See *Eroici furori*, Introduction, pp. 19–21.

52. The title is punctuated as follows: *De l'infinito, universo et mondi*, and therefore should be translated *On the infinite, the universe and worlds*. This is the punctuation recommended by Gentile (*Infinito*, p. 269, n. 1), and which we ourselves have adopted (*Eroici furori*, p. 20 and n. 8). Examination of the original edition of 1584 (where the comma is missing after *infinito* on the main title, but is present on the half-title!) leaves us in some doubt; in agreement with D. W. Singer, we now prefer *De l'infinito universo* . . . a title which seems to us more in keeping with the contents of the book which has little to say about the *infinite* apart from the *infinite universe*, whatever Gentile may say.

53. *De minimo* is prefaced only by a dedication by Johann Wechel. It says, that Bruno, being prevented by circumstances from giving final attention to this book and its successors, had instructed his printer to offer to the Duke of Brunswick: '*Tandem cum ultimum dumtaxat superesset operis folium, casu repentino a nobis avulsus, extremam ei, ut ceteris, manum imponere non potuit. Per literas igitur rogavit, ut quod sibi per fortunam non licerat, nos pro se suo nomine praestaremus. . . .' Opera*, I, iii, pp. 123–124.

54. Dedication to Heinrich Julius, Duke of Brunswick (*Opera*, I, i, p. 196).

55. This work is a summary of the theses defended at the *Collège de Cambrai* of the University of Paris (whence the adjective *camoeracensis*) by one of Giordano Bruno's pupils called Hennequin. The word *Acrotismus* is not clear. Tocco (*Opere latine di Giordano Bruno*, p. 107) relates it either to the Aristotelian term ἀκρόασις or preferably to ἀχρότης (summit): in this case it would mean that the discussion was concerned with certain of the most prominent points in Aristotelian physics.

56. The answer this time is negative; but the circumstances under which Bruno's work was written must be taken into account, not forgetting that he had not yet completed his forty-fifth year when imprisonment put an end to his activity as a writer.

57. Erminio Troilo, *La filosofia di Giordano Bruno*, Turin, 1907, p. 96.
58. For the 'aphoristic' system of Giordano Bruno, see L. Olschki, *Giordano Bruno*, p. 61.
59. Olschki (*loc. cit.*) compares Bruno with Leonardo da Vinci, for both of them, he says, affirm more than they infer. It cannot be denied that if their opinions regarding method in science, in particular as to the explanatory value of mathematics, be contrary, nevertheless those opinions themselves are never brought under discussion.
60. See F. Tocco, *Opere latine di Giordano Bruno*, pp. 91–101.
61. *Eroici furori*, I, iv, pp. 208 ff; and Introduction, pp. 53–54.

I

The universe as a subject of enquiry

Although the word 'cosmology' is unknown to Giordano's vocabulary, nevertheless it describes the subject of his investigations sufficiently well for us to have no hesitation in using it. The texts, which we propose to consider, are in effect concerned with a knowledge of the cosmos, a justification, a *logos*, an interpretation, an attempt to get back to causes and principles. A philosopher has in view not only a description, but also a systematic description, and as far as it is possible an explanation of the universe—a universe which he will consider as a whole and in all its parts, the form and dimensions, origin and future, rest and motion, structure, tangible aspects and smallest details.

All these matters involve various problems the possible solutions to which must have seemed remote to anyone in the sixteenth century. Solutions had been put forward ever since Greek Antiquity, and it was left to the freedom of the most intrepid thinker to choose in each case the one that appeared to him the best. Nevertheless, in the circumstances of genuine meditation, his originality will not fail in the first instance to manifest itself by the use he makes of multifarious sources, the motives that determine his choice of them, the style of his pronouncements, and perhaps, most of all, the extent to which he believes it possible to give a valid answer to the questions that have arisen; in other words, his conception of the universe *qua* subject of knowledge.

According to Bruno, there are two modes of study: the one is rational, the other irrational. By following the latter method, truth is sought, or else attained, by the paths of free-will, and of *love*, which is personified in *Eroici furori* by the 'irrational boy' (*il putto irrazionale*).[1] Study then implies a kind of abandon or over-stepping of oneself. On the other hand, by following the rational method, truth summons up the bare faculties of man, and proceeds by the paths of the intellect, by 'natural discourse'.

'. . . All that exists is one', according to the fourth dialogue of the treatise *De causa*, 'and knowledge of this unity is the aim and term of all natural philosophies and contemplation: allowing the highest degree of contemplation, which transcends nature, and which for him without faith is impossible and nothing, to remain at its confines.'[2] This duality of method is put forward yet again, under the transparent veil of allegory, in many passages of *Eroici furori*; for example, when it is said of the hunter Actaeon that he sets his mastiffs and greyhounds on the 'sublime prey', '. . . the latter representing the working of the intellect, which precedes that of the will, and the former representing the working of the will, which is by far the most vigorous and most efficient, considering that it is easier for a man to love divine goodness and beauty than to understand them'.[3]

L. Olschki, who is quite ready to reveal in Bruno's thought contradictions that are not always there, was struck by the fact that *De umbris idearum* and the dialogues *De la causa* maintain the impossibility of supreme metaphysical knowledge, whereas the *Eroici furori* accept 'in an inspired flight of thought, not only knowledge and vision of God, but even ecstatic union with the divinity'.[4] However, we should regard that as two complementary aspects of a single consistent thought, rather than two different modes. No doubt, *De umbris* seems to be a neo-Platonic treatise on inspiration, in which ideas are defined as metaphysical entities present in oneself and out of reach of human intelligence, but it is definitely stated on many occasions—if ony by reference to *The Song of Solomon: 'I sat down under his shadow with great delight, and his fruit was sweet to my taste'*,[5] and by the very title of the work which is the same as that of one ascribed to pseudo-Solomon.[6] Bruno does not believe in the existence of ideas, although certain poetical and symbolic developments may give the illusion; he refused to acknowledge any substance in them. What he does assert, and he does so constantly, is the cessation of *natural* knowledge at the boundaries of a forbidden domain where the essence is concealed.

As in the theological order of things God is unknowable in essence, similarly our knowledge of tangible objects is that of phenomena and relationships between phenomena: we do not arrive at the true nature of things. Although the *Eroici furori* envisages the possibility of rising to the essence and Supreme Goodness, it is made superabundantly clear that the inward light would not be obtained through the intellect, but through the will. The intellect most certainly desires, and does so ardently, but in vain. The purpose of the work is definitely to show that man by his own efforts is incapable of this metaphysical ascension and that his defeat is glorious but inevitable. Icarus, in full flight, foresaw his fall; Actaeon knew that he would be devoured by his dogs. The *De umbris*, the treatise *De la causa*, and *Eroici furori* in fact give expression to the same helplessness in different ways, which correspond in each of these works to the particular purpose in view.

In his forty-eighth sermon on the *Song of Solomon*, Saint Bernard, taking as his text, *sub umbra illius*, from the same verse, draws this lesson—that as long as we live we are in a region of shadow, which is that of faith. We cannot reach a full knowledge of supreme truths: if this knowledge is to be granted to us, it will be through an inward light which we should endeavour to merit, but which in any case will not arise till after death (*post mortem*). It would be superfluous to dwell on the gap between Giordano Bruno and Saint Bernard, the latter, indifferent to the teachings of nature, having in view only the knowledge of divine mysteries. However, the two comments include one point in common: both of them assert that here below (Bruno says *in questo stato*) we are confined to a zone, to a region of shadow, and that there are truths inaccessible to reason.

Bruno returns so often to this idea that it would be easy to gather the references. We shall limit ourselves to one last quotation and deliberately borrow it from the treatise *De la causa*, for that work is the one in which Brunonian rationalism is asserted with the greatest vigour, and the one that most readily urges anyone who wishes to stress this aspect of his teaching: 'This ultimate act, which is the same as the ultimate power, cannot be understood by the intellect except by following the mode of negation;[7] I repeat, it cannot be understood neither in so far as it can be everything, nor in so far as it is everything.... There is no power of sight that can approach it, or have access to such transcending light or to such unfathomable depths.'[8]

This text, and those previously mentioned have much interset for us, for they accurately define the subject of cosmology as conceived by Bruno, and as he expounds it in his metaphysical dialogues in the vernacular as well as in his Latin poems. Without trying to go beyond the limits of what is humanly knowable, the philosopher presents in a *natural discourse* the results of his reflections, that is to say, the fruits of 'natural contemplation', only implementing and carefully distinguished from 'superior contemplation', as much by the field in which it is exercised as by his modes. These two aspects of the matter will now be considered.

THE FIELD OF NATURAL KNOWLEDGE

It has been said, taking Bruno's texts as the basis of argument, that 'natural' knowledge—which is that of the scholar and rationalist philosopher—had, in the last analysis, the same purpose as 'superior contemplation', and that they would not differ from each other except by their methods.[9] On the contrary, we believe that in the spirit of the doctrine which we are studying they differ also in their intention. Their common aim is the truth, which is unity—and we could add that their method in common is contemplation of that which exists— but, nevertheless, their field of vision is not the same for it is not the same aspect of existence that claims their attention. It is, therefore, appropriate to define the domain of natural knowledge, to indicate its extent, and to give a preliminary survey of its limits, before fixing them with greater accuracy.

The universe propounded

To assume a difference in purpose between two modes of knowledge amounts to posing a question that one would be tempted to regard as tedious seeing that it contains within itself the terms of the answer: isn't it only too obvious that the field of natural knowledge is nature, whilst that of superior contemplation is linked with the divine? No doubt, but it is still necessary to know what is understood by the expressions 'nature' and 'the divine', not forgetting that the contrast between God and Nature, between the divine and the natural, is valid only with reservations, seeing that, in the terms of what we shall call for simplification the pantheism of Giordano Bruno, God penetrates nature, and matter itself 'is divine'. Yet, if God be everywhere, His presence does not manifest itself everywhere likewise. It is necessary to distinguish between God who is implicating and God who is explicated. 'Is implicating', He enfolds everything in his unfathomable unity; 'explicated', He is nothing else but nature. *Natura est Deus in rebus*, Nature is the art of God; God in the semblance of a material universe offered to tangible experience, of a universe propounded.

It is immediately clear that if that which is propounded is available for our investigation, then that which is not propounded is inaccessible: it is the domain of the Supreme One, the for ever secret domain of the powers of divine Grace and liberty. Forbidden to the intellect, it can only be the object of love.

It may be noted in passing that if the desire to extend the range of our rational knowledge to a maximum be found in both Bruno and Ramon Lull, the retention of a region on the threshold of which our bare knowledge is the region of our ignorance links him with Nicholas of Cusa. Consequently, as regards the problem of the relationships between faith and reason, his position is defined with respect to the two writers who have exerted the greatest influence on his thought. Endowed with a generous ambition, Ramon Lull claimed to convert infidels by proving the truths of religion through irrefutable arguments. On this point, Bruno completely parts company from him.[10] He accepts, and even earnestly asserts the existence of the unknowable, and by the same token (the universe being knowable in its entirety, at least to all intents and purposes) the existence of 'a beyond the universe', of 'a no-where', of a 'no-place'.[11]

It was not enough for him to assume a limit to the discovery of the real, and to the progress of knowledge, a state which could be reached in the more or less distant future. He intended to settle accurately and to lay out beforehand the plan of an enquiry—unfinished, continually pursued, theoretically possible, but unrealizable in practice, for it demanded superhuman faculties in order to bring it to a conclusion. He took care not to imagine the domain of natural knowledge as being susceptible of expanding beyond a moving frontier that would displace itself in proportion as our vision extended to fresh zones, penetrating further the obscurity of matter and the recesses of the firmament. One of the tasks of reason is, on the contrary, to distinguish between the unknown and the unknowable, and of itself to define the field of its possibilities and future victories.

Consequently, only the unexplored parts of its own empire will ever be open to the conquests of science. It is true that this empire extends far, and even to infinity, for it is equal to the universe—a universe that Bruno regards as an 'explication' of God under variable and manifold aspects; but which he could have defined just as well, with one of our contemporary philosophers, as 'the sum of objects within possible experience',[12] for every object being part of the universe, even though it is beyond our range, remains an object of

possible experience and by that very fact belongs to natural knowledge.

One direct consequence of these premises is to deprive the word
'heaven' of its usual, popular meaning of 'paradise'. It is not ad-
visable to hope to find 'another world' in the ultimate sphere or
beyond the starry firmament. Doubtless, it befell the philosopher-
poet to recapture the theme of the winged soul, to say that it stretches
upwards, rises and takes flight (whether it be a question of Icarus or
the sparrow);[13] but then he is speaking in metaphor. He is far from
lacking appreciation of the evocative value of an image, and he does
not fail to give the reminder that it is only an image,[14] a precaution
that may seem superfluous to us now, but which was justifiable at a
time when the ancient belief that put the seat of the gods or the abode
of the blessed on the heights of Olympus or the empyrean still survived. Giordano reacted against any conception of transcendency
that seemed coarse in his view; he was opposed to all mythology
based on cosmic dualism against which a true knowledge of nature
should thenceforth protect itself.

It has been rightly said that Brunonian rationalism, in spite of all
its intransigence, adapted itself rather well to astrology and magic.
Without making an argument of the fact that such complaisance was
shown by more than one genuine scholar[15] of the period, we must not
forget that Bruno was motivated by the desire to integrate facts with
experience and to subject them to scientific consideration, such facts,
though apparently mysterious, are none the less provided by nature,
and an observer can legitimately take account of them; for example,
hidden 'forces' in the elements, 'influence' of celestial bodies, subjects of judicial astrology and natural magic. It is only a question of
reason bringing more clarity into regions still difficult to understand,
and to areas still unsubdued, but which depend rightly on its power.

In all this we must avoid exaggerating our author's ideas. For the
Aristotelian scholastics of the thirteenth century the question of
autonomy of natural laws did not arise. Saint Thomas, without
questioning that God has full power to reverse the course of events,
notes that in fact He does nothing of the kind. He could not violate
the laws instituted by Himself. The mysticism of Avicenna agreed
with the concern 'to leave nothing outside a deterministic and rational
explanation of the universe'.[16] Saint Augustine, too, who teaches
that the action of Providence is constantly exerted on human destinies,
nevertheless accepts the existence of 'mechanisms' that subject the

material of events to a kind of historic materialism. Though all history be sacred history, that does not remove from his sight 'all reality, all causality peculiar to those instruments, those *machinamenta* which, considered in their proper character and in their rôle of subordinate ends, have their own value'.[17] No doubt, we can say that those views relate to the human order, but they are naturally applicable to the cosmic order.

For all that, Bruno adds something to these peaceful assertions: he gives them another emphasis; he colours them with bursts of his impatience and fervour, and impetuously develops the consequences therefrom. To proclaim the permanent value of natural laws signifies to him a surrender of the whole universe to an investigation by knowledge emancipated from all dogma; a challenge at one fell swoop to the intrusion of a foreign authority in the domains of physics and astronomy; and, by a ruthless rejection of a badly applied transcendentalism, a demand not only for philosophical freedom, but also that freedom which is appropriate to knowledge and which is accepted nowadays by the most religious minds.[18] He not only demands for reason the right to exercise itself in its own domain, but also the privilege of reigning there alone. A subject that belongs to natural knowledge is not to be known by other means.

From the existence of two fields and two modes of contemplation we must not conclude that a double truth exists. There are not two truths between which it would be possible to waver, for if reason lose all power on the threshold of the unknowable, nothing limits its decisions in the field of knowable nature. Consequently, acceptance of transcendency does not imply any restriction of the 'natural light'.[19] God is known by the intellect only to the extent by which He manifests Himself—where there is nature, *Deus in rebus*—but, to that extent, He demands to be known only in that manner. J. Roger Charbonnel said that Bruno, if called upon to choose between 'two truths', would finally have opted for scientific truth, an option that would have led him to the extreme penalty.[20] I believe that it would be nearer the truth to say that he was opposed, not finally but always and in principle, to the encroachment of dogma on to the field of knowledge and to the abuses of a physics improperly elevated into an article of faith. He did not have to choose between two aspects of a single truth and we do not rightly understand why he should have repudiated 'superior contemplation' the purpose of which can only be love.

63

THE MODES OF NATURAL KNOWLEDGE

Bruno preferred the expression 'natural knowledge' to 'rational knowledge' which he happened to use; they are equivalent, but the former is richer in meaning seeing that it evokes both the concept in a field of knowledge (nature) and that of an instrument of knowledge (man's natural faculties).

Natural knowledge is that of the physical universe; then again it is rational, and therefore discursive: such is its mode. Unlike the sudden flights and inspirations of faith, it is an up-hill climb, little by little, a slow operation: *intelligere est cum labore et successione, non autem fides*.[21] Looked at in this way, knowledge appears not as a grace from heaven but as a victory by man, the conquest of a truth obtained by a display of energy, the result of an effort which implies a certain duration, the conclusions of a *discourse*. Physical (*i.e.*, natural) knowledge is distinguished by these characteristics from 'metaphysical' knowledge: '. . . the divine truth, when it reveals itself to those rare minds to which it grants that favour, following a supernatural (metaphysical) mode, does not subject its advent to measurements of motion and time as happens in physical sciences (I mean those branches of knowledge that are acquired by natural learning, starting from one known thing according to sense or reason in order to arrive at something else, as yet unknown: the discursive method known as argumentation), but on the contrary appears suddenly and unexpectedly, according to the mode that suits its action.'[22]

Leaving these unforeseeable sudden outbursts aside, all knowledge is therefore subjected to measurement in time and must comprise degrees. Before passing to a consideration of these degrees, we must note the double meaning of the word *natural* in expressions such as 'natural knowledge', 'natural discourse'. Sometimes, as in the passage just quoted, it stands in opposition to *supernatural*; at other times, acquiring the meaning that we give to *physical* when we speak of the 'physical sciences', it stands in opposition to *mathematical*. Mathematics is undoubtedly discursive, too, and in this respect just as 'natural' as physics; but between these two 'discourses', physical and mathematical, the philosopher who has a clear concept of the universe in view must prefer the former. Consequently, as we already know, Bruno reproached Copernicus for his 'discourse which is more mathematical than natural' (*più matematico che naturale discorso*). He regarded mathematics at most as one of the preliminary exercises of knowledge, and often a mere intellectual game not leading to the knowledge of any concrete reality: the game of Geometry is one thing, the capture of natural truths is quite another.[23] Does this anti-mathematical prepossession, which rather baffles us and would have annoyed Leonardo, find its counterpart in a pronounced taste for experimenting? Far from it. The means that the philosopher sets to work in order to realize his cosmological construction are not those of experimental science. If he starts from experimental data, it is because he must: on the level of tangibility, data are the primary material of knowledge; but all subsequent progress towards truth is obtained through reason.

The minor works of Giordano Bruno—the *Summa terminorum metaphysicorum*, the 'Lullian' works—even more than the dialogues and the cosmological poems, proclaim this absolute confidence in the efficacy of human reason properly exercised. The *Summa terminorum*, when defining terms such as *cognito, comprehensio*, outlines a theory of knowledge which goes back to Aristotle; to the *Analytica posteriora*, and the third book of the treatise *De anima*; furthermore, this style of philosophical dictionary takes its inspiration from Book V (delta) of *Metaphysica*, the plan of which is retained. As for Bruno's admiration for Ramon Lull, it is directed to the logician whose certain method was calculated to bring unity to knowledge.[24] He does not follow him blindly; he criticizes him on occasion and makes it his duty to perfect him,[25] though he found in the *Ars magna* of Lull the fundamentals of a discipline of the mind which he used as the propaedeutics of his own teaching.[26]

The degrees of the discursus (*discursive knowledge*)—Bruno reverts six times to an enumeration of the degrees of the *discursus*, each time making some modifications to his theory. A summary of these successive schemes will now be given.

In *De umbris idearum* (1582) he distinguishes nine degrees of cognizance, namely: *animi purgatio, attentio, ordinis contemplatio, proportionalis ex ordine collatio, negatio, votum, transformatio sui in rem, transformatio rei in seipsum*. The influence of neo-Platonism is obvious. These nine degrees are in part the same as the seven degrees mentioned by Ficino in his commentary on the sixth *Ennead*.[27]

In *Sigillus sigillorum* (1583), the scale comprises only five degrees: *sensus, imaginatio, ratio, intellectus* and *mens. Ascent in the scale* takes place in such a way that each degree represents deep thought, a conscious link with the preceding one, exceeded but not eliminated, perfected rather than destroyed: sensation is only the raw material of knowledge; to imagine is to be aware of sensation; to reason is to reflect on the picture thus formed; to seize with the intellect is to be conscious of this reasoning; finally, it is in the divine *mens* that the intellect itself acquires understanding.[28]

In the vernacular treatise *De l'infinito* (1584), the moments of cognizance are reduced to four, *imaginatio* having disappeared. 'Where is truth?' asks Elpino. Filoteo, the faithful expositor of Brunonian philosophy, replies: 'In tangible things, as seen in a mirror; in reason, through the mode of argumentation and discourse; in the intellect, through the mode of principle or of conclusion; in the *mens*, in its proper and living form.'[29] Reason appears here as the 'discursive' faculty *par excellence*; it constitutes, none the less, part of the total *discursus* which proceeds from *sensus* to *mens*. This Pythagorean quadripartite division is to be found in Aristotle's *De anima*: sensation, opinion, knowledge and understanding;[30] the terms are different but the progress upwards is the same, from $\alpha \iota \sigma \theta \eta \sigma \iota s$ to $\nu o \hat{v} s$ by the intermediate and more appropriate discursive stage of $\delta \delta \xi \alpha$ and $\epsilon \pi \iota \sigma \theta \eta \mu \eta$.

In *De monade* (1591), the scheme of the *discursus* is further simplified: it is in the chapter dealing with the Triad that allusion is made to the degrees of cognizance. The first cognitive act is still sensation; then follows reason, whose effort is crowned by the intellect. The two terms *intellectus* and *mens*, having become synonyms, both in turn designate this outcome: *Principium, medium, finis, Sensus, Ratio, Mens*, and several lines later: *Sensus . . . Ratio . . . Intellectus*.[31]

The *De minimo* (1591) contains a description full of imagery of these three moments. The *sensus* from its dungeon of darkness (*in carcere tenebrarum*) perceives the universe only through vents and holes (*per cancellos et foramina*). Reason sees the light of the Sun as through a window (*tanquam per fenestram*); the intellect, in the open (*in aperto*), dominates all diversity and 'contemplates the Sun itself'. The word *mens* appears in the subsequent lines without specifying a fresh stage, and furthermore it is used as synonymous with *intellectus*.[32]

The *Summa terminorum metaphysicorum* (written about 1591, published in 1595) revives the four terms *sensus, ratio, intellectus, mens*, which signified the four stages of truth in the treatise *De l'infinito*.[33]

Intellectus and *mens* are distinguished anew. Later on, we shall see how this distinction must be interpreted; but we must consider each term in the discourse, starting at the bottom of the scale, *i.e.*, with sensation.

Sensus

The *discursus* which takes us on the path from ignorance to under-standing—and it would be as well to call it total discourse in order to distinguish it from specific rational discourse—ultimately comprises three degrees: sensation, reason, intellection; the other more or less numerous degrees being only sub-divisions or intermediate stages. Attention and imagination, without being on the level of pure sensation, do not yet rise to that of reason. Their coming into play represents a correction of the *sensus* by itself and ends in the first elaboration of the perceived impression, the result of which is to offer reason material more worthy of its consideration. The primary material of knowledge, crude sensation—scattered and fugitive—will have efficacy only by finding itself and attaching itself to some aspect of reality, and so assuring itself of some degree of permanence. Such is the rôle of *attention*. Perceptions, absent-mindedly received, leave no trace. The elements of a figure are not recognized as such, they remain without relationship.[34] They are not objects, but spots of colour. Having been fixed by attention, they will be ready to be fixed into cohesive assemblies, to constitute pictures and to receive a name. This formation of pictures susceptible of being given names is the task of the *imaginatio*, a faculty which is an organizing one in the first place; afterwards, when joined to reality, it is creative, but then the term *phantasia* is better suited to it.[35]

Even after these initial corrections, the perceived impression is still inadequate and in many respects suspect. Bruno insists a great deal on this inadequacy.[36] An experiment uncontrolled or badly controlled by the mind runs the risk of being the basis of erroneous theories. For example, because the Earth is apparently motionless we could conclude that it is indeed motionless and that the celestial vault is endowed with a diurnal motion. Objects set up by the imagination are only too often merely pseudo-objects, illusions, phantasma. Another inadequacy derives from the limited range or indifferent acuity of our senses, which are incapable of discerning the ultimate elements of matter on account of their smallness as well as of embracing the infinitely great. 'The infinite cannot be the subject of tangible knowledge', declares Filoteo at the beginning of a passage where he enumerates the reasons we have for doubting our senses. 'Then, what is the use of the senses?' asks Elpidio. The former replies: 'To stimulate the mind, to show up, to point out, to corroborate partially, but not entirely, even less to judge or to condemn. For, however perfect they may be, they are never free from some disturbance. So that truth, like a weakened principle and to a small extent, proceeds from the senses, but does not dwell in them.'[37]

Ratio

Reason performs the decisive step in passing from the plurality of images to unity of the idea. Some examples will give a general idea of its procedure and the means at its disposal for the purpose of correcting and completing a received experience.

One of the most confident assertions and, in its time, the boldest of Brunonian cosmography was that the stars as well as the suns, and that each one of them is, like our own Sun, surrounded by a retinue of planets. These latter are out of our sight, but it is from the existence, established and manifest to our eyes, of the planets of the solar system that we deduce their existence. Consequently, as we have already said, truth originates in the tangible 'but does not dwell therein'. Another example: the Earth appears to us to occupy the centre of the heavens; but on the surface of our globe are not we the sport of an illusion of the same order, when, at the centre of the circle that limits our horizon, we believe that the limits of that horizon are those of the universe? 'In my childhood', said Bruno, 'I thought that nothing existed beyond Vesuvius';[38] a childish mistake that was dispelled by his first trip to Naples. To this extent, the senses correct themselves. On the other hand, an astronomy that believes in the central position of the Earth will be corrected only if it reconciles its error with similar ones that can be exposed by experience. It is through confrontations of this kind that reason intervenes. It alone is able 'to give an account of, and to judge, things absent and separated from us by time and place'. 'It is against all reason to say that the universe is limited to that which our senses are able to attain; sensation enables us to conclude that bodies exist, but the absence of sensation does not permit us to infer their nonexistence.'[39]

Intellectus

Frequently, perhaps too frequently, Bruno has been accused of uncertainty in his terminology; we are of the opinion that in many instances a more attentive reading would have sufficed to resolve what was considered to be ambiguous. This uncertainty is none the less real and does not facilitate the task of the commentator who may find himself tempted, or even constrained, to rectify such improper and ambiguous use of the words *intellectus* and *mens*, or their vernacular equivalents *intelletto* and *mente*. Thus, in the passage quoted above, the power of judging things absent from, or beyond the reach of, the senses must be ascribed to the intellect. A judgement of that kind, always based on the interpretation of a received impression, is, however, the concern of reason. The highest degree of knowledge should furthermore require a dominant vision of things, penetrated to their fundamentals and brought, as far as possible, to unity.

Are these supreme operations going to develop in two stages marked by successive interventions of the *intellectus* and the *mens*? or, on the contrary, are the *intellectus* and *mens* only one and the same faculty, and must these two factors merge together? The texts, as we have said, exhibit several rather different accounts of the degrees of cognizance, and so justify asking the above question and suggesting one or the other answer.

The *Summa terminorum metaphysicorum* clearly distinguishes *intellectus* from *mens* and gives the two terms precise definitions: the intellect takes in at a glance and by pure intuition (*simplici quodam intuitu*) that which reason has conceived by argumentation and the discursive way; the *mens* is 'superior to the intellect *and to all cognizance*' (*superior intellectu et omni cognitione*); like the intellect, it apprehends its subject 'by pure intuition', but this intuition is not preceded or accompanied by any 'discourse' (*absque ullo discursu praecedente vel concomitante*).[40] Assuming that the *Summa terminorum* represents the final state of Bruno's thought, we may consider this statement as definitive. Furthermore, it dissipates most of the obscurities in the preceding texts and accounts for their differences.

In the *Sigillus*, the *mens* appears above the intellect as the instrument of the highest philosophical contemplation; it is already qualified as 'divine', but still dwells in the faculty of man, so that the human mind would be able to rise up to God, as neo-Platonic Gnosis would wish. On the other hand, according to the *Eroici furori*, this latter illumination is never attained through 'natural discourse'; being the free gift of the divinity and reward of faith, it depends on 'superior contemplation'. It is not 'preceded or accompanied by any discourse'; it is a total stranger to discourse; and that explains why, in certain texts, the *mens* 'superior to all cognizance', truth 'in its proper and living form', no longer appears amongst the degrees of cognizance—the word *mens* being then used only as synonymous with *intellectus*.

The intellect, which dominates and unifies concepts that reason has only elucidated and set in order, is certainly the final term of natural knowledge. The 'discourse' led to a point where it can only be transcended comes to its conclusion with and through the intellect.

The limits of the discursus

It is a consequence of what has gone before, that natural knowledge is a discourse which, rising from sensation to intellection, intends, without the support of any favour, without the intervention of any authority, to come to a view of the universe conformable with reason, simultaneously 'certain for me and valid in itself'. However, such a description is one of an ideal scheme, and we may ask, if in practice and in the particular case of Giordano Bruno, things really happen as the stated theory would wish. Now, to ask this question, is to admit the necessity of resuming an examination of the *discursus* from a point of view very different from that which we first adopted; we must no longer consider the fixed stages and the avowed claims, but the real possibilities and trend.

The notion of *discursus* implies that of a double limit; the very word discourse, which is related to a course, stipulates a starting point and an end point, a 'before' and a 'beyond'. We do not have in view here the field that extends, or should extend, to all nature, but the act or operation of discursive cognition, which *qua* operation, has its beginning and its end. The field which is assigned by it would only be covered by starting from complete ignorance and finishing with absolute knowledge. The ascent from the lowest degree of the *sensus* to the summit of the *intellectus* must identify itself with this full course; but, in fact, the universe (for it is knowledge of the universe that particularly interests us), even if it rightly depends on natural discourse, remains unexplorable not only in its infinite extent but also in its principles and innermost recesses, so that all cosmology is to some extent problematical. Furthermore, however, the *discursus*, *qua* operation, does not enclose within itself the totality of the moments of cognition. We cannot assert that it starts from naught, nor that it attains its end. Its development, which takes place between two limits, leaves outside of itself a 'before' and an 'after' the character of which we shall try to define.

The infra-terrestrial world of the discursus

Phenomenology has accustomed us to distinguish in our perceptions the immanent perceptions (*i.e.*, images of objects) of transcendental perceptions, and those of the objects themselves, which we 'constitute' starting from these images and to which the effort of our judgement will be applied. Bruno seems to have glimpsed something of the kind when he distinguished the crude sensation and the *imaginatio* as two successive periods—the image corresponding with him to that which we should rather call the constituted object, for it is not thought of *qua* image, but *qua* object.

On the other hand, even if the philosopher were not fully conscious of it, there is a constitution of the universe in its entirety, an ideal, a starting point antecedent to all interpretation of the phenomena, antecedent to any point of view.[41] When reason assembles the universe by interpreting the received impression and, especially when, exceeding this impression, it supplements its inadequacy, its creative action finds a stimulus and support in the presuppositions and haunting visions that the philosopher carries in himself. Isn't there an example of this in the conception of the reflected-universe, the shadow-universe described in *De umbris* and to which Bruno adhered right up to his final works? How can we speak here of a 'rational' hypothesis? In reality, the cosmic image is discovered before being sought. Its birth is an original event within oneself, which precedes the act of reason and modulates it; a necessary prelude to all cosmology, and which is easily seen to be of a theological order in the case of Bruno.

In connection with this preliminary event two problems arise; they are undoubtedly interesting, but we are not concerned with them here. The first would be to know to what secret motivations such a vision of the universe preceding any *discursus* responds: this problem, the information concerning which is concealed in the depths of the individual conscience, could be resolved only by the most detailed analysis of a *style*. The second might be stated in the following terms: whence comes the need for a rational explanation, for a recognition of the primitive vision by reason? We shall limit ourselves to a reminder that such a need is at the root of all rationalism that is really experienced, and if at certain periods it seems to be more urgent, then those recurrences are to be explained only by the presence of an archetype and which are not adequately accounted for by simple historical causality.

The supra-terrestrial world of the discursus

In the same way that all discursive thought is preceded by intuitions that have nothing in common with the primary material of the received impression, so it is followed—or can be followed—by inward enlightenment that has nothing in common with the knowledge, however sublime it may be, derived from 'natural' intellection. It is then dazzled by a truth 'in perfect and living form', which certainly deserves the qualification 'divine'. At this point everything is upset. The final step can no longer be accomplished by successive efforts, (*cum labore et successione*), but by an inexplicable jump. Reason gives up and abdicates; cognition becomes rather useless: 'This truth is sought as something inaccessible.'[42] 'That which unites us to it [truth], according to the Cabalists and certain mystical theologians' (this is an allusion to Dionysius and Nicholas of Cusa), 'is a kind of ignorance'[43] that accompanies disdain of the paths which have been traversed, for it is installed in the region towards which every path fails to appear.[44]

In this field of transcendency the intellect itself is transcendent, identified with the universal νοῦς. Cosmology ends in a noetic. The superior intellect alone operates independently of the effort which it recompenses. Here we see the break-through of a kind of passivity of the human intelligence in the very act of understanding: it accumulates facts from the *sensus*, organizes them by the *ratio*, unifies them by the natural *intellectus*; its task is then accomplished and full understanding depends only on an extraneous intrusion.[45]

We have endeavoured to explain how Bruno conceived the possibility of knowledge of the universe, and we have been immediately led to distinguish natural knowledge from supernatural knowledge, each of them having its own field and modes. We have seen that the field of natural knowledge was equivalent to that of all nature, to a tangible universe, that its modes were those of a *discursus*, and finally that, even when applied to its subject, this discursive knowledge was not the full knowledge, that it was, in fact, preceded by an initial vision, and, in faith, followed by final enlightenment. At the start, an *imago mundi* comes into view, like a design appointed beforehand for the exercise of reason and which must be accompanied by natural discourse.

This preliminary construction or *ante-discursus* can without any doubt be regarded as 'legitimate' if we believe in the 'spontaneous capacity, inherent in the human conscience, to discover objective truth independently of all revelation'.[46] However, this question of lawfulness seems to us to be a secondary one; we ought rather to ask ourselves if this original image, this design prefixed to the slow workings of the intelligence and to which we willingly give the reassuring name of 'hypothesis', would not spring up from the same source as the final enlightenment. In that manner the enveloping action of the superior νοῦς intervening at the beginning and end of the cycle would assert itself. At the beginning it suggests a phantasm, at the end it transforms the evidence from stated conclusions into ineffable truth. To the extent that it is *explicated*, or becomes *nature*, the Supreme Principle offers itself to natural contemplation as if it wished or demanded to be aspired to in the wrong way and identified in a mirror.

Natural knowledge can consequently appear as a prelude to knowledge of the divine to which all tangible existence refers; and it is this allusive character of the world of experience that gives a pathetic character to its exploration. Not only is the *discursus* surrounded by the irrational, but the will to discover, through it, a conception that can be established in place of the preformed image of an ideal, in other words the will to obtain rational evidence, is itself irrational. The fact that this will becomes more imperative at certain periods of history is a phenomenon that can be related to such and such set of circumstances, but in itself it is an important development. If Giordano Bruno, whilst accepting the limits of the knowable, rages so violently against those who, through sloth, place the unknowable everywhere,[47] it is because reason, in his view, is divine and that it is sacrilege to despise it as do some of the 'dogmatics'. All knowledge of the tangible universe must be based on reason alone; its ways must not be abandoned until they have been traversed.

NOTES

1. *Eroici furori*, p. 143.

2. '*. . . ogni cosa è uno, ed il conoscere questa unità è il scopo e termine di tutte le filosofie e contemplazioni naturali: lasciando ne' sua termini la più alta contemplazione, che ascende sopra la natura, la quale a chi non crede è impossibile e nulla.*' *Causa*, p. 240.

3. '*Costui* slaccia i' mastini ed i' veltri, *de' quai questi son più veloci, quelli più forti. Perchè l'operazione del' intelletto precede l'operazione della voluntade; ma questa è più vigorosa ed efficace che quella, atteso che a l'intelletto umano è più amabile che comprensibile la bontade e bellezza divina. . . .*' *Eroici furori*, I, iv, p. 205.

4. L. Olschki, *Giordano Bruno*, p. 23.

5. *The Song of Solomon*, II, 3.

6. Gabriel Naudé in his *Apologie pour tous les grands hommes qui ont été accusez de magie*, Paris, 1669, p. 431, classes the *De umbris idearum* amongst the numerous works falsely ascribed to King Solomon. Cecco d'Ascoli quotes a passage from this book in his Commentary on the *Sphera mundi* of Sacrobosco (Venice, 1499, fol. C5ᵛ). Bruno gives the same passage in chapter IX of *De monade* (*Opera*, I, ii, p. 468): '*Antarcticum circulum incolentes ita alloquitur ille* [i.e., Solomon] *in libro* De umbris: *O Antarctici manes . . .*' etc! Cecco d'Ascoli, from whom Bruno probably took this quotation, gives the full title: *De umbris idearum*.

7. Theme of Dionysius and Nicholas of Cusa.

8. '*Questo atto assolutissimo, che è medesimo che l'assolutissima potenza, non può esser compreso da l'intelletto, se non per modo di negazione: non può, dico, esser capito, nè in quanto può esser tutto, nè in quanto è tutto. Perchè l'intelletto, quando vuole intendere, gli fia mestiero di formar la specie intelligibile, di assomigliarsi, di conmesurarsi ed ugualarsi a quella: ma questo è impossibile, perchè l'intelletto mai è tanto che non posse essere maggiore; e quello per e quello per essere immenso da tutti lati e modi non può esser più grande. Non è dunque occhio ch'approssimar si possa o ch'abbia accesso a tanto altissima luce e sì profondissimo abisso.*' *Causa*, III, p. 222.

9. J. R. Charbonnel, *La pensée italienne au XVIᵉ siècle et le courant libertin*, Paris, 1919, p. 495.

10. See F. Tocco, *Fonti*, p. 512.

11. Ferdinando d'Amato ('Giordano Bruno' in *Giornale critico della filosofia italiana*, 1930, pp. 96–97) considers that all the critics agree in recognizing that Bruno '*non ha superato effettivamente la trascendenza, benché tutto il suo speculare tenda proprio a questo risultato*'; for him, God is a subject of philosophy in so far as He is revealed in this universe, but '*in quanto oggetto della teologia, esso è il Dio scisso dal mondo. . . .*'. No doubt, but this distinction far from being irrelevant to speculation by the philosopher, is itself a consequence of it.

12. E. Husserl, *Idées directrices pour une phénoménologie* (trans. by P. Ricœur), Paris, 1950, p. 15.

13. *Eroici furori*, I, iii and iv.

14. '*Apresso*, sotto forma d'un altra similitudine, *descrive la maniera con cui s'arma a la ottenzion de l'oggetto, e dice: Mio passar solitario . . .*' etc. *Eroici furori*, I, iv, p. 209.

15. For example, Kepler. See Tocco, *Opere latine di Giordano Bruno*, p. 191, n. 2.

16. Louis Gardet, *La connaissance mystique chez Ibn Sina et ses présupposées philosophiques*, Cairo, 1952, p. 52.

17. H. I. Marrou, *L'ambivalence du temps de l'histoire chez saint Augustin*, Montreal and Paris, 1950, p. 30.

18. See Dominique Dubarle, *Les conceptions cosmologiques modernes et le dogme de la création*, in *La vie intellectuelle*, December 1952, pp. 5–38, and especially section II: *Conception scientifique de l'univers et dogme religieux*, pp. 26–38. See also Ernesto Orrei, *Giordano Bruno e la sua dottrina*, Milan, 1931, p. 178.

19. See G. Gentile, *Giordano Bruno e il pensiero del Rinascimento*, Florence, 1925, pp. 43–44.

20. *La pensée italienne au XVIe siècle* . . . , p. 559. (See note 9.)

21. Nicholas of Cusa, quoted by F. Tocco, *Fonti*, p. 512.

22. *Eroici furori*, II, iv, pp. 416–418. Compare with *Spaccio*, pp. 85–86: '*La Sofia, come la verità e la providenza, è di due specie. L'una è quella superiore, sopraceleste ed oltre mondana, se così dir si puote; e questa è l'istessa providenza, medesima è luce ed occhio: occhio che è la luce istessa; luce che è l'occhio istesso. L'altra è la consecutiva, mondana ed inferiore; e non è verità istessa, ma è verace e partecipe della verità; non è il sole, ma la luna, la terra ed astro, che per altra luce.*'

23. '*Altro è giocare con la geometria, altro è verificare con la natura.*' *Cena*, V, p. 209 and see above, p. 38.

24. '*Bruno jugeait la méthode de Lulle propre à ramener la science à l'unité et à la constituer en un ensemble encyclopédique.*' Bartholmess, *Jordano Bruno*, Paris, 1847, II, p. 161.

25. *De compendiosa architectura et complemento artis Lullii* (*Opera*, II, ii, pp. 1–65), *passim*. The very title of this work makes it possible to guess its intent.

26. See E. Orrei, *Giordano Bruno e la sua dottrina*, Milan, 1931, pp. 128–130.

27. *Opera*, Bâle, 1576, p. 1793. Commentary on Plotinus, *Enn.*, VI, 7, 35. The degrees mentioned by Ficino are those for the ascent to the Supreme Principle: '*Scala per quam ascenditur ad principium septem gradus habet.*' They include: *purgatio animi* (1st degree), *contemplatio ordinis* (3rd degree), *negatio* (5th degree). Ficino's seventh degree corresponds to Bruno's eighth and ninth degrees.

28. '*Sensus in se sentit tantum; in imaginatione persentit etiam se sentire; sensus quoque, qui jam quaedam imaginatio est, imaginatur in se, in ratione imaginari se percipit; sensus, qui jam ratio est, in se argumentatur, in intellectu animadvertit se argumentari; sensus, qui et jam intellectus, in se intelligit, in divina autem mente intelligentiam suam intuetur.*' *Sigillus sigillorum* (*Opera*, II, ii, p. 176).

29. '*Ne l'oggetto sensibile come in un specchio, nella raggione per modo di argumentazione e discorso, nell'intelletto per modo di principio o di conclusione, nella mente in propria e viva forma.*' *Infinito*, p. 289.

30. 404 *b*, 18–27.

31. *De monade*, IV (*Opera*, I, ii, pp. 360–361).

32. *De minimo*, I, i (*Opera*, I, iii, p. 137).

33. *Summa terminorum metaphysicorum*, article *Cognitio* (*Opera*, I, iv, pp. 31–32). Note (p. 31) the four sub-divisions of *sensus* or degrees of tangible knowledge: *sensus communis, phantasia, cogitativa, memoria*. One arrives at rational knowledge only after having passed through these stages (p. 32).

34. This first effort of organization on the level of *sensus* is ascribed to the *sensus communis* in the *Summa terminorum*, p. 31: '*cuius est recipere et unire et comparare sensum unum externum cum altero*'.

35. '*Ailleurs, Bruno souligne la possibilité, pour l'imagination, de rectifier les représentations des réalités naturelles selon "ce qui devrait être"* (*Op. lat.*, II, 2, p. 211 [*Sigillus sigillorum*]),—*fonction de la φαντασία mise en relief par les platoniciens de tous les temps et manifestement incompatible avec le rôle de simple servante de la raison.*' Robert Klein, '*L'Imagination comme vêtement de l'âme chez Marsile Ficin et Giordano Bruno*,' in *Revue de métaphysique et morale*, 1956, No. 1, p. 20.

36. *De immenso*, I, first lines of chap. iv (*Opera*, I, i, p. 214); *De minimo*, first lines of chap. xiv (*ibid.*, I, iii, p. 182); *De minimo*, II, chap. iii and iv, etc.

37. '*Ad eccitarela raggione solamente, ad accusare, ad indicare e testificare in parte, non a testificare in tutto, né meno a giuicare, nè a condannare. Perchè giamai, quantunque perfetti, son senza qualche perturbazione. Onde la verità, come da un debile principio, é da gli sensi in picciola parte, ma non è nelli sensi.*' *Infinito*, I, p. 289.

38. *De immenso*, II, viii (*Opera*, I, i, p. 285).

39. *Infinito*, I, p. 288; II, p. 335.

40. *Opera*, I, iv, pp. 31–32.

41. E. Husserl, *Idées directrices pour une phénoménologie*, Paris, 1950, p. 69; and see p. 123, the distinction between *transcendental* perception and *immanent* perception.

42. '*Questa verità è cercata come cosa inaccessibile.*' *Eroici furori*, II, ii, p. 373.

43. Cabala, p. 266.

44. Angelus Silesius says: '*Dieu demeure en une lumière vers laquelle toute voie fait défaut.*' See Jean Baruzi, *Création religieuse et pensée contemplative*, Paris, 1951, p. 210.

45. See the *Eroici furori*, I, v, pp. 252–257, the gloss to sonnet *Trionfator invitto* . . . and the motto *Caesar adest*.

46. Pantaleo Caraballese, *L'idealismo italiano*, 2nd ed., Rome, 1946, p. 49.

47. '*Questi poltroni per scampar la fatica di dar raggioni delle cose . . . donano la colpa a la natura, a le cose che mal si rappresentano . . . Or dunque essi, volendo con minor fatica ed intelletto, e manco rischio di perdere il credito, parer più savi che gli altri, dissero . . . che nulla si può determinare per chè nulla si conosce. . . .*' Cabala, p. 290.

II

Cosmogony

The unity

The word cosmogony expresses two different ideas according as we have in mind the genesis of the universe or that of a particular world. In the latter case we should speak of Laplacean Cosmology. That of Bruno deals with universal existence.

By meditation on existence, Plotinus derived the condition for a discovery of its principle: 'He who learns who he is, will consequently know whence he comes';[1] and in the next chapter of the same treatise he acknowledges that Unity (or Oneness) is the centre of the soul, and that the soul tends thereto as though to its repose. Bruno bases his cosmogony on intuitions of the same order. He has a deep-seated feeling, a taste for unity, which constrains him to place Unity at the heart of existence, if not even to confuse one with the other. This thought was already dominant in *Sigillus sigillorum*, where it is asserted that 'all things are one, as was well understood by Parmenides';[2] and it reappears in the treatise *De causa*, where, from the existence of a primary and unique principle of the universe, Theophilus considers that we are justified in concluding 'that everything, according to the substance, is one, as Parmenides possibly understood it';[3] it occurs finally in *Camoeracensis acrotismus* (1588), where the author invokes Parmenides, as well as Xenophanes, the precursor, and Melissos, the last representative, of the school of Elea.[4]

'He who has found this oneness, I mean the reason for this unity, has found the key without which it is impossible to enter into true contemplation of nature.'[5] This sentence, taken from the argument of the fifth dialogue in *De causa* summarizes the seventh paragraph only, but it reflects the intention of the whole dialogue in which the eternal plenitude of the Unity and, correlatively, the inconsistency of the diverse and manifold: '. . . this unity is simple, it is stable and permanent; this oneness is eternal; every countenance, all appear-

77

ance, everything else is vanity; outside of this oneness all is as naught, what do I say? all is naught.'[6]

Bruno's references, sometimes neo-Platonic, sometimes pre-Socratic, seem to betray a wavering between two manners of conceiving unity and the relation of oneness to the manifold, between procession and inclusion, between the Monist oneness of Parmenides and the transcendental oneness of Plotinus, whence the diverse breaks away and proceeds.[7] As for the identification of the Unity with God, the 'sole true being and cause of causes',[8] that goes without saying. It is, moreover, frequently asserted.[9]

With regard to the relation between the unity of the primary principle and the multiplicity of appearances, that which could be interpreted as hesitation between two doctrines derives in reality from the fact that Giordano Bruno retains something from each of them: The Unity does not exclude the diverse, and it transcends the latter; it conceals and produces the latter; it implicates and explicates the latter, as Nicholas of Cusa would have it: 'God enfolds all things within Himself, so that all things are in Him; He is the development of all things, so that He Himself is in all things'.[10] 'In the simplicity of the divine essence, everything is totally . . . all the attributes are equal, or better still, they are the same', as we read in the *Eroici furori*.[11] In *De causa* (argument of the fifth dialogue) we have: Unity is infinite, it contains all, 'it contains no parts', 'although they be explicitly wanted in the universe; where, however, all that we see of diversity and difference is only a distinct and different aspect of the same substance'.[12] Other pages of the same book proclaim the coincidence of opposites in Dionysian terms (end of the third dialogue); and it fell to Theophilus, before calling on the authority of Parmenides, to invoke that of the Holy Scriptures: '*The darkness and the light are both alike to thee.*'[13]

However, if the Unity be everything, then the manifold none the less remains the subject of our experience. An illusion, perhaps, but one that must be taken into account. From the manifold implicated in the Unity to the manifold explicated in the universe, there is at least a change of aspect, and consequently a passage, a *descensus*, that the philosopher has a duty to describe.

The descensus

The second part of the *Summa terminorum metaphysicorum* is entitled *Entis descensus, seu applicatio*. This term, *descensus*, has a

Plotinian flavour, and the fact that we find it in such a late work as the *Summa* shows that Bruno never ceased to be haunted by the images and formulas of neo-Platonism, and that in spite of himself he had recourse to them whenever he endeavoured to think about, depict to himself, or describe in clear language the genesis of the tangible universe.

The first stage in the *descensus*, starting from the supreme Unity, is the separation of two principles, the 'formal principle' and the 'material principle',[14] or of two substances: the soul and matter. The descent towards the manifold starts with this separation of parts: in absolute unity, we distinguish neither matter nor form, but 'in nature, it is necessary to recognize two kinds of substance, one which is form and the other which is matter'; the power that is 'active in everything' depends on one of them, and the power that is 'passive in everything' depends on the other; 'the power to act is in one, the power to be acted upon is in the other'.[15]

We must, however, guard against inferring from this duality of principles or substances that matter without form or form without matter has a possible existence. For Bruno, thus far loyal to the data of classical Aristotelianism, matter, as we shall see later, is characterized, if we dare say so, by an absence of characteristics, or by absolute indefiniteness. In reality, these two principles, active and passive, are always coexistent; only by analysis can they be discriminated: 'One power implicates the other; I mean, having been determined, it necessarily determines the other.'[16] To assume the antecedence of one with respect to the other would be absurd: 'The absolute possibility by reason of which things in action can exist does not precede this event; nor does it follow it.'[17] Matter being coeternal with form contains in itself the possibility of every form; it cannot, as has been claimed, 'desire form', 'because we cannot desire what we possess'.[18] Consequently, the logical distinction between form and matter is not based on the fact, nor even on the possibility, of a cleavage: it is less a question of two substances than one of two aspects of the unique substance. Impelling activity and passive receptivity, inseparable from each other, are both of them inseparable from the primordial principle.[19]

The triple minimum

In the dedication to *Candelaio* (1582), Bruno wrote: 'Time removes everything and gives everything. All things change. Nothing is annihilated. Only unity is unable to change; only unity is eternal and is able to persist eternally one, uniform and identical.'[20] These eloquent phrases express an idea familiar to the ancient philosophers, namely, that only unity is incorruptible, all change being considered as a process of decomposition and rearrangement. The eternal identifies itself with the indivisible, with the atom, with the 'minimum'. This intimate bond between the concepts of unity and immutability belongs to the earliest age of Greek thought. With the atomists it became the principle of a general explanation of the material world, a 'metaphysics of dust', a term of complete destruction and itself indestructible.[21] Epicuros seized on this concept and gave it a fresh meaning; Lucretius borrowed it from Epicuros and the Renaissance borrowed it from Lucretius. Bruno, in his turn, adopted it and derived from it his theory of the *minimum*, which is developed in a Latin poem with the somewhat enigmatic title: *de triplici minimo et mensura*.

The *minimum* is put at the root of existence, the final term of the decomposition to which every compound body returns, the primary element of which, and starting from which, the universe is built. 'Everything is born of the *minimum*, and anything of bulk is reducible to the *minimum*.' It is at once unity and the source of the innumerable, the smallest and the foundation of the infinitely great. The sole permanent reality in the flux of things, it is also the *maximum*.[22]

What does 'triple minimum' mean? Why three minima? A superficial reading would readily suggest that the three minima are: *unity*, which is the smallest of the integers, the arithmetical minimum; the *point*, the geometric minimum; and the *atom*, the smallest part of material substances, the physical minimum. Let us recall the full title of the poem; it is *De triplici minimo et mensura ad trium speculativarum scientiarum et multarum activarum artium principia libri V*. According to the assumption just put forward, the three branches of knowledge in question would be arithmetic, geometry and physics; a belief that would seem to be confirmed by the title of the second chapter of the first book: *Minimum esse tum numerorum, tum magnitudinum, tum omnium utilibet elementorum substantiam*.

However, on looking closer, it will be noticed that this very title makes the minimum 'the substance of numbers, of magnitudes and of all the elements' (that is to say, of all substances). It does not, therefore, designate an abstract minimum such as would be unity in arithmetic or a point in geometry (the case of the atom in physics is different); it designates a minimum of real existence, a corporeal minimum. The subsequent text agrees moreover with the intent of the title. The terms are resumed in the opening lines: '*Minimum substantia rerum est*,' and immediately afterwards: 'Here unity, here the atom, and the whole spirit spread everywhere, not contained in any mass, but laying its imprint on all things.'[22b]

These lines clearly express the meaning of the poem: unity there becomes the monad—the living unity which the prose commentary of the preceding chapter assimilates to the supreme Unity: *Deus est monas, omnium numerorum fons*'.[23] *Monas, Spiritus, Atomus*, such are the three minima and 'substance of everything'. Translated, they are: God, the Soul and the Atom. The soul is 'spirit': it is not contained in any mass (*in nulla consistens mole*); it is indivisible in so far as it is non-spatial, like a geometric point. Finally, the atom is the ultimate element of matter. If we are to assume that the three branches of knowledge to which the title of the poem relates are indeed arithmetic, geometry and physics, then they can only be allusions to three other higher branches of knowledge more deserving of being described as 'speculative': the arithmetic of whole numbers to knowledge of the divine; geometry, the knowledge of forms, to knowledge of the soul, the principle of forms; atomism to knowledge of the corporeal principle and of the tangible universe.

Under the name of 'triple minimum' we rediscover, shortly, the three principles that a description of the *descensus* had first of all enabled us to distinguish: Unity that contains all and cannot divide itself, and the formal and material principles, both of them sprung from that divine Unity: the soul, guide and preserver of universal life; and matter, designated here—seeing that the emphasis is placed on the indivisibility of the three substances—by its ultimate element, the substratum of every material body, the atom, which is to bodies what letters are to words, and dots and strokes are to letters.[24]

The three 'minima', like the three 'principles' are, as a matter of fact, inseparable. In the universe, where God remains present—*in rebus*—there is no form without matter any more than there is matter without form: the smallest corpuscle is permeated by soul. Nevertheless, these principles, or three *minima*, are distinguished not only by analysis, but common experience also suggests this distinction.

Power and the act

The first degree of the *descensus* has led us to recognize two principles below the primary Unity: formal and material, or two powers: active and passive, or two substances: form and matter, and then two indivisibles: soul and atom. These divers pairs are but one: their different way of naming depends only on the point of view from which they are considered. In so far as they are powers, their conjunction is in fact set forth in the third dialogue of the *Causa*: 'Power is usually distinguished as active, by means of which the subject is able to operate; and passive, by means of which it can be, receive, have, or be subjected to an efficient cause in some way or other. . . .' This is a purely logical distinction, for 'there is nothing about which we can say that it is, without saying at the same time that it may be'.[25]

When, however, something results from the two powers (active and passive) and their conjunction, we pass to the act; and a fresh question immediately arises: Is the act of the two powers inseparable from those powers as they are amongst themselves? From the proposition stated above, are we justified in deducing the converse, namely: There is nothing about which we can say that it may be without saying at the same time that it is? It stands to reason that the answer is negative from the appearance of the fragmented universe, which is the appearance offered to our experience: 'Things, even though they be what they may be, might perhaps not exist, and certainly might be different from what they are; for nothing is quite what it may be. Man is what he may be, but he is not all that he may be; stone is not all that it may be, seeing that it is not lime, sludge, dust and grease. . . .' To each of these finite objects, the sum total of which constitutes the universe, there is attached a 'power of not being' which specifies its contingency. A human being is no exception to this rule. In man, as in everything, the act is not the same as the power, 'because this act is not absolute but is limited', and because 'moreover the power is always limited to a single act; even if it has every form and every act in view, it only achieves its purpose by means of certain dispositions and in a certain succession of beings'.[26]

The matter is quite different if, from a consideration of finite objects, which are partial with respect to the universe, we rise to a consideration of the Unity that comprises all, that is at once the absolute power and absolute act, that may be everything and is everything that may be. In the same way that the two principles, formal and material, were merged in the Unity which is their common source, so every distinction of power and act is obliterated: 'All power and every act in the First Principle are *interwoven*, united and one, whereas in other things they are *unfolded*, dispersed and multiplied.'[27] This indissoluble union, in God, of that which is possible and that which is accomplished had already been asserted by Palingenius in his *Zodiacus vitae* (1552)—a work which Bruno had read, which he quotes on several occasions, and which he discusses and comments upon at length at the end of *De immenso*. However, in his usual manner, Bruno seizes this idea rather than borrows it; he appropriates it and makes it the basis and fundamental axiom of his cosmogony. The consequences are developed in his two treatises *De causa* and *De l'infinito*, as well as in *De immenso*, with slight differences appropriate to the purpose of each of these works. Consequently, he gives more importance to the concept of the infinite in his cosmological books: 'How can we imagine that the agent that can do infinite good is limited in doing so.' 'In things that are changing, only power and the act are noticeable', but 'the first efficient [cause] can will only that which it wills and can do only that which it does.'[28] That is why the infinitude of God implies that of the universe and renders it necessary. There is a kind of obligation, or restraint, therein for God which seems to reduce and even destroy His liberty; but it is merely a semblance, seeing that liberty and necessity are capable of co-existence and are merged in the divine Unity in virtue of coincidence. 'Necessity and liberty are but one. There is then nothing to fear that the divine will, acting by necessity of nature will not act freely; but it would indeed be far better that the divine will should not act freely, if it did not act as required by necessity and nature, or better expressed, by necessity of nature.'[29] The necessity of the universe is the liberty of God.

The monad and numbers

'Nature is only the visible impression of the Unity', said Plotinus;[30] and Bruno said, 'The monad is the source of numbers.' The *descensus* or passage from the first principle to the diversity of the tangible universe therefore has a numerical aspect, and it is this aspect that is treated in the poem *De monade, numero et figure*. In the trilogy of Latin poems, which we know should constitute a single work, the *De monade* comes between the *De minimo* and the *De immenso*. The *De minimo* deals with principles, elements, the first-fruits; the *De immenso* deals with the universe, a kingdom without frontiers—*sine fine regnum*—wherein 'the republics of the worlds' are placed. The *De monade* deals with passing from the minimum to the total, but, because of a lack of definite knowledge of elementary combinations, this proliferation of the Unity, which results in the universe, is set forth in the form of a symbolic arithmology. In fact, *De monade* is nothing more than a digression in the Pythagorean manner on the numbers constituting the decade in which their occult properties and their relation to geometrical figures are considered.

Let us hasten to say that the author is not deceived by his game, and in no-wise conceals the metaphoric nature of his work. He claims only to give a picture that will satisfy them who have need to see in order to understand,[31] and, as he emphasized in his letter of dedication to the Duke of Brunswick, he does not rate this poem so highly as the other two. The *De minimo* is based on a doctrine and—precious secret—on inherent certitudes (*innata*); the *De immenso*, in which we find obvious, definite and very strong necessary arguments (*evidentes, certiores et fortissimae demonstrationes*), sets forth the 'discoveries' (*inventa*). Between those two is *De monade*, in which divination, faith and imagination play their parts, in which incertitude subsists (*in secundo incerti quaerimus*) and appeal is made to received opinions (*audita*).[32]

De monade contains eleven chapters. The first is a kind of introduction; each of the other ten is devoted to one of the numbers of the decade.

Chapter II, entitled *De prima (quae monadis est) figura Agono seu Circulo*, is a new hymn to the Unity, compared with the circle, the perfect figure, source and generator of all others.[33]

The dyad (chapter III) results from the first jump into the manifold, by the first stage of descending. It has acquired also a reputation of inferiority. Timaeus and Plato make the dyad an attribute of matter, preferring to reserve the monad for form:

> *Qui melius diadem tribuerunt materiam,*
> *Sed formae monadem. . . .*[34]

This doctrine was retained by the neo-Pythagoreans, as is attested by a passage in Iamblichos: '. . . a substance deprived of form and shape would be indeterminate matter, without quantity and without quality, *because of the indetermination and inequality of the dyad*'.[35] The indefinite dyad, around which oblong figures different from each other are constructed, is placed opposite the monad, around which squares similar to each other are constructed, in the Pythagorean table of contrasts. Moses, 'versed in the secret oracles of the Baby-

Ionians', refrained from commending the second day—*nulla in-signivit laude secundum*—as we read in Genesis, whereas with regard to the work of the other five days we read, '*And God saw that it was good.*'[36] Furthermore, we may note the classical identification of the monad with a point and the dyad with a line. At the beginning of the prose commentary it is recalled that 'The dyad proceeds from the monad as the line issues from the point' (*Dias ex Monade (ut ex fluxu puncti linea) procedit*) in order to express in a picturesque way the passage from essence to being: *Sic essentia fluens in aliud, facit esse*. Thus, Righteousness becomes virtue, Truth becomes true religion, etc.[37]

In the same way that unity corresponds to a point, and the dyad to a line, so the triad corresponds to a surface, especially the triangle, which is the elementary surface that gives rise to all the others.[38]

In the prose commentary accompanying the poetical text, Bruno finds an excuse to recall several common notions respecting the relationship between a thing and an idea. Every concept has a three-fold nature. For example, Virtuous Deeds, may be split into three objects of thought according as they are regarded as archetypal, real or abstract: *Archetypum, Physicum, Rationale*. 'The first is superior, external and antecedent to things; the second is linked to, in and with things; the third is inferior, and subsequent to things, being derived from them.'[39]

The chapter on the tetrad is a medley of Empedoclean, Pythagorean and Platonic recollections. Four is the number of the elements; it is also the number for a solid and the germ of the decad obtained by adding together $1 + 2 + 3 + 4$.

> *Per monadem, diadem, triadem, tetradem decas exit.*
> *Et tetrade est primum solidi natura reperta.*

The square, the symbol of justice, is the figure that corresponds to the tetrad. It has many other additional virtues which the poet is pleased to enumerate: he recalls, for example, that all nations designate God by a word of four letters. Consequently, the Pythagoreans rightly venerated the tetrad.[40]

The symbolism of the pentad is even richer. The five points of the pentagon receive an esoteric significance. God is the uppermost angle of the figure; below, to the right and left, the Intelligence and the Soul are placed; at the bottom, to the right and left, we have Form and Matter.[41] In the prose commentary to this chapter, Bruno draws upon a large number of authors, including Marsilio Ficino, whom he uses far more often than he quotes, though he names him here as one of the best Platonists,[42] and St Thomas Aquinas, 'the honour and light of Aristotelianism'.[43] The reference to Marsilio Ficino is in connection with the symbolism of the pentagon; the authority of St Thomas is quoted to justify in a general way the study of the occult sciences and magic arts, for knowledge as such should not be condemned, but only its wrong use. During his trial at Venice, Bruno declared in his defence 'that he had always esteemed and loved St Thomas as his own soul' and he gave this page of *De monade* as proof thereof.[44]

We shall not tarry over the arithmological digressions concerning the hexad, hebdomad, octad, and ennead, but will conclude this rapid survey of the poem by a note on the eleventh and final chapter, which deals with the decad. Its title is *Mundus*. The decad is assimilated to the universe. It closes and encloses the series of simple numbers:

Simplicium numerum claudit Decas atque recludit[7]

it is the 'complete and perfect' number;[45] it bears to the universe, explicated, the relation that the Monad bears to the universe, implicated. It was quite natural, therefore, that the *De monade*, a Pythagorean reverie on the genesis of diversity, should conclude with a consideration of the decad, a poetic prelude to the cosmology of *De immenso*.

The emanation

Step by step, but not without straying sometimes into the 'thick jungle' of symbolism, we have drawn near to our objective. We have, in fact, recognized that the Unity was the source of the manifold, that both the Soul and Matter were immediately derived from it, and that power was inseparable from the act in this first principle. It is already possible to guess what kind of cosmogony can be constructed on such foundations.

Seeing that matter has sprung from God, we must in the first place rule out the hypothesis of a creation that would be only the organization of a pre-existing chaos, of a genesis that would be the upthrow of a cosmos starting from an ἄπειρων, of a victory over the uncreated. This ancient concept (but it still survived with one Leo, the Hebrew) was contrary to that of the orthodox theologians and christian philosophers (down to Nicholas of Cusa and Marsilio Ficino), who established God at the centre of creation and ascribed it to Him entirely.

To the extent that he denies the existence of uncreated matter on which the creative act was performed, Bruno does not depart from the christian point of view. On the other hand, he dissociates himself from it completely when he rejects the possibility of a creation *a nihilo*. The creative act, for him, is no more a victory over the uncreated, than a victory over naught. Having assumed in principle that the power and act are merged into one another in the prime Unity, he is led to conclude that the distinction between cause and principle, which is valid when dealing with natural objects, loses all logical value on the plane of the divine. When asked what differences there is between cause and principle, Theophilus replies: 'When we say that God is the first principle and the first cause, we understand the same thing in different senses; when we speak of principles and causes in nature, we speak of different things in different senses.'[46] On the plane of nature, the principle is in the object, the cause produces the object 'but remains distinct from it'. On the other hand, God 'producing things as the first cause, remains in them as the first principle'.[47] If He were solely the cause, His creation would be cast out of Him and affected with a certain contingency, He could have created another universe. Now, this 'ability-not-to-be' rightly ascribed to the finite objects that come under our senses would not be able to influence the total universe. Consequently, Bruno shows his aversion from Duns Scotus—who thought the universe could have been different from what it is—whereas he is satisfied with the formulas of Amaury of Bêne (everything is God, *omnia esse Deum*) and of David of Dinant (God is the principle of everything, *Deum esse principium materiale omnium*).

'The essence of neo-Platonism is to represent the real as a hierarchy of all the forms of existence that are disposed between the absolute Unity and the indetermination of matter. There is a superabundant richness in the Unity by which it is compelled to spread itself by a kind of emanation.'[48] These few lines summarize what Bruno rejects from neo-Platonism and what he retains. In so far as the Plotinian movement is a necessary emanation, Bruno is akin to Plotinus. On the other hand, he discards all idea of hierarchy. Matter is no longer the final term of a degradation. Matter *proceeds* from God, without an intermediary, for the same reason as form. The emanation is purer and more direct. The universe is one aspect of God, or preferably a 'reflection', or even a 'shadow'. The universe is therefore co-eternal with God who nevertheless remains its source so that identification of the universe with God remains incomplete and it is possible to speak of creation, provided we do not understand thereby a creation *ab aeterno*, the antecedence of the creator becoming purely logical. All these views are set forth on a remarkable page of the third dialogue, *Concerning the Cause*:

> The universe, which is the great simulacrum, the great image and only begotten nature (*unigenita natura*), is itself [like the first principle], all that it can be, in these same species and principle parts [which were dealt with above], and continuity of all matter, to which nothing is added and from which nothing is lacking from its complete and unique form; but it is not all that it can be through the same differences, modes, attributes and characteristics. Furthermore, it is none other than the shadow of the first act and the first power; yet the power and the act in it are not absolutely the same thing, because not one of its parts is all that it can be ... the universe is all that it can be according to a mode of explication, dispersion and distinction. Its principle is in union and in indifference; because everything is whole and the same in simplicity, without difference and distinction.[49]

A reflection of God both transcendent and immanent—cause and principle—the universe, as a whole, does it exhaust the divine possibilities? We now come back to the question: the power to do, does it entail the doing of something?

This question, which arises in the treatise *De l'infinito* in connection with the plurality of worlds, is set down in the following terms: Must we infer the existence of several universes from the capability of God to create them? A very lively discussion took place on this topic in the thirteenth century. The Aristotelian conception of a unique and finite universe had been condemned by the Church as being incompatible with the omnipotence of God. To this the defenders of Aristotelianism—the chief being St Thomas Aquinas—replied: the divine omnipotence is irrelevant, but Aristotle is nevertheless right, for God could choose to create only one universe and, in fact, only one exists.[50] Bruno resolutely opposes this thesis, not only because he believes, in fact, in the existence of several universes, but first of all particularly because 'the first cause could not be parsimonious of its powers'.[51] The creative act is a 'pure act' and complete, exclusive of any choice between possibilities that might precede it, yet not kept entirely separate from these possibilities. God does not 'act', properly speaking: He offers Himself, He shows Himself. He shows His back, as is said in Exodus. Consequently, He is both visible and out of sight, in the universe and out of the universe, the intrinsic cause and the extrinsic cause: 'extrinsic cause through His being which is conspicuous by the substance and the essence of effects', but 'intrinsic cause as regards the act of His working'.[52] If God made a choice between possible universes, this very choice would be a work and the creation would be a completed work. Creation results only from the existence of God in His eternal repose.

The inner artificer

So far, the *descensus* has been considered from a metaphysical or theological point of view, so that in view of our lack of knowledge of the divine Unity, accepted in principle, we have hardly left the realm of hypotheses or symbols. We shall now enter the field of the knowable, by trying to define the modes of divine action in so far as it manifests itself to our senses by the production of tangible objects.

It may seem contradictory to speak of divine action in view of what has just been said about 'divine repose'. However, a distinction must be made here between the prime Unity and the spiritual principle and the active power which emanates from it and is inseparable from it, though for us logically distinct: 'The physical efficient of the universe is the universal intellect, the first and principal faculty of the soul of the universe, which is universal form.'[53] In this 'physical' efficient we recognize Nature, the inner principle of Aristotle, the quickening principle of the cosmos. Whereas, for Aristotle, nature never has 'the steadfastness of a true soul of the universe',[54] Bruno does not hesitate to use the word several times in the dialogue of *De causa*. Omnipresence and steadfastness are the essential characteristics of this efficient. Its formative activity is exercised in all places and at all times, and for that very reason we do not perceive it.[55] Philosophers give it different names which are merely metaphors: for the Pythagoreans it is 'the driving force', for the Platonists it is 'forger of the universe'; others call it the 'sower', the 'eye of the universe'; Plotinus uses the expression 'father and procreator'. Theophilus adds that among us (that is to say, according to 'Brunonian philosophy') it is called the 'inner artificer': *Da noi si chiama artefice interno*.[56]

By choosing this term, which implies a comparison between the activity of the formal principle and that of an artificer, Bruno seems to draw close to Ficino, who, in pages of great beauty draws exaltant analogies between creation by the artificer and creation by the divine.[57] Bruno's intention is quite different, however. His intention is to demonstrate particularly that which distinguishes the activity of nature from human activity. The emphasis should be placed on the adjective *interno*, rather than on the noun *artefice*.

'All forms produced by art are accidental,' said St Thomas Aquinas, 'art being able to act only on that which, through nature, is already constituted in the created.'[58] Man subdues nature, and is king over it; but he fashions it from without, he labours (in the expressive words of Bruno) 'on the surface of things' (*nella superficie della materia*), whereas the formal principle forms but one with that which is formed; it is interior to it, it acts from within (*opra dal centro*): 'We call it the inner artificer because it shapes matter and figures it from within, in the same way that from within the germ or the root it causes the stem to issue forth; from within the stem it sends forth branches; twigs from the branches; and buds from the twigs; from within it shapes, figures, entwines and innervates, as it were, the leaves, flowers and fruits.'[59]

That is only a picture. In the same way, by a comparison, the inadequacy of which he is fully aware, Bruno, in accounting for the unity and ubiquity of the soul of the universe, likens it to a voice making itself heard in a room and 'which is everywhere seeing that everything is heard perfectly everywhere';[60] in the same way he likens the profusion of the innumerable species which derive from the prime Unity to the generation of angels by fours and by twelves as is taught by the Jewish Cabala.[61]

Whether they be borrowed from the activities of man, from natural phenomena, from angelology or from heathen mythologies, these pictures can only compensate for the deficiencies of an impossible description. They will have achieved their purpose if they have enabled us to be associated with the philosopher's vision and to understand with him what must be the final stage in the *descensus*—both vital generation and artistic creation—what kind of bond unites the universe indissolubly with its principle, and finally how the universe is one whole, in the sense in which we should say that an individual expresses his whole being in each of his actions.

If nature expresses itself completely everywhere it expresses itself, that is to say, in every direction, each of the objects that it moulds is none the less partial and, by that very fact, contingent. The universe of the diverse and the manifold (broken up and explicated) remains affected, not in its totality but in each of its parts, by an ability-not-to-be, which spreads over it like a shadow. If an object should take consciousness of itself and its limits, it acknowledges itself to be both necessary and contingent, it distinguishes between its being and its necessity to be. Having in some manner crossed the threshold of non-existence, it is incapable of going back to necessary being, still less to lay hold of it, and to understand it. That is why the First Principle in advancing the universe in which it expresses itself, always present (as nature, like Diana in *Eroici furori*) and always hidden (as the universal Apollo), causes the possible to spring forth from the necessary, but, beyond the necessary, remains unknowable in its sovereign freedom.[62]

It has been said of the cosmogony which we have summarized above in its broad aspects that 'it claims to consider and define the universe as an idea existing in the mind of God, and from that to deduce the cosmological idea presented to man through his tangible experience'; that it 'theologizes cosmology and makes it impenetrable by human intelligence, contrary to his avowed (rationalist) intention'; and finally that by making everything depend on the divine act—not only form, but matter also—it gives creation a demiurgic, even magical, aspect.[63] How much can be retained of this harsh criticism will appear later. For the time being, however, we must accept that Bruno's cosmogony is, on the one hand, that of a metaphysician rather than that of an astronomer; and, on the other hand, that cosmology in the view of Brunonian philosophy is inseparable from cosmogony—in other words, that a description of the universe poses a problem which is inseparable from that of its first principle. To present the genesis of being as an emanation and the universe as an aspect of God, is in effect to give unquestionable, immediately deducible, answers to a certain number of questions concerning the nature, form, dimensions and duration of the universe, which answers would only need corroboration by experience and reason.

In subsequent chapters we shall return to the unity and necessity of the universe (considered in its totality), its eternity, and its infinitude, but without losing sight of the fact that those divine attributes, which are bestowed upon it, result from the indissolubility in God of the power and the act, as is stated in the following verses from the first book of *De immenso*:

Eligit ergo Deus quod vult, dat, scitque, facitque
Non variare potens ipsum non seque negare[6]
Quod vult atque potest est unum prorsus idemque.

. . .

Ergo alius quam sit veluti non est potis esse,
Sic aliud fieri quam fit non potest ab illo.
Est siquidem natura Dei substantia simplex . . .

'That which God wishes, gives, knows and does, that is what he chooses, for He cannot change anymore than He can deny Himself. His wish and His power are but one. . . . Therefore He cannot be different from what He is, therefore through Him nothing can be done except that which is done. The nature of God is pure substance. . . .'[64]

NOTES

1. *Enneades*, VI, ix, 7.
2. *Opera*, II, ii, p. 180.
3. *Causa*, p. 223.
4. *Opera*, I, i, pp. 96–98.
5. '. . . *chi ha ritrovato quest'uno, dico la raggione di questa unità, ha ritrovato quella chiave, senza la quale è impossibile aver ingresso alla vera contemplazione della natura.*' *Causa*, p. 143.
6. '. . . *questa unità è sola e stabile, e sempre rimane; questo uno è eterno; ogni volto, ogni faccia, ogni altra cosa è vanità, è come nulla, anzi è nulla tutto lo che è fuor di questo uno.*' *Causa*, V, p. 252.
7. In the *Causa*, Bruno refers more frequently to Parmenides (*e.g.*, p. 254: '*onde non essere inconvenientemente detto da Parmenide uno, infinito immobile* . . .'); on the other hand, we have in *Eroici furori* the Plotinian Unity, superior to the world and adored in silence.
8. '*Causa omnium causarum efficiens.*' *Summa terminorum* (*Opera*, I, iv, p. 75).
9. See *Summa terminorum*, II, *De Deo seu mente, passim.*
10. *De Docta ignorantia*, II, 3: '*Deus est omnia complicans, in hoc quod omnia in eo; est omnia explicans, in hoc quod ipse in omnibus.*'
11. *Eroici furori*, pp. 278–279.
12. '. . . *come ne l'infinito non è parte e parte, sia che si vuole ne l'universo esplicitamente; dove però tutto quel che veggiamo di diversità e differenza, non è altro che diverso e differente volto di medesima sustanza.*' *Causa* (*Proemiale epistola*), p. 144.
13. '*Sicut tenebrae eius, ita et lumen eius.*' *Causa*, III, p. 222; *Psalms*, 139, 12.
14. *Causa*, III, p. 212.
15. '. . . *troviamo che è necessario conoscere nella natura due geni di sustanza, l'uno che è forma e l'altro che è materia; perchè è necessario che sia un atto sustanzialissimo, nel quale è la potenza attiva di tutto, ed ancora una potenza ed un soggetto nel quale non sia minor potenza passiva di tutto: in quello è potestà di fare, in questo è potestà di esser fatto.*' *Causa*, III, p. 204.
16. *Causa*, III, p. 218.
17. *Ibid.*
18. *Causa*, IV, pp. 245–246. On this page, Theophilus, when referring to David de Dinant, goes so far as to assert the superiority of stable and eternal matter over *forms*, all of which it contains and assumes in turn: '. . . *parlo di quelle* [*forme*] *che*

si generano e corrompono, perchè il fonte delle forme, che è in sè [*i.e., nella materia*], *non può appetere queste forme, attesto che non si appete lo che si possiede.*' The sentence is ambiguous, but the context justifies our interpretation, which agrees with that of E. Namer, *Cause, principe et unité,* p. 188 and note 92.

19. J. R. Charbonnel, *La pensée italienne au XVI*^{e} *siècle,* Paris, 1919, p. 536.

20. '*Il tempo tutto toglie e tutto dà. Ogni cosa si muta. Nulla s'annichila. È un solo che non può mutarsi, un solo è eterno, e può perseverare eternamente uno, simile, e medesimo.*' *Candelaio,* in *Opere italiane* (Lagarde), Göttingen, 1888, p. 5.

21. G. Bachelard, *Les intuitions atomistiques,* Paris, 1933, pp. 24–29.

22. See *De minimo,* III, ii: '*Ex minimo crescit et in minimum omnis magnitudo extenuatur*', and IV, i: '*Progressio a monade ad pauca, inde ad plurima usque ad innumera et immensum.*' (*Opera,* I, iii, pp. 237 ff and 269 ff).

22*b.* '*Hinc monas, hinc atomus totusque undique fusus*
        Spiritus, in nulla consistens mole, suisque
        Omnium constituens signis.'
De minimo, I, ii.

23. *De minimo,* I, ii and I, i (gloss). (*Opera,* I, iii, pp. 138 and 136.)

24. *De minimo,* I, i and ii (*Opera,* I, iii, pp. 131–140).

25. '*La potenza comunemente si distingue in attiva, per la quale il soggetto di quella può operare; e in passiva, per la quale o può essere, o può ricevere, o può avere, o può essere soggetto di efficiente in qualche maniera . . . E così non è cosa di cui si può dir l'essere, della quale non si dica il posser essere.*' *Causa,* III, p. 218. See Nicholas of Cusa: '*Quomodo enim quid esset, si non potuisset esse*' (*Docta ignorantia,* II, 7), and Campanella: '*Dicimus esse res quia possunt esse, et posse quia sunt*' (*Universalis philosophia,* VI, vi, 3).

26. *Causa,* III, pp. 218–219.

27. *Causa,* III, p. 219. Nicholas of Cusa's vocabulary is seen here once more.

28. '*Qual raggione vuole che vogliamo credere, che l'agente che può fare un buono finito, lo fa finito? . . . onde non può* [*lo efficiente*] *essere altro che quello che è; non può esser tale quale non è; non può posser altro che quel che può; non può voler altro che quel che vuole; e necessariamente non può far altro che quel che fa; atteso che l'aver potenza distinta do l'atto conviene solamente a cosa mutabili.*' *Infinito,* I, pp. 299–300.

29. '*Necessitas et libertas sunt unum, unde non formidandum est quod cum agat* [*Dei voluntas*] *necessitate naturae, non libere agat: sed potius immo omnino non libere ageret, aliter agendo, quam necessitas et natura, imo naturae necessitas requirit.*' *De immenso,* I, xi (gloss) (*Opera,* I, i, p. 293) and see *Infinito,* I, pp. 301–302.

30. *Enn.,* V, v, 5.

31. '*Porro hinc ad malas commoda, genti Instituendo damus, quae non intelligat ipsa Omnia, sed tantum quae sunt nutrimina sensus.*' *De monade,* I (*Opera,* I, ii, p. 326).

32. *Epistola dedicatoria et clavis* (*Opera,* I, i, pp. 196–197).

33. '*Hoc de fonte fluunt primoque parente figurae.*' (*Opera,* I, ii, p. 335.)

34. *De monade,* I (*Opera,* I, ii, p. 329). As will be seen later (chap. V), Bruno declines, for his part, to accept this inferiority of matter; but, here, he echoes the opinions of others: '*secundum* [*volumen est*] *circa audita.*'

35. Iamblichos (Pistelli), pp. 77–78; trans. P. Kucharski.

36. *De monade,* III (*Opera,* I, ii, p. 350). *Genesis,* I, 8. The omission to which Bruno calls attention was made good in the Septuagint version of the Bible.

37. *De monade,* III (*Opera,* I, ii, p. 353).

38. '*Sic triquetri de fonte venit genus omne figurae.*' *De monade,* IV (*Opera,* I, ii, p. 358).

39. '*Supra, extra et ante res . . . adnexum rebus, in rebus, cum rebus . . . post res, infra res, abstractum a rebus.*' *Ibid.,* p. 367.

40. '*Sic et ex iis quas novimus linguis principes, et eae quae originalibus et primitivis proprius accedunt, quatrilitero nomine Deum significant: IEoVaH et ADoNaI enim Hebraeis.—ΘEUT Ægyptiis. ORSI Magis. SIRE Persis. ΘEOS Graecis. DEUS Latinis. ALLA Arabibus. GOTT Germanis. DIEU Gallis. DIOS*

Hispanis. IDIO Italis: et hi sunt omnes quorum hodie cultiores sunt linguae, et qui soli loqui videntur. ITA PER VENERANDAM TETRADEM iureiurando affirmabant Pythagorici.' *De monade,* V (*Opera,* I, ii, p. 387). See also the poem, pp. 380–381.

41. *De monade,* VI (*Opera,* I, ii, p. 407).

42. '*Unus e principibus Platonicis, Ficinus.*' *Ibid.,* p. 408.

43. '*Peripateticorum . . . honor atque lux, Thomas Aquinas.*' *Ibid.,* p. 415.

44. See Domenico Berti, *Vita di Giordano Bruno.* Second edition, 1889. Document XII, p. 409.

45. *De monade,* XI (*Opera,* I, ii, pp. 459 and 464).

46. '*. . . quando diciamo Dio primo principio e prima causa, intendiamo una medesima cosa con diverse raggioni; quando diciamo nella natura principio e cause, diciamo diverse cose con sue diverse raggioni.*' *Causa,* II, p. 177.

47. Note by Émile Namer in Giordano Bruno, *Cause, principe et unité,* p. 87.

48. Louis Lavelle, *Traité des valeurs,* Paris, 1951, I, p. 57.

49. '*Lo universo, che è il grande simulacro, la grande imagine e l'unigenita natura, è ancor esso tutto quel che può essere, per le medesime specie e membri principali e continenza di tutta la materia, alla quale non si aggionge e dalla quale non si manca, di tutta e unica forma; ma non già è tutto quel che può essere per le medesime differenze, modi, proprietà ed individui. Però non è altro che un'ombra del primo atto e prima potenza, e pertanto in esso la potenza e l'atto non è assolutamente la medesima cosa, perchè nessuna parte sua è tutto quello che può essere. Oltre che in quel modo specifico che abbiamo detto, l'universo è tutto quel che può essere, secundo un modo esplicato, disperso, distinto. Il principio suo è unitamente e indifferentemente; perchè tutto è il medesimo semplicissimamente, senza differenza e distinzione.*' *Causa,* III, p. 219; and see D. Berti, *Vita di Giordano Bruno.* Second edition, 1889. Document XI, p. 400.

50. See St Thomas Aquinas, Commentary to *De coelo,* Lib. I, *lectio* xix.

51. '*. . . perchè vogliamo o possiamo noi pensare che la divina efficacia sia ociosa? perchè vogliamo dire che la divina bontà la quale si può comunicare alle cose infinite e si può infinitamente diffondere, voglia essere scarsa ed astrengersi in niente, atteso che ogni cosa finita al riguardo de l'infinito è niente? . . . perchè deve esser frustrata la capacità infinita, defraudata la possibilità de infiniti mondi che possono essere . . . ?*' *Infinito,* I, p. 297.

52. *Causa,* II, p. 181; trans., Namer, p. 92.

53. '*. . . dico l'efficiente fisico universale essere l'intelletto universale, che è la prima e principale facultà de l'anima del mondo, la quale è forma universale di quello.*' *Causa,* II, p. 179.

54. H. D. Gardeil, *Initiation à la philosophie de saint Thomas d'Aquin. Cosmologie,* p. 38.

55. Angelus Silesius, V, 73, says that God acts without ceasing and that if we are unaware of it, then it is our own fault (Jean Baruzi, *Création religieuse et pensée contemplative,* p. 191); but Bruno more readily understands and ascribes this unawareness to permanent action.

56. *Causa,* II, p. 180.

57. A. Chastel, *Marsile Ficin et l'art,* p. 60.

58. '*Omnes enim formae artificiales sunt accidentales; ars enim non operatur nisi supra id quod jam constitutum est in esse a natura.*' *De principiis.* We have used the translation by H. D. Gardeil (Ref. 54 *supra,* p. 108). Once again, Bruno develops an Aristotelian theme, taking great care not to name Aristotle: the contrast between nature, inner principle and art which, in so far as it is a species of δύναμις, 'resides essentially and formally in an agent distinct from the patient'. See A. Mansion, *Introduction à la physique aristotélicienne,* Louvain and Paris, 1945, p. 230.

59. *Causa,* II, p. 180; see also pp. 180–182, close of the discourse by Theophilus.

60. *Causa,* II, pp. 195–196.

61. *Spaccio,* III, p. 191.

62. '*Però a nessun pare possibile di vedere il sole, l'universale Apolline e luce assoluta per specie suprema e eccellentissima: ma si bene la sua ombra, la sua Diana,*

il mondo, l'universo, la natura ch' è ne le cose, la luce ch' è ne l'opacità de la materia, cioè quella in quanto splende ne le tenebre.' Eroici furori, II, ii, p. 373; see also, *Introduction*, pp. 61–62.

63. Armando Carlini, '*La metafisica del Rinascimento*' in *Giornale critico della filosofia italiana*, 1948, pp. 33–34.

64. *De immenso*, I, xii, verses 7 ff (*Opera*, I, i, p. 245).

III

Ens mobile

The questions relating to the two substances that correspond to the formal and material principles, the *soul of the universe* and *matter*, will be dealt with later on; but first of all we want to give a preliminary sketch of the tangible universe such as it appears to us when we no longer consider it, as we have done previously, as an emanation from the prime Unity, but in itself, independently of the principle that renders its existence necessary, and by disregarding the divine, the unity of which it interprets and explicates. Seen, as it were, from below, it will appear to us in its contingent multiplicity and dark colours as an object of our experience, the 'grand image', the 'great simulacrum', or, to use an expression from classical Aristotelianism, like an essentially moving being, the *ens mobile*.

THE IMPERFECTION OF FORMS

When dealing with the inadequacies of tangible knowledge, one of the speakers in *Eroici furori*, Mariconda, recalls the general opinion held by mathematicians, that 'true figures' (*i.e.*, geometrically exact) 'are never found in natural bodies, and cannot be obtained by force of nature or by art'.[1] The following example is given in *De minimo*: it is impossible to produce by physical means a circle that will correspond perfectly with the definition of a circle.[2] Reason restores the perfect figure by correcting the imperfections of the real figure.[3] This distinction between *sensus* and *ratio* goes back to Plato, to whom moreover Mariconda refers, but it was adopted and given deeper meaning by the Peripatetics, and Bruno was obliged to acknowledge the fact, having 'clenched his teeth', as Tocco amusingly relates.[4]

All the same, the imperfection of forms is a fact concerning which the philosopher in search of an explanation will discover two main causes. The first—which suggests atomistic physics or at least intuition of a discontinuous reality—is that every object (hence every figure) may be decomposed into disjoint particles, if we examine it sufficiently closely. The line is replaced by a dotted line. Furthermore, it is not necessary to go right down to the ultimate elements of matter, far below tangible minima, in order to reveal certain commonplace errors. Every time that our senses give us the illusion of a perfect figure, they are deceiving us and imposing on us a double labour which consists first of all in disclosing through more attentive observation the imperfection of the figure in order that it can be subsequently corrected by reason. For example, a rainbow appears to us like a perfect semicircle, whereas in fact it is composed of droplets in which the Sun's rays are refracted.[5]

The second cause of imperfection in every realized form is found in the fact that the material universe is mobile, that is to say, animated and agitated in all its parts, even to the least, by a motion that knows no respite. According to Democritos, mobility is one of the essential characteristics of atoms: the motion is co-eternal with matter. According to Heraclitos, the universe is carried along in a perpetual flux: we never go into the same river twice. So that, even apart from any hypothesis relative to the discontinuity of the ultimate elements, the incessant motion of matter would suffice to make it impossible to realize a perfect figure—that is to say, one corresponding to a pure, stationary form, beyond the reach of flux as are mathematical things, in short, corresponding to an idea, seeing that a material object would be unable to have the stability, the permanence of the idea of which it will never be more than a fleeting reflection.

There is something more: for the want of perfect figures, we could hope to find in the tangible universe two imperfect figures equal to each other. Even this equality is a kind of perfection no example of which is offered by the *ens mobile*. From the numerous passages collected by Felice Tocco on this matter from the second book of *De minimo*,[6] we may add this curious note, taken from *Eroici furori*: 'There is no precise equality in natural objects' (*non si dà equalità puntuale ne le cose naturali*).[7] By the expression *cose naturali* is to be understood finite objects, having a boundary, a contour, for here it is a question of introducing the concept that there is no equality except in the infinite, that only two infinite magnitudes could be equal to each other. As for the word *puntuale*, it can be interpreted in two ways. If this adjective, used metaphorically, means nothing more than 'rigorously exact', then the author is merely asserting once again that perfect equality is impossible between two material objects; if, on the other hand, we ought to give it its full etymological meaning, then the sentence in question would mean that, in a discontinuous universe (where total perfection of form is impossible as a result of this discontinuity, but where we could assume that equality of two figures could become possible) this very equivalence is denied, as being incompatible with the incessant motion with which each of the 'points' constituting 'natural things' is animated.

To summarize, the irremediable imperfection of the tangible universe results from two causes, namely, the discontinuity and the mobility of its elements. Broken up and in motion, it presents itself to our experience as partial and unstable objects that never fully correspond to the idea they evoke. It is the second of these two causes of imperfection, namely, mobility, that will claim our attention.

THE *ENS MOBILE*

Heraclides and the earliest atomists taught that the essence of nature is essentially mobile; but it was Aristotle who gave full force to this concept by incorporating it into his system; so that, in spite of Bruno's aversion from Aristotelianism, in spite of his propensity on all occasions to refer to the most ancient philosophies, it is probable that his doctrine concerning the *ens mobile* at least takes its starting point from scholastic teaching. The former pupil of the Dominicans at Naples, himself a Dominican and Doctor of Theology, nurtured in his youth in Peripatetic doctrines, as he was pleased to remember, was not ignorant of the fact that, according to Aristotle, the universe of nature is one of mutability; he could not have lost all recollection of the commentaries of St Thomas Aquinas on the *Physica*, and amongst others, certain well coined formulas which he had learned by heart, such as *Et quia hoc quod habet materia mobile est, consequens est quod ens mobile sit subjectum naturalis philosophiae*: From the fact that matter because of its nature is mobile, it results that the *ens mobile* is a subject of natural philosophy. Finally, he was aware that the Peripatetics understood motion in a broad sense, the term meaning, in the universe of nature, various kinds of mutability or possible changes.

However, on this last point, Bruno starts to depart from Aristotelianism, and his disagreement with Aristotle increases in proportion as his theory of matter positively declares itself. A re-reading of the sixth chapter of *De monade* will suffice to confirm that he gives the term motion a very wide meaning, which includes every kind of mutability; the chapter in question deals with the hexad, and distinguishes six kinds of motion: 'generation and corruption, depending on substance; increase and diminution, depending on quantity; alteration, depending on quality; and translation, depending on place'.[8] One would think one was reading St Thomas Aquinas; but let us read St Thomas himself: 'If the predicaments be divided into ten categories, namely, substance, quality, etc. . . . and if motion be found in three of them, there must necessarily be three kinds of motion, namely, the motion belonging to the category of quantity, the motion belonging to the category of quality, and the motion belonging to the category of place which is called *secundum locum*.'[9] The quantitative motion (*in genere quantitatis*), being subdivided into increase and decrease, provides four of the six kinds of motion listed in *De monade*, but we no longer find (and we are not surprised) generation and corruption; these changes depending on substance definitely depend on mutation (*mutatio*) but not on motion (*motus*), for there is no motion in the category of substance (*in genere substantiae non est motus*) any more than in the categories corresponding to the other predicaments, except quantity, quality and place.

In the *Acrotismus camoeracensis* (Art. XVI), Bruno censures the Aristotelian definition of motion—'the act of that which exists potentially, in so far as it exists potentially'—because it is far too general. He claims that the definition could be applied to many other things (*non magis definitio motus est quam multorum aliorum*). Subsequently, in order to be consistent with himself, he adds (Art. XVIII) that Aristotle should have recognized the existence of motion, not in a limited number of predicaments, whether it be four or six, but in all of them.[10]

From these criticisms it emerges that Bruno rejects the Aristotelico-Thomist distinction of *motus* and *mutatio*. He regards all change as motion and all motion as local motion. It is of no little moment that in *De minimo* and the early pages of the poem he returns to this question of motion, forging a close link between the concepts of mutability and indivisibility. Every 'minimum' being unalterable, there cannot be any change in the substance of the ultimate elements of matter. This atomistic outlook—in complete disagreement with Aristotelian doctrine—entails consequences that are easy to foresee. Going back once more to the example of generation and corruption, St Thomas Aquinas rightly said that there is generation only of the compound—*generatio non est nisi compositi*; but for an atomistic kind of physics all compounding implies motion, and it is not of the compound but of that which is moved. Bruno is driven by the logic of his system first of all to broaden and then to restrict the significance of motion: to broaden it by including every kind of change, and to restrict it by reducing all motion to local motion (*secundum locum*). In short, the material universe is in a state of perpetual change; and every change, whether it be one of increase or decrease, generation or corruption, and even, in their tangible effects, that which we call birth and death, reduces itself to displacement in space.

MOTION AND INFINITY

Can these displacements be infinite? After what has been said above, it is clear that they are infinite in duration, seeing that motion is co-eternal with matter; but the question we are asking concerns only infinite space: for example, we say that the amplitude of an oscillation or of a rotation is finite, even if the oscillation or the rotation are repeated an infinite number of times. Two texts relate to this problem: several pages of the second dialogue in *De l'infinito* (pp. 319–321) and a chapter in *De immenso* (the fourth in Book II). Bruno, who teaches that the universe is infinite, sets out, here and there, to refute Aristotle's arguments against this thesis; and one of these arguments relates to the impossibility of infinite motion. In one of the vernacular dialogues, Elpidio, the spokesman for the Aristotelians, partly quotes and partly summarizes passage 274 *a–b* from *De coelo*. According to Aristotle, only a finite number of finite motions exists, each element having its proper place towards which it tends to return if it be displaced therefrom. If the universe were infinite, each of these places would be infinite and similarly the distance separating them. (Between earth and fire the infinite spheres of air and water would be interposed.) Consequently, there would be only one body to return to its natural place, and it would have to cover an infinite distance—which is impossible. Therefore, the impossibility of infinite motion becomes an argument against the infinitude of the universe.

To this, Bruno replies substantially that the argument loses its force if we assume a plurality of worlds. When Aristotle asserts: 'It is not possible for the body that is moved upwards or downwards . . . to move to infinity',[11] he assumes a unique universe having the Earth at its centre and the sphere of fixed stars for its extreme boundary. If, however, we admit the existence of an infinity of worlds and suns, every body will be able to return to its natural place without having to traverse infinite space; and it will never be necessary 'for a heavy body to tend to infinity downwards'—*da qui non bisogna che il grave vada in infinito al basso*. In an infinite universe composed of an infinity of finite worlds, there is no absolute height and depth, in spite of what Epicuros thought, when he assumed an infinite fall of atoms in an endless void.[11b]

Notwithstanding his general opposition to Aristotle, Bruno is in agreement with him on one very important point. If we can imagine a body moving itself indefinitely in a given direction in the assumed infinite universe, this motion will never be completed if its end is infinitely distant. Aristotle says: 'It is impossible for a body to be carried to a place which no moving body can reach' (274 *b*). Bruno says: 'Tending to infinity, is this any different from not tending to any end, that is to say, nowhere?'[12] Bruno, therefore, recognizes just as much as Aristotle the impossibility of infinite motion (*motion* meaning here passage from one fixed place to another fixed place); but, unlike Aristotle, he does not deduce therefrom the impossibility of an infinite universe; this conclusion, a necessity if we accept the Aristotelian scheme of a unique universe, is not imperative when we accept several universes, several centres, each body being able to find its natural place at a finite distance: 'In the same way that the borders and distances which separate bodies from each other are finite, *so are the motions finite*; in the same way that no-one leaves Greece in order to go to infinity, but to go into Italy or Egypt, so, when a body belonging to the Earth or to the Sun starts to move, the goal is not infinity, but a finite end-point.'[13]

THAT WHICH IS NOT MOVED

All motions occurring in the universe reduce to motions *secundum locum*, and they end in the displacement of finite objects in limited fields. Consequently, motion is bound and even doubly bound to the finite and the partial. It is a characteristic of the universe of the diverse and manifold as such; and if the being of nature is indeed the *ens mobile* in the sense that all parts of the universe (and among others 'the worlds') are in motion, the universe itself as a whole is motionless.[13b]

The immobility of the universe results in the first place from its infinitude. Nothing exists outside of it: no real presence that is able to enrich it with a fresh element, no space capable of being displaced. It 'does not breathe' said Xenophanes, in order to intimate that it was all that exists and that it had no need to seek sustenance for its life outside of itself in an ambient atmosphere, in an ἀπείρων, as certain philosophers would have wished. Bruno prefers a different picture, namely, that of a wheel turning on its axis, every part of which is moving, though it itself is not displaced.[14]

The immutability of the universe corresponds to the inalterability of the ultimate elements of matter; the one and the other ensure the everlastingness of the *minimum* and of the whole, whilst between the two extremes the compounded constituent part submits to the law of generation and corruption.

Another reason for the immobility of the universe is that, being a reflection of God, it participates of the divine immobility. Contrary to the being of nature, the immaterial being is essentially immobile in so far as it is non-spatial, as is pointed out, with respect to the soul, in *De triplici minimo*. On the other hand, if we accept the Aristotelian definition of motion: 'The fulfilment of that which exists potentially, in so far as it exists potentially' (Bruno criticizes this definition only on account of its too great generality, but he recognizes that it applies, amongst other things, to motion), it is obvious that it never applies to a divine act, seeing that in God the power is inseparable from the act, and this transition from one to the other, which would definitely be motion, does not exist. In the divine order, no interval of any kind exists between the repose of the power and the repose of the completed act.

THE PRINCIPLE OF MOTION

The motion that affects a sentient being even in its smallest parts must necessarily have a cause. What is this cause, and how does it act? What is the motive principle, and how does it apply its force? The answer to the first question is given by the *mens agitat molem* of Virgil: the motive force is the spirit, by whatever name it be called—

formal principle, soul of the world or, more simply, nature. The answer to the second question is summarized in the words *la natura opra dal centro* ('nature operates from the centre'), a statement that is repeated several times and developed in various ways in Bruno's dialogues. A 'natural' motion is therefore never caused by impulsion from an external force, as would be the case when our hand displaces an object on the table.[15] We must also get rid of the Aristotelian notion of motion transmitting itself by degrees starting from the ultimate sphere.

Every natural phenomenon is compounded of motions that are produced under the action of internal energy. Every natural object (plant, animal or celestial body) arranges itself and moves about a centre; so it is not surprising that circular motion should be the simplest, the most probable, and the most frequently observed in nature. Bruno is apt to emphasize this, not only in connection with the revolution of celestial bodies and their rotation on their axes, but also in connection with the strokes made by a swimmer, or the beatings of a bird's wing, and always taking care to impart a better understanding of the fact that motion propagates itself and that life radiates itself starting from an infinite number of centres and not from a unique centre.[16] To assign to the source of motion a fixed place that would be the centre of the universe, would be a misunderstanding of Aristotle by preserving his cosmic scheme. Now, it is essential to demonstrate not so much that motion does not propagate itself starting from the last sphere, but that it does not have for its source such and such fixed region where the action of the 'prime motive force' [first movent] would first of all apply itself: 'no prime motive force exists in the order of the celestial bodies'.[17] The universe comprises numberless worlds; each has its centre and therefore its own proper motion. There is no sphere surrounding the entire universe anymore than there is an impulse which, starting from the periphery or the centre, would give impetus to all motions.[18]

Just as everything is in motion in a stationary universe, so everything in the universe, except the universe itself, arranges itself about a centre. A creative energy seems to spring from the heart of every natural being; there we have the secret place in which the working of the 'inner artificer' commences.[19]

A being does not deserve the name of individual unless it has within itself this inner force which ensures cohesion of its members and controls their movements. This thought is expressed in *De monade*, and reappears in *De minimo* in another form to which is added a descriptive essay on the vital process: the soul makes us what we are; the material elements are agglomerated or dispersed, as the case may be, round about it.[20] When this internal force starts to manifest itself, it does so in the depths of a seed: a fresh centre appears around which a new being forms itself; and when this force no longer acts, it seems to withdraw itself from this very centre. 'Birth is therefore expansion from the centre; full life is enlargement of the sphere; and death is contraction to the centre.'[21]

It goes without saying that the spiritual substance, a stranger to space, is not susceptible of any motion: *expansion* and *contraction* are only appearances that interpret the appearance and disappearance (equally mysterious), of the soul in the tangible universe. On the other hand, the non-spatial nature of the formal principle makes it possible to reconcile what has already been said about its unity and the multiplicity of the 'centres' in which it exerts its action. Being non-spatial, it transcends space, dominates it, and envelops it so that it is able to appear at any point and apply its organizing power at any place. Provided that we make a definite distinction between the principle and its applications, it is then justifiable to assert the existence of a universal prime motive force, the origin of all life and all motion—*per quem omnia moventur, vegetant, vivunt.*[22]

Motion, inseparable from the partial and the manifold, is produced in the depths of a universe which is motionless because it is without bounds, and whose inner repose is not even disturbed, for motion and rest become identified in the whole. The sum of the motions issuing from an infinite number of points remains constant, or rather reduces to zero. Once more, this is the picture of the wheel, of the circle turning on itself. In that example, motion harmonizes with rest, for where one partial motion ends another begins.[23]

If there be no rest except at the source of motion, or as a result of compensation of all the motions, then there are only two ways of escaping from the moving being and gaining refuge in the immutable: either ascend to the principle, or lay hold of the totality, *i.e.*, the infinity of motions, in one single glance. As these two ways are both closed to us, immobility forms part of those divine things that can only be an object of love, and, in this universe, love without hope.

The universe with which we are familiar is only a reflection of the divine, and 'natural contemplation', of which it is the subject, cannot lead to a knowledge of the absolute. We apprehend only relationships between phenomena, we perceive only imperfect forms without ever attaining something fully conforming to the concept, the sight of which would give us repose; for we live in the partial, the incomplete, the manifold, that is to say, in emptiness, 'for all that exists outside of the unity is nothing'—*nulla è tutto lo che è fuor di questo uno.*[24]

In order to be consistent, a philosopher who expresses himself thus ought to ascribe, or so it would seem, only an indifferent, if not zero, or even negative, value to the manifold and diverse, to the partial and consequently to the movent. Yet, a poem like *De monade*, far from being that exclusive apology for the unity, as would be suggested by the title, develops into an epic on number; in *Eroici furori*, nostalgia for the Unity, the main theme of the dialogue, becomes so tenuous at times as to give place to exaltation of the diverse, a condition for concord and harmony.[25] These alternations of severity and tenderness with regard to the mobile being correspond to the impulses of a divided heart, to the contrasts of emotional feeling both classical and baroque—that of Giordano Bruno, the poet, and perhaps of any poet. The one dominant, the other more subdued, both heart-rending, the two lyrical themes intertwine one with another: the desire for the sublime, and regret at what must be abandoned in order to obtain it. The desire for death pierced by agony. The most beautiful sonnets in *Eroici furori* are particularly moving in that they interpret the hunger for the immutable into episodes that make the return to the immutable into an adventure, a symbolic exodus towards an Orient that refuses to be conquered and seems to move further away as we go towards it. What can be more moving than these descriptions of combats, hunts, flights, these journeys of sightless ones through the world, the blindness of the travellers making their effort all the more pathetic, and their movement that much purer because it is accomplished in darkness.

NOTES

1. '*Vedete a presso che li matematici hanno per conceduto che le vere figure non si trovano ne li corpi naturali, nè vi possono essere per forza di natura nè di arte.*' *Eroici furori*, II, ii, pp. 369–371.

2. '*Quampropter circus consistens partibus aequis*
   Omnino cunctis, pariter centroque relatis,
   Nulla est natura, nulla est fabrefactilis arte.'
De minimo, II, iv, 5–7 (*Opera*, I, iii, p. 196).

3. '*Perche la vertità è cosa incorporea . . .*'. *Eroici furori*, pp. 369 ff. In this passage Bruno develops a well-known thought from Plato (*Republic*, VI, 510 *d–e*; *Letters*, VII, 342 *b–c*, 343 *a*, etc.) and expressly refers to it. See also *De minimo*, II, iv.

4. Tocco, *Opere di Giordano Bruno*, p. 151, note 2.

5. *De minimo*, II, iv, verses 36 ff. (*Opera*, I, I, iii, p. 197). We are the toy of a similar illusion when we speak of the 'celestial sphere'. *Ibid.*, verses 83–86.

6. *Opere di Giordano Bruno*, pp. 150–155.

7. *Eroici furori*, II, iii, p. 393.

8. '*Sex vulgo motus species afferuntur.* Generatio *et* corruptio *secundum substantium.* Augmentum *et* diminutio *secundum quantitatem.* Alteratio *secundum qualitatem, et* latio *secundum locum.' De monade*, VII (*Opera*, I, ii, p. 429).

9. '*Si ergo praedicamenta sunt divisa in decem rerum genera, scilicet substantiam et qualitatem, etc., ut dictum est in libro* Praedicamentorum *et in V* Metaphys.; *et in tribus illorum inveniatur motus; necesse est esse tres species motus, scilicet motus qui est in genere* quantitatis, *et motus qui est in genere* qualitatis, *et motus qui est in genere* ubi, *qui dicitur secundum locum.' Physica*, V, i, 3.

10. '*Motum non in quatuor, vel in sex tantum, sed in omnibus reperiri praedicamentis dicere debuisset Aristoteles.' Opera*, I, i, pp. 111 and 114.

11. *De coelo*, 274 *b*; *Infinito*, p. 320.

11*b*. '*Nec per inane immensum atomos mundosque vagari, Ceu Epicurei, volumus sine fine deorsum.' De immenso*, II, iv, 21–22.

12. '*An tibi in infinitum tendere aliud est quam non in finem tendere, quod qui est quam contendere ad nullam partem?' De immenso*, II, iv, (*Opera*, I, i, pp. 270–271).

13. '*Onde, si come le margini e le distanze di gli uni corpi a gli altri corpi son finite, così gli moti son finiti; e siccome nessuno si parte da Grecia per andare in infinito, ma per andar in Italia o in Egitto, così, quando parte di terra o di sole si move, non si propone infinito, ma finito e termine.' Infinito*, pp. 320–321.

13*b*. '*Infinitum universum est immobile; in infinito universo infinita universorum generum sunt mobilia. . . .' De immenso*, II, iv (*Opera*, I, i, p. 271).

14. '*Questo* (Manens moveor) *vuol dire che si muove in circolo, dove il moto concorre con la quiete, atteso che nel moto orbiculare sopra il proprio asse et circa il proprio mezzo si comprende la quiete e fermezza secondo il moto retto; o ver quiete del tutto e moto secondo le parti.' Eroici furori*, II, i, 5, p. 323.

15. Bruno distinguishes, as does Aristotle, between natural motion and violent motion, the latter being the result of impact received by an inert object; but, in accordance with the theory of *impetus*, he claims (as does Telesius), that the *vis impressa* remains after impact in the body that has acquired such motion. This problem in pure mechanics is foreign to cosmology which deals only with natural motion.

16. '*Namque volae, pinnae, plumae, facilisque lacerti*
    Circulus est verus, cum bina per aequora tendunt,
    Et sublata volant tepidi per inania campi,
    In quibus ad centrum vis est motiva relata
    Omnibus; ut centrum tota est essentia cycli.'
De monade, II (*Opera*, I, ii, p. 339).

17. '*in ordine . . . aetherorum corporum nullus motor aliqua ratione primus invenitur.' Acrotismus*, Art. XLVIII (*Opera*, I, i, p. 160).

18. '*Quamvis in rerum natura circulus ullus*
    Non cluit, iccirco quia circuit undique totum:
    Quandoquidem speciem natura haud spectat in unam;
    Atqui hasce innumeras appulsu perfecit uno.
        Quare non ullum compostum simplice surrit
    In gyrum tractu, varius siquidem impetus ultro
    Ad varias tendit parteis, neque circulus est par
    Imparibus totis accitisque impare fine:
    At scopus est eadem cunctis (servarier); *hancque*
    Circuitu attendunt, intendunt, adsequitantur.'
De monade, II (*Opera*, I, ii, pp. 337–338).

19. '*Sic maxima et omnis*
    Vis posita est in centro est rerum, est anima ipsaque centrum,
    Cuius (si quiddam est) *totum explicitatio quaedam est.'*
De monade, II (*Opera*, I, ii, pp. 338–339).

20. '*Quare solum per individuam animae substantiam sumus id quod sumus. quam circum, veluti centrum quoddam ubique totum, atomorum exglomeratio fit et agglomeratio. . . .*' *De minimo*, I, iii (*Opera*, I, iii, p. 142).

21. '*Nativitas ergo est expansio centri, vita consistentia sphaerae, mora contractio in centrum.*' *Ibid.*

22. '*Est sane primus motor, id est praecipuus, unusque universalis, a quo et per quem omnia moventur . . .*', etc. *Acrotismus*, Art. XLVIII (*Opera*, I, i, p. 160). Bruno, following Plato in this matter (*Laws*, X, 896–897), makes the soul the principle of motion, and of all motion. We shall see later (chap. IX) the consequences derived from this theory.

23. '*Cumque quiete venit concurrens motus in ipso*
Praeteriti motus finemque initumque futuri
Concipit: iccirco motus est, atque quietis
Terminus: unde quies toti est, motusque per ipsum.'
De monade, II (*Opera*, I, ii, p. 338).

24. *Causa*, V, p. 252.

25. '*Non è armonia e concordia dov' è unità, dove un essere vuol assorbir tutto l'essere; ma dov' è ordine e analogia di cose diverse, dove ogni cosa serva la sua natura.*' *Eroici furori*, I, iv, p. 225.

IV

The soul of the universe

We have just seen that the universe of experience is essentially the *mobile being*; that everything in nature moves and moves without resting, whether it be a living creature, a celestial body or the smallest element of matter; that this motion, finally, does not result from an impulse received from without: its source is at the centre of things. The motion of infinite universes does not come from a motive power outside these universes, but from their own soul (*de la propria anima*), and that motive power is infinite.[1] At the origin of a motion which is both endless and unexplainable by the action of an external force, we are obliged to assume that there is a motive power which is both infinite and internal, and which we call the *soul*.

On the other hand we have acknowledged that two principles, formal and material, have issued from the prime Unity; Bruno also says, two substances, active and passive, the one 'able to act', the other 'able to be acted upon'. The substance that is able to act is the soul of the universe; that which is able to be acted upon is matter. Both are divine in the sense that they proceed directly and necessarily from the divinity. They are 'infinite' for the same reason. The soul of the universe manifests itself everywhere at all time, the universality and continuity of its action derive from the fact that 'the divine efficacy' could not be idle.[2]

Thus, by two ways, the one ascending, the other descending, the philosopher reaches the concept of soul of the universe. As the first degree of the *descensus* and suggestion of experience, the soul is the single outcome of a double effort of thought; and this convergence corresponds to the truth, seeing that the soul of the universe, as we shall see later, is situated at the limit of the divine domain 'removed from our consideration' and of the tangible domain which is that of 'natural contemplation', the extent of which it is justifiable for us to try and understand.

For the earliest Greek philosophers, the soul of the universe was nothing more than the νοῦς. On the other hand, Plotinus made a distinction, giving it third place in the progression Unity, νοῦς, soul —a grouping that reappears in Marsilio Ficino. In the christian Western civilization, the soul of the universe gave rise to the most diverse theories. It is placed more or less near to God, who is its source, and more or less close to the universe, which it endows with life. Lifted up to God, it is the Holy Spirit; lowered down to the world, it is Nature; or, yet again, distinguished from one as from the other, and sometimes personified, it is placed on an intermediate plane. This last conception was rejected in the twelfth century by the strictest theologians, on the ground of orthodoxy, as being dangerous; also certain writers, such as Alain of Lille, were led to renounce the terms soul of the universe or universal soul, and to replace them by the word Nature. For the Arabs, who endeavoured to reconcile the emanatism of Proclos and the Dionysian hierarchies with Mohammedan theology, the descent from God to the universe is carried out by a succession of ten angelic intelligences, the first of which corresponds to the νοῦς and the last to the acting intellect.

From these various systems, each of which expands into a plurality of myths and poetic visions, at the same time providing an abundant iconography, we shall retain only what they have in common. Between God and the Universe, between God and man, between the two regions of the intelligible and the tangible, the soul of the universe functions as an intermediary and link. As the principle of life, *Vita generalissima*, ἀρχὴ τῆς ζωῆς, more or less distinct from the divine, and more or less merged with it, it is in all cases the organ through which the supreme power manifests itself in the universe and by which the life of this great body, the mobility and the mutability of its parts, and its existence in time are explained. The soul of the universe as conceived by Bruno satisfies these general conditions. As to its particular characteristics, they will become evident as we consider more closely on what level it is placed and what are its methods of action.

As God is defined by His immutable Unity, so the universal Soul is defined in the first instance by its omnipresence and by its interiority. It is everywhere and within everything in this 'mobile' universe, the field of our experience. Moreover, the one does not go without the other, as is expressed in the following lines from Vergil, so aptly quoted by Bruno—and which he cited again in his defence on the occasion of his trial at Venice:

> *Totam que infusa per artus*
> *Mens agitat molem et toto se corpore miscet.*[3]

In celestial bodies as in stones, in plants, in animals and, it goes without saying, also in man, in everything and in the deepest depth of everything, this quickening principle resides, everywhere identical with itself, but assuming divers aspects and called by various names according to the consciousness that each of the beings which it animates is able to take of it.[4]

Consciousness, after all, varies from man to man; Bruno lists the degrees of it in *Sigillus*, and comes to the conclusion that all consciousness depends on one unique principle: 'Knowledge is called sense by Epicuros, intellect by Democritos and Empedocles, *mens* and superior spirit by the Pythagoreans, and they understand that this spirit is in every thing according to its reason. According to our conceptions, we judge all these terms to refer to one and the same principle.'[5] A unique principle and a superior principle whence every possibility of knowledge derives, and which is identified with that formal principle which, in us, is more inherent than ourselves. This opinion, that the Platonists are in error when, distinguishing sense from intellect, they claim that the sense is in us and the intellect is outside us, is expressed also in *Sigillus*. This illusion derives from the fact that we do not cease from experiencing sensations when we are not always exercising our intellect.[6] However, these are only intermissions of our attention. Now, how can we fail to recognize the 'formal principle', unique and ever identical with itself, even though called by various names, in that intellect, the permanence of which in us depends neither on our consciousness of it, nor on the circumstances in which it is exercised? 'The universal intelligence and the soul of the universe (wrote Émile Namer), although having functions similar to the hypostases of Plotinus, are not on different levels as are those hypostases, but are definitely on the same level as two faculties of the same spiritual activity.' Namer goes so far as to say that Bruno uses either term 'indifferently', and if he makes any distinction between 'soul' and 'intelligence', then it can be only a distinction of reason—or of function (which is something quite different)—but not of substance: 'There is only one formal principle, Soul or Intelligence, that upholds and produces all the particular forms in the womb of matter.'[7] The distinction *of function*, which has been mentioned here, is specified several times by Bruno, particularly in *De la causa*: 'As regards the efficient cause, I say that the physical efficient of the universe is universal intellect, *the first and principal faculty of the soul of the universe*. The soul of the universe is universal form'; and further on: 'The universal intellect is the most intimate and most natural faculty, the most efficient part of the soul of the universe.'[8]

From these preliminary notes it is already possible to conclude that uncertainty in Bruno's vocabulary (an uncertainty that cannot be overstressed) results from the fact that the soul of the universe is regarded as being one in substance. Bruno ignores, or accepts only as a poetic fiction, the hierarchies of the hypostases and angelic intelligences. The nomenclature used by him tends only to distinguish faculties, modalities or degrees of consciousness.

St Bernard says: 'The being that exists in itself . . . is not remote from any creature, that which is the life of every creature. . . . But is that which is the most present and at the same time the most incomprehensible.'[9] These words apply with full force to Bruno's universal soul. Permanently within every being, and always identical with itself, the soul is not knowable in itself. Its unity would conceal it even from our view and its omnipresence would become absence if we did not have the illusion of distinguishing a plurality of aspects in it, which justifies a nomenclature but which reveals in the scale of beings only a diversity of manifestation, and in us only the power and tension, variable at every instant, of our former aspect.

THE SOUL OF THE UNIVERSE AND GOD

If we attempt to imagine the soul of the universe, it appears to us, as we have seen, between the divine and the tangible in a descending perspective when we start from God, and in an ascending perspective when we start from the universe. We have noted also that a *descensus* without degrees, stages or hierarchies is immediate and to some extent precipitous. Bruno, who was not always able to resist the attraction of neo-Platonism, and who badly conceals in *Eroici furori* his borrowings from Marsilio Ficino, the translator and commentator of Plotinus and Dionysius, is far removed here from the concepts of Ficino concerning the soul of the universe (*anima mundana*). Ficino places *mens* and *anima* on different levels. A hierarchy is affirmed.

The *anima*, source of universal life, is expressed (in the Pythagorean manner) in the harmony of the spheres, whereas the *mens* 'is the articulation of intelligible essences refracted in the angelic spirit corresponding to it'. The *anima* governs a universe subjected to the rhythm of duration (and which is music), but, above the *mens*, the immutable architecture of the angelic universe emerges, timeless, into the light.[10] The contrast between architecture and music is also that of sight and hearing, priority being given to sight. These ideas, dear to Florentine neo-Platonism, and summarized by Alberti (we recall the hieroglyphic symbol of the 'winged eye'), were abandoned by Bruno: or, rather, they are foreign to him. Between the soul of the universe and the divine Unity there is no hypostasis. Furthermore, the soul, co-eternal with God, is inseparable from Him, in the same way that our faculties are inseparable from our being, so much so that it could identify itself with the Holy Spirit, rather than with an angelic power, the former of which causes life to spring and impresses the universe with its forms.

The attribution of a quickening action to the Holy Spirit is a theme that was stated by St Basil and by St Ambrose; it was resumed by Abelard, and to the extent that Bruno adopted this view, he is nearer to the christian sources than to Ficino, nearer to Abelard than to Platonic Florence of the fifteenth century. In this connection, it would certainly be most imprudent to exaggerate the significance of his confession at Venice. When pressed by his judges to answer the charges of pantheism and panpsychism, Bruno declared that the soul of the universe, as he conceived it, is nothing but the Holy Spirit.[11] This attempt to accommodate his philosophical opinions to the dogmas of established religion was rather lacking in courage, seeing that he admitted later in the course of the same confession that his teaching concerning the universal soul was still far 'from what one ought to believe'. On the other hand, and this time being under no restraint, in the *Summa terminorum metaphysicorum*, did not Bruno assert (as did St Paul) that the Spirit of God penetrates everywhere?[12] In the *Lampas triginta statuarum*, had not he assimilated the soul of the universe to the Holy Spirit?[13] So, the universal soul, aspect of God and faculty of God, is distinguished from the divinity and at the same time mysteriously merged with it.

THE SOUL OF THE UNIVERSE AND THE UNIVERSE

We shall now consider the soul of the universe from the inverse point of view, starting from the data of experience, instead of from the supreme Unity. The concept of a formal principle, without which motion and multiplicity would remain unexplainable, is imposed on us by verification of the movent and the manifold. With regard to this principle, it has been asserted:

1. That it is *unique* for all animated beings (that is to say, for all beings, because the whole universe is animated and this animation manifests itself in every one of its parts, as well as in various ways); and

2. That it is *within* each of the animated beings. These two assertions are definitely not unfounded, but, on the other hand, they are not put forward as a matter of course, either. They are the result of reflection on the data of experience and are the answers to two problems that may be justifiably propounded.

The unicity of the soul is not, in fact, immediately obvious. An effort of attention and reason is necessary in order to recognize a unique formal principle when a multiplicity of animated beings is presented to our view: men, beasts, plants and even celestial objects. Just as there is only one material principle (having passive power), one single matter sprung from the supreme Unity, one in substance in spite of its fragmentation, so there is one soul common to all beings underlying all souls. Bruno's thought on this point is clearly explained in the treatise *Cavallo Pegaseo*: 'I say that the universal efficient intelligence is one in all (*è una di tutti*) and that it is the principle of motion and of understanding (*e quella muove e fa intendere*); but over and above this there exists in all the particular intelligence from which each derives motion, light, aptitude to understand; and this intelligence is multiplied according to the number of individuals.' Bruno sheds light on his thought here, as he often does, by a comparison drawn from physical perception: '. . . in the same way that visual power is multiplied according to the number of eyes, when it is put collectively in action and illuminated by a single fire, a single light, a single sun, so the intellective power is multiplied according to the number of subjects that participate in the Soul and on which one single intellectual sun sheds its light. In this manner, then, on all animated beings there is one *active sense* which causes all to be conscious, thanks to which all are conscious in act; and an *active intellect* which endows them all with understanding, thanks to which all are intellective in act; and on the other hand, just as there are many senses and intellects, particular, passive or capable of feeling, so there are as many subjects. . . .'[14] This is not the only passage in which Bruno has used the term 'active intellect'. From this usage we should not assume assertion of a hierarchy of substances, when it corresponds only to a habit of thought or language. No intermediary of the active intellect exists between the universal soul and the individual soul, any more than a scale of the νοῦς (or of the *mens*) exists between God and the Soul. Like the νοῦς (divine intellect), the active intellect is a faculty and not an entity, it is a function and not a substance.

Bruno is not always impartial in having recourse to this term of Aristotelian origin when he considers the soul of the universe in relation to particular souls. Whatever uncertainties, so frequently condemned, there may be in his vocabulary, Bruno does not use the expressions *mente* and *intelletto agente* haphazardly (although he uses them to designate the one and the other universal soul). One is applied to the soul of the universe in so far as it is the first stage in the *descensus*, the other is applied to the soul of the universe considered starting from and as a function of the individual souls, and poetically imagined as their common summit, their common light, or as that unique and imperious 'captain', ever ready to subdue the confusion of low instincts, thought and feelings in dissension.[15]

The soul of the universe as the unique source of all life and all motion, common in this universe to all beings, to all objects, even those that we wrongly deem to be inanimate, is *within* them. This interiority does not signify, in the mind of our author, that the soul 'inhabits' the body and that it is contained by the body in some manner; although the soul is represented—no doubt by imagery, but by an image intended to suggest an unenunciable reality—as dominating the body from on high and enveloping it. It is not the soul which is in the body, 'it is the body which is in the soul',[16] whether it be a question of our body or of the body of the universe, concerning which Plotinus said: 'it is dominated by the soul and does not dominate the soul . . . it is steeped in the soul like a net in the sea'.[17]

The soul, therefore, is both within and around, at the heart of everything and around everything. This is an apparent contradiction, but it is explained by the soul's position and intermediary function between the divinity and the tangible body. 'The Spirit above everything is God, the Spirit implanted in things is Nature'—*Mens super omnia Deus est, mens insita in rebus Natura.*[18] In other words, God does not govern things from the heights of an Olympus or an Empyrean that the new astronomy would push back to infinity, but, situated in a place positively not belonging to the universe (we would almost say in another dimension, to use by way of metaphor the language of present-day science), he reaches each object through its centre and not through its surface; he quickens and governs it inside. Thus, the soul dominates and contains the bodies that it animates through its 'divine' side, whereas through its 'natural' side, it seems to be in them and to inhabit them.

Certain aspects and consequences of this 'panpsychism' will be considered later, but we can mention at this point that he tends to give recognition to natural magic, for which Bruno shows more than tolerance. Contrary to Plotinus, for whom procession is not performable, and for whom natural magic is only a piece of wizardry from which the dreamer should escape,[19] Bruno, not content with bringing reality back to God, causes God to act on everything through the intermediary of the soul; whence it follows that the 'forces' are concealed in the womb of matter, and that it is neither impossible to recognize them, nor impious to utilize them or to try and utilize them to the profit of man. It has been said that a liking for the occult sciences 'agreed with Brunonian animism'.[20] No doubt, but do the sciences which start from a general hypothesis founded on reason and appeal to verification by experience deserve also to be qualified as occult?

THE SOUL AND THE SOULS

The unicity of the soul of the universe and the fact that its action is exercised inwardly and within beings has already led us to raise the problem of the relationships between the Soul and the souls. We are now going to consider this problem and try, starting from data put forward by our author, to rediscover the solutions to which he came, though too often failing to express them with sufficient accuracy. We accept that the Soul is unity; that it is, with God and the atom, one of the three *minima*. On the other hand, it is not subject to tangible experience. On the contrary, experience provides us with a multiplicity of animated beings. We accept also that the unique Soul acts in them; but in doing so, it seems to divide itself and through this division to give birth to various, independent souls. If we assume the Soul to be indivisible, this diversity would be no more than a diversity of aspects. If the Soul, on the other hand, breaks up into parts, as matter does, then the individual souls would be its ultimate elements, comparable with atoms. Unfortunately, the poem *De triplici minimo* does not deal with the three *minima*, as its title would indicate, but deals only with the material minimum. The author sets forth his doctrine concerning the atoms, and gives ample details, but he neglects the question of the indivisibility of the Soul—or the souls. As for his other works, they provide hardly anything more than a sketch of this important problem; the facts that are left for us to interpret are scattered, and sometimes contradictory.

'It is manifest that each spirit has a certain continuity with the spirit of the universe.' There is one indication, provided by the *De Magia*.[21] No doubt the phrase 'a certain continuity'—*continuitas quaedam*—remains rather vague, yet it is interesting, if only on account of its prudence. It leaves the door open to the double hypothesis of the permanent unity of a non-divisible universal Soul (the souls then are only reflections and accidents), or of a breaking up into parts, however it takes place, which makes it possible to imagine the substantiality of the individual souls. Bruno's preference for the first solution may be guessed from various texts.[22] Luigi Cicuttini quotes several of them, including a passage from *Lampas trigenta statuarum*, where it is said substantially: 'Matter engenders the diverse, whereas form is the cause of unity. The action of the Spirit is exerted on a material, and consequently diverse and manifold universe; and the Spirit divides (or seems to divide itself) in order to animate this universe. As a result, there is a multitude of souls. If there be one single sun and one single whole mirror, we are able to contemplate that unique sun in that mirror. If the mirror be broken and multiplied in countless fragments (the material universe), the sun is reflected by each of them and appears to be multiplied, but it so happens that in some of these fragments, because of their extremely small size or of some other defect, we see only a confused image which gives hardly any idea of the universal form.'[23]

The Soul is thus compared to a unique sun and the souls to mirrors (or rather to fragments of a broken mirror) which reflect the light more or less truly, but sometimes so inadequately that they give a false impression of the splendour of the reflected object.[24] However, this comparison with a broken mirror raises a problem. Leaving aside the question of the substantially (or accidental and fugitive character) of the reflected-souls, we ask ourselves, which are the least distorting mirrors among these souls. Are they the ones most passively and most directly subjected to the action of the universal soul? We might be tempted to believe so, but we must not forget that the universal intellect, the prime function of the soul of the universe, governs the movements of ants and spiders just as much as those of human beings and celestial bodies,[25] and that, in the case of an ant or a spider, the animal organism is not moved 'by its own prudence and artifice'—*da propria prudenza e artificio*—but by the infallible divine intelligences which give it impulses usually designated by the term natural instinct. Now, these divine intelligences are answerable to the unique Soul, in substance the same, whether it govern man or an ant; and it is clear that the absolute passivity of the insect (from which the perfect efficiency of its movements derives) could not possibly be regarded as a sign of a more complete participation in the life-giving principle. The passivity and exiguity of the mirror are on a par.

The case of man is the exact opposite. The divine intelligence, of which man is both a more faithful image and more docile instrument, shines in him also and with greater brightness. His superior faculties render him capable of contemplation and discursive thought: 'God commands and directs, Nature accomplishes and forms, Reason contemplates and discourses.'[26] In another place: 'The universal intellect . . . the efficient part of the soul of the universe . . . fills everything, illuminates the universe and leads nature to produce its species as is fitting; consequently, the universal intellect is to the production of natural objects what our intellect is to the appropriate production of rational species.'[27] From the last part of this sentence it is evident that man's participation in the universal soul is quite different from that of an insect's. Man, endowed with intellect, takes cognizance of this participation, and, as far as he is able, imitates the creative action of the supreme Intelligence instead of submitting passively to its impulses and translating them into movements, undoubtedly more certain and efficacious, though more narrowly determined.

This higher degree of participation could not be put forward as a decisive argument in favour of the substantiality of the human soul. Its manifest effects mean nothing less than a superior freedom (or, if one prefers, an appearance of freedom) of that soul with respect to its principle, and in so far as it remains dependent on it, a more conscious feeling of this dependence.[28]

INTROVERSION

An intimate feeling of freedom and consciousness of dependence bring us to the problem of the soul of the universe *qua* subject of knowledge. The soul appears both as a necessary emanation from the supreme Unity and as a necessary cause of phenomena whereof the tangible universe makes us witnesses. To the deductive and inductive methods of approach, a third can be added: can an animated being participating in the universal soul arrive at a more direct knowledge of this Soul by introversion? It can indeed do so, provided that it does not submit passively to the impulse of natural instinct, but retains full consciousness of its acts, thoughts, and in short, of its person, as is the case for every being endowed with intellective life, and of man in particular; provided also that it experiences a desire to rise and return to the source of all life, as is not the case for all men, but for certain ones only who are possessed of the *furor divinus*.

Some few remarks are needed at this point.

1. Man is able to lift himself to a knowledge of his principle (called the active intellect or soul of the universe) through the intellect, that is to say, through the pinnacle of the soul, and through the whole combination of his superior faculties. However, when the *sens* acts continually (as they say), the intellect manifests itself only intermittently. Our soul, like that of every human being, were it the most experienced in contemplation, is consequently not constantly turned towards the Soul, which nevertheless still remains in the utmost depth of our being. In *Eroici furori*, Bruno describes the two aspects of the human soul, the one turned towards the body and the lower powers which it governs, the other turned towards the sovereign Intellect with which it aspires to be connected.

2. This very aspiration and the rare instants of union that it achieves when it is satisfied are shared with the soul, which is trying to find

how far it is from its goal. As a result, we have suffering, nostalgia, the feeling of insufficiency of being and a soaring towards plenitude. From the fifteenth century onwards, and particularly after Ficino's commentary on the *Banquet* of Plato, this great theme of intellectual love gave rise to countless variations with which we are not concerned here, except in so far as they relate to Giordano Bruno. It is not our purpose to describe the Passion of love, but to define its aim and the method of union to which it should conduce.

3. There are two possible hypotheses. Either the divine unity is absolutely simple; in which case the soul of the universe merges with God, and the final outcome for a soul rising to this supreme Soul can only be to lose itself there and come to naught; or this divine unity is organic, as certain of Bruno's expressions lead us to assume. The *Deus complicans* encloses the manifold; the universal Soul emanating from Him contains all souls from all eternity, and it is one of those souls, enclosed in the *Anima*, though as a distinct entity, that our soul must rediscover and with which it must unite in order to resume its place in the celestial choir. From the beginning, christian thought wavered between two conceptions of Paradise: pure monism, or an assembly of souls, each of which would for ever retain its own countenance.[29] The problem, resumed at the close of the Middle Ages and during the sixteenth century, is propounded allusively, if not resolved, in *Eroici furori*. The soul that has fallen in love with God cannot attain its end, for, at its own summit, identified with its perfect nature, but still living (like Actaeon devoured by his hounds),[30] it remains outside of absolute perfection in which it could be able only to blend and disappear. It limits itself to reflecting the light of the divine Unity, attenuating it like a veiled mirror; and it is this veiling that preserves the soul from total death. The mystery of its proper being and the safeguard of its everlastingness reside in a defect of existence.

THE LIMIT OF THE KNOWABLE

From what we have said, it follows that on the way for a return to the First Principle, the soul of the contemplator discovers a limit to the soul of the universe beyond which it cannot pass. That is evident if it be swallowed up there, and no less evident if it establish its dwelling there. Both hypotheses provide the same outcome of its effort, before a wall of silence beyond which there reigns only a dazzling clarity which is darkness for the soul.

Observation of the universe surrounding us would lead us no further than to introversion. The existence of beings endowed with life or motion permit us to deduce with certainty the presence of a life-giving energy, and as the source of this energy is concealed from us, we are justified in assuming that it is to be found within the bodies which it animates, an assumption that agrees with the direct experience we have of ourselves and others.

As for the deductive method, which by a consideration of the supreme Unity leads us to that of the formal principle and of the soul of the universe, it is outside the range of experience and beyond the reach of reason. There we enter the domain of metaphysical conjecture or of faith.

From now on, we have a better understanding of why the soul of the universe is set as the final term of natural contemplation, as the limit of the knowable and the unknowable. Reason, interpreting tangible experience, rises up to this summit, but no higher; introversion descends to this depth, but stops there on the threshold of the unfathomable. On many occasions Bruno has expressed the opinion that progress of cognition towards the First Principle encounters unpassable boundaries. Some of the important relevant texts will be mentioned here.

First of all, there is the passage in the third dialogue of *De la causa*, which asserts the irremediable disparity between the finite intellect and the divine, the infinite object: 'This absolute act, which is identical with the absolute power cannot be understood by the intellect, except by the way of negation. . . . Indeed, the intellect, if it wants to understand, must mould the intelligible image, assimilate, measure and raise itself to equality with that power; but it is impossible, for the intellect is never so great that it cannot be greater. . . . Consequently, the eye does not exist that is able to approach or have access to such an exalted light or to so deep an abyss.'[31]

In the second dialogue of the same work, it is explicitly stated that it is given to us to contemplate the inaccessible only in its reflected image or in the impressions it leaves behind: 'We can know nothing of the divine substance, either because it is infinite, or because it is very far removed from the effects which are the final term in the progress of our discursive faculty, except through its residual impressions

... from remote effect ... through a mirror, shadow and enigma. ...'[32]

In the *Eroici furori*, one of the speakers in the second dialogue of the second part talks of theologians in search of the 'truth of truths' —a subject that cannot be turned into a subject (*oggetto inobiettabile*), 'situated beyond all possibility of being caused to assume the character of a subject as of all comprehension'. Therefore, he adds, 'not one of them believes it possible to see the Sun, the universal Apollo, the absolute light', and their gaze is directed only 'to its shadow, to its Diana, that is to say, to the world, the universe, *nature which is in things*, the light hidden in the opacity of matter'.[33] By a name and character borrowed from heathen mythology, we have no difficulty in recognizing the soul of the universe. It is Diana—harmonization of the reflection of Apollo and the Nature of things.

Finally, it is expressly designated in a passage in the fourth book of *De la causa*: 'You can raise yourself up to the concept, I do not say of the supreme and sovereign principle, which is excluded from our consideration, but of the *soul of the universe*, in so far as it is the act of all, the power of everything, and is all in everything.' In that power we lay hold of the unity of the diverse, knowledge of which is the goal 'of all philosophy'. As for contemplation of that which is above the power, or beyond, it is 'impossible and useless' without faith.[34]

THE TWO ASPECTS OF THE SOUL OF THE UNIVERSE

The first part of the *Figuratio aristotelici physici auditus* (printed at Paris, 1586) lists the main concepts of Aristotelian physics: principle, matter, form, cause, motion, etc. Each of these abstractions is related to a mythological illustration intended to represent it and fix it in the memory. It is no more than a pleasantry, but each term is accompanied in addition by a definition which is never uninteresting. The following nine characteristics are ascribed to *Form*, the principle of nature:

1. *In esse simpliciter;*

2. *Immediate subjecto adveniens;*

3. *Ex quo fit aliquid per se;*

121

4. *In re facta permanens;*

5. *Ad cujus analogiam materia est cognoscibilis;*

6. *Per substantiae physicae;*

7. *Ingenerabilis;*

8. *Incorruptibilis;*

9. *Quoddam divinum, optimum et appetibile.*[35]

In this Form, unbegotten, incorruptible, eternal and divine, thanks to which matter becomes a subject of study and which gives rise to the being through a simple act, we recognize the residual impressions of the soul of the universe.

On the basis of some of Bruno's expressions of opinion, it has been said that he regarded the soul of the universe as merging with God and making one with Him; and that, if he distinguished between them (it is undeniably so), then it was a purely logical distinction, introduced for the convenience of the discourse. Ignoring the fact that a feeling for the opportunity of making such a distinction is in itself significant, we believe that identification of the soul of the universe with God attributed to Bruno is the result of an inaccurate interpretation of the texts where it is stated that the soul of the universe is the ultimate goal of contemplation; for it is then a question of 'natural' contemplation, in other words, an effort of reason. The soul of the universe is located between God and the universe. Those forms that it contains in itself, it impresses them on matter, or better expressed, acting from within it causes them to burst out and so render them accessible to sense and reason. The soul delivers up its secrets to attentive minds, and it is not even forbidden to intercept its forces, as is shown by the efficacy of the magic arts—and of all arts.[36] The superior realm, that of divine preparation, the *ante res* where every form is hidden in the mind of God, remains, however, inaccessible to rational knowledge; for it is only through nature (*i.e.,* the soul) that God acts on the reason: *Influit Deus per naturam in rationem.*

In *De minimo* we read: 'God is love, efficience, clarity, light; Nature is worthy to be loved, it is object, fire and ardour; Reason is loving, it is a subject that is kindled by Nature and illumined by God.'[37]

The Soul of the universe has two aspects, like the human soul of which it is the supreme model; one aspect is towards the Supreme Unity whence it receives light; the other (and it is this aspect which takes the name of Nature) is towards the lower regions which it quickens, towards the tangible universe, towards the souls to which, by transmitting the reflection of divine light, the Soul dispenses warmth, and in which it awakens the desire for love.

NOTES

1. '... tutti [gli astri] se muoveno dal principio interno, che è la propria anima ...; e pero è vano andar investigando il lor motore estrinseco ... preposti cotali averti-menti ... non siamo forzati a dimostrar moto attivo nè passivo di vertù infinita intensivamente; perchè il mobile ed il motore è infinito, e l'anima movente ed il corpo moto concorreno in un finito soggetto; in ciascuno, dico, di detti mondani astri.' Infinito, I, 2nd part, argument viiie, p. 304.

2. '... perchè vogliamo o possiamo noi pensare che la divina efficacio sia ociosa?' Infinito, I, p. 297.

3. Ennead, VI, 726–727; see Cause, principe et unité (trans. E. Namer), p. 89, note 16.

4. The permanence of imaginary objects which are not entities 'superimposed on the real', but which are repeated indefinitely entro il mutare sensibile (see Nicola Badaloni, La filosofia di Giordano Bruno, Florence, 1955, pp. 38 and 24) is itself assured by the unity of the universal soul and by its permanence.

5. 'Epicurus ... cognitionem appellat sensum, Democritus et Empedocles in-tellectum, Pythagorici mentem et spiritum altiorem, ipsumque intelligunt esse in omnibus pro sua ratione. Et certe ex nostris principiis nos haec omnia in unum con-currere principium judicamus.' Sigillus, section 31 (Opera, II, ii, p. 174).

6. 'Sensum quidem (quia sentimus semper) iudicamus esse nostrum, de intellectu vero ambigunt Platonici, et quia eo non semper utimur, et quia est separatus, separatus inquiunt.' Sigillus, section 31 (Opera, II, ii, p. 173).

7. Cause, principe et unité (La philosophie de Giordano Bruno), p. 17.

8. Causa, II, trans. E. Namer, pp. 88–89.

9. Sermons sur le Cantique des cantiques, IV, 4. Trans. A. Béguin, Paris, 1953, p. 108.

10. See A. Chastel, Marsile Ficin et l'art, Geneva and Lille, 1954, p. 89.

11. Domenico Berti, Vita di Giordano Bruno, Turin, 1889, p. 40.

12. De Deo seu mente (Opera, I, iv, pp. 73–101), passim; in particular see articles I (Substantia) and XXI (Medium).

13. Opera, III, p. 54.

14. Cabala, pp. 277–278.

15. See Eroici furori, I, v, 5 (emblem Caesar adest), pp. 252 ff, and Introduction, pp. 56–57.

16. 'Cicada.—Dunque il corpo non è luogo dell'anima? Tansillo.—No, perchè l'anima non è nel corpo localmente, ma come forma intrinseca e formatore estrin-seco; come quella che fà li membri, e figura il composto da dentro e da fuori. Il corpo dunque è ne l'anima, l'anima ne la mente, la mente o è Dio, o è in Dio, come disse Plotino.' Eroici furori, I, iii, p. 191.

17. Ennead, IV, iii, 9.

18. De minimo, I, i (Opera, I, iii, p. 136).

19. Ennead, IV, iv, 43–44.

20. J. R. Charbonnel, La pensée italienne au XVIᵉ siècle, pp. 560–562.

21. Opera, III, pp. 408–409.

22. *Acrotismus* (*Opera*, I, i, p. 180); *De immenso* (*Opera*, I, i, p. 372). See Luigi Cicuttini, *Giordano Bruno*, pp. 155–159. Cicuttini, who is in agreement with Tocco and Gentile on this point, does not doubt that the unicity of the soul asserted by Bruno is incompatible with the substantiality of individual souls.

23. See *Lampas trigenta statuarum* (*Opera*, III, p. 59).

24. '*Quod ita ferme est quemadmodum si unus sit sol et unum continuum speculum, in toto illo unum solem licet contemplari; quod si accidit speculum illum perfringi et in innumerabiles portiones multplicari, in omnibus portionibus totam repraesentari videbimus et integram solis effigiem, in quibusdam vero fragmentis vel propter exiguitatem vel propter figurationis indispositionem aliquid confusum vel prope nihil de illa forma universali apparebit, cum tamen nihilominus insit, inexplicata tamen.*' *Ibid.*

25. See *Cena*, p. 210 and *Summa terminorum metaphysicorum* (*Opera*, I, iv, pp. 120–121); the latter refers to bees and spiders, but the idea is the same. Aristotle (*Physica*, II, 199a) quotes the spiders and ants as examples of animals acting through natural impulses.

26. '*Deus dictat et ordinat, Natura exequitur et facit, Ratio contemplatur et discurrit.*' *De minimo* (*Opera*, I, iii, p. 136).

27. '*L'intelletto universale è l'intima, più reale e propria facultà e parte potenziale del'anima del mondo. Questo è uno medesimo, che empie ill tutto, illumina l'universo e indirizza la natura a produre le sue specie come si conviene; e così ha rispetto all produzione di cose naturali, come il nostro intelletto alla congrua produzione di specie razionali.*' *Causa*, II, p. 179.

28. These views are developed in the 'moral' dialogues. The *Spaccio* dwells more on liberty, the *Eroici furori* on awareness of dependence.

29. This wavering is apparent in the divergent concepts of the Fathers of the Church. In this way it has been possible to compare '*la vision orchestrée et synesthésique de saint Ambroise (surtout dans l'*Hexaemeron*) à la sensibilité plus stricte, plus purement monothéiste de saint Augustin (dans le* De musica*); les deux attitudes se maintiennent dans la cosmologie chrétienne, jusqu'à la Renaissance, et bien au delà. . .'*. A. Chastel, *Marsile Ficin et l'art*, p. 127, note 6.

30. '*. . . fà estraordinaria vita . . . comincia a vivere intellettualmente, vive vita de' dei. . . .*' *Eroici furori*, I, iv, p. 209.

31. '*Questo atto assolutissimo, che è medesimo che l'assolutissima potenza, non può esser compreso dal'intelletto, se non per modo di negazione. . . . Perchè l'intelletto, quando vuole intendere, gli fia mestiero di formar la specie intelligibile, di assomigliarsi, di commesurarsi ed ugualarsi a quella: ma questo è impossibile, perchè l'intelletto mai è tanto che non possa essere maggior. . . . Non è dunque occhio ch'approssimar si possa o ch'abbia accesso a tanto altissima luce e sì profondissimo abisso.*' *Causa*, III, p. 222.

32. '*. . . della divina sustanza, sì per essere infinita sì per essere lontanissima da quelli effetti che sono l'ultimo termine del corso della nostra discorsiva facultade, non possiamo conoscer nulla, se non per modo di vestigio . . . di remoto effetto, . . . di specchio, ombra ed enigma. . . .*' *Causa*, II, p. 176.

33. *Eroici furori*, II, ii, p. 372.

34. '*Possete quindi montar al concetto, non dico del summo ed ottimo principio, escluso della nostra considerazione; ma del'anima del mondo, come è atto di tutto e potenza di tutto, ed è tutta in tutto; onde al fine (dato che sieno innumerabili individui), ogni cosa è uno e il conoscere questa unità è lo scopo e termine di tutte le filosofie e contemplazioni naturali: lasciando ne' sua termini la più alta contemplazione, che ascende sopra la natura, la quale a chi non crede e impossibile e nulla.*' *Causa*, IV, p. 240.

35. '*Elle crée par un acte simple; elle atteint immédiatement son sujet; elle donne à chaque être son être propre; elle subsiste dans la chose faite; la matière est connaissable en tant qu'elle lui est analogue; elle s'indentifie à la substance physique; elle est inengendrable; incorruptible; elle est quelque chose de divin, d'excellent et de désirable.*' *Figuratio aristotelici physici auditus*, I, ch. ii, art. 4 (*Opera*, I, iv, p. 153).

36. In the opening pages of *Theses de magia* (*Opera*, III, p. 455 ff), Bruno recalls that magic involves not only knowledge, but action. It involves consideration

of the natural order on the scale of beings ('*Principium magiae est considerare ordinem influxus seu scalam entium*', *Opera*, III, p. 457) and the application of that consideration.

37. '*Deus est amor, efficiens, claritas, lux; natura est amabilis, objectum, ignis et ardor; ratio est amans, subjectum quoddam quod a natura accenditur et a Deo illuminatur.*' *De minimo*, I, i (*Opera*, I, iii, p. 136).

V

Matter

With regard to matter we know already that, together with form and ranking equally therewith, it is one of the two substances that sprang directly from the prime Unity, themselves inseparable and both inseparable from their common principle.[1] We know, too, that matter (or, at least, its ultimate element, the atom) appears with God and the Soul among the three indivisibles, the three indestructible minima to which everything is finally reduced and which ensure the everlastingness of the universe.

'All bodies reduce to one single principle of substance: Matter. All forms and all souls reduce to one single principle of subsistence: the divine Intelligence. These two principles reduce to a common substance.' That is how one expositor of Bruno[2] expresses himself, using Spinozistic terms, before recalling that David of Dinant, an obvious and admitted source for Bruno, had formulated the theory of the three indivisibles in the twelfth century: 'The first indivisible of which bodies are constituted is called Hyle; the first indivisible of which souls are constituted is called νοῦς or Mens; the first indivisible in eternal substances is called God.'[3]

St Thomas Aquinas, drawing freely upon Aristotle, defined matter as 'prime subject, essential and non-accidental principle of all things and subsisting in the thing that is wrought'.[3b] We cannot but notice the similarity of this definition with that given by Bruno in respect of form, and which has been quoted above. They seem to be based on each other, and that is not fortuitous, for the similarity of the definitions corresponds to the indissolubility of the two principles. In this respect, Bruno hardly departs from scholastic tradition. St Thomas Aquinas taught that 'the true subject of existence is compounded of matter and form'.[4] On the other hand, matter *qua* principle is infinite (it is substance, and therefore infinite: as Spinoza declared). Matter is divine, and therefore infinite, participating in the infiniteness of its principle. It possesses this infiniteness in common with form, in which respect neither exhausts the other, as is explicitly stated in *Sigillus*: 'Form is not exhausted in any matter, matter is not exhausted in any form', which means that it is always susceptible of fresh forms.[5]

So far, as regards matter, we have revealed those characteristics that it possesses in common with form: its immediate dependence on the prime principle, its indivisibility, its infiniteness. The fact that they are indissolubly linked together could also be considered as a property held in common. In reality, the one does not exist without the other. They are different, however, and their distinguishing characteristics must be defined. Unfortunately, the first quality of matter is the absence of any quality, when we have isolated it in our mind from form. It no longer becomes the subject of our senses, its indeterminism is absolute.[6]

Matter, which the philosopher has in mind, is not in fact a specific matter already in possession of a form (as, for example, clay, a potter's raw material), but the prime matter ($\pi\rho\dot{\omega}\tau\eta$ $\ddot{v}\lambda\eta$), the principle of tangible being. Bruno emphasizes this important distinction, which was familiar to him from his instruction in Aristotelianism and Platonism, which agree on this point.[7] With regard to marble, we can say: 'Will it be God, a table or a basin?', but whatever be the object that is made, it will never be other than a marble object: the infinity of forms is not exposed to our view, for marble is itself, like clay or wood, one form exclusive of the others. However, there is one matter of which we can say: will it be marble, clay or wood? 'That matter, which is conceived without any form . . . is called the prime matter, for no other matter is antecedent to it' (*Dicitur materia prima propter hoc quod ante ipsam non est alia*).[8] It is called also *Hyle*. Bruno enters so thoroughly into these Aristotelian views that he outdoes Aristotle, refusing the name of matter to anything that is not prime matter: '*Materia non prima, quae improprie materia dicitur.*'[9] Nevertheless, he recognizes that this non-prime matter is of two kinds: either it possesses its form completely (*e.g.*, honey with its sweetness), or it serves as a material support for some object, as in the case of wood used to make a statue of Mercury; a distinction for which Bruno was indebted to Themistios.[10]

POWER AND LATENCY

Every tangible object (whether it be an object possessing its form completely, or matter incorrectly called prime and which serves as a support for it) is secondary matter. Prime matter, or more simply the Matter, forms no part of tangible existence. It is not being, but the possibility of being, and absolute possibility. Isolated, deprived of all form, it is virtually pure. To compensate for this lack of being it possesses an infinitude of virtualities. It is nothing, but may become everything; it has the power only 'to be wrought', but with this reservation it has every power; and it desires the fulfilment of the virtualities carried within itself. It has the appetite for them, as Polihimnio, one of the speakers in the dialogue *De la causa*, says in a discourse where he compares matter to a woman, bewailing her changing humour and the infinite diversity of her desires: he asks, 'Do not you believe that if matter were content with the present form, then no change or passion would have dominion over us, and that we should not be liable to die, but be incorruptible and eternal?' To which, Gervasio, wisely replies: 'If matter were contented with the form which it possessed fifty years ago, what would you say, Polihimnio? What would you be?... It is the wish of nature which orders the universe that all forms give place to all forms. I concede the fact that it is far more dignified for this our substance [matter] to become everything by accepting all forms, than to be partial by retaining one of them only.'[11]

This availability which excludes nothing takes account of cosmic development and incessant change of the *ens mobile*, of which it is one of the aspects. By reason of the absolute virtuality of matter, all motion is possible, that is to say, every kind of change, whether it be of place, quality or quantity. Being concerned to make sure that nothing is left obscure, Bruno returns to this question in the course of the same dialogue and repeats, in respect of dimensions, what he has already said about forms: matter contains them all. In the same way that he had distinguished between prime matter and secondary matter, he discriminates between 'absolute' matter and 'contracted' matter: 'Absolute, it is above all dimensions and comprises them all; contracted, it is constituted by and within some of them.' Dicson echoes these words of Theophilus: Matter, in itself, has no dimension, anymore than it has form; but it contains in itself the possibility of all dimensions as well as of all forms. Polihimnio declares: 'That is definitely why we say that it has no dimension at all.' Dicson says: 'We, we say, if matter has none at all, then it is for the purpose of having them all: (*ideo habet nullas ut omnes habeat*).' Is that a play on words? Not at all, and the continuation of the dialogue is ample proof thereof. What, in fact, it is important to define, is how the Matter, without having any dimension, carries 'within itself' the potentiality of every dimension. Gervasio asks: 'Why do you want it to include them all rather than that it should exclude them all?' and Dicson replies: 'Because it does not receive the dimensions as from the outside, but makes them issue and rise as though from its womb.'[12]

All the wise men of Antiquity agree on this point—the Pythagoreans as well as Anaxagoras, the Babylonians, Moses himself[13]— 'they want things to result from matter by separation and not by addition or reception. It is then necessary to say that the Matter contains the forms and includes them, rather than to imagine that it is empty and excludes them'.[14] We guess that Bruno, having said that matter 'received' all forms, was afraid of being misunderstood. For that reason he emphasizes the fact that his uncertainty of mind was resolved, not by an external influence but by one which, though quite foreign to him (seeing that matter, essentially passive, 'receives' the influence), was within him and sprang from his breast. Matter is not a block of marble awaiting the sculptor, and whose form is produced by his chisel. Indissolubly linked with the active forces of nature, it is sculptured from within and has never ceased from being sculptured. Its powers reside in itself: they are latencies. Now we are closer to the *Enneads* than to Aristotle's *Physica*.[15]

IMMUTABILITY AND SUBSTANTIAL UNITY

As support for tangible being and first state of its mutability, matter is itself unchangeable. Throughout all the changes, it does not change, it does not renew itself. 'In the products of our arts, when a statue is made from wood, we do not say that a new being has been added to the wood, for it remains wood exactly as it was before; but that which receives being and reality is the new object that is produced, the composition, the statue.'[16] Now, what the wood is to the statue, so the prime matter is to the wood. Furthermore, it is always identical with itself: 'It is that around which and in which change takes place, rather than that which changes itself.'[17]

An objection now arises. If the Matter, persisting in the compound (as the material support for the statue persists in the statue), is unchangeable; and if, on the other hand, the tangible being is such for us only to the extent that it is a movable being, and if all tangible knowledge be knowledge of change, how can we perceive the Matter? Patricius put the question to Telesius, as was noted by Dorothea Singer.[18] The answer is ready to hand, or rather, the objection disappears, in view of the fact that it has been admitted that the prime matter is not apparent to our senses, and comes within the field of our perceptions only as something that has been enquired after, that is to say, animated by the other principle from which it is in fact inseparable. Both are eternal and unchangeable; consequently, the one as well as the other being inaccessible to our experience, if we assume them to be isolated from each other, it follows that matter and form are, through their alliance, the source of all change, that is to say, of all perceptible things.

Consequently, we must beware of underestimating matter, and form just as much; we must avoid saying, as has been done, that Bruno regarded form 'as an accident of matter' which alone, being both cause and effect, would be eternal.[19] Bruno expressly contradicts the statement thus ascribed to him when he criticizes Avicebron through the person of Theophilus and declares the doctrine of those, such as 'this Moor', who 'have concluded that forms are only accidents and circumstances of matter', to be erroneous. It would be, moreover, just as false to regard matter as an accident of form. Accident implies the manifold, and is conceivable only on the level of compounds. Now, there exist one single formal principle and one single material principle—one spirit and one matter, which are likened in *De monade* to the male and the female. 'This unique spirit, not proper to each body but common to them all, united with certain materials would produce gold, in the same way that man is born of the seminal vital spirit received and nourished in the female womb.'[20]

The image evoked by these words involves the risk of some misapprehension, but we must not forget that matter is one and unchangeable just as much as the spirit, and that the existence of various, definite bodies assumes their union. The Matter is a 'minimum', and on that score is exempt from change. Without form, nature is indivisible:

Ergo atomam tantum naturam dixeris esse
Perpetuo, cuius nulla aut propria una figura est.[21]

The substantial unity of matter is thus asserted, and if it happens that Bruno speaks of the four elements, we must realize that in his view they are not primary bodies or simple bodies, but already forms in which spirit and pure matter are indissolubly united.[22]

Without taking further notice of the rather coarse image of the male and the female, it remains to be seen how the internal energy acts on the matter, which is substantially one, in view of the production of various bodies.

It is only too obvious that an account here cannot relate to the source of the act but only to its development and its results. We start from two principles concerning which we know that each of them is eternal and unchangeable. We must, therefore, put aside any idea of substantial transformation of the matter, and consequently assume that the ceaseless changes presented to our gaze by the universe are necessarily linked with local motions, displacements, processes of dissociation and recombination of elements. Then again, being given that the common substratum not only of all objects but of all bodies —even those that seem to us to be elementary—is one absolutely indeterminate matter capable of assuming all forms, the philosopher is left with only two solutions: either to accept as a fact, without seeking an explanation thereof, the possibility of the generation of various, definite substances starting from one unique indeterminate substance,[23] or to assume that bodies owe their forms and determination to a method of grouping of elementary particles, which finally ends in atomism. Aristotle regarded mixtures as true substances within which the constituents undoubtedly subsist, but which nevertheless cannot be likened to aggregates of pre-existing corpuscles. Bruno, on the other hand, considered that any solution involving a substantial alteration in the matter must be set aside; in the same way he refused the concept of a springing forth of new substances: the universe being unchangeable as a whole as well as in its ultimate elements is not susceptible of augmentation or diminution; it is what it is *ab aeterno*. In short, every change reduces to a displacement, every tangible body is vitalized matter; transmutations and changes of all kinds are the appearances that clothe for us the hidden reality of the displacements and combinations of particles which are in themselves unchangeable and inaccessible to our senses: 'When we consider more profoundly the being and substance of that

131

in which we are unchangeable, we shall find that there is no death, either for ourselves or for any other substance; in substance nothing diminishes, yet everything, altering its position in infinite space, changes its appearance.'[24] The transformations undergone by a living being in the course of its life are only one example, though a particularly striking one, of this universal rule: 'We are in a state of continual transmutation: fresh atoms are continually being incorporated in us, whilst others that we received in former times escape from us.' These changes which condition birth, life and death take place by virtue of the 'general Intellect'.[25]

CONTINUITY AND DISCONTINUITY

From some of the passages previously quoted we know already Bruno's answer to the question concerning continuity and discontinuity in the material universe. It must be admitted that this answer was not rigorously asserted. Consequently, it must not be put forward as a logical result of what has been advanced and set down in principle concerning indetermination, substantial unity, the inalterability and permanence of the prime matter. Aristotelian physics accepts both the continuity and existence of an indeterminate $\pi\rho\acute{\omega}\tau\eta\ \ddot{\upsilon}\lambda\eta$, the substratum of all bodies. Bruno, too, was content to speak of the discontinuity of matter in passing, as though it were a matter of course. Such an assertion would sooner or later be surrounded by polemical arguments, be more closely defined, and developed into a system.

It was in 1586, during his second stay in Paris, that Bruno first put forward his objections to infinite divisibility. They are recorded in two small works, one, printed at Paris in the same year, has the title *Centum et viginti articuli ... adversus Peripateticos*; the other—*Camoeracensis acrotismus*—was printed two years after, at Wittenberg. The latter is merely a reissue of the former with several additions.[26]

Article XLII of the *Acrotismus* is directed to proving the physical impossibility of continuity which according to Aristotle's definition would not be composed of indivisible particles.[26b] Continuity implies, in effect, infinite divisibility. Now, any magnitude whatsoever, if it be infinitely divisible, is infinite. Two infinite magnitudes being equal to each other (we have seen that, for Bruno, only infinite magnitudes can be equal to each other), it follows that all magnitudes will be equal, and as a result all objects will be of the same magnitude: the Earth will be just as large as the whole universe, and this apple, which is infinitely divisible, will be just as large as the Earth.[27] Bruno concludes that the concept of infinite divisibility must be rejected both by the physicists, and (this may seem stranger) the mathematicians. The former recognize that every body is composed of ultimate elements (*ex minimis illis corporibus omne corpus componitur*), the latter would not push their division beyond certain limits.[28]

The charge against mathematicians of accepting infinite division of finite magnitudes is repeated in several passages in *De minimo*. The author there refers so often to logical impossibilities that it would be tedious to stress the matter. One example will suffice: to claim that a finite magnitude is able to diminish indefinitely, is to fall into the same absurdity as to assume that two straight lines, when produced indefinitely, would never meet although the distance between them were continuously decreasing.[29] The mathematical digressions in *De minimo* are of little importance, even for their author, who is far more concerned, as he frequently proclaims, with the realities of nature than with the imaginings of geometers. The doctrine of discontinuity, based on the notion that the minima are the only permanent substances in the flux of things, disappears in an atomistic physics doubly opposed to Aristotelian physics, seeing that it assumes indivisible ultimate elements in an infinite universe, whereas, according to Aristotle, the infinite is contained within the limits of a finite universe.[30]

With regard to atomism, we feel that it is necessary to give an answer to the following question before considering the system in detail: What is the place of atomism in Bruno's cosmology considered as a whole? At what point does it appear? How important is it?

According to Tocco, atomism, following after a neo-Platonizing mysticism and a Parmedian monism, would represent the final stage in Bruno's thought. According to Olschki, it appears, though fleetingly, in the London dialogues (1584–1585) and in *De immenso*; is stated precisely during his second stay in Paris (1586); and only fully expressed at a later date in *De minimo*.[31] Olschki concludes that atomism is, in short, only an 'episode' and quite late in this development. We do not share that opinion. We agree rather with the

opinion of Gentile and Olgiati who see in atomism the natural conclusion of a collection of earlier reflections on the universe and matter.
We would go even further. For, accepting the fact that the development of an atomistic theory was late (and late in the very restricted
period of ten years, 1582–1592, during which all Bruno's known works
were printed), and taking into account the fact that this theory did
not start to find expression until 1586, that is to say, roughly in the
second half of the short period under consideration, we must recognize also that atomism was not only prepared or envisaged, but also
stated and on occasion asserted during the first half of that same
period (1582–1586). At the time he was writing the London dialogues
Bruno was familiarizing himself with Nicholas of Cusa, whom he
quotes frequently, and he could have been struck by certain opinions
of that great mind concerning the indivisibility of the ultimate
elements.[32] Undoubtedly, that is mere conjecture, but it cannot be
denied that many passages in the treatise *De l'infinito* (printed at
London) and in *De immenso* (which is acknowledged to have been
written partly at London) already betray an atomistic intuition of
matter, which is too clearly stated to be regarded as episodic or
marginal, though it is not developed into a theory, for it would be out
of place in these works.

Here, for example, is a curious passage in which Philotheus, the
leading character in the dialogues of *De l'infinito*, shows how it
happens that a discontinuous mass may have all the appearances of
continuity when the elements of which it is composed are intimately
blended together. For example, mud is formed out of water and
earth, 'but as we do not distinguish the collection of the smallest
parts of the earth and the smallest parts of the water, we do not have
the impression of discreet quantities or of several continua, but of
one single continuum, which is neither water nor earth, but mud'.
Dorothea Singer, who has rightly pointed out the importance of
these lines, is not justified in translating *le minime parti di terra e
minime parti d'acqua* by *atoms of earth, atoms of water*.[33] That rather
distorts the text. Furthermore, earth and water being bodies that
come within the range of our senses are already forms, and, according
to Bruno's doctrine to be developed later, atoms can only be the
ultimate elements of the indeterminate prime matter. If we wish to
avoid the anachronism, 'molecule of water', *le minime parti* must be
translated simply as 'the smallest parts'. It is indeed most interesting
for us to realize that during the period when he was writing his

vernacular dialogues, Bruno accepted the existence of minimal quantities of earth and water. We may add that on the two pages preceding this comment on mud, the word 'atom' is used four times (in connection with changes and alterations in various bodies) and that it is said that 'infinitude [of matter] is not continuous, but is made of discreet parts, which are in an infinite continuum which is space': (*questa infinitudine non è come di continuo, ma come di discreti; li quali sono in un continuo infinito, che è il spacio*).[34] This passage seems sufficiently clear to make it unnecessary to quote others. However, we can recall the following sentence, a parenthesis in a discourse by Philotheus in the fourth dialogue of the same work: 'As for the indivisible prime bodies of which the whole was originally composed' (*quanto . . . al i primi corpi indivisibili, de quali originalmente è composto il tutto . . .*),[35] or again those lines in *De immenso* which deal with the atom *qua* permanent and unalterable element.[36]

ATOMISM

State of the problem. Léopold Mabilleau in his *Histoire de la philosophie atomistique* devotes only the briefest of paragraphs to Giordano Bruno. He is mentioned only to be excluded from the topic. He admits that certain passages in *Acrotismus*, *De immenso* and *De minimo* (which he quotes from Lange and Lasswitz) seem to make Bruno 'the most conscious and most resolute of atomists'; but against these passages he cites another taken from the treatise *De la causa* in which is expressed an idea so often repeated by its author to the effect that 'the infinite variety of forms under which matter appears to us are not borrowed from another being . . . they emanate from its own womb . . . it contains them all'. This assertion (which relates to the internal action of the formal principle) puts Bruno among the supporters of hylozoism, a doctrine deemed to be incompatible with atomism, 'rather on the side of Thales than Democritos'.[37]

Writers who have specially studied Bruno's philosophy have not been able to avoid the problem quite so easily; though we have the impression that the doctrine set forth in *De minimo* as regards the structure of the material universe has embarrassed some of them. Olschki gives a rather brief analysis of the matter, treating it as an 'episode'.[38] He says, it is not quite clear that it is the atom in this extraordinary 'physics'. All the same, we see what it is not: it is not the atom of Democritos, because it is 'animated'; in so far as it is the centre of energy, it is more deserving of the name of monad. Nevertheless, it is not comparable with the monad of Leibniz, seeing that he believed in the infinite divisibility of matter. Bruno refers sometimes to Democritos, sometimes to Epicuros and to Lucretius, not without an appeal on occasion to the Pythagoreans, Anaxagoras, Paracelsus or the Arabs. Hence, a state of inextricable confusion for the critic. These facts, he says, are valuable, because they reveal the spiritual character of the thinker, though it is impossible to build a coherent system from them.[39]

For our part, we do not think that there is cause for despair, and we feel that the confusion which is so much deplored derives in great part from the fact that we endeavour to relate Bruno's atomism to earlier (and sometimes later) systems. It is not that the question of sources is in itself without interest, or that the works of Felice Tocco are not of great use in this respect, but it must not be put in the foreground. The tradition of atomism of Antiquity was perpetuated in the Middle Ages by the Arabs in the East, and by the alchemists in the West; it was revived at the dawn of the Renaissance in various forms by Nicholas of Cusa, Agrippa von Nettesheim, Basil Valentine, Paracelsus, then by Cardanus, Fracastoro, Telesius. These writers were not known to Giordano Bruno, but he sought suggestions rather than models in their works. If he seems to follow first one and then the other, then this eclecticism is not a sign of hesitation on his part, and even less of an attempt at reconciliation, which would not be in accordance with his character. When he agrees with one or the other of them on a particular point, he does not hesitate to say so, but when he disagrees on some point he proclaims the fact just as loudly.

Whether it be a question of Democritos, Copernicus or Palingenius, his expressions of admiration are rarely given without reserve, and his approvals are sometimes followed by severe criticisms. His sole purpose is to set forth, or cause to be set forth, the Brunonian philosophy through speakers in his dialogues. Such independence in respect of sources is only to be expected in his opinions concerning the nature of the atom. As Gaston Bachelard has pointed out, atomism is a doctrine that is not transmitted.[40] In this field, successive schools of thought have scarcely been connected with each other; the influences were quite weak—at least until that period, still far from the sixteenth century, when positive experiments came into play—each thinker started from an initial intuition which he developed in original concepts.

Giordano Bruno is an example. Therefore, our method will be to keep to that which he asserts in *De minimo* and all the other works in which he speaks of the atom, even though it be incidentally. The passages will provide sufficiently clear answers to the questions put forward to account for their apparent contradictions.

The minimum and the term. The *De minimi existentia*, which is the first of the five parts comprising *De minimo*, reveals in a series of sketches or partial definitions what the chief characteristics of the atom will be. We learn that atomism is certainly a theory of matter, that the atom is a material body and not an ideal limit. A point may be defined in two different ways according as we regard it as the extremity of a line or as the smallest part of that line, as a limit or as an ultimate element.[41] Only in this latter sense can the atom be compared to a point. It is a 'minimum' and not a 'term'. The term has no dimension, it is nothing. The minimum has all dimensions potentially, it is the principle, the $\alpha\rho\chi\acute{\eta}$, the unity, the source of number.[42]

Elsewhere the material universe is likened to a written passage which would contain an infinite number of words; in order to form these words, it suffices to have a very limited number of signs (letters or accents) and these signs themselves consist of points. Atoms are not likened here to letters and *then* to points, as Tocco says. The words represent an infinite variety of tangible objects; the letters are the elementary bodies from which these objects are composed; the points are the ultimate elements into which, finally, everything resolves.[43]

These few remarks already inform us about the essential characteristics of the atom: it is the material minimum, the physical unity; principle and non-limit, it is the sub-stratum of all simple and compound bodies; all division when pushed sufficiently far is reduced to it and stops there.[44]

Atoms and the void. The indivisibility of the atom implies its impenetrability: to penetrate would be to separate. Impenetrability in its turn implies discontinuity—not so obviously perhaps, but necessarily all the same. The unit-points of Pythagorean arithmo-geometry were surrounded by a 'field' without which these arithmetical atoms would not have been representable. Points juxtaposed without any interval between them would form only an indistinct mass, unsuitable for representing a number. Furthermore, a point having no parts, two points, strictly speaking, cannot touch without merging. Bruno's aim being to make known what exists in nature, he retains from this abstract atomism only that which he deems applicable to a 'physics'. The atom is not a mathematical point without dimension, but a *body*. Nevertheless, there are some precautions. One body does not touch another body, nor one atom another atom, *toto aut parte* (in whole or in part), but by the term or extremity of the whole or of the part: *aut totius aut partis termino . . . seu extremo.* Now, this extremity itself is composed of parts, and gradually we establish that the contact between two material bodies is produced only by a 'minimum'. Seeing that the atom is indivisible and unchangeable, nothing exists and we can conceive of nothing that is truly and properly 'miscible'. Sometimes we have the illusion that two bodies mix together to form a third, but what is produced is in reality a different arrangement of the most subtle elementary particles, which remain distinct. All contact is effected by impenetrable elements of extreme smallness; and that which touches never merges with that which is touched.[45] 'As the extremities of two bodies in contact do not form one continuum, it follows that two surfaces are separated by an indivisible space, the interstice between bodies that Democritos has called the void'; however close their contact, atoms do not merge together: 'the extremity of the one is distinct from the extremity of the other'; and, apart from indivisibility itself, which has no parts, nothing can be regarded as a continuum.[46]

This passage calls for some comment: there is the question of 'indivisible space' (*individuum spacium*), and, further on, that of the internal continuity of the atom—an impenetrable material body without constituent parts, therefore continuous and a single continuous body. Consequently, in this description of the universe of the manifold and discontinuity, there exist, for all that, two continua, two kinds of continuity: that of the atom itself, and that of the medium in which the atoms are placed, the intermediate space, which, with Democritos (and Bruno, too) we shall provisionally call the 'void'. If atoms occupied all space, they would no longer be distinguishable; they would not be able to evolve, move, or form bodies. It follows that the material universe is formed of two elements, each equally necessary to each other, each possessing the other, and alone having the privilege of continuity: 'Apart from atoms nothing is simply a plenum, and there is nothing apart from space that is simply a void.'[47]

What is the nature of this ambient space, the interstice between atoms, this immensity between universes? According to the Pythagoreans, this 'void' is still a substance, an element, a kind of matter surrounding everything; they likened it to air and it was accorded continuity. It was only at a later date that it became an absolute void for the atomists of the school of Abdera. Bruno seems to waver at times between these two possibilities. However, it is to be noted that he never resolved to assert the existence of a true void, which would have safeguarded the unity of matter so often proclaimed by him; perhaps we have there a result of his Aristotelian upbringing. When he uses the word 'void', it is for the sake of convenience and the want of something better in order to indicate briefly that which in nature is not the atom, the substratum of material bodies. In connection with the vast regions of the firmament in which the celestial bodies evolve, he speaks of 'an immense space, which we can certainly call void' (*che chiamar possiamo liberamente vacuo*); but a little later, it becomes 'an infinite aether, containing and penetrating everything'.[48] Four words are used to designate the medium surrounding material bodies and which infiltrates between their indivisible parts: they are, *void, air, aether and space*, but they are not used with the same shade of meaning. *Space* prejudges nothing. *Air* and *void* are the general expressions, but unsuitable. *Aether* suggests an hypothesis finally regarded as indispensable. In spite of Leucippos and Democritos, we cannot form a picture of the cosmos conformable with reality using atoms and the void. Between these indivisible elements there must exist a 'certain matter' that binds them together: *Nobis vero vacuum simpliciter cum atomis non sufficit, certam quippe oportet materiam qua conglutinentur.*[4] Elsewhere it is stated that Plato was wrong to make space a substance; and, in yet another place, the Ancients receive approval for having called the aether 'this void' in which the celestial bodies move around.[50]

The aether, explicitly distinguished from the absolute void, is none the less distinguished from the air which we breathe. This discrimination is already present in the *Cena de le ceneri*, the first of Bruno's cosmological treatises; it reappears in *De immenso* and in the dialogues of *De l'infinito*, where we read that the aether is distinguished from air 'in so far as it is pure and does not enter into the composition of tangible bodies' (*in quanto è puro e non si fa parte di composto*).[51]

Air is a body; aether is not a body properly speaking, but it is not a void. It is simple and continuous. Impalpable, it offers no resistance to motion, whether it be motion of the celestial bodies or of the ultimate elements of matter. Better still, it is the necessary condition for motion, and that is why, on the basis of a rather rash etymology, the name aether is appropriate for it.[52] As a substance without material being, does it depend on the materialistic principle? It would seem so, but Bruno's insistence on the substantial unity of matter raises a difficulty here. Tocco says that the aether is the body of the cosmic soul, which would remove it from the region of the formal principle. Lasswitz regards it as the *spiritus*, substituted for the αενόυ of Democritos—the vehicle for the soul of the universe, the agent for transmitting this vitalizing force which must, however, act within matter. Unfortunately, neither Lasswitz nor Tocco is able to quote any passage in support of his claim.[53] We must resign ourselves: in Giordano Bruno's physics, this substance which is neither matter nor void, but is a 'certain matter' 'which we think proper to call void', retains its ambiguous and mysterious character.

Let us now forget the aether, or rather let us profit by the freedom we have of calling it the void, in order to consider matter properly so-called: matter which is dense, solid (*i.e.*, impenetrable), discontinuous, and composed of indivisible elements. These elements—the atoms— are extremely small, but not infinitely small, and the consequence of their discontinuity will be, as we have already pointed out, the non-existence and impossibility for existence of 'perfect figures', a theme that is developed several times in *De minimo*, particularly in Book II (*Contemplationum ex minimo liber*) and interspersed with remarks on the imperfection of our senses. The perfect circle is a creation of the spirit: *Definit cyclum tantum mens*, our senses are unable to receive it: *Sensus verum circulum non apprehendit*.[54] Nevertheless, elsewhere it is said that our senses perceive perfect (continuous) curves which do not exist in reality, for example, the rainbow which is composed of drops of water.[55] These and other apparent contradictions concerning the mathematical problem of incommensurability demand a certain effort on the part of the reader in order to reconstruct a thought that is sometimes confused and which may be summarized as follows: perfect figures do not exist in nature by reason of the fact that the ultimate elements of matter are discontinuous and mobile (discontinuity excludes perfection in the irrational, mobility excludes perfection in the rational).[56] These perfect figures are therefore creations of the spirit, and at the same time illusions of our senses, when we believe we discover them in nature.

The atom, the monad and the 'minimum'. L. Olschki, one of the severest modern critics of Giordano Bruno considers it to be 'stupid' to maintain a theory which, he says, makes the atom a material point whilst assuming that every geometrical figure (square, triangle, etc.) has its own proper minimum, and which at the same time allows an unfortunate confusion between the atom and the monad to remain.[57] On the other hand, Enrico de' Negri considers that the atom and the monad are clearly distinguished by this very same theory, the atom being pure matter, whereas the monad, being matter and form, assumes 'a particular aspect'.[58]

In fact, Bruno never failed to state precisely what he meant by *atom*, *monad* and *minimum* whenever he considered it necessary to do so; and if he happens to use these terms indiscriminately, it is because they can be applied to one single object in certain instances. Everything becomes clear if we abide by the etymological meaning: the atom is an indivisible material element; the monad is the unity; the minimum is the smallest being or the smallest figure of a given kind. So that there shall be no possible ambiguity, Bruno illustrates his definition of the minimum by an inelegant example, even burlesque although classic: the smallest bull. There exists a bull which is the smallest of all existing bulls, and we can imagine a bull which would be the smallest of all possible bulls. It would, however, be larger than such an animal of another species, for example, an ant, for it would be the smallest 'of its kind', and not the ultimate smallest, which is something quite different.[59] There is nothing to prevent the minimum *in genere* from being a complex organism; consequently, it is not necessarily an atom, an indivisible thing. Similarly with the monad, subject to the requirement that it cannot be divided without being destroyed. However, again, it is necessary to guard against confusing the ultimate indivisible with the indivisible *in genere suo*. An object when it is cut in two ceases to exist as such but not *qua* matter. The atom, on the other hand, is indivisible by definition, whereas by definition it is not a minimum: Democritos assumed atoms of different sizes. Nevertheless, in Bruno's system the atom is, in fact, always minimum *in genere* (all the atoms being of the same size) and the ultimate minimum matter, 'a special case of the Simple', of the *metaphysical minimum* in which Bruno saw the condition for all measure, the starting point and the ultimate term of all speculation.[60] It is likewise 'unity' and, as we shall see later, it is worthy of the name monad, even if this word must designate a living unity. To summarize, the ultimate element of matter is *at one and the same time* atom, monad and minimum. That is why one or other of the three terms is used indiscriminately to designate the ultimate element, though they possess quite distinct meanings.

The substance of atoms. The knowledge that we have already about the substantial unity and the indetermination of the 'prime matter' which, without having any form, contains them all potentially, makes it unnecessary to revert to this question in connection with atoms. What has been said about matter can only be repeated in respect of its ultimate elements. Loyal in this respect to the earliest tradition of Greek atomism, Bruno assumes, as did Democritos, that atoms are all of the same substance, thereby discarding the hypothesis of an infinity or plurality of simple bodies. The use made of the word 'element' and the standard nomenclature of the 'four elements' should not, as mentioned above, be regarded as contradicting the statement about the substantial unity of matter. When, for example, Bruno says that the elements constituting our Earth are to be found again in the celestial bodies, he is dealing with a quite different problem, namely, that of the homogeneity of the universe. However, on Earth as well as in celestial bodies, the elements remain as forms, or bodies having their own qualities and fixity of purpose. They are comparable with the letters of the alphabet, whereas the indivisible material minima, the end-point of all decomposition, are the points, all identical but put together in different ways, that make up these same letters.[61]

Shape or form of atoms. Because atoms are all composed of the same substance, it does not necessarily follow that they all have the same form. Plato distinguishes two fundamental forms, Epicuros admits a limited but very large number of them, Democritos says the number is infinite. For Bruno the atom is also a *minimum*. To the property of indivisibility, by which the atom is defined, he adds that of being the absolute material minimum, and on that basis the atom can have only one form. Furthermore, in view of what has been said about the indetermination of matter—simple virtuality, potentiality of being wrought—we could be led to think that its ultimate element in which all forms lie hidden (*qui complicat omnes formas*) is itself without form. Yet, when Bruno speaks of 'pure' matter, he does so as a metaphysician and not as a physicist. Matter without form is only one aspect of our intellect. In reality, the smallest element is already a thing and cannot exist without having the attribute of form. The atom is a solid, the smallest of solids.[62] Bruno goes so far as to identify the atom with earth, the dry element, whilst water and air, regarded as two other 'material principles' become 'abyss' and 'spirit' respectively.[63]

Should we then be justified in questioning whether water and air, which are classed as humid according to Aristotelian physics, are composed of atoms? Elsewhere, in the letter of dedication prefixed to *De monade*, light and air are designated as prime elements (*praecipua elementa*).[64] From these passages, or from others that could be adduced, we must refrain from concluding that Bruno's atomism would be applicable to solid bodies only. In the first place, we must remember that according to Aristotelian physics, which is based on the unity of matter, each of the four elements can give rise to three others through transformations; and, above all, we must not forget that when Bruno speaks of 'elements' he is considering only the tangible universe, and he takes care to say so definitely. We are on the scale of the tangible and not on the plane of *minima* which is beyond reach of our experience. In the same way that the aether binds the atoms together, so water binds particles of earth together; in the same way that bodies are formed from discontinuous atoms, so the rainbow is formed by droplets of water; but these facts are not of the the same order, and to make a comparison between them is merely borrowing a rough image of the invisible from the visible.

In short, all bodies, and throughout all possible changes of physical state, are and remain composed of solid atoms. These atoms being solids have a proper form, and although it does not come within range of our senses, this form can be the subject of thought, and an object of contemplation.[65] Bruno then proceeds to 'contemplate the minimum', once again mixing mathematical and physical ideas, in order to arrive at the assertion that the atom is a sphere, the sphere being the smallest of solids in the same way that the circle is the smallest of surfaces.[66] In support of this opinion he quotes the classical arguments: perfection of the sphere, equality of its three dimensions, simplicity and unity of form.[67]

Experience, duplicating reason, moreover suggests this spherical form for the material minimum, seeing that every object in nature tends to become spherical in shape as it becomes worn and whittled down: for example, stones rolled over and over in water;[68] it is a tell-tale tendency, suitable for confirming an aspect of the spirit, but it can end only in an approximation, for we know that a tangible object will never attain the perfect sphericity reserved for the *minimum* and the *maximum*, *i.e.*, for the atom and the infinite.

The atoms, being all spherical, therefore do not have the infinitely diverse forms of the bodies of which they are the constituent parts. Consequently, some expositors of Brunonian thought have found it surprising that each geometrical figure should have its proper minimum. Now, that is contrary to an obvious consequence of atomism as it is understood here, provided that by 'figure' we understand a realized material form and not a pure form that would be only an aspect of the spirit. If the atom be a minimum, the minimum is not always an atom; and if, for example, a minimum-square exists, there is no such thing as an atom-square, any more than there is a square atom. The minimum-square is, in reality, composed of four 'absolute' minima, the ultimate elements of matter, that is to say of four small spheres in contact on the same plane; and the imperfection of such a figure would leap to view if its extreme smallness did not place it beyond the perceptible. As for the ultimate element, it carries within itself all forms; its sphericity abounds with them, but it still remains a sphere. Unity for the mathematician is the prime whole square, as it is for the prime triangle and the prime cube. In true reality, however, the prime figure, subject to its inevitable imperfection, which deserves the name of a square is composed of four elements. Similarly the prime triangle requires three, and the prime cube, eight. Consequently, for each figure, as for every body or object, there is a minimum below which it cannot be divided without changing its nature, though it is still divisible. Lasswitz has remarked that this intuition heralded the chemistry of molecules.[69]

Atomism having been extended into the domain of geometry, it will be accepted that the ultimate elements of a plane figure are circles, in the same way that the ultimate elements of a solid are spheres. The minimum-square will then be represented by four circles, the minimum-cube by eight spheres. Every figure, plane or solid, is a 'minimum' when it is formed from the smallest possible number of ultimate elements which are positively *in contact*. Bruno refers several times to this concept of contact between atoms, which is an essential requirement, as far as he is concerned; it hardly contradicts his views on the discontinuity of matter, but on the contrary helps him to define the mode of this discontinuity. What he definitely rejects, is the possibility of a contact that would be adherence, which would affect the whole, or part, of the surface of two material objects. Any two bodies whatsoever—and that includes two atoms, because the atom is a body and not a dimensionless point—do not touch each other in any circumstance wholly or partially, but only at the extremity of the whole or of the part.[70] They can be tangents only, and they must be such in order to be able to form the smallest figures or the smallest possible bodies of a given kind.

The atom and the point of contact between two atoms differ consequently in magnitude; they do not have even a common measure: the atom is a material mass, the point of contact is nothing. Thus, the general distinction between the minimum and the term is applied to the physics of the ultimate elements, which distinction Bruno applies rather surprisingly also to geometrical figures. Rejecting infinite divisibility, he accepts the concept of the indivisible mathematical point, which has magnitude, however; this concept would not have been accepted by the earliest Pythagorean arithmo-geometry, in which unit-points were surrounded by a 'field' and would not have been able to touch each other without merging together.[71]

This unwarranted distinction in geometry between the minimum point and the ultimate point no doubt betrays Bruno's unfitness for certain kinds of mathematical reasoning, but on the other hand it is interesting because it enables us to have a better understanding of the nature and sources (I mean his own inward sources) of his atomism. For him, as for Nicholas of Cusa, to think and to measure are but one. However, in order to measure one must have a unit of measurement, a *minimum*. The quest for the 'minimum' is therefore the basis of all knowledge, whether it be metaphysical, physical or mathematical.[72] Without a minimum, nothing is knowable, and therefore nothing exists, seeing that in this universe in which we are placed the conditions of existence merge with those of awareness, and the physical order is to the intellectual order what the foot-print is to the foot and the shadow is to the body.[73]

By making a distinction between the minimum and the term, Bruno thought he could confound the contemporary mathematicians and triumph over the perplexities of the irrational. He deceived himself, for this very distinction had a quite different meaning on the plane of physical reality. In the same way that the minimum-point is extended and occupies a certain area, so the minimum-body remains a volume, indivisible in fact, because it is indivisible, but divisible by the mind, because it can be a tangent to another body; so that this doctrine presents, whilst it denies, and in the very moment of denying, the concept of the infinitely divisible.

Conversely, in the 'void continuum', which is space (or the aether), the minimum indispensable to all thought will reappear under an unexpected aspect.

Certain passages in *De minimo*, when taken out of context, would let us assume that the triangle is the smallest of plane figures, and that the pyramid on a triangular base is the smallest of three dimensional figures; or that the triangle and the pyramid share this privilege with the circle and the sphere.[74] Is this to be regarded as indecision on the part of the author, or homage to Plato? Taking an argument from *De minimo*, we could with greater justification say that, without prejudice to the circle and the sphere (which are forms of the point-atom and the material atom), the triangle and the tetrahedron are the smallest possible of all geometrical forms reduced to a minimum, because they require only three points or four spheres in order to be defined and constituted. In fact, when Bruno speaks of minima triangles and pyramids, what he has in mind are not material bodies or figures composed of points, but empty spaces. Atoms and points, assumed to be in contact, leave interstices between them. Now, the smallest of these interstices are those left by three points arranged in a triangle or by four spheres arranged as a tetrahedron. In the former case, the interstice has the form of a triangle with curved sides; in the latter, of a pyramid with curved surfaces. We believe that the following lines from *De minimo* should be understood: He who regards things as a mathematician or a logician will accept that the circle and the sphere are the smallest figures, 'but he who regards them as a physicist (*physice*) will note that the minima are a curved triangle and pyramid, seeing that a minimum gap must remain between the atoms (which are the smallest bodies and are round), which gap is an empty triangle'.[75]

The accompanying diagram will remove all ambiguity. The three circles are the three 'point-atoms'; the triangle *ABC* formed by them is the smallest realizable 'whole' figure; the triangle *abc* bounded by them is the smallest 'void' figure, in other words, *the smallest space* which it is possible to bound or define by material bodies. It is only necessary to replace the three circles by four spheres to realize that when the smallest body is a sphere, then the smallest 'whole' figure is a pyramid formed by four spheres and that the smallest 'void' figure is a pyramidal interstice between these same four spheres assumed to be tangential.

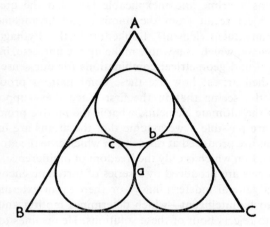

Size and number of the atoms. Seeing that the atom has form, it obviously has dimensions also; and the fact that two atoms can touch in a point (we mean, ultimate-point) implies that the dimensions are not zero. Atoms have magnitude; and, seeing that they are all of the same form and substance, they have all the same size, which is a consequence, moreover, of the fact that this size is a 'minimum'. *Est atomus minimum longum, latum atque profundum corporis.*[76]

The atom is the smallest of all material bodies, but it is not infinitely small. To assume the existence of a material infinitely small, a *given* infinitely small, would be contradictory, and Bruno is right in rejecting this possibility. He is less right in rejecting it from the domain of mathematics, and to declare, as he does in a peremptory manner, that the concept of the infinitely small is the cause of all the mistakes made by mathematicians.[77]

As regards the number of atoms, it is necessarily infinite, seeing that matter is infinite.

From the atom to the tangible object. As the atoms are all equal in size, all of the same form and substance, it follows that only their method of arrangement can account for the variety of tangible objects. How does the passing from indeterminate matter to distinct objects take place? At what moment do the attributes of tangible objects appear? Bruno gives no answer to this question, or rather he replies only by the arithmological phantasies of the *De monade.* Briefly, he invites us to accept as a prime and inexplicable fact that the qualities of a tangible object result from the number and arrangement of the ultimate constituent elements. Looked at in this Pythagorean way, all phenomena, which as a whole make up the universe, interpret the arithmetical and geometrical combinations for our senses. Another question then arises: how are these combinations produced? Or, more exactly, seeing that in the first place they suppose a local motion of the ultimate elements, what is the motive principle? Two solutions are possible if we assume that the atoms are inert; either the motions are produced at random, in which case the atoms enjoy a kind of freedom which is only the freedom of indifference, and all the possible forms are produced by a series of fortunate encounters as a result of a general indeterminacy; or there is an external action—assumed to be intelligent—which determines motion and composition. Bruno rejects both of these solutions. He declines to relate the production of forms to chance in the disordered motion of inert corpuscles; he accepts neither the *clinamen* of Epicuros, nor the *impia elementa* of Democritos. He excludes the possibility of external action just as firmly, though perhaps with less indignation. One of the guiding principles in his cosmology is that matter is worked upon from within: he says, the infinite variety of the forms in which matter appears is not borrowed from another being, 'it does not receive them from without', it produces them from within its own being. It is not that *prope nihil,* that 'almost nothing' to which certain philosophers have wanted to reduce it; it is not a naked, pure, empty force without efficacy, perfection and action. It resembles rather a woman in child-bed who by her convulsive efforts expels the child from her womb.[78] This internal action must be located within the ultimate element and must be exerted in the first place within the atom. Nevertheless, he frequently says that matter is 'passive', that it has the 'potentiality of being wrought'. We ought, therefore, to assume that it is moved by a 'foreign' force, but this strange force acts from within. The source of an atom's motion is not to be sought in another atom any more than in a privileged region of space, but in nature that is fundamentally different from material nature. We are now brought to animism. The atom is a centre of life, a point in which the soul of the universe is inserted. Co-eternal with God, matter is not a pre-existent chaos that the νοῦς should gradually organize; nor was it created in time. Like the soul and God, and for the same reasons, it is located outside of the temporal. It is not identified with God, but is 'close to God', as Émile Namer has so rightly expressed the matter:[79] 'Thus, as far as possible, it has the similitude of Him who is all in all.'[80] It is 'something divine'. *Quoddam divinum est materia.*[81]

NOTES

1. 'Matter is not separable by the act, save by reason.' *Lampas trigenta statuarum* (*Opera*, III, p. 29).

2. Émile Namer in his Introduction to *Cause, principe et unité*, p. 21.

3. *Ibid.*

3b. '*Primum subjectum ex quo aliquid fit per se et non secundum accidens, et inest rei jam factae*' (*Physica*, I, c. 9, 192a).

4. H. D. Gardeil, *Introduction à la philosophie de saint Thomas d'Aquin*, II, *Cosmologie*, p. 25.

5. '*Est . . . forma infinita quia est ita omne esse, ut non ad hoc et ad illud esse finiatur . . . sicut ex opposito infinita dicitur materia, quae non hoc vel illo esse per fornam finiatur.*' *Sigillus sigillorum* (*Opera*, II, ii, p. 203).

6. See Aristotle, *Metaphysica*, VII (Z), 1029a, 20–21. For the meaning of the word ὕλη in Aristotle, see A. Mansion, *Introduction à la physique aristotélicienne* (1945), pp. 240–241.

7. St Thomas Aquinas, *De principiis naturae* (Gardeil, *op. cit.*, ref. 4 *supra*, p. 111); Plotinus, *Ennead*, II, iv, 8.

8. St Thomas Aquinas, *De principiis naturae* (Gardeil, *op. cit.*, ref. 4 *supra*, p. 111).

9. *Summa terminorum metaphysicorum*, viii, *Materia* (*Opera*, I, iv, p. 21).

10. '*Hanc differentiam adducit Themistius in paraphrasi Phisici.*' *Ibid.*

11. 'Pol. —'. . . *Non credete che, se la materia si contentasse, della forma presente, nulla alterazione o passione avrebbe domino sopra di noi, non moriremmo, sarremmo incorrottibili ed eterni ?* Gerv. —*E se la si fosse contentata di quella forma, che aveva cinquanta anni addietro, che direste ? sareste tu, Polihimnio ? . . . cosi è in volontà de la natura, che ordina l'universo, che tutte le forme cedano a tutte. Lascio che è maggior dignità di questa nostra sustanza di farsi ogni cosa, ricevendo tutte le forme, che, ritenendone una sola, essere parziale.*' *Causa*, IV, p. 231.

12. '*Perchè non viene a ricevere le dimensioni come di fuora, ma a mandarle e cacciarle come dal seno.*' *Causa*, IV, p. 238.

13. *Genesis*, I, 20, 24.

14. '*Tutti dunque per modo di separazione vogliono le cose essere da la materia, e non per modo di apposizione e recezione. Dunque si de' più tosto dire che contiene le forme e che le includa, che pensare, che ne sia vota e le escluda.*' *Causa*, IV, p. 242.

15. 'The concept of *force* does not have the same meaning for Plotinus as for Aristotle: the former regards it not as indetermination for completion exercised from without, but as latency (απχρύπτουτα, VI, 4, 16[29]), retarded activity, positive perfection, though dormant (ἥσυχα, VI, 2, 20[27]).' J. Trouillard, '*La présence de Dieu selon Plotin*', in *Revue de métaphysique*, 1954, p. 44.

16. '*Come nelle cose artificiali, quando del legno è fatta la statua, non diciamo che al legno vegna nuovo essere, perchè niente più o meno è legno ora che era prima;*

ma quello che riceve lo esser e l'attualità, è lo che di nuovo si produce, il composto, dico la statua.' Causa, IV, p. 244.

17. *'Non è dunque la materia in potenza di essere o la che può essere, perchè lei sempre è medesima ed immutabile, ed è quella circa la quale e nella quale è la mutazione, più tosto che quella che si muta.' Causa,* IV, pp. 244–245. As pointed out by E. Namer in his *Cause, principe et unité,* p. 187, note 88, 'It is not inertia, but immutability of the essence of matter that Bruno asserts.'

18. *Giordano Bruno,* p. 75, note 73.

19. E. Orrei, *Giordano Bruno e la sua dottrina,* p. 137.

20. *'Però si son trovati di quelli che . . . hanno concluso al fine che quelle [le forme] non son che accidenti e circostanze della materia. . . .* Teo. *—A questo errore son stati ammenati quelli da non conoscere altra forma che l'accidentale; e questo moro [Avicebron] . . . considerandola come cosa corrottibile, non solo mutabile circa la materia, e come quella che è parturita e non parturisce, fondata e non fonda, è rigettata e non rigetta, la dispreggiò e la tenne a vile in comparazione della materia stabile, eterna, progenitrice, madre. E certo questo avviene a quelli che non conoscono quello che conosciamo noi.'* In *De monade,* ch. V (on the Tetrad) (*Opera,* I, ii, p. 297), after having distinguished four spirits and four bodies, Bruno asserts that these four spirits have sprung from a Spirit and the four bodies from a Matter. He adds: *'Vides ut non ex homine, vel hominis carne et formatione actuali, fit homo, sed ex spiritu qui est in semine hominis, si in matrice proprii fomenti, et nutriminis adiectione, circumstantiis adiuvetur.'*—For a comparison of form and matter with male and female, see Aristotle, *Physica,* I, p. 192a, 23.

21. *De minimo,* II, iv (*Opera,* I, iii, p. 208).

22. See *De monade,* V (*Opera,* I, ii, pp. 396–399); paragraph entitled: *Natura quatuor elementorum in mundo spirituali;* and *De immenso,* V, i, *De compositione omnium ex elementis, utque quodammodo omnia sint in omnibus* (*Opera,* I, ii, pp. 111 ff).

23. *'Pour Aristote . . . il faut affirmer que dans toute génération il y a apparition d'une substance nouvelle. . . . La nouvelle substance ne pourra donc avoir à son principe ni un substrat qualifié, ni une pluralité d'éléments déjà constitués, mais une matière absolument indéterminée.'* H. D. Gardeil, *op. cit.,* ref. 4 *supra,* pp. 22–23.

24. *'Ma mentre consideramo più profondamente l'essere e sustanza di quello in cui siamo immutabili, trovaremo non esser morte, non solo per noi, ma nè per veruna sustanza; mentre nulla sustanzialmente si sminuisce, ma tutto, per infinito spacio discorrendo, cangia il volto.' De l'infinito, Proemiale epistola,* argument of the fifth dialogue, p. 282. This agrees with Aristotle in recognizing in matter the passive indispensable principle of the changes to which the being is subject; it detaches itself completely from the being when it is a question of defining the processus of the changes.

25. *De l'infinito,* II, p. 321.

26. See F. Tocco, *Opere di Giordano Bruno,* p. 107.

26b. *'Nunquam physico propositio vera est, continuum . . . ex indivisibilibus non componi.' Acrotismus,* art. XLII.

27. *'Quomodo totum universum aequaliter sit divisibile cum terra ista, et totus iste globus cum hoc pomo.' Acrotismus,* art. XLII (*Opera,* I, i, p. 151).

28. *Ibid.,* and p. 154.

29. *De minimo,* II, xv (*Opera,* I, iii, pp. 230–231).

30. See *De minimo,* I, vi: *Ad eos qui continuum in infinitum divisibile accipiunt* (*Opera,* I, iii, pp. 150–154).

31. L. Olschki, *Giordano Bruno,* p. 84. *De immenso* and *De minimo* were published in the same year (1591), though the former had been written, at least partly, some years before.

32. See *De mente idiotae,* III, 9. Nicola Badaloni sees atomism as one of the constants in Brunonian thought; before reaching maturity as a philosopher, he reverted to his earliest reflections on the structure of matter. See *La filosofia di Giordano Bruno;* I. *Il pensiero di Giordano Bruno nel suo sviluppo storico,* Florence, 1955, p. 21 and *passim.*

33. *De l'infinito,* II, pp. 323–324; D. W. Singer, *Giordano Bruno,* London and New York, 1950, pp. 72–73.

34. *De l'infinito*, II, pp. 322–323.
35. *De l'infinito*, IV, p. 375. Note the use of the word 'atom' in the same discourse, several lines later.
36. *'Talis certe est substantia rerum. Utpote quae sola est constans, natura atomorum.'* *De immenso*, VI, xviii (*Opera*, I, ii, p. 218).
37. L. Mabilleau, *Histoire de la philosophie atomistique*, Paris, 1895, pp. 398–399.
38. L. Olschki, *Giordano Bruno*, pp. 65–71.
39. *Ibid.*, p. 69. See also L. Cicuttini, *Giordano Bruno*, Milan, 1950, pp. 193–196.
40. *Les intuitions atomistiques*, Paris, 1933, p. 10.
41. *' Duplicitur punctum distinguimus, ut sit Terminus hoc, illud vero pars ultima.'* *De minimo*, I, xi, vers 10–11 (*Opera*, I, iii, p. 175).
42. *'At minimum est ex quo dimensio constat,*
    Cuis pars prima est vere, velut, et numeri unum.'
De minimo, I, xiii (*Opera*, I, iii, p. 180).
43. *'Non aliter rerum simplex substantia prima est,*
    Corporibus minimum corpus, quod et omnia tandem
    Attingunt resoluta.'
De minimo, I, ii (*Opera*, I, iii, p. 139). Bruno gives more definite expression to his thought in the prose commentary (p. 140): *'Neque multa oportet esse minimorum genera atque figuras, quemadmodum neque literarum, ut innumerabiles exinde species componantur. . . .'* In connection with the problem of atoms compared with the signs used in writing, see R. Cadiou, *'Atomes et éléments graphiques'* in *Bulletin de l'association Guillaume Budé*, October 1958, pp. 54–65.
44. *'Naturae et artis subiectum et obiectum, compositio et resolutio agendo et contemplando ex minimo oritur, in minimo consistit et ad minimum reducitur.'* *De minimo*, I, ii (*Opera*, I, iii, p. 140).
45. *'Tactum esse in minimo, et differentiam esse inter quod et quo tangit.'* *De minimo*, II, x, chapter heading (*Opera*, I, iii, p. 222). See also (*ibid.*,) the end of the preceding chapter: *'Inalterabilibus ergo impenetrabilibusque existentibus atomis non est quod vere proprieque miscibile possimus intelligere; ast corporum quaedam, dum-secundum subtiliores partes coacervantur, in tertiam videntur quandam speciem transire. Sed veritas ista extra sensum non excurrit.'* The last sentence means that 'this truth' (namely, the appearance of a third body) is truth only for our senses.
46. *'Cum quippe duorum se contingentium termini non sint unum continuum, consequens est inter utramque superficiem individuum mediare spacium, quod inane corporibus interiectum Democritus appellavit; quod plane inter quascunque (quantumcunque arcte concurrant) atomos oportet mediare, sicut extremum unius ab extremo alterius est distinctum, et praeter ipsum insectile, cuius non ulla est pars, nihil vere continuum possis intelligere.'* *De minimo*, II, x (*Opera*, I, iii, p. 223).
47. *'Praeter atomos nihil esse simpliciter plenum, nihil simpliciter vacuum praeter spacium intra coeuntium . . . atomorum concursum intermedians.'* *De minimo*, II, iv (*Opera*, I, iii, p. 200). The omitted words are not important, but they introduce another theory which will be considered later.
48. *De l'infinito*, V, pp. 404 and 412.
49. *De minimo*, I, ii (*Opera*, I, iii, p. 140). On aether 'binding' matter, see K. Lasswitz, *Geschichte der Atomistik*, 1890, I, pp. 377–379.
50. *'. . . inane . . . illud*
    Nomine quod proprio, atque antiquo dicitur aether.'
De immenso, II, x and IV, xiv (*Opera*, I, i, p. 297 and I, ii, p. 77).
51. *Cena de le ceneri*, pp. 172–174; *De immenso*, IV, xiv (*Opera*, I, ii, pp. 77 ff). (*Distinctio aeris et aetheris*); *De l'infinito*, V, p. 412.
52. *De l'infinito*, p. 412; see Plato, *Cratylos*, 410 *b*, Aristotle, *De coelo*, I, 3, 270 *b* and *Meteorologica*, I, 3, 339 *b*.
53. Tocco, *Le opere latine di Giordano Bruno* (pp. 377–378) gives no reference, and the only passage cited by Lasswitz (*Geschichte der Atomistik*, I, 379–380) relates to air and not the aether.
54. *De minimo*, II, ii and iii (*Opera*, I, iii, pp. 189 and 190).
55. *V. supra.*
56. One of the reasons why a perfect circle cannot exist is that all its radii are

equal; now, the equality of two figures is impossible in nature. *De minimo*, II, iv: '*Verum circulum finitum non esse in natura possibilem*', and v: '*Duas figuras vel lineas in materia omnio aequales ostendere vel bis eandem repetere, est impossibile*' (*Opera*, I, iii, pp. 196 ff).

57. L. Olschki, *Giordano Bruno*, pp. 65–71.

58. '*Il principio dialettico della monade leibniziana*' in *Giornale critico della filosofia italiana*, 1925, p. 262.

59. '*Distinguitur minimum in genere a minimo absoluto.*' *De minimo*, I, x (*Opera*, I, iii,, pp. 171–174).

60. K. Lasswitz, *Geschichte der Atomistik*, I, pp. 365–366.

61. *Ibid.*, I, p. 394 and see note 43 *supra.*

62. '*Est minimum solidum, quod atomum corpusque primordiale est.*' *De minimo*, I, x (*Opera*, I, iii, p. 173).

63. '*Materialia principia (mundi sensibilis) sunt Terra, seu Atomi, seu Arida, Abyssus, seu Styx, seu Oceanus, Spiritus, seu aer, seu coelum seu firmamentum.*' *Acrotismus* (*Opera*, I, i, p. 81).

64. *Epistola dedicatoria et clavis* (*Opera*, I, i, p. 198).

65. '*Minimum, quamvis sit insensibile, nihilo tamen minus contemplationis obiectum esse potest.*' *De minimo*, I, xiv (*Opera*, I, iii, p. 184).

66. '*Figura minimi plani circulus est, minimi solidi globus.*' *De minimo*, I, xii (*Opera*, I, iii, p. 179).

67. '*Sed spherae e centro lungum, latum atque profundum,
Concentrae ut partes, minimum referuntur ad unum.*'
De minimo, I, xiii (*Opera*, I, iii, p. 180).

68. '*Minimum vero esse ritundum manifestatur, primo sensu et imaginatione . . .*; *secundo ipso extenuante natura (lapides enim et durissima quaeque primo cornibus atteruntur). . . .*' *De minimo*, I, xii (*Opera*, I, iii, p. 179).

69. '. . . *Anderseits ist sein Minimum dasjenige, was keine Teile gleicher Art mehr enthält, und bedeutet, physisch genommen, dasselbe wie die Molekeln der neueren Chemie.*' Lasswitz, *Geschichte der Atomistik*, I, p. 399.

70. '*Atomum ab atomo, corpusque omne a corpore non toto aut parte, sed aut totius aut partis termino contingitur seu extremo.*' *De minimo*, II, ix (*Opera*, I, iii, p. 222).

71. With regard to the unwarranted distinction between the minimum-point and the ultimate-point in mathematics, and generally on the dangerous application Bruno makes in mathematics of concepts borrowed from physics, see Lasswitz, *Geschichte der Atomistik*, I, p. 371, note 1 and p. 376.

72. *Ibid.*, pp. 368, 377, 389 and 401.

73. '*Corporum . . . ordo non aliter sequitur ordinem intellectus quam pedis vestigium ipsum pedem, et umbra corpus.*' *De immenso*, V, i (*Opera*, I, ii, p. 117).

74. '*In plano . . . sunt duae primae minimae (et maximae) figurae, triangulus videlicet et circulus; in solido totidem istis repondientes, pyramis et sphaera.*' *De minimo*, I, xii (*Opera*, I, iii, p. 179).

75. '. . . *physice vero contemplanti, ubi inter atomos (quae sunt minima rotundaque corpora) coeuntes oportet minus quoddam (quod inane est triangulare) intermediare, triangulus et pyramis curvilinae recurva simpliciter comperientur esse minima.*' *De minimo*, V, *Sectio* III, *cap.* ii (*Opera*, I, iii, p. 332). Compare the passage in *De minimo*, I, xii (*Opera*, I, iii, p. 179): '*Inter coeuntes circulos sunt trianguli recurvi, inter coeuntes sphaeras pyramidalia spacia recurvarum similiter hedrarum.*'

76. *De minimo*, IV, vii (*Opera*, I, iii, p. 285).

77. '*Principium et fundamentum errorum omnium, tum in physica, tum in mathesis, est resolutio continui in infinitum.*' *De minimo*, I, vi (*Opera*, I, iii, p. 153).

78. *De causa*, IV, p. 239.

79. *Cause, principe et unité*, p. 165, note 18.

80. '*Cosi, al suo possibile, ha la similitudine di che è tutto in tutto.*' *De causa*, IV, p. 231, trans. Namer, p. 165.

81. '*Et divinum ego quoddam est materia, sicut et divinum quoddam existimatur esse forma, quae aut nihil est aut materiae quiddam est. Extra et sine materia nihil sicut posse facere et posse fieri tandem unum et idem sunt, et individuo uno con-*

sistunt fundamento, quia simul datur et tollitur potens facere omnia cum potente fieri omnia; atque una potentia absoluta atque simpliciter (quicquid sit potentia in particulari et compositorum et accidentaria, quae sensus et mentum Peripateticorum fascinavit, cum asseclis quibusdam cucullatis), quemadmodum pluribus in his quae De infinito *et universo diximus et in dialogis* De principio et uno *exactius, non stultam concludentes Davidis de Dinantho et Avicebronis in libro Fontis vitae sententiam ab Arabibus citatam, qui ausi sunt materiam etiam Deum appellare.*' De vinculis in genere (*Opera*, III, pp. 695–696). See *De causa*, p. 139 (*Argomento del terzo dialogo*): '*. . . prima si mostra che non fu pazzo nel suo grado David de Dinanto in prendere la materia come cosa eccellentissima e divina.*' See also *De causa*, end of the dialogue, pp. 237–246.

VI

The infinite universe

Giordano Bruno makes the problem of the infinite universe peculiarly *his* own problem, though he is not in the least disconcerted by appealing to ancient and modern philosophers, and quoting the authority of the pre-Socratics as well as that of Nicholas of Cusa; he gives his arguments a polemical quality that allows the originality of his mind to be portended. We come now to one of the central themes of his anti-Aristotelianism.

Though, indeed, the notion of an infinite universe had been defended by numerous theologians and lay thinkers before his time, it had none the less been rejected by the uncompromising attitude of the Schoolmen. For a long while, technical astronomy remained stubbornly faithful to, and based its calculations on, an Aristotelian scheme of a closed universe, bounded by the sphere of fixed stars, beyond which there was no place, no space, not only no existence, but no possibility of existence.

The immediate forerunners of Bruno, who will be sought in vain amongst the astronomers, are found amongst the metaphysicians and cosmologists of the fourteenth, fifteenth and sixteenth centuries. A rapid survey of this recent past will enable us to have a better understanding of our author's position. Four individuals will be considered: Thomas Bradwardine, Crescas, Nicholas of Cusa and Palingenius.

Thomas Bradwardine (1290–1348), Doctor Profundus, was primarily a theologian 'of the divine Omnipotent',[1] for whom the condemnations of the thirteenth century against Aristotle in the name of orthodoxy were still valid. He accepted as a fact that the universe is one and finite, but he refused to deny that God had the power to create other universes. The boundary of the universe is not therefore an absolute limit of all possible existence and motion. Adopting from Philoponos a picture of the universe as an 'island of matter', he extends an infinite space beyond the final sphere of the fixed stars, which space is a place prepared for future eventual

154

creations and where nothing would act as an obstacle to rectilinear motion of the whole body of the universe.

Later, at a time when Aristotelianism was triumphant, Hasdai Crescas, a Jew of Barcelona, (1340–1410) put forward a remarkable criticism of Aristotelian cosmology in a work entitled *Or Adonaï* (*The Light of the Lord*). The Hebrew text of this work was first published at Ferrara in 1556, then at Vienna in 1860, and finally in 1929, under the editorship of H. A. Wolfson, with an English translation.[2] Crescas declares the infinitude of the universe. Beyond the firmament which limits our view there is an endless space; it is not empty, but is strewn with other universes similar to our own, that is to say, geocentric and conforming in structure to the data of Ptolemaic astronomy. Bruno makes no mention of Crescas whom he could not have read, and it is permissible to ascribe the similarity of their systems to the possibility of two minds having meditated on the same problems. We may also suppose, as Wolfson is inclined to assume, that Bruno had some indirect knowledge of the theories of his predecessor. It is a fact that on more than one point (such as the homogeneity of the universe in opposition to the double physics of Aristotle) the two writers maintain the same theses using the same arguments. Wolfson lists no less than fifteen examples.[3]

We shall not dwell on Nicholas of Cusa (1401–1464): it would be superfluous to repeat that Bruno's concepts regarding the infinite universe, the plurality of worlds, and cosmic homogeneity are to a great extent derived from him—Tocco, and many other expositors of 'Brunonian philosophy' are unanimous on the matter.[4] The relationship is obvious, and moreover acknowledged.

Marcellus Palingenius Stellatus (born between 1500 and 1503, died about 1543) gave his cosmic vision in the form of a Latin poem, *Zodiacus vitae*. It was first printed at Venice (before 1550) and reprinted many times during the century;[5] in spite of being placed on the *Index* (1558), the work long enjoyed a fame that was not extended to its author. Bruno was well acquainted with *Zodiacus vitae*, which he quotes and discusses at length in the eighth book of *De immenso*; but, like most of his contemporaries, he knew nothing about Palingenius, who he thought was a German, and whom he designates, on a level with Nicholas of Cusa, Paracelsus and Copernicus, as one of the great minds that have brought honour to Germany.[6] Palingenius, whose real name is Pietro Manzoli and whose identity was not established until 1725, was in fact born at Stellata, a village near

Ferrara (whence the surname Stellatus). His universe remains conformable to the teachings of the Schoolmen: closed universe, completely enclosed within the sphere of the fixed stars. However, beyond this boundary, the void of the Aristotelians becomes space, and even more than space: it becomes infinite light, the dwelling-place of God.

Not one of the writers we have just mentioned was an astronomer and not one of them ventured to cast doubt on the data of a branch of knowledge to which he was a stranger. In their view, the universe was exactly as described in the *Almagest*. They were content to deny, and they did so resolutely, that the totality of actual and possible existence reduces to this universe. They wanted to surround it by an infinite ultra-universe: a great void for Bradwardine, light for Palingenius, space populated by other universes similar to our own for Crescas and Nicholas of Cusa.

It was only in the seventeenth century that technical astronomy, acknowledging the intuitions of philosophers, brought this beyond into the scope of its investigation. It has been said of Spinoza 'that he was no longer backward in combating the Aristotelian theory of celestial spheres and the finiteness of the cosmos, which was vigorously combated by Crescas and Bruno'.[7] Now, if 'he was no longer backward', it was because science gave a verdict. However, the great merit of Bruno is that he tried to speak in the name of a science that was still mute (the heliocentric cosmos of Copernicus differs little in its structure and limits from the geocentric cosmos of Ptolemy). Without being an astronomer, he clearly saw the scientific nature of the problem of the infinite. It was no longer enough for him to assert the existence of other universes, simply assumed or conjectured, beyond a universe that remains closed. In order to enter upon unexplored paths, he claims to throw down what he calls 'the walls of the firmament'; and he pursues this purpose with such boldness that we may be permitted to smile, but in the history of science it marks nevertheless a new period—a subsequently completed period in which stand out the fear of a Pascal, the peaceful certainty of a Spinoza or a Fontenelle, the proud assurance, already impaired, of the nineteenth century.

The opening lines of *De immenso*, like the preliminary sonnets of the dialogue *De l'infinito*, express the joy that the poet-philosopher experiences on being liberated from the 'dark prisons' of error to discover and conquer space, to fly towards the depths of a firmament become completely aetherial, 'without fear of encountering any obstacle of glass or crystal'.[8]

These lyrical preludes to long, detailed and frequently pedantic refutations of Aristotle's arguments imply that the problem of the infinite was solved before it was stated: the heart spoke before reason. Thought of the infinite 'animates the system', as Troilo rightly said. It springs forth at every turn, and expresses itself on every occasion. In the *Figuratio aristotelici physici auditus*, a disputation in the style of the Schoolmen is initiated on the question of ascertaining if the infinite exists as a substance, a property, or as both;[9] elsewhere, infinity is invoked in connection with the concept of number: 'In everything that we see and in each object by itself, we find the vestige, the simulacrum and the mirror of infinity.'[10]

In order to dispose of such rich and scattered material we shall first of all consider the philosophical problem of the infinite, which will be the subject of the present chapter; and then, in the following chapters, we shall deal with the physical and astronomical theories connected with this problem. The essential texts are the Italian treatise *De l'infinito* and the Latin poem *De immenso*. There is much repetition in these two works, the first of which was completed, and the second started, at London; but in more than one respect they complement and explain each other. Reference will be made to both works simultaneously, and the minor works, especially *Acrotismus*, will not be neglected.

THE THEOLOGICAL ARGUMENT

The condemnations pronounced in 1277 by Étienne Tempier, Bishop of Paris, in respect of 219 Aristotelian propositions, as well as other condemnations which struck at the reviving Aristotelianism of the thirteenth century, were mainly concerned with the infiniteness of the universe, the plurality of worlds and the possibility of rectilineal displacement (*motu recto*) of the cosmos in ambiant space. In every instance, Aristotle was charged with imposing a limit to the divine power. These strictures were not based on physical theory but solely on the dogma of the divine Omnipotent; therefore they were not made to intimidate the Aristotelians, who had a ready answer: God is able to do everything in the absolute, but his power relative to nature is limited to that which nature, created by Him, is able to endure. It is inconceivable that God should disown Himself and infringe His own law. It is only necessary then to prove that the infiniteness of the universe, the plurality of worlds or the existence of an ambient void are incompatible with the laws of nature in order to demonstrate their impossibility.

In the fifth dialogue of *De l'infinito* (number eight in the series of twelve arguments put forward by the Peripatetic Albertino against the plurality of worlds) we find the following argument: the limited passivity of nature would itself limit the creative act. Though God may have the power to create several universes, it does not follow that they exist, 'for, besides the active power of God, the passive power of things is required'. The same statement reappears in almost the same words in book seven of *De immenso*.[11]

Now in a lyrical mood, now in a facetious mood, but always vehemently, Bruno rejects any opinion which he finds to be doubly absurd. If, in effect, we assume that the passive power of nature is limited, whilst accepting that the power of the creator is infinite, we are really saying that the finite imposes limits on the infinite and claiming 'with supreme inconvenience that the prime and highest principle is similar to a man who wants to play a guitar, but does not learn because he has no guitar; or, to someone who is able to do something but does not do it, because the thing that he can do cannot be done by him, which is an obvious contradiction'.[12] Furthermore (and this second objection makes the former one superfluous), the statement of the Aristotelians assumes, but in no wise proves, that there is not an infinite passive power in nature corresponding to the infinite active power of God. It is permissible to think otherwise, and, for Bruno, it is evidence that matter, which is itself divine and animated from within by the formal principle, ought to lend itself without limit to all God's operations.[13]

The hypothesis of an external obstacle susceptible of opposing conversion into reality by an infinite power being disposed of, it would seem that we are left with the right to assume, if we believe that we can establish a limit to creation, that that limit was fixed by the Creator Himself. Consequently, we assume at one and the same time the possibility of an infinite universe and the fact of a finite universe. Such is the position of Thomist Aristotelianism (God could have created several universes, but it appears that He created one only); it is also the position of Plotinian neo-Platonism which is not at all disconcerted by accepting the existence of an infinite God and a finite universe. The finiteness of the universe would then be a kind of divine reticence—an internal obstacle, the thought of which Bruno discards with as much indignation as that of an external obstacle. God could not be 'miserly in his powers', He must give all that He can give without parsimony, without restrictions. 'Why do you wish that this centre of divinity which can amplify itself infinitely into an infinite sphere should remain sterile and envious . . .' asks Philotheus, 'why do you wish it to communicate itself in a restricted manner, as much as to say, not as a whole and not according to the reason of its glorious power and being?[14] We take this word 'envious' (*invidioso*) in the sense of miserly. It will be found again in *De immenso*, where it is said that if God, being infinite, created the finite, he would be not only envious but infinitely envious, whereas His bounty would, on the other hand, be finite.[15]

This notion of envy, and even the word itself, are to be found in the writings of Nicholas of Cusa: '. . . seeing that the maximum is far removed from all envy, it cannot communicate with a lesser being, as such.'[16] Nevertheless, Nicholas of Cusa and Bruno have very different conceptions of the coincidence of the divine power and the divine act. For Nicholas of Cusa, all things that can happen are *in act*—and not only in the state of possibles—*in God's providence*; but it does not follow that these things are in act in the universe. The universe of Nicholas of Cusa is infinite in the sense that it is without limit, but it never realizes the infinity of divine possibilities: 'it is a privative infinity'; as for 'infinite actuality, which is absolute eternity, it cannot emerge from the possible'.[17] Bruno, on the other hand, does not hesitate in defiance of all logic to make the universe a realized infinity, a given infinity. When speaking in this connection of avarice or envy, he makes use of a metaphor. If God is not miserly with his powers, it is because He cannot be so. The universe is not a creation detached from Him and then reduced to itself: as a reflection of God, it participates simply and harmoniously in the divine infinity, in which the contrarieties power-act, valid for finite beings, are transcended like all contrarieties.

THE INFINITE AND THE HUMAN SOUL

A little known passage in *Oratio valedictoria* refers to the three dwelling-places of Wisdom, which are God, the universe and the soul: 'The sun of the Intelligence may be considered in three ways: first, in the essence of the divinity; secondly, in the substance of the universe which is the image of it; thirdly, in the light of the sense of beings who participate in life and knowledge.' According to the third method, Wisdom 'is set in our spirit, seated on the poop of our soul, holding the tiller of the ship which it navigates across the tempestuous sea of the century'; '. . . the divine Wisdom has then three dwelling-places, the first, unerected, eternal, the seat of eternity itself; the second, and first begotten, which is this visible universe; the third, and second begotten, which is the soul of man'—*tertiam, secundogenitam, quae est hominis anima.*[18]

One of the dominant themes of *Eroici furori* is precisely the search for this wisdom that dwells within us. The Intellect, emanation from the divinity and participant of the divine infinity, reigns at the summit of the soul. The infinite, we discover it in ourselves; or, rather, we feel a presentiment of it and seek it through an irresistible and hopeless movement, insatiable as we are of an inexhaustible goodness, both present and absent, whose nature is to overwhelm us and yet leave us unsatisfied.

Furthermore, we project this internal infinite out of ourselves. Our mind demands limitlessness in the sequence of numbers, in space, in the universe; and from this demand Bruno draws an argument regarded by Aristotle as the strongest that could be advanced against the notion of a finite universe: 'It is, he said, because consideration does not exhaust the subject that number appears to be infinite, besides mathematical magnitudes and that which is beyond the firmament. If the external region be infinite, then the body also must be infinite, and the universes. . . .'[19] Naturally, Aristotle arrives at this conclusion only in order to refute it. Thought, he declares a little later (208 *a*) 'is only an accident', on which it would be absurd to base any certainty: we can imagine a man of colossal size, but that is not a reason for his existence.

Consequently, the infinite would exist only in our imagination; we believe in it because we can always in our mind add magnitude to magnitude. And why not? asks Bruno. Why should not this power of imagination correspond to reality? If it were otherwise, imagination, which in itself is natural, would exceed nature, which is impossible: '*Non enim plus debet habere imaginatio naturalis . . . quam natura.*'[20]

THE INFINITE ADAPTED TO THE UNIVERSE

The statement is undoubtedly daring. At least, it has the merit of exposing the difference that exists between the infiniteness of the soul or of the intellect (possibility of always adding number to number, or magnitude to magnitude) and the infiniteness of the universe which this possibility inclines us to assume, but which is a real infinity. A similar distinction is made in *Eroici furori* between the 'infinite potentiality' of the human intellect and the infiniteness of its object, the one being 'infinite according to the mode of the finite', the other 'infinitely infinite'.[21]

In any case, the infinite exists only potentially in the human soul. Whether its effort tends to make the soul think of the universe as 'explained' or to raise it up to the supreme Unity, the pursuit of the object in both cases takes place gradually, whereas the infiniteness of the object is pre-existent.

Seeing that each of the three dwelling-places of wisdom has its own characteristics (in spite of what has been adduced on the subject of Brunonian 'monism'), a final distinction has to be made between the two objects that are pursued, namely, between the cosmic infinite (characteristic of the universe) and the divine infinite.

According to St Thomas Aquinas, God alone is infinite in essence. 'There is no obstacle to the infinite intervening in God's handiwork; but it will always be a relative infinite (*secundum quid*); the infinite in the absolute sense (*simpliciter*) is impossible in that connection.'[22] In number as in magnitude, the infinite is always virtual: a multiplicity being proposed, we can propose another and so continue without end, but it is impossible to arrive at a total infinity, an infinite multiplicity in act.[23] *Non est possibile esse aliquam multitudinem actu infinitam.*[23]

Nicholas of Cusa remained loyal to these principles, for when he accepts the infinity of the universe, it is only a question of a virtual infinity 'without possible comparative relation with the absolute infinity'. The infinite power of God has no limit, the universe could be larger: 'however, as the possibility of being, or matter, is not in act extensible to infinity, the universe cannot be larger; if it has no limit, the reason is that we cannot give *in act* something larger that will be the limit: it is a privative infinity'.[24]

Bruno, on the other hand regards the infinity of the universe not only as virtual but indeed actual; the infinity implicated in the prime principle is explained in its infinite simulacrum;[25] the contrast is therefore no longer between the actual and the virtual, but between the implicated and the explicated: God is infinite *complicatamente e totalmente*; the universe is 'quite infinite, but not totally infinite, for that is incompatible with dimensional infinity'. Elpidio asks Philotheus to explain more fully this distinction which he does not properly understand. Philotheus replies: 'I say that the universe is quite infinite because it has no border, no end, no surface; I say that the universe is not totally infinite, for in that universe each of the parts that we are able to consider is finite and each of the countless worlds contained within it is finite. I say that God is quite infinite because He excludes all limit from Himself and because everything that can be attributed to Him is one and infinite; and I say that God is totally infinite, for He is everywhere in the whole universe and in each of its parts, infinitely and totally.'[26] In other words, the supreme Principle is indivisible, whereas the universe is composed of parts which are infinite in number but are finite in themselves. That is how it is infinite 'according to the mode of the finite' in plurality and in dimension. The characteristic of cosmic infinity is to express itself in multiplicity and magnitude: *it implicates infinite number and infinite space*.

EVIDENCE OF THE SENSES

From the foregoing it is easy to deduce that cosmic infinity, though different from divine infinity, nevertheless has this in common with it, namely, that it is inaccessible to experience. In the same way that the supreme Unity, the object of love pursued by the way of introversion, remains for ever out of each, so the boundless universe offers and withdraws itself at the same time from exploration by our senses. At the beginning of the dialogue in *De l'infinito*, one of the first questions put by Elpidio to Philotheus is the following: 'If we put our faith in tangible facts, are we really justified in concluding in favour of the infiniteness rather than the finiteness of the universe?'

Philotheus replies: 'No sense perceives the infinite, this consequence is not required by any sense, for the infinite cannot be the object of sense; to claim to know it through tangibility would be as though one wished to see with one's own eyes both the substance and the essence; and he who would deny a thing [that is to say, the existence of a thing in itself] because it is not tangible or visible would be ready to deny his own substance and being. Yet there must be a means of claiming the evidence of our senses.'[27]

Broaching of this subject demands some attention. We are told that our senses are incapable of perceiving the infinite, and at the same time we are told that it is possible to accept the concept of infinity starting from a tangible fact, provided that the evidence for it is referred to certain precautions and corrections that will be indicated later. We are surrounded by a field of perception (or, more simply, a field of view), which is limited by the weakness of our organs, but most of all by the very nature of a universe infinite in size and whose infiniteness is broken up into universes. The impossibility we have of discovering it entirely is compared with that of perceiving the essence of things—a simple comparison, but one whose intention is to show quite clearly that it is a question of absolute impossibility. On the other hand, if we know how to interpret the evidence of our senses according to a suitable mode, our necessarily partial vision of the universe will allow us to take cognizance of the infinite. The sense invites the intellect to transcend the tangible: the sense 'confesses and reveals its weakness and insufficiency through the appearance of the limitation given by its horizon, the nature of which shows its fickleness'.[28]

THE HORIZON

This word calls to mind a passage in *De immenso*, where the author, haunted by childhood memories, recalls the time when Vesuvius was the end of the world for him, a childish illusion shared by the Peripatetics when they restricted the universe to the boundaries of a firmament, whereas for any serious-minded person the sight of an horizon suggests, however far the horizon extends, the thought of a beyond.[29]

In *Axiomata sphæræ*, which form part of the preliminaries to *Cent soixante articles contre les mathématiciens de ce temps*, we find the idea of a revelatory connection between tangible experience of an horizon and mental vision of the infinite, expressed in another form. These axioms are nine in all. Certain ones, especially the second, relate to the question in hand: 'On the surface of a sphere any point whatsoever is the centre of the horizon, in the same way that in the infinite [sphere] the middle is everywhere'; the third axiom says: 'It is necessary for two kinds of spheres to exist in nature, namely the finite and the infinite spheres; the latter is more truly spherical than the former'; the fourth says: 'The infinite sphere is much more truly possessed of a centre: it is everywhere; whereas the finite sphere is more truly possessed of a circumference; furthermore, for him who divides the mass (assumed to be continuous) indefinitely, it is a circumference everywhere through division of its surface'; and finally, the fifth, which is most surprising: 'The finite sphere has no centre, properly speaking; the infinite sphere has no periphery for him who divides it indefinitely.' This last axiom seems to have discouraged commentators; Tocco refrains from quoting it and no doubt classes it amongst those concerning which he said that 'they would not be accepted by mathematicians'.[30] However, let us try and see something more than absurdity in the statement 'the finite sphere has no centre'. Bruno considers that the characteristic of the finite sphere, which distinguishes it from the infinite one, is the fact that it possesses a surface. Furthermore, in this series of axioms, he never speaks of the *volume* of the finite sphere (except when it is specified, as in axiom IV), but of its surface; consequently, the *finita non habet centrum* of axiom V is only a repetition of *in sphæræ plano quilibet punctus est horizontis centrum* of axiom II. As for the infinite sphere, which has no surface, it must be considered in its three dimensions and assumed that every point of this sphere is really a centre (and not only 'the centre of the horizon'), because every point of it can be taken as the origin of infinite radii, that is to say really equal (we must not forget that 'there is not equality except in the infinite'). On the other hand, as the centre is more essential for the sphere (*de ratione sphæræ*) than the periphery, we come to the conclusion that the infinite sphere is more truly a sphere than the finite sphere (axiom III); and that the universe is more truly spherical than any other universe or globe (axiom VI);[31] and finally that the 'true sphere', that is to say, the universe, is not within reach of our senses: *vera sphæra non est sensibilis* (axiom IX).[32]

This brings us to tangible experience and more particularly to that 'illusion of finitude' given by the horizon. The position of the spectator is always central; it is apparently so on the surface of the globe where we are; it is really so in the infinite universe. In both cases our view is limited by an horizon but suggests by that very fact the thought of a beyond, for we can pass over that horizon either simply by changing our position (for example, by crossing over the mountains), or in thought by imagining that we are carried far from the Earth to another celestial body. In one case experience shows, and in the other reason forces us to conclude that we are and always shall be at the centre of the horizon, seeing that this centre changes its position with us and that we discover it to be everywhere because it is everywhere. The extremely meaningful comparison between the surface of the sphere and the infinite sphere, between the universe and the surface of the globe is used by Bruno as a means of making the infinitude of the universe intelligible by causing the horizons of the firmament to appear just as illusory as those on Earth. On the contrary, it could have suggested to him the idea of a universe both finite and without bounds, exactly like the surface of the Earth; but in Bruno's mind the infinite was a certainty rather than a problem: the answer was there before the question had been asked.

THE THEORY OF PLACE

Unfortunately, opponents are at hand to remember that the discussion is open and that other answers would be possible; but Bruno is not short of objections and arguments any more than he is of persuasive comparisons. Criticism of the Artistotelian conception of the finite universe, which fills the first two dialogues in *De l'infinito*, is resumed point by point in *De immenso*. Bruno proclaims that the infinite is out of reach of our senses, not as a concession to Aristotelianism, but as something that stands to reason: *Vera sphæra non est sensibilis*. Now, seeing that all natural knowledge is acquired through sense-perception, we are obliged to admit that the infinite cannot be a subject of study. Can we draw an argument from that and say that the universe is finite rather than infinite? Certainly not! and such a conclusion is prohibited by the very reason of the inaccessibility of the object whose existence is under discussion. Such was the thought that inspired the early replies of Philotheus. To the question with which Elpidio opens the dialogue: 'How is it possible for the universe to be infinite?' he replies with the same question:

'How is it possible for the universe to be finite?' The play continues: 'Do you claim that this infinitude can be demonstrated?—What is the meaning of this expansion?—What is the meaning of this barrier?'[33] Philotheus, however, is not satisfied with putting on the same level two hypotheses that seem to be justified equally by the impossibility of a trial. Intellect comes to the aid of failing sense and declares: a limit to the universe is unthinkable. What, then, would be the path of an arrow shot against the ultimate firmament? Would it go beyond the universe, or would it encounter an obstacle? In neither case would it have reached the extremity of the universe. This objection to Aristotle's system goes back to Antiquity. Bruno borrowed it from Lucretius, whom he quotes and paraphrases.[34] Closer in time, Nicholas of Cusa, whilst refusing the universe the absolute infinity that belongs only to God, had asserted the impossibility of assigning a limit to it: 'If the universe had in itself its beginning and its end, it would be bounded with respect to something else ... it is not infinite, nevertheless, *it cannot be conceived as finite* seeing that it has no limits between which it is enclosed.'[35] That is suggested by our own senses, as Philotheus expresses the matter in his eighth argument: 'No sense is able to deny the infinite: negation of the infinite cannot be based on the fact that we are unable to comprehend it through the sense; but as, on the other hand, the sense is comprehended by the infinite [*i.e.*, as the infinite overlaps the domain of the tangible], which is something that is confirmed by reason, we ought to assume the infinite. Furthermore, if the matter be well considered, sense establishes the infinite, because we see that an object is always contained by another object, whereas it never happens that we see or imagine an object that is not contained in another.'[36]

The Aristotelians were content to answer these objections by saying that beyond the ultimate firmament no body can exist (like a container) nor have motion (like an arrow shot towards the exterior of the cosmos) because there is no *place*: space is, so to speak, closed upon itself. Burchio, who is one of the opponents of Philotheus in the first dialogue of *De l'infinito*, says: 'If someone stretched his hand beyond this convexity [of the last celestial sphere], that hand would not proceed to any place, it would not be anywhere, and consequently it would not have being.'[37] By means that Aristotle could never have suspected, modern physics has made the hypothesis of a finite universe conceivable by introducing a fourth dimension. So the brilliant conceptions of the Stagyrite find their supporters again; but in the sixteenth century it was easy to show that for a long time every fresh advance in knowledge made the theory, according to which the heavens were 'nowhere', more and more untenable, and it was safe to forecast that it would become even more so in the future. On this matter, Bruno with some maliciousness dwells on the difficulty in which it placed Aristotle's commentators, whether ancient or modern —whether it be Gilbert de la Porrée, Themistios, Avempace, Averroes or even St Thomas Aquinas; and it has to be admitted that it was a real difficulty.[38]

In the fifth dialogue of *De l'infinito*, a new speaker appears; he is Albertino, a sincere Aristotelian, whose part is to present the arguments of the Schoolmen against the plurality of worlds in a less summary way than the previous opponents of Philotheus. This last mentioned question, without being merged into that of the infinite universe, is connected with it in so far as we seek to establish that nothing exists beyond the sphere that limits our universe. 'Heaven, says Albertino, is unique, perfect and complete; whence it follows that, outside this body, there cannot be place, either full or void, nor time.'[39] This doctrine excludes not only the existence of a body (a plenum) outside the 'perfect' universe, but even the possibility of this existence (a vacuum); consequently, it does not admit motion outside the universe, any more than time which is the number of motion.[40]

Neglecting the problem of time, we shall now examine the answers of Bruno's philosophy to the two questions raised by the double negation of all space and of any body beyond the ultimate firmament.

The solution provided for the first of these two questions concerning space will obviously depend on the definition of *place* (without prejudice to the presence or absence of material bodies in 'that general place which we shall be permitted to call void'[41]). According to Aristotle, place is limited by that which contains. Bruno, who does not accept this definition, tries to show that it was not always accepted by the Aristotelians themselves, and cited the authority of St Thomas Aquinas, who, according to him (Bruno), refused to confuse place with the surface of that which contains, or with that which is contained, but situated between the two.[42] After St Thomas Aquinas he invokes the 'numerous Peripatetics who have not thought it necessary to adhere to Aristotle's propositions against a void, and in the first rank of those who must be mentioned he cites Philoponos as the boldest'.[44]

According to Aristotle, the true principle of place is finally the last, supposedly motionless, envelope of the universe. In other words, place is 'the motionless limit of that which was the first to contain' (or of that which was first contained): *terminus immobilis continentis primum*,[44] which definition is rejected by Bruno, for whom place is a portion of space. He said, it is not the *locus* which defines the *locatum*, but conversely it is the *locatum* which defines the *locus*. A body occupies in virtue of its mass a space which is its place and beyond which infinite space extends: 'Place cannot be the centre or the periphery of a sphere, though space can fill it.' That is what he said in *Acrotismus*.[45] As a matter of fact, Bruno gives a rather different definition of place elsewhere, seeing that it no longer refers to the portion of space occupied by a body, but to the space which surrounds it and separates it from what is contained, with which it cannot be in immediate contact in view of what has been said above about matter.[46] These definitions, however, are complementary rather than contradictory; both say that every body fills a certain space and necessarily finds itself surrounded by a space which separates it from that which is contained or from any other neighbouring body; 'and if we wish to determine the surface, we shall be obliged to seek a finite place at infinity'.[47]

To summarize, we cannot conceive of a body not surrounded by space. This slightly confused process of reasoning, the terminology of which is sometimes uncertain, ends with two very clear statements:

1. Space, independently of the bodies contained within it, is abstractly defined by its three dimensions.[48]

2. If the void is that in which there is nothing, it is not possible to conceal the void by establishing a finite universe.[49]

SPACE AND MATTER

Affirmation of an infinite space, 'a general place', homogeneous, three dimensional, having neither 'up' nor 'down', neither centre nor periphery, the affirmation, in short, of a space independent of the body of the universe is of prime importance: it leads to affirmation of the infinite universe. The passage from one to the other takes place by one of the simplest of reasonings, the meaning of which may be easily guessed.

If we assume the universe to be finite, 'we do not conceal the void', which means that we are constrained to assume, being given our definition of 'place', that there is a boundless space—an 'exterior region'— beyond this universe. 'But if the exterior region is infinite, the body must be infinite also, and the universes; in effect, why a void here rather than there? . . . If void and infinite place exist, there must also be infinite body; in fact, between possibility and being, there is no difference in eternal things.' It is not Bruno who is expressing himself in those terms, as we might think, but Aristotle himself.[50]

Bruno agrees with Aristotle in not being disturbed by assuming a useless void; and he would be if motion were possible within a *plenum*[50b]. That must be conceded to the Aristotelians: 'We must not assume a void which is repugnant to nature if there is no reason for our being obliged to do so.' However, it happens that this reason exists as soon as the void (here we part company with Aristotle) is indispensable for motion: 'all motion is accomplished either starting from a void, or towards a void, or in a void'.[51]

The void (whether we mean thereby an absolute vacuum or an 'aether' offering no resistance to local motion of material bodies) has, therefore, its proper function in nature: it is the medium favourable to the motion of atoms and to universes, which are the heavenly atoms; it is a continuum that surrounds bodies, it separates them seeing that it is distinct from them, and it permeates them because it penetrates between their ultimate elements.[52] The universe, conceived in this way, is not imagined as an infinite body, but as an infinity of finite bodies. The space in which our universe is contained is suitable for containing other universes;[53] we must therefore assert that it does contain them otherwise we shall be brought back to the inadmissible hypothesis of a finite universe in infinite space, of a universe which, however vast and enormous it may seem to us, would, in the sight of the divine presence, be only a point, or to be more exact, nothing.[54]

Whereas Aristotle denies both the infinite universe and infinite space, Bruno asserts them both. One certitude is common to them both—and perhaps Bruno owes it to his Aristotelian upbringing— it is, that we cannot assert one and deny the other. Between the finite and the infinite there is no proportion, no *ratio*, to use a term from the language of the mathematicians of Antiquity, such that the measure of a finite object, however large it be in our view, becomes irrational and inexpressible with respect to the infinite. To assume both an infinite possibility of being and a finite universe, is to suppose a god 'infinitely sparing of his powers', and to reduce his creation to a work of naught.

It may be mentioned that this absolute lack of proportion between the finite and the infinite is transposed on to the plane of spiritual life in *La Querelle des yeux et du cœur*, a poetic allegory whose purpose is to show that the privative infinity of the soul's potentialities must agree with the positive infiniteness of its object.[55]

THE INFINITE AND THE GOOD

The concept of the infinite was not unknown to Aristotle. He asserts the infinity of time, of number (a number, however large, can always be increased), and, as regards *the body of the universe*, if he does not accept infinity in the sense of size (the universe having an absolute limit), he does accept it in the sense of smallness (infinite division). As for the pre-Socratic physiologers to whom Bruno so readily refers they thought of the infinite as a 'principle', as a primordial substance which nourishes our universe, a chaos, an ἄπειρων in the midst of which the universe organizes itself and at the expense of which it progresses without ever exhausting the possibilities. Whether it be the enveloping infinity of Anaximander, or the enveloped infinity of Aristotle, in both cases we are confronted with pure possibility. To claim infinite greatness or infinite smallness is equivalent to acknowledging that a supreme degree does not exist in greatness or in smallness. The infinite, if it were to become actual, would cease to be the infinite. The ancients and the moderns are unanimous on this point. According to Leonardo da Vinci, the infinite 'is that thing which does not give itself, and which, if it were to give itself, would cease to exist'.[56] In another place, he notes: 'That which is divisible in act is so also in potential. That is to say, a division having been made, a fresh division is still possible, but that is not to say that what is actually divisible is also potentially so.'[57] So much for the infinitely small; as for the infinitely great, we have only to take Nicholas of Cusa: 'There is no difference in saying that the universe can always be larger and saying that *to be able to be* exceeds *to be infinite in act*, which is something impossible. . . .'[58]

According to the usual opinion of philosophers, the infinite is that which is not; so much so that the words by which it is designated (*infinitum*, ἀπείρων) have a negative form that brings out the degree of inferiority by which it is characterized. The concept of infinity implies incompletion, imperfection. In the table of Pythagorean opposites, πέρας (limited) is contrasted with ἀπείρων (unlimited), as is one to the multiple, and good to evil.

The first of the three objections (in abridged form) put forward by St Thomas Aquinas to God's infinity is: 'All infinity is imperfect. . . . But God is most perfect. Therefore He is not infinite.'[59] The reply is immediately forthcoming: the Ancient philosophers, said St Thomas, were right in attributing infinity to the prime principle whence flows the endless universe, but some of them fell into error as to the nature of this principle, for they saw a material principle in it. Nevertheless, the concepts of infinitude and perfection appear to be contradictory: God alone, mysteriously and inexplicably, is both infinite and perfect.

Bruno has no hesitation in conceding these two attributes to the universe, the reflection of God. As it is impossible to imagine *one* infinite and perfect universe, in other words *one body* having form and no limit, his 'unimaginable' universe will consist of an infinite plurality of finite worlds in infinite space.

That is substantially the reply made by Philotheus to the twelfth and final argument of Albertino in favour of Aristotelian cosmology. 'To the perfect, one adds nothing', says Albertino. If, then, the universe be perfect, it is finite and unique. A point develops into a line—*corre in linea*—which is 'a kind of continuum'—*una specie di continuo*; the line develops into a surface, the surface into a volume, 'but the volume does not develop into another kind of continuum'—*non migra o discorre in altra specie di continuo*. Consequently, if a body, *i.e.*, a volume be part of the universe, it finds its limit in another body, 'but if it be the universe it is limited to itself'. The argument would be valid, and even unanswerable, if the universe consisted of a single world, a unique body, but nothing is more arbitrary than such a supposition. Philotheus, too, extricates himself from the impasse into which his opponent thinks he has driven him by pleading the possibility (in his opinion the certainty) of a plurality of worlds. That is the meaning of his final answer. Not only does the existence of other worlds raise no obstacle to the perfection, but an infinite number of worlds is necessary for the perfection of the universe.[60] Or better expressed, the perfection of each world taken separately necessitates the immensity of the universe. In a remarkable chapter in *De immenso* 'Where is proved the perfection of the immense', a distinction is made between absolute perfection (*simpliciter perfectum* and perfection in kind (*in genere*). Each world is perfect 'in its kind', only the infinite universe is absolutely perfect. On the other hand, nothing is absolutely imperfect, for what we believe to be defective in the narrow field of view which we are permitted to explore takes on its true worth as part of the infinite universe.[61]

Evil is privation: it can affect only the partial; but the partial itself is free from it if we consider it as functioning with the whole, in harmony with the whole. We could say these are common-places, but they incur remarkable consequences as soon as the whole becomes the infinite universe. In the Pythagorean table, the infinite is contrasted with what is limited, as the multiple is contrasted with unity, good with evil, the moving with the motionless; whereas in Bruno's system the order of the first two terms only being reversed, the infinite passes over to the side of unity, the motionless and good. According to Nicholas of Cusa, the word 'universe' means 'unity of several';[62] Bruno recaptures this maxim: the universe for him is unity of the infinitely numerous. It is therefore both one and infinite. The fifth dialogue of *De la causa* opens with this statement, which is presented as a logical consequence of everything that has been said previously: 'Therefore the universe is one, infinite, motionless'; and further on: 'The universe is one, infinite, indivisible; and if in the infinite we find no difference, as between the part and the whole, as between one and the other, assuredly the infinite is one.'[63] The words *infinitum, unum, immobile* are similarly associated in *Acrotismus*, as well as in the treatise *De l'infinito*.[64] At the close of the second dialogue of this same treatise, Philotheus, without reverting to the futile discussion on the possibility or impossibility of rectilinear motion in the cosmos, states that 'the whole is motionless', that it is 'no more affected with circular motion than with direct motion';[65] and in *Acrotismus* again (article 23): 'the infinite as such does not move', it is everywhere; 'infinity is the supreme reason for immobility'.[66] Many other passages could be quoted here, but none is more explicit than the chapter on 'the perfection of the universe' in *De immenso*: 'the unity and infinity of God become attributes in it of *universal nature*, his perfect image, his great simulacrum, carefully distinguished from the tangible universe (hence finite and imperfect) in which good and evil, matter and form, light and darkness, sadness and joy mingle.'[67]

Cassirer has noted that the problem of space is an ethical one for Bruno.[68] It is the same and even more so with respect to the problem of the infinite which in *Eroici furori* is brought on to a moral plane: 'In the simplicity of the divine essence . . . all attributes are equal; or better still, they are the same, they are but one thing. . . . The summit of wisdom constitutes but one with the abyss of power and the breadth of goodness. All these perfections are equal seeing that they are infinite.'[69] It is only necessary to apply to the infinity of the universe what has been said of the divine infinity in order to come to the paradoxical conclusion that the infinite is truly finite, whilst every finite object, *i.e.*, every object that we can fully apprehend in the tangible universe, or whose limits we can imagine, is necessarily partial, unfinished, and affected with all the negative attributes that we are accustomed to regard as being those of the ἀπείρων. 'All that is finite is imperfect'—*finitum quodlibet est imperfectum*— and all the things that we see subjected in this limited universe to alteration and motion pass under the sense of unity, truth and goodness in that infinity that we rightly call universe.[70]

The poems and dialogues in *Eroici furori* exalt the effort of the soul to ascend to its prime principle: a hopeless attempt, high-minded above all, but doomed to failure from the start.[71] Would exploration of the universe offer man in love with the divine a round-about means of reaching the supreme Unity that hides itself from the conjoint enterprises of will and intellect? Would not it be possible for man to contemplate the back of the divinity, in default of the 'noble face', through the aspect of universal nature, which is the reflection and explanation of God? One might think so, but it is nothing of the kind for the reason that the universe, if it participates in the perfection of God participates also in His infinity. Furthermore, Bruno's cosmological treatises, in spite of the fervour and joy, suitable to the expression of a splendid truth, at last discovered, bring us to the same unpassable threshold and to the same confession of impotence as his moral treatises. To place the good beside the infinite, is to put it out of reach for ever.

The infinite is not a subject of knowledge: overflowing the field of the tangible, it baffles natural discourse. It will be noticed on reading the treatise *De l'infinito* (and the same comment could be made in respect of *De immenso* and *Acrotismus*) that the existence of the infinite is never proved, and for good reason. On this point, the opening replies of the dialogue give the tone: 'How is it possible for the universe to be infinite?—How is it possible for it to be finite?' Philotheus satisfies himself with an absurb proof: he concludes in favour of the infiniteness of the universe by disclosing the vanity of the contrary thesis. The Aristotelians invoke the impossibility of a finite object to act upon the infinite body, and *vice versa*; similarly they invoke the impossibility of rotation by an infinite sphere: if the body of the universe were infinite, the radius of the ultimate sphere would be so also, as a result of which motion of the said sphere would be unable to be completed in a given time.[72] How, then, is it possible not to see that these arguments, like all others of the same kind, presuppose a certain cosmic order? They are valid only if we assume that a certain number of rigid spheres, encased one within the other, move around the Earth which is motionless at the centre of the universe. If we reject this picture, as the progress of knowledge invites us to do, a new astronomy is going to suggest, and on reflection is going to impose on us an infinite universe. This makes us understand the importance attached by Giordano Bruno to a discussion of geocentrism.

NOTES

1. A. Koyré, *'Le vide et l'espace infini au XIVe siècle'* in *Archives d'histoire doctrinale et littéraire du moyen âge*, 1949, p. 81.
2. H. A. Wolfson, *Crescas, critique of Aristotle*, Cambridge, Mass., 1929.
3. *Ibid.*, pp. 35–36.
4. See especially, D. W. Singer, *Giordano Bruno*, London and New York, 1950, pp. 57–58.
5. The original edition (Venice) has no date. The first one to bear a date seems to be that of Bâle, 1548. The work was reprinted at Bâle, Lyons, Paris, London, and again at Venice up to the end of the sixteenth century and again in the seventeenth century.
6. *Oratio valedictoria* (*Opera*, I, i, p. 17).
7. A. Ferro, *'La filosofia di Spinoza e la filosophia ebraica medievale'* in *Giornale critico della filosofia italiana*, 1935, p. 56.
8.   '... l'ali sicurea l'aria porgo
       Ne temo intoppo di cristallo o vetro
       Ma fendo i cieli e a l'infinito m'ergo.'
De l'infinito, p. 286; see *De immenso*, I, i (*Opera*, I, i, p. 201).
9. *Figuratio aristotelici physici auditus, lib.*, III, *cap.*, iii, *art*, i (*Opera*, I, iv, pp. 166–167).
10. '*Vestigium, simulacrum et speculum infinitatis in omnibus quae vidimus atque singulis experimur.*' *De immenso*, I, xiii (*Opera*, I, i, p. 250).
11.   '*Quaeritur activam praeter passiva facultas,*
        Non et tot natura potest portare, quot ille
        Condere ...'
De l'infinito, V, p. 399; *De immenso*, VII, vi (*Opera*, I, ii, pp. 252–253).

12. *De l'infinito, Proemiale epistola*, p. 280.
13. *De l'infinito*, V, pp. 399 and 415; eighth argument of the Aristotelians and refutation of this argument under number 9; *De immenso*, VII, vi and xv (*Opera*, I, ii, pp. 252 and 276): twelfth argument of Aristotle and refutation.
14. '... *perchè volete quel centro della divinità, che può infinitamente in una sfera ... infinita amplificarsi, come invidioso, rimaner più tosto sterile ... voler più tosto communicarsi diminutamente e, per dir meglio non communicarsi, che secondo la raggione della gloriosa potenza ed esser suo?*' *De l'infinito*, I, p. 297.
15. '*Deus infinita potens et finita faciens infinite esset invidus, finite bonus.*' *De immenso*, VIII, iii (*Opera*, I, ii, p. 295). See also the last verses of the same chapter: '*Ergo qui potuit facere infinita, putandum est-Fecisse, ac totum sancte explevisse vigorem—Nec servasse in se vanum, vel inutile quicquam.*'
16. *Docta ignorantia*, II, 2; trans. Mouliner, p. 107.
17. *Ibid.*, II, i, p. 106 and see I, 22, p. 86.
18. *Oratio valedictoria* (*Opera*, I, i, pp. 13–14).
19. *Physica*, III, 203 *b*.
20. *Acrotismus, art.* xxi, *Ubi de infinito* (*Opera*, I, i, p. 217): and some few lines later: '*Unde ex parte hujus potentiae naturalis est infinitum, ut imaginatio quantitatem quantitati addendo non quiescat, neque illi terminetur dimensio simpliciter, et aliquid extra mundum nequeat non fingere, sive vacuum sit illud, sive plenum. Unde etiam alicui naturali talis tantaque potentia inest non secundum naturam certa ratione illi respondentem?*'
21. *Eroici furori*, p. 284.
22. *Summa theol., Prima pars, quaestio VII, De infinitate Dei* (trans. Sertillanges, p. 193).
23. '*Non est possibile esse aliquam multitudinem actu infinitum.*' *Ibid.*, p. 209.
24. *Docta ignorantia*, II, i and 4 (trans. Moulinier, pp. 106–107 and 118).
25. *De l'infinito*, I, p. 294.
26. '*Io dico l'universo tutto infinito, perchè non ha margine, termino, ne superficie; dico l'universo non essere totalmente infinito, perchè ciascuna parte che di quello possiamo prendere, è finita, e de mondi innumerbili che contiene, ciascuno è finito. Io dico Dio tutto infinito, perchè da sè esclude ogni termine ed ogni suo attributo è uno e infinito; e dico Dio totalmente infinito, perchè tutto lui è in tutto il mondo, ed in ciascuna sua parte infinitamente e totalmente.*' *De l'infinito*, I, p. 298.
27. '*Non è senso che vegga l'infinito, non è senso da cui si richieda questa conclusione; perchè l'infinito non può essere oggetto del senso; e però chi demanda di conoscere questo per via di senso, è simile a colui che volesse veder con gli occhi la sustanza e l'essenza; e chi negasse per questo la cosa, perchè non è sensibile o visibile, verebbe a negar la propria sustanza ed essere. Però deve esser modo circa il dimandar testimonio del senso.*' *De l'infinito*, I, p. 288.
28. '... [*il senso*] *fa evidente e confessa la sua imbecillità ed insufficienza per l'apparenza de la finitudine che caggiona per il suo orizonte, in formar della quale ancora si vede quanto sia incostante.*' *De l'infinito*, I, p. 289. Compare with the passage in *De immenso*, I, iv (*Opera*, I, i, pp. 214–218).
29. *De immenso*, III, 1 (*Opera*, I, i, pp. 313–315).
30. F. Tocco, *Le opere di Giordano Bruno*, p. 123 and note 3.
31. '*Verior sphaera est universum quam mundus vel quicunque globus.*' Compare axioms III and VI with *De minimo*, I, xiii (*Opera*, I, iii, p. 181). The formless infinity may be likened to a sphere more than to any other figure, seeing that the sphere is defined by the equality of the distance of all points on its surface from a common centre. In the infinite sphere, every point is a centre.
32. *Articuli adversus mathematicos. Axiomata sphaerae* (*Opera*, pp. 14–15).
33. *De l'infinito*, I, pp. 287–288.
34. *De rerum natura*, I, 968 ff; *De l'infinito, Argomento del primo dialogo*, p. 271; *De immenso*, I, vii (*Opera*, I, i, p. 227).
35. *Docta ignorantia*, II, ii.
36. '*Ottavo, da quel che nessun senso nega l'infinito, atteso che non lo possiamo negare per questo, che non lo comprendiamo col senso; ma da quel, che il senso viene compreso da quello e la raggione viene a confirmarlo, lo doviamo ponere. Anzi se oltre ben consideriamo, il senso lo pone infinito; perchè sempre veggiamo cosa*

compresa da cosa, e mai sentiamo, nè con esterno nè con interno senso, cosa non compresa da altra, o simile.' De l'infinito, Argomento del primo dialogo, p. 272.

37. '... se uno stendesse la mano oltre quel convesso, ... quella non verebbe essere in loco, e non sarebbe in parte alcuna, e per consequenza non avrebbe l'essere.' De l'infinito, I, p. 290.

38. De immenso, I, vi (Opera, I, i, pp. 223–224).

39. 'Cossi è cosa manifesta vhe non son molti mondi, perchè il cielo è unico, perfetto e compito, a cui non è, nè può essere altro simile. Indi s'inferisce, che fuor di questo corpo non può essere loco nè pieno nè vacuo, nè tempo.' De l'infinito, V, p. 296. See Aristotle, De cælo, I, 9, 278b–279a.

40. 'Non vi è tempo, perchè il tempo è numero di moto.' De l'infinito, V, p. 296.

41. De l'infinito, V, p. 404.

42. '... ad Aquinatem redeo, cui jam proprius locus non erit superficies corporis continentis neque contenti, sed quod circa utraque vel circa illa utraque est.' De immenso, I, vii (Opera, I, i, pp. 229–230).

43. De immenso, I, viii (Opera, I, i, p. 321).

44. Physica, IV, 4, 212a.

45. 'Neque sphaerae medium aut ultimum locus esse potest, sed spacium quod implet illa.' Acrotismus, art. xxxi (Opera, I, i, p. 128). See also art. xxix, pp. 125–126.

46. 'Quinto, da che la definizione del loco che poneva Aristotele non conviene al primo, massimo e comunissimo loco, e che non val prendere la superficie prossima ed immediata al contenuto, ed altre levitadi che fanno il loco cosa matematica e non fisica; lascio che tra la superficie del continente e contenuto che si muove entro quella, sempre è necessario spacio tramezante a cui conviene più tosto esser loco.' De l'infinito, Argomento del primo dialogo, p. 272. See De immenso, II, x (Opera, I, i, p. 293 ff).

47. '... e se vogliamo del spacio prendere la sola superficie, bisogna che si vada cercando in infinito un loco finito.' De l'infinito, Argomento del primo dialogo, p. 272.

48. 'Est ergo spacium quantitas quaedum physica triplici dimensione constans.' De immenso, I, viii (Opera, I, i, p. 231). The continuation of the passage stresses the abstract and 'indifferent' character of a space which is nothing more than Euclidian space, though Bruno regards it as a physical reality.

49. 'Non si può fuggir il vacuo ponendo il mondo finito se vacuo è quello nel quale è niente.' De l'infinito, Argomento del primo dialogo, p. 272.

50. Physica, III, 4, 203b.

50b. 'Nulla necessitate (inquit Aristoteles) si motus est, vacuum esse oportet.' Acrotismus, art. xxxv (Opera, I, i, p. 135).

51. 'Omne ... movetur aut e vacuo, aut ad vacuum, aut in vacuo.' Ibid.

52. 'Vacuum tum separatum quid a corporibus, tum ipsis imbibitum, tum unum continuum dicere non formidamus.' Acrotismus, art. xxxvii (Opera, I, 8, p. 142).

53. 'Come dunque in questo spacio, equale alla grandezza del mondo ... è questo mondo, cosi un altro può essere in quel spacio ed in innumerabili spacii oltre questo equali a questo.' De l'infinito, I, p. 292. See De immenso, I, vii (Opera, I, i, pp. 225 ff).

54. 'O che repugna che l'infinito, implicato nel simplicissimo ed inviduo primo principio, non venga esplicato più tosto in questo suo simulacro infinito ed interminato, capacissimo de innumerabili mondi, che venga esplicato in sì anguste margini, di sorte che par vituperio il non pensare che questo corpo, che a noi per vasto e grandissimo, al riguardo della divina presenza non sia un punto, anzi un nulla?' De l'infinito, I, 294—Note that what is here compared with a point is not the finite universe but a universe supposed to be finite.

55. Eroici furori, II, iii, pp. 392–394.

56. Les carnets de Léonard de Vinci (trans. Louise Servicen), Paris, 1942, I, p. 509.

57. See Pierre Duhem, Études sur Léonard de Vinci, 2nd series, Paris, 1909, pp. 51–52.

58. Docta ignorantia, II, i.

59. 'Omne infinitum est imperfectum ... Sed Deus est perfectissimus. Ergo non est infinitus.' Summa theologica, I, quaestio VII, art. i.

60. *De l'infinito*, V, p. 400: Albertino's argument, and p. 416; reply by Philotheus.
61. 'Nihil est absolute imperfectum.
*Quidquid enim exiguum est, imbecille, inque minutum
Totius incurrit complendam ad nobilitatem.*'
De immenso, II, xiii, *Utcunque probatur perfectio immensi*, poem and gloss (*Opera*, I, i, pp. 309–312).
62. *Docta ignorantia*, II, 4.
63. '*E dunque l'universo uno, infinito, immobile.*' '*Dunque l'universo è uno, infinito, impartibile,*' *De la causa*, I, pp. 247 and 248.
64. *Acrotismus* (*Ubi de infinito*), art. xxi (*Opera*, I, i, p. 119); *De l'infinito*, II, pp. 313–314.
65. *De l'infinito*, II, p. 336.
66. *Acrotismus*, art. xxiii (*Opera*, I, i, p. 120).
67. *De immenso*, II, xii (*Opera*, I, i, pp. 302–308).
68. E. Cassirer, *Individuum und Kosmos in der Philosophie der Renaissance*, Leipzig, 1927, pp. 197–200.
69. *Eroici furori*, I, v, pp. 278–280.
70. '*Quae omnia in infinito in rationem unitatis, veritatis et bonitatis veniunt.*' *De immenso*, II, xii (*Opera*, I, i, p. 307).
71. See *Eroici furori*, Introduction, pp. 42–43.
72. See Aristotle, *De cœlo*, I, 5, and the discussion on the Aristotelian arguments in *De immenso*, II, ii (*Opera*, I, i, pp. 252–257).

VII

The solar system

Bruno's knowledge and ignorance of astronomical matters have been the subject of equally excessive praise and scorn, both to some extent justified, for if we can admire the boldness of his cosmological intuition, we must admit also that this intuition was not supported by any very certain knowledge; whence all the mistakes and inadequacies that have been revealed in his descriptions of the planetary system (taking into account the state of knowledge in his day) and in the judgements that he did not hesitate to pass on the greatest astronomers, past or present. His cosmology is based on two principles: the infinitude of the universe and its homogeneity. It is therefore just as incompatible with the 'Ionian' conception of a limited cosmos resting within an infinite ἀπείρων as with the Aristotelian scheme of a closed universe, unique and divided into zones each having its own particular physical properties.

No doubt this *Stufenkosmos*, as Cassirer calls it,[1] this 'storied' universe, which is just as much that of the pseudo-Dionysios as of Aristotle, retained a symbolic value in Bruno's eyes, as may be judged from the episode of the nine blind men in the final dialogue of *Eroici furori*. However, in his letter of dedication to Sir Philip Sydney, our author, who seems to have wanted to avoid any possible contempt as regards his views on the cosmic architecture, definitely states that if the nine blind men 'represent the number, order and diversity of all things that are enveloped and dominated by the absolute unity, and in which and above which are disposed the intelligences which similarly . . . [distributed in nine orders] are subject to the prime and unique intelligence', then it must be understood to mean 'according to the *popular conception* of the nine celestial spheres'.[2] So we are warned that a statement of Brunonian cosmology must not take any notice of poetical discourses borrowing their descriptions from the data of a repudiated astronomy.

Would it be perfidious, or at least an abuse of language, to speak of a *system* of the universe? Does not this term, which is foreign to Bruno's vocabulary evoke the idea of an organic universe, whereas the infinite universe is 'formless' and 'unrepresentable'? 'Thou knowest as little of God's extension as of the universe when thou sayest that it is a circle.' That was how Angelus Silesius expressed the matter in a couplet which clearly shows the direct influence of Giordano Bruno.[3] Nevertheless, there is an astronomy, a science of the celestial objects, which is well-founded in so far as it is concerned with the study of that which comes within range of our vision and is limited to the horizon of the sky. The Earth, the Moon, the Sun and the planets are so many 'worlds' which, taken as a whole, definitely constitute a 'system' and an 'organism' whose laws we are permitted to know.

We now come to a distinction between the *universe* and *worlds*, so frequently stated and even written into the title of the dialogues *De l'infinito universo et mondi*, and furthermore emphasized in the title of the Latin poem *De innumerabilibus, immenso et infigurabili, seu de universo et mundis*—'Concerning the innumerable, the immense and the unrepresentable, or Concerning the universe and worlds.' If it should happen that we ascribe the meaning *universe* to the term 'world', we 'are following popular usage'. 'If, on the other hand, thou speakest the language of true philosophers, world means any globe, any celestial body like our Earth, or the body of the Sun, or the Moon, or others.' As for the universe, 'without dimension or measure', it is the sum of these worlds, 'the place of an infinity of worlds . . . it contains within its infinite space all those great brutes we call celestial bodies'.[4] Consequently, there is a plurality of worlds in a universe which is necessarily unique because nothing exists outside of it. The universe, according to an etymology borrowed by Bruno from Nicholas of Cusa, is 'the unity of many'.

Astronomy will therefore be the knowledge of *worlds*, and, amongst these worlds, it will be knowledge of those that come within range of perception by our senses. Seeing that such knowledge will be all the more certain if it can be based on more numerous and conclusive experiments because of the proximity of what is being studied, it will be convenient to make a distinction on that account between the planetary system and what is beyond, *i.e.*, the starry firmament known to traditional astronomy as the 'sphere of fixed stars'. With regard to the planetary system, Bruno's criticism bears on classical geocentrism, which is opposed by a heliocentrism inspired by Copernicus; and his criticism extends to Copernicus himself whose heliocentrism is opposed by the hypothesis of innumerable worlds. These aspects of Brunonian cosmology will be treated in two separate chapters.

THE ARISTOTELIAN SYSTEM

Aristotle's cosmos differs little in its main features from that of Plato, at least as regards the planetary system. Aristotle was not the only one, nor the first to be responsible for the geocentric system adopted by astronomers from the time of Eudoxos and retained by them till the dawn of modern times, though with various corrections that were rendered necessary from time to time by the progress of their knowledge. Aristotle, however, is not only a symbol. If Bruno regards him as the chief enemy to be conquered, if he takes so much trouble to refute his arguments whilst he hardly bothers to mention the name of Ptolemy, it is undoubtedly because he is more familiar with *De cælo* than with the *Almagest*; but, in addition, it is also because Aristotle is, like himself, 'more physicist than mathematician', and so they have something in common, namely, the field of battle. Leaving others with their calculations to take account of the apparent motions of celestial bodies, Aristotle wanted to give a physical significance to the system of homocentric spheres devised by Eudoxos. In his opinion, it was not only a question of 'saving the appearances', but of saying what exists: the Earth occupies the centre of the universe; around it are ranged the regions of water, air and fire, each element having its proper 'place' to which it ceaselessly tends to return; this collection of layers constitutes the sublunary world, beyond which extends the zone of the incorruptible aether and the celestial spheres; the lowest sphere, the one nearest to the Earth, is that of the Moon; then follow the spheres of the Sun, Mercury, Venus, Jupiter and Saturn; finally, a separate sphere, the sphere of the fixed stars is merged with the planetary system, it envelops all the other spheres and sets them in motion; it is the boundary of the universe.

HELIOCENTRISM

The system described above, like every geocentric system, was opposed by heliocentrism, which from Antiquity had likewise appeared in various forms. In the sixteenth century Giogio Valla, Calcagnini,

Copernicus himself gave credit to certain early philosophers for having stated and supported this cosmological hypothesis.[5] Copernicus, however, was the first to give heliocentrism the character of a scientific theory, with the result that, after publication of *De revolutionibus orbium coelestium*, astronomers who till then had been unanimous in their respect for a tradition which had held sway since the time of Ptolemy were now divided into two camps. In siding with the heliocentrists, Bruno gives tribute to his predecessors both ancient and contemporary, and in particular to Copernicus whom he hails as a 'new dawn' and whose genius he exalts; but he limits his debt to them and is even close to reducing it to nothing when, using Theophilus as a mouthpiece, he makes the following eulogy: 'Copernicus was not satisfied to make assumptions as a mathematician; as a physicist he proved the motion of the Earth. However, though Copernicus, Nicetas of Syracuse, Philolaos, Heraclides of Pontos, Ecphantos the Pythagorean, Plato in *Timaeus* (but rather timidly and without vigour seeing that he relied on faith rather than on knowledge), the divine Nicholas of Cusa in the second book of *Docta ignorantia*, as well as other rare minds have previously asserted, taught and proved the matter, all that means little to Bruno, for it is from other more solid principles, which are peculiarly his own that (without recourse to authority but through the exercise of sense and reason) he derives his certainty in so far as this as well as any other truth which he feels able to hold as certain.'[6]

The immobility of the Earth and its central position in the universe are two distinct things: there is nothing to prevent us from assuming that the Earth is at the centre of the universe and from explaining its rotation on its axis by the apparent motion of the celestial vault. That was the theory of Heraclides. On the other hand, if the Earth is not allowed to occupy the central position, then its immobility becomes unthinkable. Bruno hardly troubles to discriminate between the two problems. In the passage from *La cena* quoted above, it was only a question of terrestrial motion, but immediately afterwards[7] the other question is raised and resolved in the way we would expect, using arguments that are resumed in a chapter of *De immenso* whose title is: 'The Earth, in the infinite universe, is not at the centre, except in so far as everything can be said to be at the centre.' In this chapter it is explained that the Earth is not central amongst the planets. That place is reserved for the Sun, for it is natural for the planets to turn towards its light and heat, and accept its law.[8]

It will be noted that the argument as put forward has a finalist and Aristotelian pungency, and that it could be turned round by the supporters of geocentrism. When Marsilio Ficino says that the Sun reigns in the median region like the king in the middle of the city,[9] he means that the Sun is equidistant from the Earth and the furthermost planets, and definitely situated in that manner so as to distribute light and heat to them uniformly. Bruno, however, bases his heliocentrism on other more convincing reasons, which are developed in *La cena* as well as in the third book of *De immenso*. The irregularity of planetary motions and their variable distances with respect to the Earth are explained only with difficulty if the Earth be placed at the centre of the system; they can be accounted for only by introducing the most complicated corrections, whereas revolution of all the planets and the Earth round the Sun satisfies the mind, simplifies calculations and saves the appearances.[10]

As for the Earth, if it thereby lose the privilege of its position at the centre of the cosmos, it is at the same time relieved of all its former misfortunes: it is no longer the lowest region, the here-below, the inferior world, subject to and alone subject to corruption. Restored to the firmament, it rediscovers its character of a celestial body: 'We are a celestial body for the Moon and for every other celestial body, and we are the firmament just as much as they are for us.'[11]

HOMOGENEITY OF THE PLANETARY SYSTEM

This statement as to the homogeneity of the universe, a universe which we shall reduce to the planetary system for the sake of clarity in our account, is regarded by Giordano Bruno as one of the essential themes of his doctrine. The importance he attaches to it may be gauged by the extent of the developments involved and the exceptional vigour of the Aristotelian polemic to which it gives rise.

According to Aristotle, the cosmos is divided into two zones, the sublunary world and the celestial world. The former is that of generation and corruption. The matter of which it is composed may assume four chief forms: the four Empedoclean elements of earth, water, air and fire. Each of the four is capable of producing the other three by a direct or indirect change ($\dot{\alpha}\lambda\lambda o i \omega \sigma\iota s$), and their combinations give rise to all the infinitely diverse bodies that are found in nature. On the other hand, each element has its proper 'place'; it occupies one of the four sublunary spheres—of earth, water, air or fire—and tends to return there if it is displaced, with the result that the properties of bodies are strictly 'localized'. Beyond the sphere of fire are ranged the crystalline spheres of the various heavens, which taken as a whole constitute the celestial world. The celestial bodies are composed of a fifth element, the quintessence, the incorruptible aether, and cannot undergo any change except that of local motion— *secundum ubi*—with, in addition, the restriction that this motion must be uniform and circular, rectilinear motion being possible only in the inferior world.

The 'double physics' based on these topographical distinctions had been attacked long before Copernicus by William of Occam, by the French Occamites and by Nicholas of Cusa.[12] Bruno merely resumed and continued a controversy that had been going on during three centuries, but he was justified by the bitter resistance of the Aristotelians. The discussion which had started long before was not yet closed; and was not to be closed until the seventeenth century, in spite of later survival of geocentrism.

At the beginning of *La cena de le ceneri*, Smith, a studious English gentleman, asks Theophilus, 'what opinion he has of Copernicus';[13] and Theophilus replies by a panegyric of the great astronomer, which soon leads to one of Bruno. Copernicus becomes the forerunner of Giordano Bruno, 'the dawn that must precede the rising of that sun of the ancient and true philosophy buried for so many centuries in the dark caverns of a blind, malignant, impudent and envious ignorance'. 'But what do you say of Bruno?' 'He is so close to me— Theophilus amusingly confesses—as close as I am to myself— *quanto io medesimo a me stesso*—that it is unbecoming for me to sing his praises.' Nevertheless, he submits and owns that the glory of this restorer of good doctrines is 'to have penetrated the firmament, pursued the celestial bodies, stepped beyond the margins of the universe, and caused the imaginary walls (*le fantastiche muraglie*) of the first, eighth, ninth, tenth and other spheres to vanish'. These ramparts born of the calculations of vain mathematicians and illusions of vulgar philosophers he overthrows with his mind. He proclaims the unity of the firmament: 'If we were on the Moon or on any other star, we should not be in a place very different from this', perhaps it would be better, or it might even be worse.[14]

The fourth book of *De immenso* is entirely devoted to a refutation of the double physics. The arguments in favour of that doctrine, summarized in the first chapter,[15] are prefaced by a lyrical piece inspired by the mythological story of Enceladus, who was punished for his revolt against Jupiter. Weighed down by the enormous weight of Sicily (*sub pondere vasto Trinacriae*), the unvanquished giant awakes to proclaim his freedom, regained through men endowed with great gifts, who braving the anger of the gods, feared not to break those 'painted ceilings' (*laquearia picta*) that limited the firmament and to discover universes beyond the universe. Realizing that the Earth is a celestial body, the giant proclaims his joy: 'I belong to a star, a famous luminary; henceforth, no Etna will oppress me, seeing that the Earth, secure in its own members, is without weight. I am unfettered, I am free. . . .'[16]

A statement and refutation of the 'seven arguments' follows this song of victory. According to the Aristotelians, there is a difference in substance between the sublunary world and the celestial world; the former is composed of the four elements which by combining and dissociating amongst themselves give rise to infinitely varied bodies, the most stable of which are subject to possible 'accidents', change and destruction; the latter, on the other hand, is composed of one single element, whereby all possibility of combination and consequent change is excluded. Bruno believed, with Aristotle, in the substantial unity of a 'prime matter' which potentially contains all the forms, that is to say, all possible objects, simple elements or compound bodies; but, in addition, and contrary to Aristotle, he believed that those combinations were the rule in all parts of the universe. The unity of the prime matter and the diversity of the bodies in which it abounds exist without any kind of distinction equally on Earth and in the firmament.

Burchio, a character in the dialogues of *De l'infinito*, who represents the popular common-sense, changed and spoilt by the teaching of the Schoolmen, refuses to accept this identity of matter between the bodies of this lower world and the celestial bodies. 'What difference do you see between them?' he asks Fracastoro, the Veronese astronomer who is the author's mouthpiece in this argument. Burchio is content to reply: 'These are divine, those are of base matter (*materialacci*).' Fracastoro. 'How can you make me believe that they are more divine?' Burchio. 'Because they are impassive, unchangeable, incorruptible and eternal.'[17]

Burchio's mistake is not in proclaiming the incorruptibility and eternity of matter, but in not seeing that there is no difference in this respect between the matter of celestial bodies and that of the objects which are around us; and, furthermore, it is not only on Earth, but everywhere that the various elements and compound bodies originate from the unique prime matter. Bodies subject to accidents can only be compound bodies; now, the celestial bodies are subject to accidents, as we shall see later on in the case of sunspots and comets; but, without taking into account these exceptional phenomena, is not it evident that the celestial bodies give light and heat every day? and that light and heat, being accidents, can only be assigned to compound bodies?[18]

The differences that are able to subsist and which certainly do exist between the Earth and other celestial bodies are those that we are able to ascertain between particular individuals of the same kind, for example between two men of different race. Bruno returns insistently to the particularly instructive comparison of the Earth with the Moon. For the inhabitants of the Moon, the Earth is a luminary in the sky; it gives light to their nights, it occupies a place in the firmament, it forms part of the world above, and all transport from the Earth to the Moon, which would be ascent for us, is descent for them: *Quae a nobis ascendunt, lunaribus descendunt.*[19]

One chapter in *De immenso,* entitled *De ascensu in coelum et vera mundi contemplatione,*[20] provides an imaginary and picturesque account of a journey to the Moon. To the eyes of the traveller, the landscape gradually becomes indistinct as he moves away from the Earth. Whilst the dimensions of our planet get smaller, what happens to our forests? 'Where are the rivers, the mountains, ponds and towns?'[21] All these familiar objects merge together and disappear, and in their place the forests and mountains of the Moon stand out and become conspicuous. In this inverted perspective, the Earth, through an illusion caused solely by the position of the spectator, becomes a celestial body, unchangeable and of absolute purity, whereas the Moon is henceforth the centre of the universe, the herebelow, the world of diversity and change, of rectilinear motion and of accident.

What is said of the Moon is repeated for the other planets, which are globes similar to our own, and inhabited in like manner.[22] From Venus, the Earth and Moon will appear merely as brilliant points.[23] Mercury, which in Brunonian cosmography forms a 'couple' with Venus similar to the Earth and Moon, forms the night-star for the inhabitants of Venus, in the same way that Venus will be for the inhabitants of Mercury.

Finally, there is the Sun, which, too, is restored to elementary nature. Bruno does not hesitate to take this final step; but he is perhaps aware of giving evidence of greater boldness, seeing that on two occasions, once in *La cena* and then in *De l'infinito*, he takes care to shield himself under the authority of Cardinal de Cusa, 'who supposes that the Sun has dissimilar parts like the Earth and Moon' and 'is compounded of its elements'.[24] Indeed, one would be tempted to believe, even after abandoning the quintessence, that one single element, namely, fire, would suffice to constitute this blazing globe. However, Bruno has not forgotten the lesson of the early Milesian physiologers, for whom 'the fire of the Sun and the stars is maintained by exhalations from the waters': *Ignisque est nullus nisi quispiam suppetat humor.*

This statement is developed in the poetical text of *De immenso*, Book IV, Chapter VII, and is resumed in a more general way in the prose commentary; a composition of elements is necessary in order to produce the fire; the Sun, as well as the Earth, is a complex organism in the formation of which all elements must unite. In the same way that the Earth has its torrid zones, so the Sun has its cold regions and those favourable to the development of life.[25]

THE EARTH

a) *The four elements.* Like the celestial spheres, the four sublunary spheres corresponding to the four elements exist only in the imagination of 'vulgar philosophers'. According to Aristotle, the localization of the elements and the tendency of each of them to return to its proper place had to take account of the vertical motion of tangible objects. Solids, which are dominated by the element 'earth', tend towards the Earth; if a body is transformed into fire through combustion, the flame rises in order to get closer to the sphere of fire, which is the highest one. Water and air occupy the intermediate regions. On the other hand, each element is characterized by two fundamental qualities. Earth is cold and dry; water is cold and humid; air is hot and humid; fire is hot and dry. On these principles there is based a physics which is easily shown to be incompatible with factual experience.

They speak of a 'sphere of water'; but the mass of water spread over the surface of the Earth, not excepting the deepest oceans, is very little in relation to the total mass of the globe; at most it may be compared to a layer of perspiration on a living being, or to the thickness of a thin membrane.[26] Water certainly constitutes a very considerable portion of the composition of our planet, but it is not necessary to reduce it to the small dimensions of an alleged enveloping sphere. Water is everywhere: *sphaerae jacet intra viscera pressa*. 'It is manifest that the waters play the same part in the entrails of the Earth as do the humours and blood in ours . . .'; the natural place of water 'is no more above or around the Earth than the humidity of our substance is above or around our body'.[27]

Earth, water and fire no longer have their own sphere or natural place. All the elements intermingle; they are everywhere and are nowhere at rest: the winds blow in all directions; earth spreads and flies about in the great void of air in the form of fine dust.[28]

Another mistake of the Aristotelians was their choice of characteristic qualities ascribed to each of the elements. For example, how can we accept that earth is a cold element? According to Aristotle's reasoning, cold being removed as far as possible from hot, the coldest regions would be found at the centre of the globe and the hottest regions on the tops of mountains; experience contradicts this, seeing that mountainous regions are colder than the plains and that hot springs rise from the depths.[29]

In order to maintain the fine Aristotelian architecture, it would also be necessary to disregard the fires of Hell, or at least to deprive them of the property of rising, as Campanella recalls was done by Lactantius.[30] This argument, as we may imagine, does not appear in Giordano Bruno's treatises; but we find others penned by him, which without going beyond the limits of 'natural discourse' are hardly less curious. So we find that in *De immenso* (eighteenth and last chapters of Book IV, *De figura Telluris*) the author makes the observation that the theory of 'natural places' assigned to the four elements is incompatible with the Earth's sphericity. The heat of the tropics and the intense cold of the polar regions could in fact only be explained, if we accept the existence of a 'zone of fire', by ascribing a non-uniform depth to the said zone which would be very thick at the equator and absent at the poles where the layer of air would be directly in contact with the first of the celestial spheres, namely, that of the Moon. Consequently, it would not be really correct to speak of the 'sphere of fire'. As for the mass of air, it would assume a shape approximating to that of a cylinder—and no doubt that is why there are some (such as Thales) who have given the Earth itself a cylindrical form: *secundum quam forte rationem aliqui hanc figuram huic nostro globo tribuerunt.* This curious argument is developed in a gloss several pages in length, and the conclusion is reached that cylinders of air or fire do not exist any more than do spheres of the same, that they are phantastic concepts, and that one uniform aetheric space surrounds the Earth, Sun, Moon and all celestial bodies.[31]

b) *The geocentric error.* The central position of the Earth in the universe is another error of classical astronomy. It is to the credit of Copernicus that he finally made short work of the notion.[32] Those who exhausted themselves in fruitless efforts throughout the centuries in order to remain loyal to Aristotle's cosmology and to correct Ptolemy's calculations by multiplying the number of spheres and tangling up their orbits accounted for the phenomena at the expense of very improbable arrangements, whereas heliocentrism obtains the same end result by much easier ways. The common purpose of both systems being to explain the apparent irregularities of planetary motions, is not it in fact more satisfactory for the mind to see 'secondary effects' in these irregularities as 'projections of the motions of the Earth itself on the sky?'[33]

Numerous objections were raised by the Peripatetics to that; one of them being that if the Earth were not at the centre of the universe but, for example, nearer the East than the West, then the celestial bodies would not have the same apparent size on rising as on setting.[34]

This curious argument, that presumes the form of the cosmos and presupposes terrestrial immobility which would be a matter of proving in the first place, is not found in Aristotle's writings, but it must have been generally assumed by the defenders of geocentrism, for it appears in the *Trattato della sfera o cosmografia* written by Galileo in 1597 for the use of his students at Padua.[35]

The fact remains that geocentrism is based on some kind of experience, though it is a crude experience insufficiently controlled and corrected by reason, in other words, it is based on sensory illusions. There lies the weakness, and Bruno did not fail to stress the matter. In this connection he distinguishes two particularly deceptive illusions, equally difficult to eradicate.

The first is the optical illusion we have already mentioned in connection with the *horizon*: no matter where we are, that place is the centre of our field of vision, just as much on the Earth's surface as in the infinite space of the firmament; and that is why we are encouraged to ascribe to the planet we inhabit a privileged position to which it is not entitled any more than is any other celestial body.

The second illusion derives from gravity, which causes us to conclude that there is an absolute above and below in the universe, the below being the centre of the Earth. The fall of heavy bodies is a daily observational experience from which Aristotle draws the argument against the plurality of worlds. The motion that draws heavy bodies towards the Earth is a natural and not a forced or violent motion. It is, in fact, faster the greater the mass of the body that is moved, and the nearer it approaches its end point. In the case of violent motion, the contrary result is produced: 'the rapidity of motion would not increase towards the end, for a forced motion always slows down when the body that has given the impulse becomes more distant'.[36] However, if fall be a natural motion, then portions of earth located in another world would be attracted towards our centre, and consequently should naturally proceed upwards in the world to which they belong; similarly, heavy bodies belonging to our Earth should move naturally from the centre when they are attracted towards the centre of the other world.[37] Aristotle refused to accept such a contradiction in natural motions. Unfortunately, his theory resulted in untenable consequences: a heavy body cannot be moved away from the Earth except by violent motion; this motion will become weaker as the body gets further away from its centre, and conversely the centripetal force will increase in direct ratio to the distance; this conclusion is contrary to experience which shows (and Aristotle himself notes the fact) that the velocity of a heavy body increases during fall as it approaches the Earth.[38] The acceleration during fall proves that the heaviness of a body is less the further it is away from its centre; and Bruno gives the following explanation of this decrease in heaviness, which he attributes to the earliest Greek philosophers: 'It appears to me that the Ancients were right in thinking that the further a body is removed from the Earth, the more its heaviness is decreased on account of the thicker layers of interposed air.' That is in *De l'infinito*. He resumes the same theme in *Eroici furori* in order to illustrate the enhanced facility for contemplation when the soul approaches its principle: 'At the beginning the effort is very difficult, but it becomes easier according as the progress of contemplation becomes more fruitful. The further anyone flies away from the Earth, the more air will he find beneath him for his support, and so he will be less inconvenienced by gravity; it would be even possible to carry his flight so high, that without troubling to cleave the air, he would be unable to redescend, although it is generally considered easier to cleave the depths of the air in the direction of the Earth than in the direction of the other celestial bodies.'[39]

Whatever, after all, may be the reason for this phenomenon, we accept, although the fact has not yet been established by accurate experiments, that the tendency of a body to approach the Earth becomes weaker the further away it is, and that at a certain distance the tendency will disappear. Copernicus had already formulated this law. According to him, says Galileo, 'the natural propensity of the elementary bodies to follow the Earth's motion has a limited sphere, outside of which that natural inclination would cease.'[40] Bruno expresses the same idea, and he contradicts Aristotle, as he often does, by borrowing his language: 'Portions of earth come towards us from the air, because their sphere is here; but if their sphere were in the opposite direction [that is to say, if it belonged to the organism of another planet] they would go away from us and move in that direction. So also the waters, and fire. Water in its proper place is not heavy, and is not a burden on the beings that are in the depths of the sea.'[41]

As for the Earth itself, taken in its total mass, it is no heavier in the vast aether than a grain of dust floating in the air.[42]

What is true of the Earth is certainly so of the other celestial bodies: 'Know, then, that the Earth, nor any other celestial body is absolutely heavy or light; no body in its proper place is heavy or light. These differences [in weight] and condition have no import for the principal bodies, the perfect, particular individuals of the universe; they are suitable only for the separate parts of the whole when outside of their material limit, as though on a journey; nevertheless, they tend to the place of their conservation, like iron towards a magnet.'[43] It is therefore absurd to say of a body that it is in itself heavy or light; the Earth is no heavier in its region than Venus, Mars, the Moon, the Sun, Jupiter, Saturn and Mercury are in theirs.[44]

c) *The Earth's motions.* The question of terrestrial immobility is intimately linked with that of geocentrism. If the Earth lose its central position, it is obvious that it moves. However, the feeling that we have of being on a motionless Earth is sufficiently strong to make us sure of this lack of motion; so it becomes necessary to expose the sensory illusion which, once again, is the source of our error. If, wherever we may be, we are tempted to believe ourselves at the centre of the universe, by reason of the confusion that arises in spite of ourselves between the universe and our field of vision, a similar confusion inclines us to consider ourselves as the stationary reference point for all motion: 'As has been noted by the true contemplators, ancient and modern, of nature, and as is made manifest in a thousand ways by our senses, we are able to apprehend motion only by comparison with, and in relation to, some fixed object; he who finds himself on a moving boat in the middle of a river will not be aware of the movement of the boat, unless he knows that water flows its course and he can see the river banks. Therefore I have doubt and uncertainty about the repose and stillness of the Earth, and I believe that if I were on the Sun, the Moon or some other star, I should always seem to occupy the stationary centre around which all the surrounding bodies are revolving, when this globe where I am would on the contrary revolve about its own proper centre. That is why I am not sure of the difference between the mobile and the fixed.'[45]

In all this doubt, the arguments in favour of the immobility of the Earth remain to be refuted, and some of them are worth consideration. According to Aristotle, 'the Earth is necessarily stationary ... because heavy bodies when thrown upwards in a straight line[46] by violent motion fall again to their starting point'.[47] If the Earth had motion, it would be displaced during the ascent and fall of the heavy body, which would not return to the same point. This objection to terrestrial motion long remained a difficulty for the opponents of geocentrism. Copernicus gave a rather unsatisfactory explanation as to why a solid thrown vertically upwards falls to the same place: according to him it results from the identical nature of terrestrial things and the Earth. This is a return to the Aristotelian theory of natural places, for which Bruno substitutes the *impetus* of the Parisian Nominalists. The Earth is for him an 'organism'; we should say: a closed system. A moving body is not linked to the place of origin of its motion by the nature of that place (the Earth is not of a different nature from that of the other planets), but by the motion through which it is itself animated. A comparison of the Earth with a ship will make the matter clear: 'Suppose there are two men, one of whom is on the moving ship and the other is not; let us assume that each has a hand at about the same point in the air and that from this same point and at the same moment each allows a stone to fall without giving it any impetus. In the former instance, the stone will fall in a straight line without any deviation to the predetermined point, and in the latter instance, it will be left behind. . . . We cannot give any other reason for this difference except that things which are attached to the ship, or form part of it in some way or other, move with it; one of the two stones therefore carries within itself the impulse from the motive force which moves with the ship. The other stone does not share in this impulse. Whence it is manifest that the direction taken by a moving body is not determined by the starting point, nor the end point, nor by the medium through which it passes, but depends on the efficacy of the force impressed in the first place. . . .'[48]

Another objection to terrestrial motion, taken from the same passage in Aristotle's works as the one above, is summarized thus: all parts of the terrestrial whole tend by natural motion towards the centre of the Earth; a contrary motion, from the centre to the remotest part, can only be a violent motion; what is true of any portion of the Earth is *a fortiori* true of the whole Earth; consequently it would only be able to move as a result of a violent motion and 'under the action of a superior force', so that 'it must necessarily remain at the centre'.[49]

Bruno does not adopt the argument in that form. He goes straight to the alleged evidence implied in the passage from Aristotle but which the Aristotelians fail to state, namely that a force capable of moving the terrestrial globe does not exist: 'Some consider it difficult for the Earth to move, seeing that it is so large, so dense and so heavy a body.' What reply will you give them? asks Smith, already convinced of the inanity of the objection, but curious to know the arguments of Theophilus. The latter gives them immediately: no body, when in its proper place, is heavy or light. If we consider that the Earth is prevented from moving on account of its own mass, what shall be said about the other celestial bodies, which are just as large and even larger? We consider it impossible for the Earth to rotate on itself in twenty-four hours and revolve round the Sun in a year, and we assume 'that all these large and countless celestial bodies accomplish inordinately long circuits round the Earth, and so quickly'.[50] It will be noted that Bruno does not refute Aristotle's argument. As for that of Ptolemy relating to centrifugal force, he doesn't even allude to it. He is content to show that any argument put forward against terrestrial motion can be turned round because he demonstrates the absurdity of the hypothesis of diurnal motion of the whole firmament.

Having accepted as a fact that the Earth moves, it now remains to define the simple motions into which we can split its motion, which must be assumed to be complex, seeing that we have to account not only for the diurnal rotation of the celestial vault, but also for all the other phenomena that we can see: digression of the planets, sequence of the seasons, precession of the equinoxes. Seeing that Bruno takes the *De revolutionibus orbium coelestium* of Copernicus as his basis, we shall first of all very briefly summarize the Copernican theory so that we can then examine what Bruno retains, what he omits, and what he adds.

According to Copernicus, the Earth's motion is complex and results from three simple motions to which he adds, hypothetically, a fourth motion which he introduces for the purpose of making his observations agree with those of his predecessors.

The first motion is the diurnal rotation (*revolutio quotidiana*). 'It appears to carry round the whole universe, except the Earth. Now, if it is agreed that the firmament has no part in this motion, but that the Earth itself rotates from West to East (in the opposite direction to the apparent motion of the firmament) we can easily convince ourselves that it must really be so.'[51]

The second motion is the Earth's revolution round the Sun. It explains the apparent annual motion of the latter. The restricted digressions of Mercury and Venus had already suggested to Martianus Capella (Book VIII, chapter, *Quod tellus non sit centrum omnibus planetis*) that these two planets revolved round the Sun. That remark, said Copernicus, is not to be set aside as naught.[52] However, it is necessary to go further: 'Ptolemy claims that the Earth is in the middle both of the planets that deviate most from it and those whose digressions are restricted, such as Mercury and Venus; but the argument fails when we recall that the Moon [whose orbit is closest to us] is not restricted at all in its digression.'[53] Copernicus resolved the problem by making the Sun the centre of the system, and the Moon a satellite of the Earth carried along in the orbit of the latter.

The third motion was devised by Copernicus to explain the maintenance of the obliquity of the Earth's axis to the plane of the ecliptic, and, in consequence, the alternation of the seasons. From the time of Galileo it had been axiomatic in mechanics that the axis of a body rotating about a centre in simple translatory motion always remains parallel to itself, so that any point of a revolving body always faces the same direction in space (Fig. 1). Copernicus believed, as did

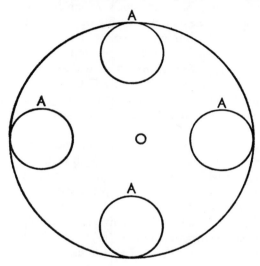

Figure 1

Ptolemy and in conformity with Aristotelian views on motion, that simple circular motion of a body should be such that if a point A were directed towards the centre, it would remain fixed in that direction, as though the body had been linked to the centre of its orbit by some kind of rigid tie-rod (Fig. 2).

The Earth's rotation about its axis (first motion) combined with simple translation as defined (second motion) certainly accounted for the succession of days and nights (at least as far as the polar regions), but not their variable duration in any region. As a result of such motion of translation, the Earth's axis would take the form of a frustum of a cone in the course of a year; one of the two hemispheres then enjoying perpetual summer and the other undergoing the rigours of endless winter. As that did not happen in reality, Copernicus resorted to the hypothesis of the third motion. He said, 'It is necessary to assume that the equator and the axis of the Earth have an interchangeable inclination [to the plane of the ecliptic]; for if they were fixed and only followed the motion of simple translation of the centre [of the Earth], inequality of the days and nights would not result. . . . A third motion in declination therefore exists, and it, too, is an annual revolution though in the opposite direction to the motion of the centre [that is to say, of translation). As a result of the effect of

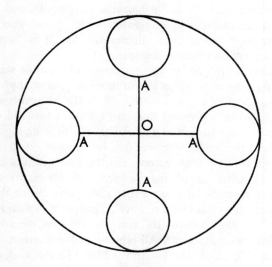

Figure 2

these two equal and opposite motions, the axis of the Earth and its equator always face very nearly the same region of space as if they were stationary.'[54]

If parallelism of the Earth's axis during its annual revolution is not strictly maintained, but is only 'very nearly' so, the reason is that the precession of the equinoxes must also be taken into account. Being in agreement with his predecessors as to the amplitude and regularity of that phenomenon, Copernicus proposed a fresh explanation: instead of relating it to a trepidation of the celestial sphere as did Thebit ben Korrah, he ascribed it (and he was the first to do so) 'to librations that cause the Earth's poles slowly to describe lines similar to a twisted garland'.[55] These 'librations' are linked with the 'third motion' of the Earth and must not be confused with the fourth motion, intended solely to reconcile the heliocentric system with certain observations of Ptolemy, Albatenius and Abraham Arzachel.

Whenever Giordano Bruno's opinion on a given subject seems to be sufficiently constant, we are always obliged to consult his various works in conjunction in order to determine the general doctrine. Here, we must alter our method, for we find two essays describing terrestrial motion in Bruno's writings: the first is in *La cena de le ceneri*, dialogue V, the second is in *De immenso*, chapters IX and X of Book III, and these two passages, written with several years' interval between them,[56] reveal such differences that it is impossible to summarize them in a single description.

In *La cena de le ceneri*, it is naturally Theophilus who has the honour of giving instruction in 'Brunonian philosophy' on such a delicate matter. Smith, fully convinced of the absurdity of geocentrism after all the arguments that had been put forward during the discussion (we are in fact at the end of the fifth dialogue and the final pages of the book), declares that he considers it as 'something most certain that we must accept that the Earth moves rather than believe in the existence of this platform with lamps riveted to it'; nevertheless, he adds, 'if you want to satisfy me, define the motions that are peculiar to this globe of ours'. Theophilus willingly complies as he feels sure that defining the motions will have the advantage of making their necessity clear. All regions of the Earth must have in turn all possible associations with the Sun. 'To this end, it is fitting and necessary that the Earth's motion be such that the ocean make way for the continent and conversely, that the cold regions become hot and conversely, that an habitable, temperate zone, become less habitable and less temperate and conversely: in short, that each part take the position of every one of the others with respect to the Sun, so that all participate in full life, all generation, complete happiness.'[57]

This preamble, whose insistence on final causes agrees as we shall see later on with Bruno's animistic conceptions, is followed by a detailed statement of the terrestrial motions asked for by Smith. They are four in number. The first is the diurnal rotation of the Earth about its own centre in twenty-four hours; the second, its revolution round the Sun in approximately three hundred and sixty-five days; the third results in the 'superior hemisphere' of the globe taking the place of the 'inferior hemisphere' 'relative to the universe'. The fourth, inadequately distinguished from the preceding one, brings about a complete inversion of the poles. Theophilus then describes which apparent motions of the firmament correspond to these four motions: diurnal rotation of the celestial vault, passage of the Sun through the various signs of the Zodiac, slow rotation of the eighth sphere (contrary to the diurnal rotation and completing itself in 49,000 years), and 'trepidation' of the same eighth sphere.[58]

It is not surprising that the passage in question has been the subject of severe judgements. Tocco has no trouble in finding 'grave errors' in it, but being unwilling to make a decision without having the advice of a competent judge, he appealed to Schiaparelli. The reply from this famous astronomer was in line with what was expected. Bruno, said Schiaparelli, 'describes the Earth's motions in accordance with the system of Copernicus, not as it is described in the book *De revolutionibus orbium coelestium*, but as his own imagination interprets it. For the want of a proper notion of geometry and being ignorant of the language of that subject, he gives his confused and indefinite ideas, which are put forward in even more confused sentences, explanations wrapped in such great obscurity that I believe it would be a hopeless task to try and clarify them.'[59]

This judgement is only too well founded and it is unnecessary to go over the matter, but we should like to add some remarks drawn from the same text of *La cena de le ceneri*:

1. The very short and very clear definition of the first motion—rotation of the Earth about itself in twenty-four hours—eliminates the useless corrections introduced by Copernicus.[60]

2. On two occasions Bruno insistently reminds his reader that the Earth's motion remains, for all its complexity, *one* motion, which is resolved into a number of simple motions only by our analysis: 'Whereas we were speaking of four motions, nevertheless they must be regarded as all merging into one compound motion.'[61]

3. These four simple motions are said to be circular, though in fact not one of them is truly so: *nullo però di quelli è veramente circolare*. We must be careful here not to imagine an anticipation of Kepler. Theophilus merely wants to draw the attention of his audience to the imperfect nature of the motions in respect of which ancient astronomy from the most remote times, had demanded that they be 'ordered and regular'; he does not intend to let his audience forget that im-

perfection and 'very nearly', in motions no less than in figures, are the rule in the tangible universe.

4. On account of this general rule and despite the opinion most widely held amongst the 'vulgar philosophers' (amongst whom we are constrained to count the Pythagoreans and Plato), astronomy, like all the other 'physical' sciences does not depend on mathematics: 'Many have endeavoured to find the true law governing these motions; their effort has been in vain and those who will give themselves the same trouble will not be any more fortunate, for not one of these motions is entirely regular and susceptible of a rigorous geometrical interpretation.'[62]

If it be hardly of interest for the progress of knowledge, at least the discourse of Theophilus has the merit of being particularly revealing as regards several presuppositions in Brunonian philosophy. He shows that if Bruno does not follow Copernicus in his calculations, then it is not only through ignorance, but also because he feels some hostility to all mathematical physics, which is explained, and justified in his view, by the way in which he understands the possibilities of matter on the one hand, and the free, constant action of the spiritual principle in every place on the other.

When he returned to the question of terrestrial motion in *De immenso*, Bruno had completed his astronomical knowledge in many respects. *La cena de le ceneri* was printed at London in 1584, the *De immenso* at Frankfurt in 1591. It is obviously difficult to give exact dates for the writing of those two works, but it has been established that Bruno had written some parts of his Latin poem during the time he was living in London. Nevertheless, it would seem that there can be no doubt but that several years separated the writing of the two passages which interest us: the fifth dialogue in *La cena* and the third book of *De immenso* (chapters ix and x).

Chapter ix, devoted to a panegyric of Copernicus, is one of the shortest (31 lines only), but the prose text which follows it occupies no less than about ten pages, borrowed entirely from *De revolutionibus orbium coelestium*, partly from the Letter of Dedication to Pope Paul III, and partly from the second chapter of Book I (pp. 382–385 and 385–389 of the Fiorentino edition). The second passage is divided into three paragraphs to which Bruno gives the following titles: 'Definition of the Earth's triple motion according to Copernicus;

Proof of the triple motion; That the [annual] motions of the centre and the inclinations (*sic*.) are not absolutely uniform.'[63] These two long quotations—which show his concern to give the reader an authentic survey of the matter under discussion, and concerning which reservations are made in the following chapter—are preceded by several lines of preamble in which Bruno thanks Copernicus for having been the first in a century lacking intellectual perception 'to declare boldly that which Nicholas of Cusa before him had been content to say in a whisper in his book *Docta ignorantia*'.[64]

We come then to chapter x, whose prose commentary is noteworthy in several respects. With regard to terrestrial motion, we note first of all complete absence of the fourth Copernican motion, which had been the subject of a confused interpretation in *La cena*, and which Bruno abandoned for the future; in addition, denial of the necessity for the third motion is particularly to be noted. In so far as it was designed to explain the maintenance of a parallelism by the Earth's axis, the hypothesis concerning this motion is in fact superfluous, as was shown by Galileo: it is the consequence of an erroneous idea of what a simple circular translatory motion should be.[65]

Did Bruno have an inkling of, or foresee, Galileo's principle? Tocco puts the question and remarks that the 'third motion' of Copernicus had already been rejected by Christoph Rothmann in a letter to Tycho Brahe dated 18 April 1590: He says, 'Seeing that the Earth is freely suspended in the air, why, if the centre be endowed with translatory motion, should not the inclination of the axis on this same centre be that which is required by Nature?... To my mind, Copernicus is most obscure at this point, and difficult to understand. These facts can be explained much more easily in another way without resorting to a triple motion, diurnal and annual, of the Earth.'[66] Bruno makes the same claim, if not 'almost in the same terms' (as Tocco says), at least in substance: '... The Earth achieves its purpose, namely the sequence of the seasons, the allotted amount of light and darkness, heat and cold if, in conjunction with the diurnal motion, it performs an oblique circuit round the Sun; there is no need to introduce a third motion.'[67]

We do not know when these lines were written, but the date and circumstances of their publicaton are known. The facts are as follows: the three Latin poems *De minimo*, *De monade*, *De immenso*, which form a trilogy, ought to have appeared in a single volume. Printing was started in the early months of 1591 by Wechel and Fischer at

Frankfurt, but Bruno had to leave that town when the final pages of *De minimo* were coming off the press. This poem was put on sale separately at the Spring fair; the work of printing was continued and completed during the year, with the result that the other two poems appeared in one volume at Frankfurt in time for the Autumn fair. There would not appear to have been any alteration to the text of the manuscript. In the circumstances, for Bruno to have derived any inspiration from Rothmann's letter, he must have had knowledge of it before the end of 1591—a possibility which cannot be entirely excluded. Nevertheless, as Tocco has pointed out, we should then have to assume that Bruno was well placed to know the secrets of contemporary astronomers for him to have been informed of a private correspondence so quickly. We shall be nearer the truth by crediting him with an intuition that does him more honour seeing that his ideas on astronomy were dubious. That was the opinion of Tocco and Schiaparelli.[68] The fact remains that Rothmann and Bruno could have had the same source of information about which we know nothing; but that is a gratuitous hypothesis, and we have no reason to suspect Bruno's sincerity here, for immediately before the sentence which we have just quoted Bruno states that the variable inclination of Copernicus *never* 'seemed to him to fit in with nature'. It might be convenient for the computator, but it did not occur in the reality of things.[69] Finally, we may add that simple circular motion of translation as understood by the Aristotelians evokes the picture of two bodies linked together, connected one to the other by a rigid link, which notion is quite contrary, as we shall see later, to the idea Bruno has of the freedom enjoyed by celestial bodies in the infinite space which is open to them.

It now remains to speak of one final motion which does not merge with, which does not *compound* with the preceding ones, and which, furthermore, is not peculiar to the Earth, but is common to all the celestial bodies. It is of a quite different nature from the others and is directly linked with divine action: it no longer depends on astronomy. No allusion to it occurs in *La cena* or in *De immenso*. A description of it is outlined in the treatise *De l'infinito* at the end of the first dialogue, where Philotheus, in a discourse which is rather obscure at first sight, describes the two principles of all motion.

> It is appropriate, I say, to consider, if you please, that there are two active principles of motion in everything: the one finite, according to the reason of the finite subject, and which moves in time; the other infinite,

according to the reason of the soul of the universe, or of the divinity, which is like the soul of the soul, which is complete in everything and makes the soul complete in everything; and this moves in an instant. The Earth, consequently, has two motions. Similarly, all bodies that move have two principles of motion, of which the infinite principle is the one that simultaneously moves and has moved, whence according to that reason, the moving body retains the utmost stability in its extreme mobility. This will be seen from the accompanying figure which represents the Earth, which is moved in an instant through the impulse of a motive force of infinite power (Fig. 3). Its centre moves from the point A to the point E, and turns from E to A, and as this displacement is instantaneous, it is simultaneously at A and E and at all the intermediate points; it departs and returns simultaneously; and seeing that conditions are always thus, the Earth is consequently always most stable. Similarly with respect to its motion about the centre, the East is at I, South at V, West at K and North at O; each of these points describes a circle as a result of an infinite impulse, so that each of them has simultaneously departed and returned; consequently, it is always fixed, it is where it was. So that, in fine, for these bodies to be moved by an infinite force is the

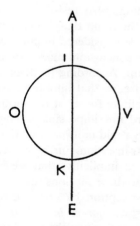

Figure 3

same as not to be moved; because to move instantaneously and not to move are one and the same thing. As for motion that depends on the other active principle, it proceeds from the intrinsic force, and consequently takes place in time and involves succession; it is therefore distinct from rest. That is how we are able to say that God moves everything, and that

201

is how we must understand that He gives the faculty of motion to everything that moves.[70]

Concerning the two motions distinguished by Philotheus, it goes without saying that the first one can be compounded of simple motions, as in fact is the case with the Earth. This first motion depends just as much as the other on the soul of the universe, and through this soul, on the divinity; but it 'requires time', for the immediate source is in the 'intrinsic force' of the moving body, a material body which obeys the laws of nature and to which a certain freedom is permitted. On the other hand, the second motion is immediately dependent on the divine action, and as potentiality and act, in God, are but one, it has no need for time for its development. To move and to have moved are but one for the infinite principle: *insieme insieme muove ed ha mosso*. The merging of time with instantaneity, *motus sine motu*, recalls the *creatio sine motu* of St Thomas Aquinas (*in his quae fiunt sine motu, simul est fieri et factum esse*) for which he gives the instantaneity of light as a physical symbol (*simul aliquid illuminatur et illuminatum est*).[71] According to Aristotle, the velocity of a moving body being inversely proportional to the resistance of the medium in which it is travelling, zero resistance ought to correspond to infinite velocity, with the result that the velocity would be infinite in a vacuum; but Aristotle considered infinite velocity to be an absurdity, and from that conclusion made an argument against the possibility of a vacuum. According to Bruno, velocity is related to the force of the impulse, so that infinite velocity of a moving body corresponds to the 'infinite force' of the motive agent; which statement is neither absurd nor impossible seeing that it envisages the reality of two infinitely rapid motions, one the rotation of the sphere about itself, the other translation. Furthermore, it must be recognized, and Philotheus does so implicitly, that we have left the realm of knowledge seeing that these motions are not observable; they are completely beyond perception by our senses, and we cannot distinguish them from rest: *movere in instante e non movere è tutto medesimo ed uno*. This lack of distinction between *quies* and *motus* in the extreme state is evidence of their identification with God; it is, as has been remarked, one aspect of the coincidence of opposites in the heart of the prime principle.[72]

Motion 'in an instant', not distinct from rest, reappears in *Eroici furori*, where it becomes a symbol of eternity. The Sun is its emblem, and the word *circuit* the motto. In fact, the expression *insieme*

insieme si fà ed è fatto, an exact translation of *simul fieri et factum esse* used by St Thomas Aquinas, is applied this time to the Sun's rotation and no longer to the Earth's; but it is of little moment, for the 'infinite' motion impressed by the Divine Wisdom, itself 'most mobile and most stable', is assumed to affect all the celestial bodies: 'thus the Sun always finds itself again in all points of the path it has traversed, for if it move in an instant, it follows that it moves and is moved as a whole, that it is likewise present at every point of the circumference and that motion and rest conjoin and unite in the Sun.'[73]

THE SUN

We know already that the Sun occupies the central position amongst the planets and that its diurnal revolution round the Earth is an illusion, as well as its annual passage through the Zodiac. Must we therefore conclude that it is stationary? or admit that is has a proper motion? Naturally, we are no longer speaking of infinitely rapid motion, supernatural as it were, and resulting from the divine impulse, but of a physical motion, a motion that should be observable, or at least one whose existence should be detectable from the facts of tangible experience. That is what Smith means in the fifth dialogue of *La cena de le ceneri*, when he puts a question to Theophilus about solar motion, expressing or feigning surprise that one could say that the Sun is a fire and at the same time claim that it is 'stationary and fixed in the midst of those wandering bodies amongst which we place the Earth'. Fire is the most mobile of all the elements: when we prevent the flames, 'the parts of the fire', from rising, when we retain them 'in the bowels of the furnace', they twist impatiently about themselves, whereas it is easy to keep portions of earth or water in position. If we judge the whole according to its parts, then motion is better suited to the Sun than to the Earth. The distinction that follows, relating to the 'mobility' of the various elements, is not of great interest, anyhow, seeing that it has been accepted that the Sun is not composed solely of fire; but Theophilus admits, rather apprehensively and only as an hypothesis, a rotatory motion of the Sun about itself and not about some other centre.[74] He speaks for himself, without committing the author: He says, 'Let this suffice, for as far as I can see Bruno has not wished to make any precise statement as to the motion or rest of the Sun.'[75] On the other hand, this statement is very clearly given in the third book of *De immenso*, chapter X: *De solis motu astrorumque fixorum ejusdem generis*. Bruno parts company here with Copernicus and proclaims Galileo.[76]

It was by reflecting on the causes of solar heat that he was led to adopt this position at a later date. When he wrote the dialogues in the vernacular, he claimed that the Sun consisted of various elements, that it contained water and earth, in the same way that the Earth contains water and fire, but that in its fiery parts it must be made of a non-fusible, non-liquefiable metal, luminous and hot in its own right.[77] Now, to accept the existence of this perpetually hot block of material, was not this a round-about way of returning to the incorruptibility of celestial bodies and the error of the Aristotelians that had been so often denounced?

A way must be found out of the impasse. So, in *De immenso*, Bruno again takes up the problem of solar heat and suggests an original solution—even though it has some relation to the earliest concepts of Greek cosmology. According to Thales, 'the fire of the Sun and of the celestial bodies is maintained by exhalations from the water'; but if the Sun be composed of all the elements, there is nothing to prevent us from assuming, without resorting to the myth of the generative ocean, that its fire is the result of combustion, exactly like the fire on our hearths. 'Light cannot be a simple substance'; 'its roots are in the opaque, as we can verify every day when we see a body burst into flame'.[78] There is no light without water (*neque usquam est ignea lux sine aqua*), and it is not in itself, but in the water that the flame finds its nourishment:

Flamma etenim lympha, non sese vescitur ipsa.[79]

That would explain the constancy of the Sun's light and heat in a far more satisfactory manner than by assuming an eternally incandescent mass; but we must assume:

1. The presence in the Sun of the same elements as are on the Earth (this is laid down as a principle).

2. The possibility that the Sun has to recover the nourishment absorbed by its fire and dispersed by its radiation throughout space.[80] This recovery does not seem to create a difficulty: Bruno compares it with the benefit derived by terrestrial oceans from rain and rivers which together replenish the water lost by evaporation;

but, curiously enough, he makes it depend on the rapidity of solar motion, as did the earliest Greek atomists who regarded the celestial bodies as 'revolving round the Earth and being enflamed by the rapidity of their motion'. There is one difference, however; having recognized this apparent revolution as an illusion, we are necessarily led to replace it by a rotation of the Sun itself.[81]

Sunspots. 'If we consider the body of the Sun, the centre looks like a world, there is a brilliant light like fire at the circumference, and in the intermediate zone there is a kind of watery cloud and a clearer air.' This passage from *De docta ignorantia*,[82] in which the Cardinal of Cusa stated the existence of sunspots long before the discoveries of Johann Fabricius, Galileo and Christoph Scheiner,[83] could only arouse the enthusiastic attachment of Bruno who quotes it first in *La cena de le ceneri*, and gives a full translation of it in the third dialogue of *De l'infinito*. 'The black colour of the Earth does not prove that it is inferior', said Nicholas of Cusa, and if there be dark regions in the Sun, we must assume that it is composed of different elements. Bruno made use of all that in his battle against Aristotle, and pressing his advantage he came to the conclusion not only that the Sun 'has regions of water like the Earth and regions of fire', and that humid, temperate and even cold regions are to be found there, but also that it is habitable and inhabited by living creatures. No doubt the fiery element dominates there, but life could be favoured by the influence of other celestial bodies. Such is the theory described by Philotheus: 'As animals live through the heat and light of the Sun on this cold and opaque Earth, so also do they live on that torrid and luminous celestial body through the coolness that is poured forth by the neighbouring cold celestial bodies.'[84]

THE MOON AND THE PLANETS

The third, fourth and fifth books of *De immenso* provide a survey of the planetary system, or rather the elements of a somewhat disordered description in which the author only too often betrays his ignorance and his suspicion of mathematical astronomy. On reading these passages, in which some happy intuitions are mixed with the most fantastic interpretations, one assumes that the supporters of geocentrism could not have regarded Bruno as a particularly dangerous opponent, and it is understandable why the heliocentrists were careful in making any appeal to his favourable testimony.

Some of his bold statements are accompanied by a sketch and an attempt at a proof: for example, the one concerning the Moon's motion round the Earth. It is a matter of experience that the Moon presents always the same face to the Earth, and it is also a proof that celestial bodies are not fixed to their spheres, as claimed by classical astronomy, but are free to move at their convenience.[84b] If the Moon were in fact fixed to its epicycle $ABCD$ (Fig. 4), it would present the same face N always to the centre F of the epicycle and not to the Earth. When the centre of the Moon is at A, the point nearest to the Earth will be the point G. This same point will, on the contrary, be the furthest away from us when the Moon is at C.[85] It seems superfluous to point out the weakness of this objection to the theory of

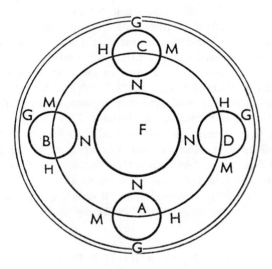

Figure 4

epicycles: the reasoning would be valid only if the point F were stationary with respect to the Earth, whereas it moves over the deferent.

The cosmography of *De immenso* completely misunderstands the nature of the Moon as a satellite, for not only does it make the Earth and the Moon two associated globes, each revolving round the other and neither having a privileged position with respect to the other, but in addition it postulates that these two heavenly bodies must be nearly equal in size: they differ no more than do two animals of the same species, or two adult men. This rule is extended, moreover, to all the planets in the solar system.[86]

MERCURY AND VENUS

There were reservations in the panegyric upon Copernicus in *De immenso*. The great astronomer is charged with four 'errors', two of which have already been mentioned: ignorance of the Sun's proper motion and the unnecessary hypothesis of a terrestrial 'third

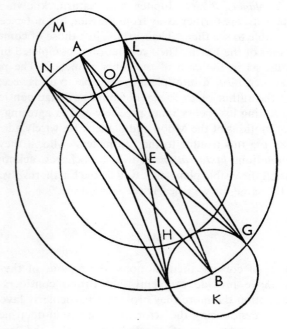

Figure 5

motion'; the third, which will be considered later, was retention of the sphere of fixed stars; and the fourth is to have given Mercury and Venus smaller orbits than the Earth and Moon possess, which is something Bruno says he cannot accept.[87]

According to Bruno, the two inferior planets should form a pair similar to that provided by the Earth and Moon; they should revolve about each other maintaining the same distance from the Sun as the other pair to which they would be diametrically opposed on their common orbit. This curious construction is shown on the accompanying diagram (Fig. 5). The circle with centre A is the orbit of the Earth and Moon; the circle with the centre B is that of Mercury and Venus; the large circle AB is the common orbit of the two pairs which revolve about the centre E (the Sun); their revolutions are completed *aequali passu* in one year. This arrangement is intended to explain why the 'inferior' planets are always seen in the vicinity of the Sun and why they appear to us to be nearer the Sun than the Earth.[88]

The superior planets. Mars, Jupiter and Saturn, known as the 'superior' planets, are further away from the Sun, but not excessively so, as we are able to see them. Their orbits, like those of comets, are inclined to that of the Earth. Their revolution is completed in about the same time as in the case of the other planets.[89] The possible existence of other, more distant planets, invisible to us, is accepted.[90]

No doubt the author of *De immenso* would have had considerable difficulty in stating his theory more precisely and in agreeing it with the apparent motions of the Moon and planets. He wisely adopts the course of leaving this trouble to the 'geometers' who, if they make their interpretations *juxta rationem*, will, he believes, acknowledge the fact that all the visible planets, as well as the Earth, revolve about the Sun in the same, or very nearly the same, time.[91]

COMETS

The substance of comets, their motions, the regions of the sky in which they move provide problems that Bruno considers to be worthy of attention the more they provide a particularly favourable opportunity of denouncing the error of Aristotelian doctrines concerning the incorruptibility of celestial bodies and the crystalline nature of the spheres.

Several brief allusions in the vernacular treatises (*La cena*, *De l'infinito*) to cometary theory tend rather to arouse than to satisfy the reader's curiosity. Still, in the fourth dialogue of *De l'infinito*, Philotheus 'takes proof from the comets' to show that it is not true that a heavy body, whatever its distance, is drawn towards the centre (or the organism) to which it is attached (*al suo continente*). If the comets be, as Aristotle claims, 'of terrestrial matter', then they ought to fall on the Earth and not maintain themselves in the sphere of fire. We know, as Bruno says in his foreword, that he is merely concerned here with getting the Aristotelians to contradict themselves: 'The argument is not based on true physical principles but on suppositions in Aristotle's philosophy.'[92]

As to the true nature of comets, Philotheus says that he will talk about it later, *facendo propria considerazione di quelle*, and that he will prove that these 'blazes' (*quelle accensioni*) are not meteors belonging to the sphere of fire, but are celestial bodies, 'as was truly said and well understood by the Ancients.'[93] This promise was kept, not by Philotheus, for the remainder of the dialogue is not concerned with comets, but by Bruno—who in the circumstances is indistinguishable from his spokesman—in the poem *De immenso*, Book IV, chapters ix and xiii, Book VI, chapters xix and xx. Whilst writing *De immenso*, Bruno had to make himself conversant with the work of Tycho Brahe, whose name is not once mentioned in the vernacular dialogues, but is mentioned several times with the greatest praise in the Latin poem. If Bruno then designates Tycho Brahe as 'the first astronomer of his times'—*astronomi nostri temporis, quorum Thico Danus nobilissimus atque princeps*—in spite of what he regards as his (Tycho's) adherence to geocentrism, it is on account of his observations on comets and his anti-Aristotelian conclusions, as is proved by the context.[94]

Contrary to the opinion of the 'earliest philosophers', called 'the Ancients' by Bruno, amongst whom Anaxagoras, Democritos, the Pythagoreans, Hippocrates of Chios may be mentioned, Aristotle links comets as well as meteors and the Milky Way with the sublunary world. According to him, they originated in 'the upper part of the universe surrounding the Earth' as a result of collision between a dry exhalation and a fiery element. He says, 'It is rather as though one threw a fire-brand on to a heap of straw'; and this blaze, being close to the celestial spheres, is 'carried along in their circular motion of translation'.[95]

Bruno not only does not accept this theory, but it seems of the utmost importance to him to refute it, for if Aristotle is mistaken on this point, then his whole cosmic architecture must collapse. Consequently, he appeals more than usual to the authority of other learned men. Several pages of *De immenso* are devoted to reporting their observations and opinions. First of all, he notes that the Peripatetics have abandoned the theories of their master, the most recent of them being convinced that the appearance of comets happened *ultra solem*, and very frequently round the orbits of Venus and Mercury; he recalls that Albumasar, alone amongst the Arabs, had located a comet *supra Venerem*; but he expatiates especially on the observations of the 'author of *Homocentrica*' (Fracastoro) and of Cardanus on the comet of 1531, as well as those of another Italian astronomer on the comet of 1532, which it was impossible to locate *infra lunam*. He makes three references to the New Star, which appeared *supra Saturnum* in November 1572 and was first observed by 'the astronomers of Oraniborg'—that is to say, by Tycho Brahe and his assistants —and which remained visible for sixteen months, from the beginning of November 1572 until April 1574.[96]

The appearance and disappearance of the unusual celestial body struck the imagination of contemporaries; Cardanus identified it with the star that guided the Three Wise Men to Bethlehem, and Théodore de Bèze, captivated by this hypothesis, concluded that it announced the Second Advent of Christ. Tycho Brahe established that it could not be a comet, any more than a planet, seeing that the complete absence of parallax made it necessary to place it in the region of the fixed stars. It was, in any case, a *celestial body*, and its momentary appearance provided the opponents of Aristotle with yet another argument against the dogma of the inalterability of the heavens.[97]

Bruno does not make use of this argument: he seems to be unaware of Tycho Brahe's conclusions on the matter; he quotes Cornelius Gemma only, whom he accuses of Aristotelian prejudices. In his (Bruno's) opinion, the celestial body that appeared in 1572 is a comet *sine coma*, and it was this absence of coma that determined the astronomers not to call it a comet, but, more prudently, to call it the *sidus novum*.[98]

As for the comet of 1577, Bruno refers to the descriptions given by Helyseus and Cornelius Gemma, which showed that it, too, was a celestial body.[99] Finally, he depends on the observations of Claus Cimber, assistant of Tycho Brahe, and of Christoph Rothmann of the comet of 1585.[100]

From these writers, with whom he is imperfectly acquainted, Bruno is principally concerned to have a confirmation of his own doctrine, as he had outlined it in the treatise *De l'infinito*, and which may be reduced to the following four statements:

1. Comets are not cones of fire, but are solid celestial bodies of the same nature as planets.[101]

2. Consequently, they cannot belong to the terrestrial organism (that is to say, to the sub-lunary world), otherwise they would be drawn towards the Earth by reason of their weight.

3. Not only do they have a physical constitution in common with the planets, but also their motion round the Sun; there is this difference, however, their orbits are inclined with respect to those of other planets.

4. As a result of this inclination of their orbits they must cross the planetary orbits in order to complete their revolution; and that is incompatible with the Aristotelian hypothesis of solid, impenetrable spheres.[102]

Tocco is of the opinion that Bruno, being better informed of Tycho Brahe's work, had probably abandoned his theory of comet-planets in favour of that of fugitive comet-apparitions, unstable celestial bodies, composed of a less solid matter, for in this latter theory he would have found a very strong argument against the dogma of the immutability of celestial bodies; whereas, following his own doctrine, the occultation of comets simply results from their passage into a part of the sky in which they disappear from our view.[103] All the same, it seems difficult to prejudge Bruno's ignorance on this particular point. Being primarily concerned to prove that all celestial bodies are of the same nature, all composed of the same elements as the Earth, and believing that he had sufficiently established this truth in respect of the planets, the assimilation of comets to planets with their orbits inclined to each other was sufficient to enable him to demolish three fundamental assertions of Aristotelian cosmology: uniform circular motion of celestial bodies, unchangeability of the firmament, impenetrability of the crystalline spheres.

In the light of the passages that we have mentioned or quoted, we are now in a position to describe the planetary system as understood by

Bruno. The Sun is at the centre; stationary, that is to say, lacking all motion of translation seeing that it is inside the system, though it is endowed with a proper motion of rotation on itself. Seven planets move around it, and their times of revolution are practically the same. The nearest four planets form two pairs: Earth–Moon and Venus–Mercury. The remaining three, called superior planets, are only slightly more distant. Beyond, we may assume that there are other, invisible planets. Comets, of the same nature as planets, revolve also round the Sun; their occultation is the result of the inclination of their orbits; sometimes they are in the vicinity of the Earth, but more often they are at such distances that they are out of sight.

It is only too obvious that this picture does not reproduce reality; but the inherent mistakes will be judged quite differently according as we compare them with the data of traditional astronomy, with the progress accomplished during the sixteenth century, or with the latest acquisitions to knowledge. In the last instance, it is furthermore necessary to distinguish the unquestionable acquisitions that may be treated as definitive from the general hypotheses on which our concept of the universe rests at the present time and which it may be assumed are not exempt from modification. The conclusions advanced by Felice Tocco on this matter are most significant.[104] Tocco has the credit of giving a balanced judgement on Bruno; it is midway between that of those who in their excessive enthusiasm as apologists have sought to make Bruno one of the initiators of modern science, and of those who refuse to accord him any position in the history of science, because they consider that his intuitions, even if confirmed, were not supported by adequately certain knowledge. On the credit side, Tocco puts Bruno's vision of a boundless universe on the same level as his bitter fight against Aristotelian double physics; on the other hand, he believes it right to take him to task for an animism on which 'modern science has turned its back'. However, to us at the present time, does not it seem that Tocco, when he formulated those criticisms, was limited by the views of Euclidean geometry and the very strict mechanicalism that was current when he wrote his work (between 1880 and 1890)? Today, perhaps, we might be tempted to appraise Bruno's doctrines on infinite space and the internal energy of matter in a quite different way, but experience has made us careful and more disposed to fear the contradictions of the future than was the case in the last century. The history of science, like that of the arts, has ceased to be normative.

We feel that we are in a better position to pass a valid judgement on Brunonian cosmology if we restrict ourselves to relating it to the disciplines of his period: that is what was then accepted and taught, what had just been found out by science, what was the subject of discussion; here then is what an educated man round about 1580 could know, what the author of *De immenso* ought to know or would have been wrong not to know. Even on this more solid ground caution is needed. Bruno is frequently in disagreement with contemporary astronomers, not excepting those for whom he expressed the greatest admiration (Copernicus, Tycho Brahe); and when this disagreement is stated it may be the result of misunderstanding, but not of complete ignorance. On reading a book such as *De revolutionibus orbium coelestium*, it happened more than once that Bruno had the feeling of a mistake (quite incapable as he was of carrying on the discussion on a truly scientific plane), and of finding himself nearer to the truth. Such was the case, for example, when he rejected the terrestrial third motion of Copernicus or when he refused to accept perfect circularity of celestial motions as a prescribed rule.

'To account for the appearances' was the unanimous desire of cosmologists since ancient times, but they are divided into two groups according to the degree of reality they ascribe to their systems. Whereas the ambition of the 'mathematicians' is limited to converting the universe into symbols, the 'physicists' have its laws in mind and sometimes flatter themselves by stating them, that is to say, they endeavour to relate all the phenomena of the universe to their true causes. On this score, it is obvious that Bruno must be placed, together with Aristotle, in the group of 'physicists', and beside his great opponent; however, that does not detract from the vigour of his anti-Aristotelian polemics, which could only be rendered more bitter from the fact that the disagreement depended on the order of things and not on the results of calculation. Bruno would certainly have opposed Aristotle and the Aristotelians less arduously if they had regarded geocentrism as no more than a convenient explanatory hypothesis without prejudging the realities.

As a reaction to the tendencies of the Academy, Aristotle showed a certain suspicion in regard to mathematics; for present-day philosophers, he said, 'mathematics has become the whole of philosophy', whereas it should be cultivated only with 'a view to the rest'.[105] Bruno goes even further in that direction. He never misses an opportunity to oppose 'mathematics' and 'physics', and he does so with all the more tartness, the less he understands the importance of mathematics as the preliminary requirement for all knowledge of nature. He cannot even glimpse the fruitfulness of theories which, in his view, are mere chimeras and vain imaginings.

In the anonymous preface 'To the Reader' in the first edition of *De revolutionibus orbium coelestium*, Andreas Osiander, when dealing with 'the hypotheses contained in this work', takes the precaution of distinguishing between the Copernican interpretation and reality of which it does not claim to be a picture. 'It is unnecessary', he said, 'for these suppositions to be true, or even probable. . . .' They are admirable in that they facilitate calculation, 'but he who would hold as true those things invented for another purpose would be even more foolish after that study than before he had started it'.[106] At the beginning of the third dialogue of *La cena*, Bruno gives a free translation of the passage from Osiander and accompanies it with commentaries the tone of which is easily detected. He doesn't know 'what ignorant and presumptuous ass' was so bold as to attach 'this super-preliminary epistle' to the work of Copernicus. 'What a fine janitor! Consider the way in which he opens the door in order to introduce you to this most honourable knowledge [of nature], without which measurement, calculations, geometries and perspectives are but the diversion of clever fools.' Copernicus himself, however, in his preface of dedication to Pope Paul III was not afraid to assert the motion of the Earth, which he treats 'not only as a mathematician who assumes, but as a physicist who proves'.[107]

Bruno was undoubtedly quite right in what he said about Osiander, in the sense that, safely entrenched behind anonymity, Osiander, whose idea of the subject was different from that of Copernicus, had allowed it to be assumed that his preface was the work of the author of *De revolutionibus orbium coelestium*. In fact, several historians of astronomy, even Delambre, have been deceived by it.[108] All the same, Bruno has not acknowledged, or rather did not want to acknowledge the interest of an otherwise noteworthy passage, the main purpose of which was to show that an astronomer must make suitable hypotheses on which to base an accurate calculation—*ut calculum recte instituant*—and that he must select the one which is easiest to understand from those that occur to him—*quae comprehensu sit quam facillima*.

In the same spirit and with significant relentlessness Bruno opposes the theory of epicycles; appended spheres, attached to planetary orbits in order to explain their retrograde motions. The subject irritates him and he continually reverts to it: in *La cena, De l'infinito, De minimo* and several time in *De immenso*.[109] Indifferent to the brilliancy of the theory, he becomes indignant at those 'who invent this stuffing and filling of unequal orbits, of various diameters, and other plasters and medicaments with which nature is treated to such a point that it becomes amenable to Master Aristotle, or some such one, to conclude that all motion is continuous and uniform about the centre'.[110]

This quotation is one of the most revealing as regards Bruno's mind. Not only does he not accept that this architecture of the spheres could be in accordance with reality, but he regards the purpose for which it was assumed and the presuppositions giving rise to that purpose as being absurd. Aristotle laid down the unchangeability of celestial bodies and the simplicity of their essence as a principle, and he was led to the idea that simple natures agree with simple motions.[111] In addition to the unchangeability of celestial bodies, Bruno rejects the perfect circularity of their motions, being in disagreement on this latter point with both Aristotle and Copernicus. The planets, according to him, do not describe circles round the Sun, but describe something like spirals, the complex combinations of arcs of circles. This idea had already been mooted by Fracastoro, and it is possible that Bruno borrowed it from the *Homocentrica* of the Veronese astronomer. Even so, he would have had a quite different purpose in view, for he is less concerned with defining the laws governing celestial motions than in showing that these laws are peculiar to the bodies themselves and that they discover for themselves, so to speak: '*per suas gyrent methodos*'.[112] Splitting up the planetary motions into perfectly circular simple motions is not only unnecessary when these wandering bodies cease to be attached to their spheres, but is also against nature. Perfect motion in the physical universe is just as inconceivable as perfect form. 'No body is absolutely spherical'— *semplicemente rotondo*, and similarly there is no motion by natural bodies that does not deviate, and to a great extent, from simple, uniform revolution about a centre.[113]

This theme is merely outlined in *La cena de le ceneri*; it is developed on one page in *De immenso*, where its source is indicated: 'The Platonists have said, and they were not entirely wrong, that there is no form, properly speaking in the material universe'—*neque ullam formam vere in materia esse dixerunt Platonici (et non omnino male)*; nor does 'a true man or a true horse' exist in this world (*scil.*, the

215

idea, or perfect figure of a man or a horse) any more than does circular motion in the mathematical sense of the word: *Mathematice . . . circularis motus non est in materia.*[114]

If circles be replaced by spirals or ellipses, the impossibility of a strict path still remains; the impossibility is valid for any perfect motion: there is no celestial body that describes a definable geometrical figure in the course of its revolution. That is Bruno's belief. Must we, consequently, decide in favour of a universal disorder? No! because the celestial bodies, freed from all fetters, choose the paths that suit the necessities of their life and abide by them, *secondo l'anima propria.* The description of the planetary system no longer depends on cosmic geometry but on astrobiology which makes the motion of celestial bodies a function of their nature; and if the irregularity of this motion reveals the imperfection of the tangible being, it is equally a sign of its freedom.

NOTES

1. E. Cassirer, *Individuum und Kosmos,* Leipzig, 1927, p. 9.
2. *Eroici furori, Argument,* p. 112.
3. See Jean Baruzi, *Création religieuse et pensée contemplative,* pp. 137–138.
4. *Eroici furori,* I, iv, p. 232.
5. See *La cena de le cerneri,* III, p. 149, note by Giovanni Aquilecchia.
6. '. . . *dove* [i.e., in the first book of *De revolutionibus orbium coelestium* by Copernicus] *non solo fa ufficio di matematico che suppone: ma anco di fisico che dimostra il moto de la terra. Ma certamente al Nolano poco se aggionge che il Copernico, Niceta Siracusano Pitagorico, Filolao, Eraclide di Ponto, Ecfanto Pitagorico, Platone nel* Timeo (*benchè timida, et inconstantemente per che l'avea più per fede che per scienza*) *ed il divino Cusano nel secondo suo libro* De la dotta ignoranza, *ed altri in ogni modo rari soggetti, l'abbiano detto insegnato e confirmato prima: perchè lui lo tiene per altri proprii e più saldi principii, per i quali non per autoritate, ma per vivo senso e raggione, ha così certo questo, come ogn'altra cosa che possa aver per certa.*' *La cena,* III, pp. 149–150.
7. *La cena,* III, pp. 164 ff (*Terza proposta del dottor Nundinio*).
8. '*Nonne ad lucem diam, atque calorem*
    Est ut vertantur potius, legemque capessant ?'
De immenso, III, iii (*Opera,* I, i, p. 330).
9. *Theologia platonica,* XVIII, 3.
10. The Aristotelians themselves were forced to admit it: '*Dicunt tellurem esse in medio, et hoc nulla luce demonstrare possunt eorum quae circumcurrere videntur; neque enim magnitudinem, neque motus regularitatem eandem planetae servant ad illam, sed* (*et ut omnes quoque peripateticis imbuti principiis mathematici observant*) *ad solem.*' *De immenso,* III, iii (*Opera,* I, i, p. 337).
11. '*Non etenim nos minus lunae et cuicumque astro, astrum coelumque semus, quam universa ipsa nobis esse possint.*' *Acrotismus* (*Opera,* I, i, p. 69); see *La cena,* I, p. 100: '*Atteso che nonpiù la luna è cielo a noi, che noi alla luna.*'
12. See Maurice de Gandillac, *La philosophie de Nicolas de Cues,* Paris, 1941, p. 51 and note 55.
13. *La cena,* I, p. 92.
14. *Ibid.,* I, pp. 94–100.
15. Under the title *Septem argumenta quibus Arist. et alii probant diversam esse substantium corporum superiorum et inferiorum istorum. Opera,* I, ii, pp. 1 ff.

16. '*Pars ego sum stellae atque illustris lampadis, et quem*
Aethna premit nullus, siquidem est sine pondere tellus
In membris comperta suis. Sic ergo solutus
Liberque . . .'
De immenso, IV, i (*Opera*, I, ii, pp. 1–3).

17. *De l infinito*, III, pp. 248–249. On the question of the elements and the quintessence, see also *De immenso*, III, iv and ix; IV, ix (beginning of the chapter); V, i (*De compositione omnium ex elementis, utque quodammodo omnia sint in omnibus*) (*Opera*, I, i, pp. 341 and 380; I, ii, pp. 46 and 111); *De monade*, V (*Natura quatuor elementorum in coelo*) (*Opera*, I, ii, p. 394).

18. '*Repetivimus ut astrorum partes etherogeneas esse oporteat: lux enim et calor similia accidentia, atque iis contraria, non nisi in corpore composito esse possunt.*' *De immenso*, IV, vii (*Opera*, I, ii, p. 36).

19. *De immenso*, III, *title* of chapter iv (*Opera*, I, 8, p. 341); see *De immenso*, III, ii (*Opera*, I, i, p. 328); *La cena*, III, pp. 163–164.

20. *De immenso*, IV, iii (*Opera*, I, ii, p. 15 ff). The full title of the chapter reads, *De ascendu in coelum et vera mundi contemplatione, et primo Telluris species ab orbe Lunae prospicitur*. The first part of this title indicates the scope of chapters iii to vii.

21. '*Dic: ubi sylvarum species? ubi flumina, montes,*
Stagna, lacus, urbes, brumae discrimen, et aestus? . . .'
De immenso, IV, iii (*Opera*, I, ii, p. 16).

22. *De immenso*, IV, chap., iii *et seq*. (*Opera*, I, ii, pp. 23 ff). Title of chapter iv: *Hinc Telluris species ab orbe seu astro Veneris, haud aliter quam Venus a nostro orbe declaratur*.

23. *De immenso*, IV, iv; *De l'infinito*, III, pp. 350–351.

24. '. . . *mi ricordo de aver visto il Cusano di cui il giodizio so che non riprovate, il quale vuole che anco il sole abbia parti dissimilari come la luna e la terra.*' *La cena*, III, p. 163; see *De l'infinito*, III, pp. 343–345; Nicholas of Cusa, *De docta ignorantia*, II, 12.

25. '*Sicut vero non est sine suo calore, luce et igne Tellus, ita neque omnino Sole sine sua opacitate et frigore, cum accidentibus aliis circa aquam, quae communis est omnium substantia.*' *De immenso*, IV, vii (*Opera*, I, ii, p. 42). In the last paragraph of this chapter, which starts as follows—'*Ita etiam animalibus nostri generis crediderim partes habitabiles illic* [*i.e.*, *in Sole*] *esse raras*'—the author tries to show how and to what extent the Sun is habitable.

26. '*Sudor . . . extra animalibus pellem, aut membranae exiguae spissamen.*' *De immenso*, V, xiii; *Comparatio maris ad corpus Telluris* (*Opera*, I, ii, p. 162). See *De l'infinito*, III, pp. 354–355.

27. *De immenso*, V, xiii (*Opera*, I, ii, p. 160); *De l'infinito*, III, p. 354.

28. *De immenso*, VI, xviii and V, xi (*Opera*, I, ii, pp. 215 and 151).

29. '*Proinde cur frigidum maxime distare dicunt ab extreme calido nempe igne, quod est illis in orbis lunae concavo, quando alti montes sunt frigidiores quam planities, et planities frigidior interioribus terrae partibus? (In membris quippe subterraneis aquae non glaciantur, non nivescunt, non inspissantur, sed potius accenduntur, sed potius multos undique de subterraneis locis ignes cum liquidissimis fluminibus et calidissimis interdum erumpere qui concrescunt in superficie telluris:) constantius in altioribus ejus regionibus, constantissime vero, aut saltem primo in media ipsa regione aeris, quae frigidarum impressionum mater est.*' *De immenso*, III, v (*Opera*, I, i, p. 353).

30. '*Propterea Lactantius igni infernali aufert exhalationem.*' Tommaso Campanella, *La prima e la seconda resurrezione* (*Theologicorum libri xxxvii–xxxviii*). Edit. Romano Amerio, Rome, 1955, p. 208.

31. '*Stat enim circa Tellurem, Solem, Lunam et omnia unum idemque aethereum spacium.*' *De immenso*, IV, xviii (*Opera*, I, ii, pp. 100–110).

32. The eulogy on Copernicus, outlined in *La cena*, I, pp. 92–94, is resumed and followed by a long quotation from *De revolutionibus omnium coelestium* in *De immenso*, III, ix (*Opera*, I, i, pp. 380–389).

33. A. Koyré, '*Les étapes de la cosmologie scientifique,*' in *Revue de synthèse*, July–December, 1951, p. 18.

THE COSMOLOGY OF GIORDANO BRUNO

34. *'Phebus*
    Mane oriens mundo majorem ostenderet orbem
    Et serotino tenuatior iret in axe.'
De immenso, III, v (*Opera*, I, i, pp. 347–348).
35. The *Trattato della sfera, ovvero Cosmografia* (*Opere*, Edizione nazionale, II, pp. 203 ff), published after Galileo's death, was long considered to be apocryphal because of the arguments from Peripatetic astronomy which were developed in it. Its authenticity was established by the editors of the *Edizione nazionale* of Galileo's works. See the *Avvertimento* to the work in Vol. II, pp. 205–209.
36. *De coelo*, I, 8, 277 *b*.
37. *Ibid.*, I, 8, 276 *b*–277 *a*.
38. *De immenso*, VI, xix (*Opera*, I, ii, p. 220).
39. *'Ma pur mi par oltre vero quello che è de credere che volesser dir gli antichi, che un corpo per maggior lontananza acquista minor attitudine (che loro chiamorno proprietà e natura per il lor frequente modo di parlare); perchè le parti, alle quali è soggetto molto aria, sono meno potenti a dividere il mezzo e venire al basso.' Infinito*, IV, p. 376.—'. . . *il principio è durissimo, e secondo che si fa più e più fruttifero progresso di contemplazione, si doviene a maggiore e maggior facilità. Come avviene a chi vola in alto, che quanto più s'estoglie de la terra, vien ad aver più aria sotto che lo sustenta, e conseguentemente meno vien fastidito dalla gravita; anzi tanto può volar alto che, senza fatica de divider l'aria, non può tornar al basso, quantunque giudicasi che più facil sia divider l'aria profondo verso la terra che alta verso l'altre stelle.' Eroici furori*, II, i, p. 335.
40. *Dialogo dei massimi sistemi, Giornata seconda* (*Opere*, Ed. naz. VII, p. 264).
41. *'Le parti della terra da l'aria vengono verso noi: perchè qua è la lor sfera. La qual però se fusse alla parte opposta, se partirebbero da noi, a quella drizzando il corso. Così l'acqui, così il fuoco. L'acqua nel suo loco non è grave, e non aggrava quelli che son nel profondo del mare. . . .' La cena*, V, p. 211.
42. *'Nec Tellus plus immenso gravis aethere habenda est,*
    Quam quae sic vacuo corpuscula in sere pendent.'
De immenso, VI, ix (*Opera*, I, i, p. 188).
43. *'Sappi che né la terra, né altro corpo è assolutamente grave o lieve: nessuno corpo nel suo loco è grave né grave né leggiero. Ma queste differenze e qualità accadeno non a' corpi principali, e particolari individui perfetti dell' universo: ma convegnono alle parti che son divise dal tutto, et che se ritrovano fuor del proprio continente, e come peregrine: queste non meno naturalmente si forzano verso il loco della conservazione, che il ferro verso la calamita. . . .' La cena*, V, p. 211. See Copernicus, *De revolutionibus orbium coelestium*, I, 8: '*Rectus ergo motus non accidit nisi rebus non recte se habentibus dum separantur a suo toto et ejus deserunt unitatem.'*
44.   *'Non gravis est igitur Tellus magis in regione*
        Hac, quam sit propria in regione Venus, Pyroentes,
        Cynthia, Apollo, Dios, Saturnus, Mercuriusque,
        Quotquot in immenso sunt scintillantia campo,
        Unus, continuus, quae circumplectitur, acr.?'
De immenso, II, iii (*Opera*, I, i, p. 262).
45. '. . . *come han notato gli antichi e moderii veri contemplatori della natura e come per esperienza ne fa manifesto in mille maniere il senso, non possiamo apprendere il moto se non per certa comparazione e relazione a qualche cosa fissa: perchè, tolto uno che non sappia che l'acqua corre e che non vegga le ripe, trovandosi in mezzo l'acqui entro una corrente nave, non avrebbe senso del moto di quella. Da questo potrei entrare in dubio ed essere ambiguo di questa quiete e fissione; e posso stimare che, s'io fusse nel sole, nella luna ed altre stelle, sempre mi parrebe essere nel centro del mondo immobile, circa il quale tutto il circostante vegna a svolgersi, svolgendosi però qual corpo continente in cui mi trovo, circa il proprio centro. Ecco come non son certo della differenza di mobile e stabile.' De l'infinito*, III, p. 349.
46. χατά στάθμην, *perpendiculariter.*
47. *De coelo*, II, 14, 296 *b*, 20–25.
48. *'Se dumque saranno due, de quali l'uno si trova dentro la nave che corre, e*

218

l'altro fuori di quella: de quali tanto l'uno quanto l'altro abbia la mano circa il medesimo punto de l'aria; e da quel medesimo loco nel medesimo tempo ancora, l'uno lascie scorrere una pietra, e l'altro un'altra; senza che gli donino spinta alcuna: quella del primo senza perdere punto, ne deviar da la sua linea, verrà al prefisso loco: e quella del secondo si trovarrà tralasciata a dietro. Il che non procede da altro, eccetto che la pietra che esce dalla mano del uno che è sustentato da la nave, e per conseguenza si muove secondo il moto di quella, ha tal virtù impressa quale non ea l'altra che procede da la mano di quello che n'è di fuora, benche le pietre abbiano medesima gravità, medesimo aria tramezzante, si partono (se possibile sa) dal medesimo punto, e patiscono la medesima spinta. Della qual deversità non possiamo apportar altra raggione, eccetto che le cose che hanno fissione o simili appartinenze nella nave, si moveno con quella: e la una pietra porta seco la virtù del motore, il quale si muove con la nave. L'altra di quello che non ha detta participazione. Da questo manifestamente si vede che non dal termine del moto onde si parte; né dal termine dove va, né dal mezzo per cui si muove, prende la virtù d'andar rettamente: ma da l'efficacia de la virtù primieramente impressa, dalla quale depende la differenza tutta.' Le cena, III, pp. 180–181.

49. *De coelo*, II, 14, 296 b–297 a.

50. *Le cena*, V, pp. 210–211 and see p. 223.

51. *De revolutionibus orbium coelestium*, I, 5.

52. '*Minimum contemnendum arbitror quod Martianus Capella scripsit existimans quod Venus et Mercurius circumcurrent Solem in medio existentem.*' *Ibid.*, I, 10.

53. *Ibid.*

54. *Ibid.*, I, 2. Passage reproduced by Bruno in *De immenso*, III, ix (*Opera*, I, i p. 386) under the title *Definitio triplicis Terrae motus per Copernicum*.

55. '*. . . librationes concurrentes invicem efficiunt, ut poli terrae cum tempore lineas quasdam describant corollae intortae similes.*' *De revolutionibus orbium coelestium*, III, 3.

56. According to a conjecture of F. Fiorentino, which is now universally accepted, parts of *De immenso* were written at London, that is to say, during the same period as *La cena* (1584); but the Latin poem (published in 1591) was continued and finished during Bruno's stay in Germany. The chapters to which we refer undoubtedly belong to this later period of writing.

57. *La cena*, V, pp. 224–225.

58. *Ibid.*, V, pp. 225–227.

59. F. Tocco, *Le opere latine di Giordano Bruno*, p. 313, note 3.

60. Copernicus still believed that the terrestrial globe, like that of the other planets, was *solid*. In order to account for the different motions of the Earth, it was therefore necessary for him to have a motion which restored the Earth's axis to the same extent as the motion of the globe caused it to tilt. See A. Koyré in Copernic, *Des révolutions des orbes célestes*, Paris, 1934, p. 148.

61. '*E da considerare che quantumque diciamo esser quattro moti nulladimeno tutti concurreno in un moto composto.*' *La cena*, V, p. 226; see also p. 227.

62. '*. . . benchè molti si siano affaticati di trovar la vera regola de tali moti; l'han fatto, et quei che s'affaticaranno lo faranno in vano: p[er] che nessuno di que' moti è fatto regolare et capace di lima geometrica.*' *Le cena*, V, p. 227.

63. *Definitio triplicis Terrae motus per Copernicum; Demonstratio triplicis motus; Quod non omnino aequales sint motus centri et inclinationis.*

64. '*Mirum, o Copernice . . . ut ea quae suppressiore voce proxime praecedente aetate in libro* De docta ignorantia *Nicolaus Cusanus enunciarat, aliquanto proferres audacius. . . .*' *De immenso*, III, ix (*Opera*, I, i, p. 381).

65. Galileo Galilei, *Dialogo dei massimi sistemi*, *Giornata terza*. Ed. naz. VII, pp. 424–425.

66. Tychonis Brahe, *Epist. astron.*, pp. 186–187; quoted by F. Tocco, *Le opere latine di Giordano Bruno*, p. 315, note 2.

67. '*Satis enim Tellus assequitur finem suum varandorum temporum, et mensurae lucis ac tenebrarum, calidi atque frigidi, si cum motu diurno componat obliquum circa solem circuitem absque tertio illo motu. . . . Tertius ergo ille declinationis motus contra centri motum reflectens, hoc tantum quaerit ut axis terrae et in ipso maximus*

parallelorum aequinoctialis in eandem fere mundi partem spectent: hoc autem non ad naturam rei et momenta pro quibus Tellus moveatur, sed astronomica phaenomena, idque (quod ego capere possum) magna cum difficultate atque Genii remurmuratione quadam.' De immenso, III, x (*Opera*, I, i, pp. 393–394).

68. Cf. F. Tocco, *Le opere latine di Giordano Bruno*. p. 316.

69. '*Centrum quippe Telluris secundum ipsum verius inter polos zodiaci discurrit: et hoc pro quadruplici anni tempestate poterat ei sufficere; sed reclamantibus mundi polis et tota illa reliquarum stellarum constantia cum verticali circulo et horizonte (quos in proposito statarios congoscere oportet) quasi a natura revocante ad suppositiones divertere coepit cum sua illa inflexione, quam convertibilem inclinationem appellat: quam licet mathmatici pro eorum usu non incommodam inveniant (utpote qui magis implicitis et abstrusis et absurdis naturae torminibus assuerint alias suas construere tabulas pro cujusque motus regula et anomalia), mihi tamen nunquam satis naturae adcommodata visa est.'* De immenso, III, x (*Opera*, I, i, p. 393).

70. '*Dico, dunque, che nelle cose è da contemplare, se così volete, due principii attivi di moto: l'uno finito secondo la raggione del finito soggetto, e questo muove in tempo; l'altro infinito secondo la raggione dell'anima del mondo, overo della divinità, che è come anima de l'anima, la quale è tutta in tutto e fa esser l'anima tutta in tutto; e questo muove in instante. La terra dunque ha dui moti. Così tutti gli corpi che si muoveno, hanno due principii di moto; de quali il principio infinito è quello che insieme insieme muove ed ha mosso; onde, secondo quella raggione, il corpo mobile non meno è stabilissimo che mobilissimo. Come appare nella presente figura, che voglio significhe la terra; che è mossa in instante in quanto che ha motore di virtù infinita. Quella, movendosi con il centro da A in E, e tornando da E in A, e questo essendo in uno instante, insieme insieme è in A ed in E ed in tutti gli luoghi tramezzanti; e però insieme insieme è partita e ritornata; e questo essendo sempre così, aviene che sempre sia stabilissima. Similmente, quanto al suo moto circa il centro, dove è il suo oriente I, il mezzo giorno V, l'occidente K, il merinozio O; ciascuno di questi punti circuisce per virtù di polso infinito; e però ciascuno di quelli insieme insieme è partito ed è ritornato; per consequenza è fisso sempre, ed è dove era. Tanto che, in conclusione, questi corpi essere mossi da virtù è medesimo che non esser mossi; perché movere in instante e non movere è tutto medesimo ed uno. Rimane, dunque, l'altro principio attivo del moto, il quale è dalla virtù intrinseca, e per conseguenza è in tempo e certa successione; e questo moto è distinto dalla quiete. Ecco, dunque, come possiamo dire Dio muovere il tutto; e come doviamo intendere, che dà il muoversi al tutto che si muove.'* De l'infinito, I, pp. 305–306.

71. St Thomas Aquinas, *Summa theologica*, I, quaestio 45, art. 2, ad tertium.

72. D. W. Singer, *Giordano Bruno*, London and New York, 1950, p. 85.

73. *Eroici furori*, I, v, p. 260.

74. '*Si potrebbe concedere che il sole si muova circa il proprio centro, ma non già circa altro mezzo.'* La cena, V, p. 214.

75. *La cena*, V, p. 215.

76. *Opera*, I, i, pp. 389 ff. See Galileo, *Istoria e dimostrazioni intorno alle macchie solari*, Ed. naz. V, p. 133.

77. '*Bisogna . . . che il sole, secondo quelle parti che in lui son lucide e calde, sia come una pietra o un solidissimo infocato metallo.'* De l'infinito, III, pp. 345–346.

78. '*. . . radices in opaco lux habet, ut sat,*
        Commonstrant nobis flammantia corpora semper.'
De immenso, IV, ix (*Opera*, I, ii, p. 49).

79. *Ibid.*, IV, vii, gloss and line 56 (*Opera*, I, ii, pp. 37 and 34).

80. '*Materieque opus est aeterna in corpore tanto,*
        Quae quoties absumpta fuit, resolutaque in auras,
        Sit toties iterum certum renovata per orbem . . .' and the continuation.
Ibid., IV, vii, lines 57 ff (*Opera*, I, ii, pp. 34–35).

81. '*. . . se circum convertitur ille.'* Ibid., IV, vii (*Opera*, I, ii, pp. 35–36).

82. *De docta ignorantia*, II, 12.

83. Their observations on sunspots date from 1610 and 1611.

84. *De l'infinito*, III, pp. 344–346; *La cena*, III, p. 163. See the notes by G. Gentile and G. Aquilecchia in the editions quoted.

84*b*. '*Quod vero astre non sint affixa orbibus, sed suo ipsamet centro, animoque adpellant quo illis condicit atque lubet, in libro illo, tabellaque illa, quae est in vultu lunae legere possumus.*' *De immenso*, III , iii (*Opera*, I, i, pp. 338–339).

85. *Ibid.*

86. '*Cum tellus sit ejusdem speciei atque luna, reliquique planetae, et unaquaeque species (ut omnes cognoscunt) sit determinata ad maximam minimamque quantitatem, sicut adultorum hominum est ratio qua non sit statura minor, et ratio qua non sit statura major (monstris nihilominus in tanto rerum illustriorum ordine praetermissis), ita et in ordine planetarum, atque constantium astrorum non ad quantamlibet, sed ad certam latitudinem alia aliis majora intelligere oportet et minora.*' *De immenso*, III, iv (*Opera*, I, i, p. 345).

87. '*Proinde nec in eam possum currere sententiam qua Mercurium atque Venerem minores circulos a Telluris atque Lunae circulo comprehensos, constituit efficere.*' *Ibid.*, III, x (*Opera*, I, i, p. 395).

88. *Ibid.*, pp. 395–398; see also IV, v and V, vii (*Opera*, I, ii, pp. 25–29 and 142–144).

89. '*Conveniens est, omnium planetarum motum circa solem annuum esse vel aequalem, ut Lunae, Telluris, Mercurii, Veneris, qui sunt in eodem circulo, vel quasi aequalem. . . .*' *De immenso*, V, viii (*Opera*, I, ii, p. 145).

90. '*Plurima perpetuo credenda latentia cursu
     Quae non ad speculi veniunt rata munia nostri.*'
De immenso, V, viii (*Opera*, I, ii, p. 144).

91. *Ibid.*, p. 145.

92. '*Settimo, da le comete si prende argomento che non è vero che il grave, quantunque lontano, abbia appulso o moto al suo continente. La qual raggione corre non per gli veri fisici principii, ma dalle supposizioni della filosofia d'Aristotele, che le forma e compone da le parti che sono vapori ed exalazioni de la terra.*' *De l'infinito, Argomento del quarto dialogo*, p. 279.

93. *De l'infinito*, IV, pp. 379–380.

94. *De immenso*, I, v (*Opera*, I, i, p. 221). The comets of 1577, 1585 and 1590 had been observed by Tycho Brahe.

95. Aristotle, *Meteorologia*, I, 6–7.

96. *De immenso*, IV, ix, gloss (*Opera*, I, ii, pp. 51–53). A Latin translation of the works of Albumasar had been printed at Augsburg (1488 and 1489), and subsequently at Venice (1506 and 1515). The works of that writer must have been known to Giordano Bruno who had read, amongst others, the *Flores astrologiae* (perhaps apocryphal), in which it is said that all the planets at the moment of creation were in the sign of the Ram. Bruno refers to this belief in *Eroici furori*, II, i, p. 300—Fracastoro's *Homocentria* had been published in his *Opera omnia*, Venice, 1555; and the *De subtilitate* of Cardanus at Lyons in 1580—The star of 1572 had been observed by Tycho Brahe and his assistants, but not at Oraniborg, as the expression ab *Uraniburgicis astronomis* might lead one to believe. Building of the observatory at Oraniborg was not started before 1576.

97. See F. Hoefer, *Histoire de l'astronomie*, Paris, 1873, p. 329.

98. *De immenso*, IV, xiii and VI, xx (*Opera*, I, ii, pp. 74 and 226–227).

99. *Ibid.*, IV, xiii (*Opera*, I, ii, pp. 70–71).

100. *Ibid.*, VI, xx (*Opera*, I, ii, pp. 228–229)—The comet to which reference is made in *De l'infinito* (written before 1585) could be that of 1582, also observed by Tycho Brahe. That is the assumption made by Kuhlenbeck, as well as by Gentile (*De l'infinito*, IV, p. 379 and note 3).

101. Tycho Brahe in his treatise *De cometa anni 1577* (printed in 1588) did not give a clear pronouncement on the physical constitution of comets. F. Tocco considers that Bruno could not in any case have known of that work (see *Le opere latine di Giordano Bruno*, pp. 318–319). There is, however, some doubt on the matter.

102. '*Nunc satis est quod pereat illud non fissile, non penetrabile coelum.*' *De immenso*, I, v (*Opera*, I, i, p. 221).

103. *De immenso*, IV, xiii (*Opera*, I, i, p. 74). At the period when Bruno was writing, many Aristotelians had already ceased to look upon comets as sheaves of fire *intraconcava Lunae*, as Bruno himself points out; for example, Jan Édouard du

Monin in his poem *L'uranologie ou le Ciel*, Paris, 1583, maintains 'that a comet is a star, contrary to the opinion of Aristotle':

> *Que si me detraquant du sentier ancien,*
> *Je n'en suis le parti de mon Stagirien,*
> *C'est tout un à present: ma Verité jurée*
> *Me promet saufconduit à la maison sacrée.*
> *Et quoi? si plus hardi je fiche de mes clous*
> *L'astre crinier sanglant, la Comete, chez vous?*
> *Que les grans promeneurs [i.e., the Peripatetics] bâtissent*
> *De seche exhalaizon pour tourner en fumée . . .*
> *Nous n'oterons donc pas par semblable moien*
> *A l'astre chevelu le droit de Citoien*
> *En la Cité des cieus . . .* (fol. 80 and 84).

104. *Le opere latine di Giordano Bruno*, pp. 414–415.

105. *Metaphysica*, I, 9, 992 a.

106. *Des révolutions des orbes célestes, Livre premier* (edited and translated by A. Koyré), Paris, 1934, pp. 28–31.

107. *La cena*, III, pp. 146–149.

108. Nevertheless, contemporaries (Tiedemann Giese and Pierre de la Ramée, amongst others) had suspected that the *Preface* could not have been written by Copernicus. The real author's name was revealed by Kepler (*Astronomia nova*, Prague, 1609).

109. *La cena*, III, p. 165; *De l'infinito*, III, p. 338; *De immenso*, III, v and vi (*Opera*, I, i, pp. 363–364 and 368), etc.

110. '... *forzeni quantosivoglia color che fingono queste borre ed empiture de orbi disuguali, di diversità de diametri, ed altri empiastri, e recettarii, p[er] medicar la natura sin tanto che venga al servizio di Maestro Aristotele, o d'altro, a con[c]hiudere che ogni moto è continuo e regolare circa il centro.'* *La cena*. III, p. 165.

111. *De immenso*, III, vi (*Opera*, I, i, p. 365). See Aristotle, *De coelo*, I, 3, 270 b.

112. *De immenso*, III, vii (*Opera*, I, i, p. 369).

113. '*Così ... de moti che noi veggiamo sensibile et fisicamente ne' corpi naturali, non è alcuno che di gran lunga non differisca dal semplicemente circulare, et regolare circa qualche centro.*' *La cena*, III, p. 165.

114. *De immenso*, III, vi (*Opera*, I, i, p. 362). See also chapter vii (pp. 367 ff).

VIII

The countless universes

The planets, comets and even the Sun having been accorded the same nature as the Earth, and being composed likewise of elements, Aristotle's double physics then found itself overthrown, and the homogeneity of the universe was affirmed within the limits of what we call the solar system. It remains to be shown and, if possible, proved, that this homogeneity extends to the infinite universe. Bruno makes no distinction between the two questions, which are but one, as far as he is concerned. If we have so far avoided discussing the ultimate sphere or the sphere of fixed stars, it was because we did not want to tackle all the difficulties at once, and also in order to make a better distinction between the domain in which Bruno, during his contest with the Aristotelians, took his bearings from Copernicus, and that other domain in which he had to venture, if not alone, then at least without any support from well-informed astronomy.

As regards his argument, it is inspired by the same methods. In the first place it consists in showing that the objections of the Aristotelians to the homogeneity of the universe, whether it be a question of the lower spheres or the sphere of fixed stars, as well as to its infiniteness imply certain presuppositions, and that the objections fall to the ground as soon as these presuppositions are no longer accepted. We shall revert to this in the first dialogue of *De l'infinito*: —*Che dilatazione è questa?—Che margine è questa?*[1] a preliminary skirmish which makes it clear that Brunonian philosophy just as much as the adverse doctrine is based on an act of faith. A problem concerning the infinite universe will never allow of one rigorously definite solution. Whatever the solution of which there may be an inkling— and may be desired—the argument must be based on a general hypothesis that can be shown to be more or less plausible by reasoning and observation of the phenomena. The starting hypothesis of traditional astronomy, and of even the more recent Copernican astronomy, is that of a finite universe, organized round a fixed centre, the Earth or the Sun; Bruno's hypothesis is that of an 'infinite and unportrayable' universe.

THE ILLUSION OF THE CELESTIAL VAULT

The weakness of a system that claims to assign a limit to the universe becomes apparent from the fact that this limit varies from century to century and seems to be more and more difficult to define. Spheres are added to spheres. The last sphere for Aristotle was the eighth. His followers were constrained to add a ninth, and then a tenth, which contains no stars but is responsible for motion. The eleventh sphere had recently been introduced, and a twelfth was already raising its head.[1b]

These uncertainties and continual modifications provided Bruno with material for raillery[2] and valuable confirmation of his own doctrine into the bargain. The horizon of the firmament widened itself even to the eyes of those who would have restricted it; the supporters of error were set upon the path of truth in spite of themselves.

Nevertheless, their hesitation related only to the detail of cosmic architecture and did not prevent them from clinging blindly to the certainty that the sphere of fixed stars, whatever the number assigned to it, is not a mere appearance but is a physical reality whose very name of firmament expresses its solidity. This vault, or 'ceiling' as Bruno is pleased to call it, is strewn with stars all of which are supposed to be at the same distance from the Earth—a convenient representation, and one which is justified to a certain extent by the remoteness of those celestial bodies. That very remoteness, however, provides Bruno with a prime reason for suspecting that observers of the sky have once more been deceived by an optical illusion. He compares them to a man of little discernment looking at the trees of a forest, and being aware that the nearest ones are at different distances from him, yet thinking that the most distant ones are all on the same line. Sueh a lazy interpretation of appearances gives rise to error which is supported by the musings of the imagination. Here, I see 'unequal distances', therefore they exist; there, they cease to be detected by me, therefore they no longer exist.[3] Further penetration into the depths of the forest would no doubt suffice to undeceive me, but I prefer to exercise the mind rather than make that effort to undeceive myself: the mind creates an illusory world which satisfies me so long as it is coherent, and which I then appraise as such provided the evidence of my eyes agrees with an arbitrary geometrical construction that has been substituted for the realities of nature.

Seeing that the depths of the firmament are not accessible to us, as they are in the case of a forest, we are unable, as regards stellar distances, to correct the errors of a first impression by subsequent experience, namely through a better view. Whenever reason comes to the aid of senses, it deduces the necessary conclusions from trials made in accordance with the means at our disposal.

If the stars be located at unequal distances from the Earth, then the distances between them will be very different from those assigned to them, when they are shown projected on the celestial vault. To an eye at O, a star B will merge with star A; or, if it is not situated exactly on the radius OA produced, it will seem to be very close, even if it be much further away than stars C and D, viewed at different angles.[4]

THE DIMENSION OF THE UNIVERSE

The errors that persisted in 'vulgar' astronomy in respect of stellar distances from the Earth as well as the distances between individual stars have a common origin in the extreme remoteness of the alleged 'sphere of fixed stars'; so, we are now brought back to the problem of the dimensions of the universe, a problem which has undoubtedly been resolved by the affirmation of infinite space, but it may be raised anew starting from cosmographical data and forgetting the theological or philosophical arguments that have been urged already.

The dimensions ascribed to the universe have increased continually from the time of Plato to Ptolemy. (By *universe*, we mean here the cosmos, or more simply the visible sky, neglecting any hypothesis about the existence of an ἀπείρων.) In this respect, the history of ancient astronomy is one of continual progress, hardly interrupted by several backward trends. For example, take the distance of the Earth from the Sun. According to the *Timaeus*, the celestial bodies are located in the sphere of fire. The nearest is the Moon, whose orbit marks the lower limit of that sphere; the Sun follows immediately after, and the distance between it and the centre of the Earth, which is also the centre of the universe, barely exceeds eight terrestrial radii. The *Epinomis* assumes it to be much further off, seeing that the Sun is admitted to be larger than the Earth; whereas,

THE COSMOLOGY OF GIORDANO BRUNO

according to the calculation from *Timaeus* and being given its apparent diameter, it ought to be noticeably smaller.[5] Aristarchas (third cent., B.C.) moved the Sun to a distance of 360 terrestrial radii; Ptolemy, using a method devised by Hipparchos, gave a figure of 1210. This figure was scarcely subjected to any revision up to the end of the Middle Ages. The matter came under consideration again in the sixteenth century, but starting from the same uncertain data.[6] A contemporary of Galileo, by name, Joseph Gaultier de La Valette, astronomer at the college of Aix-en-Provence, repeated the calculation of Hipparchos, and thought that he had a result nearer the truth; he published it in 1618, giving his result as 1218 terrestrial radii; this corrected value was just as illusory as the earlier ones, for the required answer is 23,452. It was not till the close of the seventeenth century that Cassini obtained an almost correct result by using a totally different method.

As regards the extreme limits of the universe, they were placed according to the *Timaeus* at the limit of the sphere of fire, that is to say, at a distance of 18 terrestrial radii. Being moved further back in succeeding ages, the limits of the universe appeared much more remote to sixteenth-century astronomers, but not enough to make it possible to imagine the Earth revolving round the Sun. The resistance to geocentrism in the time of Copernicus, as well as in the time of Aristarchas, was based on objections of a scientific nature considered to be insurmountable, rather than on religious convictions. François de Foix, Bishop of Aire, gave a sympathetic description of the Copernican system in his commentary to the *Pimander* (1579); and Cardinal de Bérulle, no doubt drawing upon François de Foix, wrote concerning heliocentrism: 'This new idea, hardly popular for a knowledge of the stars, should be so for a knowledge of salvation.'[7] He thought that a universe with the Sun, the source of all light, at the centre, would be better suited to the divine majesty, and he lets us conjecture his regret that geocentrism should have become so firmly established as the truth.

Indeed, it seemed to be the case. The opponents of Copernicus had no need to resort to the authority of dogma in their refutation of heliocentrism. The absence of stellar parallax and the invariance of the angular distances of two given stars, whatever be the point of observation on the Earth's surface, were already giving rise to the thought that the dimensions of our globe are negligible in ratio to the distances between it and the sphere of fixed stars. If we assume

226

that the Earth is endowed with motion of revolution round a stationary Sun, points of observation may be chosen at the two extremities of the diameter of the terrestrial orbit. We should then be able to confirm the *annual parallax* of a fixed star. This annual parallax, however, is almost unobservable. The greatest that has been determined is less than one second and relates to a star in the constellation Centaurus. Parallelism of two visual rays was absolute for the contemporaries of Copernicus. To accept the annual revolution of the Earth round the Sun, then made it necessary to accept also, as regards the fixed stars, their displacement to infinity 'which seemed contrary to common sense and scientific spirit'.[8]

Neither the suggestions of common sense, nor the demands and strictness of scientific spirit embarrassed the intrepid champion of the 'true philosophy' who, having laid down the infiniteness of the universe as a principle, saw no difficulty about the distances to which the heliocentric system necessarily removed the stars. Bruno, as has been pointed out, was 'almost the only one' of his time to make a physical reality of infinity, but precisely for the reason that he was 'neither astronomer, nor scientist'.[9] That is a severe criticism, but its severity indicates that ignorance is capable of opening the paths of discovery when it passes beyond the obstacles that only await a fresh progress in knowledge in order to be overthrown. After having denied to the Sun itself the privileged position so long accorded to the Earth, Bruno ends by dehumanizing the universe, reduces the final resistance to anthropocentrism and obliterates its last vestiges by removing the nearest stars to unmeasured distances.

In doing so, he was only responding to a desire of his times. For, if he should be the only one, or 'almost the only one', to assert the infinite 'in act'—an untenable paradox for the metaphysician, and a superfluous hypothesis for the scientist—he none the less expresses thereby the spirit of an epoch whose tendency was to enlarge the celestial horizon beyond all measure. Astronomers, who were faithful to geocentrism, found themselves constrained to free the Earth from the henceforth uncertain, mobile limits of a universe whose plan, but not the scale, was maintained by the Copernicans, who were more daring.

This extension of the frontiers of the universe announced by the philosophers was a scientific revolution whose effects were not slow in making themselves felt beyond the realm of science: in poetry and the fine arts. Man saw the firmament with other eyes, and painters gave witness to this new vision which they were the first to interpret. The geometrical skies of Romanesque paintings, symbolically decorated with circular orbits against golden Byzantine or Gothic backgrounds gave place to less abstract skies, still restrained, but with the quiet rhythm of urban or rustic scenery, prudently encircled with foliage or architectural motifs. These gave place in ever increasing numbers to animated skies, deep and gaping, which disturb more than they reassure, and certain of which fill with terror: the chaos from which St Michael breaks free, by Tintoretto in the Dresden Museum; the sky of the Trinity, by Bassan at the Church of Angerano, in which the mantle of the Eternal Father rises in a spiral as though caught up in an immense void; the impetuous whirlwinds in the Assumptions by Malosso; chasms of brilliance from which the Holy Spirit of Pentecost falls in a rain of fire.

THE PLURALITY OF WORLDS

Although the problems of the plurality of worlds and of the infinite universe are closely connected and, to certain minds, are hardly to be differentiated, nevertheless each of them involves solutions independent of the other.

Thomas Digges, the earliest astronomer to support the hypothesis of an infinite universe, put forward a heliocentric scheme in 1576 in an enlarged edition of *Prognostication Everlastinge*, written by his father Leonard Digges; his scheme was very similar to that of Copernicus, except for the last sphere, which was replaced by an endless field strewn with stars. On the other hand, Leonardo da Vinci, whilst dismissing the possibility of a 'given infinity', logically contradictory, accepted the existence of several universes comparable with ours and obeying, like ours, the general laws of Ptolemaic astronomy, each of them being organized about an 'earth', the centre of attraction and stationary pivot of the concentric spheres.[10]

Bruno, for his part, does not separate the two problems of the infinite universe and of the plurality of worlds; and the positive solutions he provides seem to him to imply each other. The so-called 'fixed' stars distributed throughout space are so many universes and mobile worlds. Their immobility which it is fitting to substitute for their impossible diurnal revolution round the speck of dust that is our globe, is only a semblance. If the constellations seem to form unchangeable patterns in the sky, the reason is simply that any change in their relative positions is undetectable by us on account of their extreme remoteness.[11] In the 'unimaginable' universe, it becomes possible to accommodate not only one Earth revolving round the Sun, but an infinity of other suns and other earths.

This doctrine, described at length in the fourth and fifth dialogues of *De l'infinito*, had already been outlined in *La cena*, and no doubt had been taught by Bruno at Noli in 1576 and at Toulouse in 1581.[12] On this point, it is unlikely that Bruno's opinion had ever altered. As for the arguments on which it is based, they are to be found in his criticism of Aristotelianism, more particularly in his twofold, detailed refutation of *De coelo*. The most important ones may be grouped under three headings: the theory of place and heaviness; the void and tangent universes; the problem of the one and plurality and of the superiority of the one ('theological' argument).

a) *The theory of place and heaviness.* According to Aristotle, every element has its proper place from which it cannot be displaced except by violent motion and to which it tends to return. The light elements rise to the upper or peripheric regions; the heavy elements fall downwards, or towards the centre. In this way we have earth, water, fire and air as strata in the sublunary world, and above we have the quintessence, the subtle and unchangeable matter which constitutes the celestial spheres up to the final one, beyond which there is no place. We have already seen how Bruno rejected this theory in so far as it applies to the sublunary world and the planetary system.[13] He considers it just as inapplicable to the alleged sphere of fixed stars, which is now no longer the envelope of the cosmos, but the 'immense region of the aether', homogeneous space stretching to infinity, the receptacle of more distant worlds of the same nature as the Sun, Earth and planets, formed from the same elements, and obeying the same laws.

The distinction between the *universe* and *the worlds*, which is emphasized by the very titles of Bruno's cosmological works, was not new. The possibility of a plurality of worlds had already been formulated in the thirteenth century by Aristotle's opponents, who were careful not to restrict the divine power by laying down the oneness of the cosmos as an absolute principle. Seeing that there was then no reason to doubt Ptolemaic astronomy, the other possible worlds were imagined as being similar to the geocentric universe of the Aristotelians, with the same stratification of spheres of elements and celestial spheres.

That was how Albertino described matters when he put the point of view of the Aristotelians in the fifth dialogue of *De l'infinito*. The arguments relating to the arrangement of the elements round the centres of the many other supposed worlds are the fourth and fifth: if two universes are in juxtaposition (argument 4) the centre of the one will be further away from the centre of the other than from its own periphery;[13b] consequently there will be a greater distance between similar elements than between contrary elements, which is absurd.[14] Let us now suppose that seven universes are in contact, one being in the middle, and the other six forming a circle round the first (argument 5). The difficulty is the same as before, but is aggravated, for this time the centre of the innermost universe is equidistant from the six points of contact between its periphery and those of the tangent universes. 'This being so, it follows that there will be several *horizons* . . . round one single centre . . . so that the upper elements will become more powerful than the lower ones, and will have an advantage over the latter, thereby provoking dissolution of the entire mass.'[15]

These two arguments are repeated in *De immenso* (VIII, v), but they will be sought in vain in Aristotle's *De coelo* and in the works of the early commentators.[16] They were only put forward in order to introduce the refutations that follow, and in order to link the problem of the plurality of worlds with that of the multiplicity of 'centres' and 'horizons', that is to say, in the last analysis, with the problem of heaviness. The interdependence of the two problems had, moreover, long been recognized. Leonardo da Vinci brought it into the open; when he envisaged the possibility of a mass in equilibrium in space, he asked, what will be the motion of a heavy body 'placed at the same distance from two worlds far apart from each other'.[17]

The plurality of worlds consequently implies that of centres of gravity, which Copernicus had already asserted as far as the celestial bodies composing the solar system are concerned. When, indeed, he puts the Sun at the centre of the universe, he refrains from making it the unique centre of attraction for all heavy bodies. He said, 'For myself, I consider heaviness to be nothing more than a certain natural craving with which the architect of the universe in his divine providence has endowed the parts of each one of them so that they can exist in unity and integrity, coming together in the form of a globe. We may believe that this tendency is shared in the same way by the Sun, the Moon and the other wandering celestial bodies.'[18] Copernicus, faithful in this matter to the principles of the Ancient cosmologies, still regarded the attraction of like to like as one of the great laws of nature, and even retained recollection of the theory of 'natural places', to which he made the important correction that these natural places are everywhere, their number being equal to the number of celestial bodies, each of which has its natural place. It follows that the planets do not attract each other and are not in danger of coming together. We might even suppose that, as an extreme consequence of the theory, 'a piece of the Moon transferred to the Earth would leave it in order to return to the Moon, and conversely'.[19]

Bruno gives heaviness a definition which is closely cognate with that of Copernicus, but with this difference, that the tendency of matter to come together in the form of a globe is not limited to the restricted realm of the 'wandering celestial bodies', but extends to the realm of the fixed stars, that is to say, to infinite space.

On the other hand, one of the axioms of Brunonian cosmology is that celestial bodies lack weight. The *siquidem est sine pondere tellus* of Enceladus has already enlightened us on this point as regards the Earth. 'To be heavy or light is not suitable to worlds, any more than to parts of worlds, for these differences do not depend on the *nature* of the things, but on their *position* and their *relation* to each other.'[20] This passage from the fourth dialogue of *De l'infinito* does more than confirm those from *De immenso* and *La cena*, which have already been quoted;[21] it reveals the full significance by giving a better explanation of the generality of the rule that they set forth. *La cena* compared 'the chief bodies of the universe' (*i.e.*, the celestial bodies) with their individual parts, namely, with the heavy bodies whose heaviness we can experience and whose ability to fall we can verify. The former were said to be 'neither heavy nor light'; the latter, on the other hand, could be 'affected by differences of weight'.

Bruno's thought on this matter did not alter, but Philotheus in *De l'infinito* expresses it more fully than Theophilus in *La cena*. The latter went so far as to say that 'no body is heavy or light in its place', but the former, eliminating all trace of Aristotelian vocabulary, states that no body is heavy or light 'by nature'. Heaviness is no longer a permanent quality in bodies; it exists only in virtue of their respective

231

positions. Therefore, the 'principal' bodies—the celestial bodies—separated from each other by vast extents are, are 'without weight', whereas 'their parts'—the heavy bodies—tend to draw near to the place 'of their conservation', a tendency which becomes weaker moreover as the distance increases, because a heavy body far removed from the Earth would no longer fall back and would be unable to draw near to it except by an effort in order to pierce the interposed layers of air. Consequently, heaviness seems to be merely relative, and if Bruno is still far from being able to formulate this relationship in the form of a physical law, at least he perceives the two variables (mass and distance) of which heaviness is a function.

The fifth argument of Albertino relating to the impossibility of existence of several universes grouped round and in contact with a central one is countered by Philotheus who says that such contiguity, even if we should accept the 'fantastic' hypothesis of mobile spheres, would not have dissolution and collapse of the whole assembly as a result. Each of these great organisms would continue to exert its influence on its parts and ensure their cohesion: 'If several animals were pressed one against another, it would not follow that the members of one animal would merge with those of another, so that some might have several heads or several bodies.'[22] This reply gave Bruno an opportunity to introduce into the discussion a thought that was very dear to him, and which is one of the main pieces in his cosmology; it is, that the celestial bodies are living beings; but the thought takes on a note of condescension, seeing that the vision of universes composed of concentric spheres is set aside beforehand, and *a fortiori*, the hypothesis of possible contiguity between them. Therefore, Philotheus takes care to prevent any suspicion of acquiescence on his part in doctrines which he rejects, by straightway adding: '. . . but we, thanks be to God, are freed from the painful necessity of begging such excuses, because in place of so many heavens, so many orbs, rapid or restive, upright or inclined, to the east or to the west, on the axis of the universe or on the axis of the Zodiac, in this or that, in high or low declination, we have one single firmament, one single space through which this celestial body on which we are and all the others accomplish their proper revolutions according to their proper courses.'[23]

Finally, abandonment of any absolute system of localization in space eliminates the objection which involves making heaviness incompatible with the plurality of worlds, seeing that the heaviness of a body no longer depends on its position relative to a fixed region of the cosmos, but definitely on its position relative to a 'principal body', the centre of the organism of which it is itself a part.

b) *The void and tangent universes.* Following the arguments about heaviness, Albertino puts forward two fresh arguments (numbers 6 and 10)[24] against the plurality of worlds, which claim to derive their force from the insurmountable difficulties that would be raised by the hypothesis of tangent universes. Seeing that Aristotelian physics excludes all possibility of a void, it follows that the universes, if there be several of them, must be in closest proximity, even in contact; but because of their spherical form, they would touch each other only in one single point, leaving gaps between them; and these gaps, represented by triangles with curved sides in the same way that spheres are represented by circles, must necessarily be filled. Such is the sixth argument, which is resumed in *De immenso* as number 8.[25]

We are then forced to assume either that there are other elements not belonging to any one of the universes in contact, but constituting another universe, which supposition only begs the problem; or we must accept the void.[26]

On the other hand, the universes as imagined by Albertino, following Aristotle's scheme, would be formed like ours of a stationary Earth and concentric spheres endowed with rotatory motion which would be progressively more rapid for the outer spheres. Under these conditions it is obvious that the points of contact between the ultimate spheres would be so many points of friction, so many obstacles to the action of the motive intelligences. Such is Albertino's tenth argument (resumed in *De immenso* as number 14).[27]

It is easy to guess Bruno's replies to these two arguments. They merely repeat what has been said with regard to three dimensional, homogeneous, boundless space (*spacii ingentis dimensio triplex*), void if we wish (*non ergo absurda est vacui sententia*), unless it is assumed to be filled with a subtle aether; that space in which the celestial bodies can move freely, separated from each other by sufficiently great distances so that all risk of contact is avoided.[28]

c) *The problem of the one and plurality and of the superiority of the one* ('*theological*' *argument*). The objections against the plurality of worlds which have been summarized above are valid only if we exclude from the discussion certain postulates of Aristotelian physics and astronomy: rotation of the celestial spheres, theory of 'natural places', impossibility of a vacuum. Rejection of these fundamental hypotheses is sufficient to render the subsequent argumentation null and void. Similarly, there are no longer 'theological' objections, which do not depend, or depend less strictly, on the adopted cosmic scheme.

Having accepted that matter, itself divine, would be no obstacle to the 'explanation' of the formal principle from which it is inseparable (see above, chapter IV), we have no need to revert to the limitation that the passive power of matter would impose on the active power of the divinity (Albertino's argument number 8).

One argument remains: the twelfth and last, which Albertino reserved for the end, as he judged it to be the most suitable one to convince an opponent who has so often asserted the superiority of the one over the multiple: the universe is perfect and that which is perfect must be unique. To the perfect, no addition is made. This argument, after all, only completes that which had been stated under number 7: 'If there be several universes, they are either finite in number or infinite. If they be infinite in number, an infinity in act exists, which is considered impossible for many reasons. If they be finite in number, then this number is fixed.' We are then led to enquire, why one number any more than another? Must we stop at an even number or at an odd number? Why assume four, six or ten Earths rather than a single one, 'when unity, all other things being equal, is preferable to plurality' and more conformable to the wish of nature?[29] These themes are resumed and developed in much the same terms in the sixth book of De immenso.[30]

We already know Bruno's answer: it goes without saying that nothing is added to that which is perfect, but the perfect being paradoxically identified with the infinite,[31] it is no longer incumbent on us to stop at such and such a number: we are spared from making this impossible choice. Seeing that the universe reflects the infiniteness of its principle, the real infinity is accepted as a divine mystery. As for the preeminence of the unity, it is no longer in question. The unity expresses itself in the multiple without ceasing to be the Unity. What is it in the plurality and diversity of universes that causes such indignation? Ought there to be only one star in the sky, one man on Earth? That is a strange notion of unity. In the infinite universe, unity and omnipresence of the formal principle manifest themselves as an upthrow of existence in all places and causes life to open up everywhere in its most varied forms: *Anima ubique est una, spiritus unus mundanus, totus in toto . . . ubique omnia producit.*[32]

On our Earth, is not it easy to verify and justifiable to explain certain revealing facts concerning this universal law? The variety of animal species should be sufficient to enlighten us; but let us go further: the presence of a certain species in islands isolated from any continent forces us to admit that it must have appeared simultaneously everywhere on land, that there was not a first wolf, a first lion, a first ox from which all individuals of the same species have descended 'and been transported to the islands'. Similarly, the diversity of human races, the existence of men different from us in height or colour, such as the negroes, the American Indians or the pygmies, allows us to assume a multiplicity of families in the beginning. Adam was only the father of the Jewish race, as is stated, contrary to popular belief, by certain Hebrew monuments, according to which the other races were descended from two other protoplasts, created at an earlier time.[33] In support of this polygenism, Bruno quotes in the *Spaccio* the discovery of America and the existence there of evidence of a civilization 'more than ten thousand years' old. Now, those regions were unknown to the Ancients, and it is hardly likely that the sons of Adam were able to transport themselves thither in order to found a family, as Jupiter expresses it in an ironic antiphrasis in the *Spaccio*, when he declares that 'if human families are found in various continents, their presence there is not explained, as in the case of so many other animal species brought forth from the maternal womb of nature, but through the crossing of seas and in virtue of navigation, having been transported thence on vessels that existed before the first ship was invented'.[34]

If it be difficult to accept that all men are descended from a common ancestor when during many centuries the various human families were unable to have the least contact with each other, then the impossibility of a common origin for the inhabitants of the various planets is even more obvious. This impossibility appears moreover amongst the arguments put forward by Albertino against the plurality of worlds (argument number 9); the hypothesis is described as 'preposterous, because those multiple worlds would be deprived of the benefit of civil life, which consists in commerce between human beings'. Philotheus, refusing to lay down as a principle that all thinking beings ought to have the means of communicating with each other, replies that relationships between the inhabitants of the various worlds are by no means indispensable to the public good (*bontà civile*), and that one could say exactly the same thing about relationships between the men who populate the various regions of our planet: 'Experience teaches us that it is best for the inhabitants of this our world that nature has placed the obstacle of seas and mountains between their families; and when it happened that relationships were established between the said families through human artifice, then they have lost rather than gained, seeing that the result of the contacts has been to double the vices rather than to increase the virtues.'[35] The same scepticism with regard to the alleged benefits of universal commerce is expressed with just as much force and even more tartness in one page of *La cena*, where Christopher Columbus, the idol of the century (*ai nostri tempi vien magnificato il Colombo*), is described as one of the 'new Tiphys' whose discoveries had been proclaimed by Seneca in his tragedy, *Medea*. These audacious navigators have in reality only 'disturbed the peace of others . . . merged together that which a foreseeing nature had kept apart, increased the vices of nations, spread fresh follies by violence, introduced unheard-of ones where they never existed . . . taught men a new art and new means of tyranny and assassination amongst themselves'.[36]

Even when they are not purposely intended to interpret cosmology by way of parables and so make its truth understandable, these oft repeated diatribes, always with the same degree of vehemence, against explorers, against conquerors, and against all who dream of causing one single law and one single faith to reign on Earth,[37] express a vision of the universe. They tend to turn the reputedly invincible argument of the superiority of the Unity against the opponent; Bruno does not hesitate to accept this superiority which he had never ceased from proclaiming, but he conceives it in such a way that it peremptorily demands diversity in the tangible universe. On Earth, where our view may dilate, as well as in infinite space, the Unity that contains all is *explicated* in the multiple, and 'omniparent' nature engenders the diverse everywhere; it manifests itself in a variety of aspects that it would be impious to wish to reduce by violence or by artifice, a task moreover just as impossible as levelling a mountainous ground. The unity that we must seek and discover is that of the ever living, ever present, principle common to every being. It is not the goal of a conquest conducted throughout space; it is not the close of an exordium, but of a road,[38] of a journey to the inside, towards the totally immanent infinity of each finite being and in which all diversity is resolved.

THE FABRIC OF THE FIRMAMENT

Bruno's polygenous teachings are connected with his views on the plurality of inhabited worlds, which views are themselves inseparable from the physical hypothesis that says that the realm of the elements is not limited to the Aristotelian sublunary spheres, but extends to the countless celestial bodies which occupy infinite space beyond the furthest planets. Nicholas of Cusa had already outlined a picture of a universe entirely peopled by living beings, but, it must be added, different from ourselves and concerning the nature of which we can only make indefinite conjectures.[39]

Bruno seems to have no doubt about the existence of an infinite number of inhabited worlds. First of all, there are the visible planets and the Sun itself; then the other planets, invisible though certainly forming part of the solar system; celestial bodies conjoined with Mars, Jupiter and Saturn in the same way that the Moon is conjoined with the Earth and Mercury is with Venus;[40] or located beyond Saturn, being hidden from our view, as the case may be, by their remoteness, their small size, their opacity, or because the waters occupy a too small portion either of the total surface or of the face turned towards the Sun, as a result of which they are unfit to reflect the light.[41] Finally, there are the planets and satellites associated with the fixed stars, the countless suns,

Sideraque totidem soles quae fixa videntur . . . ,

which we see because they are larger, because they are extremely large bodies, whereas the worlds surrounding them are invisible to us, because they are much smaller (*per esserne corpi molto minori*), as well as for other reasons that are detailed in one chapter of *De immenso*: *Cur planetae quae sunt circa alios soles non videntur.*[42]

These reasons are the self-same ones that account for the invisibility of certain planets of the solar system, but, when applied to more distant worlds, they acquire more force; and whoever is able to correct by an effort of reflection the evidence of the senses and to draw from the scenes most commonly offered to our sight the lessons they offer, will not hesitate to compensate the inadequacies of a limited perception by an hypothesis which is soon changed into certainty. It happens that we see a procession of small boats round a ship; from afar, we should still be able to see the ship but not the boats. Similarly, can we see the birds flying about that laurel tree which we can barely distinguish in the coppice?[43] and, if we do not see them, must we doubt the possibility of their presence? Again, are we to conclude that there are no other birds in the air except those that we see in flight from one single open window? He who would deny the existence of invisible celestial bodies would argue in that way. On the other hand, he who will judge with a lively intelligence and clear reason will understand that the near and the distant obey the same rule.[44]

An objection could be raised against the existence of planets round the stars. How does it come about that these opaque bodies do not hide from view the luminous celestial bodies round them? Bruno got rid of that difficulty beforehand by assuming them to be of much smaller size; but subsequently, no longer taking this pertinent precaution into account, he assumes that there are opaque bodies larger than the luminous ones, and endeavours to show that occultation of the latter would still not occur. In his desire to establish his theory on unshakeable ground, he tries to prove too much, and instead of sticking to the remark that a body interposed between two stars *does not prevent them from being seen*,[45] he claims to make the occultation of a star depend on the distance between them and no longer on the size of the interposed planet. This thesis, defended by Theophilus in *La cena de le ceneri*, is resumed at length in the chapter in *De immenso* entitled *Cur soles non eclypsentur, et quod intermediante maiore opaco non sequatur eclypsatio*. It is illustrated both times by an explanatory figure intended to show that as the distance between the luminous source and the opaque body increases, so an occultation becomes less perceptible and tends to become of no account. This persistency in error provides evidence of a singular lack of knowledge of the laws of geometry and of optics.[46]

To tell the truth, these erroneous proofs are mainly superfluous, and they are marginal in the descriptions of Brunonian cosmography. What is important is to make the unity of the universe obvious as is affirmed by the obedience of the plurality of worlds to one single law, *unam ad normam*. . . . The same causes produce similar effects everywhere and the similitude of planetary systems corresponds to the homogeneity of sidereal space within which they are organized.[47]

This universal receptacle (Dorothea W. Singer calls it *universal envelope* in her English translation) has a double claim to be called homogeneous, for it is everywhere identical with itself in so far as it is three dimensional space—deprived of any local property that would permit of distinction between a centre and a periphery, above and below, west and east—and in so far as it is the *subtle medium* of celestial bodies and of all material bodies.

What is the substance of this medium? Bruno, as we know, admits that we can designate it by the term *void*, but that is a kind of metaphor intended to indicate its extreme subtlety and to take account of the fact that it offers no resistance to the free motion of celestial bodies, rather than a piece of really adequate nomenclature. It would be more appropriate to speak of *air* or *aether*. A certain amount of confusion seems to be permitted between these two words to begin with, and it happens that they are used as being nearly equivalent. For example, in this sentence from *De immenso*: 'Is not the Earth in the air or the aether like the Moon, the Sun and all the celestial bodies?'[48] Elsewhere, this uncertainty disappears. The heavy, dense terrestrial atmosphere with its winds, clouds and humid vapours is first described in *La cena*.[49] A distinction is made between air and aether in the fifth dialogue of *De l'infinito*, but rather as two states of the same substance than as two substances; it is called *aether* 'when the substance is pure' as it is in celestial space; *air* when it is closer to us; and *spirit* (*spirito*) when it enters into the composition of our organism and is distributed throughout 'our lungs, arteries and other cavities and pores'.[50] Finally, in the fourth book of *De immenso* (chapter xiv), under the heading *Distinctio aeris et aetheris*, the meaning of the two terms is more exactly defined. Air, 'the humid substance' that we breathe, 'forms part of our Earth, which it envelops, and it may be assumed that the other planets are similarly enveloped. The aether, on the other hand, forms part of the firmament, or rather, it is nothing but the firmament, the void, the absolute space that penetrates bodies, and which embraces them all through its infiniteness.[51]

This gloss certainly betrays some uncertainty as to the nature of the aether, but instead of being almost merged with the air (. . . *aere vel aethere*), the aether is assimilated to the void, the absolute space, without, however, the condition that this space should be pure nonbeing; it exists in so far as it is a receptacle, and a suitable medium for the movement of celestial bodies; it is properly the fabric of the firmament. It stretches and penetrates everywhere, and seeing that it remains similar to itself everywhere, its apparent variations can only result from its degree of purity. There is a most interesting annotation at the end of the gloss. Three zones are distinguished, and each receives a particular name:

1. *Coelum telluris*, the ambient space surrounding our planet, and, naturally, of every other planet or star.

2. *Coelum coeli*, the space in which a group of celestial bodies is collected together, for example, the solar system: *spacium unius synodi sicut in quo hic sol est cum suis planetis*.

3. *Coelum coelorum*, the immense space separating these assemblies or synods, and which, being open everywhere for the passage of celestial bodies, offers no resistance to their movements. Thus, with remarkable intuition, Bruno anticipates the discoveries of technical astronomy and discriminates between the proper atmosphere of a celestial body, interplanetary space and interstellar space on the basis of the greater or less rarefaction of the matter present.[52]

These differences, which reveal the presence of a non-uniformly distributed matter that has nothing in common with the *aether* and is simply humid air or air charged with vapours, do not in the least affect the homogeneity of *absolute space* so frequently asserted by Bruno. In his view, this point is so important that he reverts to it again at the end of his cosmological poem, the eighth and last book of which is entirely devoted to a criticism of Palingenius and his *Zodiacus vitae*.

The universe of Palingenius is infinite, but not homogeneous. Like that of Aristotle, it consists of a sequence of homocentric spheres round the Earth; but the last sphere, that of the fixed stars, is no longer the boundary beyond which, in the absence of 'place', nothing can exist and no motion can be produced: a region of light whose extent is boundless is substituted for this emptiness. The universe is therefore no longer divided into two, but into three, realms: the firmament, that which is below the firmament, and that which is beyond the firmament:

Ergo triplex regnum est mundi portio triplex.[53]

We can easily imagine that such a picture of the universe will give Bruno the opportunity for a commentary in which praise and criticism are mingled—warm praise and severe criticism. Palingenius was right to proclaim the infinitude of the universe; he was wrong in not recognizing its homogeneity. At the outset he seems to escape the slumber which delights all those who lazily accept the tradition of error: 'Palingenius is almost awake';[54] but he is comparable with a sleeper who opens his eyes through being conscious of dreaming, and believing himself to be awake then falls into even more deceptive dreaming: so, Palingenius dozes off to sleep again and abandons himself to aberrant imaginings. He distinguishes three kinds of light: that of our world; that of the heavens, the dwelling place of the inferior divinities (or angelic hierarchies); and that of the infinite Empyrean; a distinction that is incompatible with the unity of the prime principle, which, in so far as it is present in the universe, identifies itself with Nature, the source of all species, which acts at the centre of everything, and is the same everywhere, no matter what name it be given: Spirit, God, Being, Unity, Truth, Destiny, Reason or Order:

Mens, Deus, Ens, Unum, Verum, Fatum, Ratio, Ordo[55].

What is the significance of this fringe round the universe, this light 'without matter' to which the author of the *Zodiacus vitae* seems to relegate God? If we speak of divine light, it can only be as a figure of speech, in the same way that we speak of the light of wisdom, virtue or justice; but in the physical order of things light is no longer separable from luminous bodies—luminous sources or opaque bodies which reflect their light—any more than goodness is separable from that which is good.[56] Finally, does not the imprudent poet-cosmologer concur in the errors of the Manichees and Gnostics in assigning two realms impenetrable each by the other to Good and Evil?[57]

If the universe is indeed divided and if a zone of pure light becomes the dwelling place of God, then the worst has happened for our world: evil alone reigns there; it is wicked and therefore sprung from an evil principle: *Si hic mundus esset malus, a malo esset principio*. On the final pages of *De immenso* the Monist affirmation is forcefully repeated: God is everywhere and in everything, not above, not below, but in the heart of everything. Besides the closed universe of the Peripatetics, it becomes necessary to reject this 'imperceptible', 'super-aetheric' light from which the stars would derive their fire as from a foreign source, and recognize the existence of an infinite field strewn with countless suns.

HOMOGENEITY OF THE UNIVERSE

It is worth noting that *De immenso* ends, as do the two treatises *De causa* and *De l'infinito*, with a hymn to unity, the obvious intention of which is to destroy completely the objection, raised in the name of unity, to the plurality of worlds. This infinite plurality, which is inseparable from perfect homogeneity, far from being incompatible with the unity of the formal principle and the material principle, is the sole adequate expression of them. Coherence of the system is consequently assured through agreement between a metaphysics and a cosmography.[58]

The concepts of infinity and homogeneity are certainly not implied by either: the only example of Palingenius shows that we can conceive of an heterogeneous and infinite universe; but the premises of Brunonian philosophy being accepted (unity and omnipresence of the formal principle, itself participating in the divine infinity), their separation becomes a disgrace, and their union becomes a logical necessity, the consequences of which are shown in the last book of *De immenso*; they are more easily deduced and more fully developed in other works.

On the plane of human knowledge, infinitude placed the universe out of range of scientific investigation, but homogeneity restores it to a certain extent to 'natural contemplation'. Bruno's universes do not have those individual differences in size and structure that characterize, for example, those of Democritos; their diversity, which is infinite, remains comparable with that of individuals of one single species; so that our Earth and Sun within their narrow limits provide us with a picture, no doubt imperfect, though sufficiently revealing of the infinite universe. These considerations bring us back to the *quodlibet in quodlibet*, or the 'all in all' of Anaxagoras 'who desired that everything should be in everything because, the spirit or the soul or the universal form being in everything, all can be produced from all'.[59] Both in the *Sigillus sigillorum* and the treatise *De causa*, Bruno unduly urges the opinion of the Clazomenian philosopher, for whom 'all in all' meant the presence of all qualities in no matter how small a fragment of matter, indefinitely divisible, though unknown to the νοῦς to whose organizing influence it is subjected. Anaxagoras said 'In everything there is a small portion of everything, except Intelligence';[60] whereas, on the other hand, according to Bruno, matter is deprived of every quality, so that introduction of the whole into the part results, and uniquely at that, from formal affinities whose origin is to be sought in the influence of a common principle. Bruno ought to have invoked the *Deus totus est in omnibus et singulis* of St Thomas Aquinas,[61] rather than the 'all in all' of Anaxagoras.

On the moral and religious plane, homogeneity of the infinite universe, which results from the unity of its principle, involves two consequences:

1. Omnipresence of the Good. The evil that we believe we discern is an illusion; it appears to us in the perspectives of the finite, that is to say, of the partial. A total sight of the universe would eliminate the shadows from it. The criticism of Gnostic dualism levelled at Palingenius provides Bruno with an opportunity of reverting to this familiar theme. If we distinguish a region of Good and a region of evil in the universe, we accept two contrary principles; furthermore, as these two principles are hostile, if the Good does not triumph over the evil, and if the evil force operating in the lower region is able to resist the infinite Good, then it must itself be infinite. Indeed, we cannot imagine how a finite force would be able to maintain an infinitely unequal contest against an infinite force.[62]

2. The presence in each of these innumerable worlds (of which our Earth is a very illuminating example) of imperfections which are linked with the partial; consequently, a region which would be that of the absolute Good is incapable of existence in the 'explicated' universe. As Gentile pointed out, the concept of nature as unity is not in itself something uncommon: it is found in various guises in the *Laudi* of St Francis, in the writings of Ficino, Pico della Mirandola, and Campanella;[63] but Bruno, by adding infinitude to unity, definitely puts the threshold of paradise outside of tangible existence.

The texts that have been considered in this chapter have provided us with a cosmic picture whose conformity with reality we may challenge, but it is one to which we shall really have access only by following the paths at whose end it appears. Bruno had thought out the genesis and meaning of the universe before working out its structure, and the latter must have seemed to him as a necessary consequence of the former. In his view, the tangible universe is neither creation, nor even emanation, but the direct and immediate expression of its principle. The simple does not generate the complex; the former expresses itself in the latter; the multiple does not *develop* the infinite richness of the Unity: it *reflects* it. If it were otherwise, the universe could be divided into two zones, in truth, into multiple zones; it could be centred and shaped; include an Earth and a Firmament; a here-below and an on-high between which the spheres would be ranged in ascending stages, the stages of a journey of the soul towards a mystical orient. In a universe which never withdraws from its principle, these localizations, however, lose all *raison d'être*; the divisions of time and space are applicable to limited universes, to planetary systems, but not to an infinite universe, which is always one in its multiplicity, unchangeable in its changes. In the foreword to his treatise *De causa*, Bruno wrote: 'In it, the century does not differ from the year, the year from the moment, the foot from the furlong, the furlong from the parasang, any more than in its essence any specific being differs from another such; therefore, there is no number in the universe: the universe is one.'[64]

The universe has no centre any more than it has number. 'The machine of the universe', said the Cardinal of Cusa, 'has its centre everywhere and its circumference nowhere'; and also: 'The universe has no circumference.'[65] As for the ubiquity of the centre (and speaking of a centre, that is to say, of a point, ubiquity is equivalent to absence), Bruno is in agreement with the writer from whom he drew inspiration; but as regards the circumference, he contradicts him: 'The universe is all centre and all circumference'—'*L'universo è tutto centro e tutto circonferenza.*'[66] The idea is undoubtedly the same; nevertheless, it seems that the change of formula reveals some secret intent of the doctrine. In a universe that is centred on nothing, neither on the Sun any more than on the Earth, we are able to believe and say that we are at the centre, but we can say also that we are always really much nearer the limit, always on the edge, always on the point of breaking loose. The limit of the universe which we shall seek in vain in space, however far we go, nevertheless exists, and that is where we are.

We shall obtain a better idea of the meaning of this picture of a limit that is encountered everywhere, if we consider that of broken mirrors, symbols of distinct beings each of which reflects its principle, howbeit imperfectly. The true method of the soul's journey will then be defined: it is not a flight into space but a withdrawal on itself, a descent into the depths, not a vain chase from one mirror to another, but an effort to pass from the reflection to the reflected object, every individual in the diversity of the explicated universe being only 'a countenance of the unique substance'.[67]

At this point a reversal takes place and the assured monism of the natural philosopher who contemplates nature wavers and is disowned. The Good, which is everywhere and is completely grasped, is everywhere in danger of taking on the character of the evil, so that the universe, in every place, reveals through its own transgression an exigency which is all the more pressing in every individual the more it becomes the subject of more lucid thought. Thus, the formless universe rediscovers an Orient. The prime principle, that was so close to us through its omnipresence, seems to withdraw itself until it becomes inaccessible; our supreme desire being henceforth to pass from the Simple as it reveals itself in the guise of the multiple to the Simple as it dwells in itself; to flee from a dimension of shadow in order to reach an inconceivable region which, outside of space of which it is the complete epitome, is to space what eternity is to time.

The poems of *Eroici furori* compare the trials and sufferings of man who has ventured on the trail of the divine prize to the joy of the giant Enceladus when he discovered that he is in heaven, having realized that the Earth is without weight, and proclaimed the fact by a song of triumph. The joy of not being confined to a lower-world, but of belonging to a celestial body that deserves the name of star just as much as any other, is mingled with a yearning for somewhere else. The universe in its infinitude remains what the Earth was: a place of exile.

NOTES

1. See above, chap. VI, p. 166 and note 33.
1b. *'Est operae ergo almo doctori mobile primum*
 Jam nonam ac decimam sphaeram superaddere, nullis
 Illustrem stellis, sed motum suppeditantem:
 Undecima est niviter superaddita susidiatrix:
 Nec data propterea est populo pax grata sophantum;
 Nam duodena caput jam jamque efferre videtur.'
De immenso, III, i (*Opera*, I, i, pp. 316–317).
2. For example *La cena*, I, p. 98; *Acrotismus* (*Opera*, I, i, p. 67).
3. *'Haud aliter stultus, quem circum sylva coronat*
 Undique plantarum, septem ex iis ille propinquas
 Iudicat, imparibus devinctas intervallis,
 Namque et apparent: non sic reliqua omnia, namque
 Non etiam apparent. Neque plus rerum esse deinceps,
 Namque apparent: quasi finiat omnia sensus.'

De immenso, V, ii (*Opera*, I, ii, p. 122); see *La cena*, V, p. 205: '*Come a noi che dal centro dell'orizonte voltando gli occhi da ogni parte, possiamo giudicar la maggior et minor distanza da, tra, et in quelle cose che son più vicine: ma da un certo termine in oltre, tutte ne parranno equalmente lontane: cossi alle stelle del firmamento guardando, apprehendiamo la differenza de mot ie distanze d'alcuni astri più vicini: ma gli più lontani e lontanissimi, ne appaiono immobili, e equalmente distanti, e lontani quanto alla longitudine.*'

4. *La cena*, V, pp. 205–206.

5. See Ch. Mugler, '*Les dimensions de l'univers platonicien d'après le Timée 32b*', in *Rev. des études grecques* (1953), pp. 56–88.

6. The results obtained were as follows: 1179 terrestrial radii according to Copernicus; 1150 according to Tycho Brahe; 1208 according to Galileo (*Systema mundi*). See P. H. Michel, '*Giordano Bruno et le système de Copernic d'après la Cène des cendres*', in *Pensée humaniste et tradition chrétienne aux XVe et XVIe siècles*, Paris, 1950, pp. 318–319.

7. See J. Dagens, *Bérulle et les origines de la restauration catholique*, p. 22.

8. A. Koyré, '*Les étapes de la cosmologie scientifique*', in *Revue de synthèse*, Juillet–décembre, 1911, p. 15.

9. *Ibid.*, p. 22.

10. See P. H. Michel, '*Léonard de Vinci et le problème de la pluralité des mondes*' in *Léonard de Vinci et l'expérience scientifique au XVIe siècle*, Paris, 1953, pp. 31 ff.

11. See above, note 3.

12. See D. W. Singer, *Giordano Bruno*, London and New York, 1950, pp. 13 and 16.

13. See above, chap. VII, *L'erreur géocentriste*, pp. 123–125.

13*b*. '*Averrò allora che il mezzo dal mezzo sarà più distante ch'il mezzo da l'orizonte.*' *De l'infinito*, V, p. 397.

14. *Ibid.*

15. *Ibid.*, pp. 397–398.

16. Unless we regard them as a free interpretation of *De coelo*, I, 8, where Aristotle proves the unity of the firmament through the nature of the elements.

17. P. H. Michel, ref. 10 *supra*, pp. 36–37; and see P. Duhem, *Études sur Léonard de Vinci*, II, pp. 57–59, Paris, 1909.

18. *De revolutionibus orbium coelestium*, I, ix.

19. Note by A. Koyré in his translation, Copernic, *Des révolutions des orbes célestes*, Paris, 1934, p. 146.

20. '*Esser grave o lieve non conviene a mondi ne a parte di quelli; perchè queste differenze non sono naturalment, ma positiva- e respettivamente.*' *De l'infinito*, IV, p. 378.

21. See above, chap. VII, notes 16 and 43.

22. '*Come se più animali fussero ristretti insieme e contigui l'uno a l'altro, non per questo seguitarebe che gli membri de l'uno potessero appartenere a gli membri dell'altro, di sorte che ad uno ed a ciascun d'essi potessero appartener più capi o busto.*' *De l'infinito*, V, p. 410.

23. '*Ma noi, per la grazia de dei, siamo liberi da questo impaccio di mendicare tale iscusazione; perchè, il loco di tanti cieli e di tanti mobili rapidi e renitenti, retti ed obliqui, orientali ed occidentali, su d'asse del mondo ed asse del zodiaco, in tanta e quanta, in molta e poca declinazione, abbiamo un sol cielo, un sol spacio, per il quale e questo astro in cui siamo, e tutti gli altri gli proprii giri discorsi.*' *De l'infinito*, V, pp. 410–411. See *De immenso*, VII, xvii (*Opera*, I, ii, p. 280): '*Nos quippe ab hisce angustiis liberi sumus unum continuum ponentes spacium immensum, certis in locis corpora complectens.*'

24. According to the author's numbering which is sometimes imperfect. The tenth argument is really the eleventh for two consecutive arguments have been given the number 'seven'. See *De l'infinito*, V, pp. 398 and 400.

25. '*Praeterea attiguos puncto quoniam decet esse,*
    Est operae precium, spacium remanere triquetrum . . .
    In quo nimirum spacio est opus esse quod implet. . . .'
De immenso, VII, v (*Opera*, I, ii, p. 251).

26. '*Bisogna dunque fingere novi elementi e novo mondo, per empir quel spacio.* . . .
Over è necessario di ponere il vacuo, il quale supponemo impossibile.' *De l'infinito*,
V, p. 398.

27. *Ibid.*, V, p. 400; *De immenso*, VII, vi (*Opera*, I, i, p. 253).

28. *De immenso*, VII, xii (*Opera*, I, ii, p. 273).

29. *De l'infinito*, V, pp. 398–399 (argument 7) and p. 400 (argument 12).

30. '*Impar de numeris mavult celebrarier, an par?*
Ut libet esse putet, fugiet te causa.
. . . in plures cur massa haec materiei
Dispersa est mundos? Cur non glomeratur in unum?
. . . Inclita nempe monas numerum apponitur ultra. . . .'
De immenso, VI, vi (arguments 9, 10 and 16) (*Opera*, I, ii, pp. 251, 252 and 254).

31. See above, chap. VI (*The infinite and the good*). In his reply to Albertino's twelfth argument, Philotheus goes so far as to say that an infinite number of worlds is necessary so that the universe may *subsist* and be perfect: '. . . *per la propria sussistenza e perfexion dell'universo è necessario che* [*i mondi*] *sieno infiniti.*' *De l'infinito*, V, p. 416.

32. *De immenso*, VII, xviii (*Opera*, I, ii, p. 284).

33. '*Quia multicolores*
Sunt hominum species, nec enim generatio nigra,
Aethiopum, et qualem producit America fulva,
Udaque Neptuni vivens occulta sub antris,
Pygmeique iugis ducentes saecula clausis,
Cives venarum Telluris, quique minaerae
Adstant custodes, atque Austri monstra Gigantes,
Progeniem referunt similem, primique parentis
Unius vires cunctorum progenitrices.'
De immenso, VII, xviii (*Opera*, I, ii, p. 282). '*Propheticum est illud et populi cuiusdam celebritas, quod omnia hominum genera ad unum primum genitorem referantur, vel ad tres, ut ex Ebreorum monumentis accipimus et firmiter credimus, quorum quidam solum optimum genus, id est, Iudaeorum, ad unum protoplasten referunt; et reliquas gentes ad duos priores, qui biduo ante creati sunt. Echinensium religio recens compertorum tres alius nominis protoplastes numerat ab annis vigenti millibus. Aethiopum genus ad illum protoplasten nemo sani iudicii referet. Porro sicut omnis terra producit omnia animalium genera, ut in insulis patet inaccessis, neque enim fuit unus primus lupus et leo et bos, a quo sunt omnes leones, lupi, et boves geniti et ad insulas omnes transmissi, sed quaque ex parte tellus a principio dedit omnia.*' *Ibid.*, p. 284.

34. '. . . *è frescamente scuoperta una nuova parte de la Terra che chiamano Nuovo Mondo, dove hanno memoriali di diece mila anni e più.*' *Spaccio*, III, p. 203. '*Oltre che le generazione de gli uomini si trovano in diversi continenti non a modo con cui si trovano tante altre specie d'animali usciti dal materno grembo de la natura, ma per forza di transfretazione e virtù di navigazione, perchè, verbigrazia, son stati condotti da quelle navi che furono avanti che si trovasse la prima.*' *Ibid.*, p. 202.

35. *De l'infinito*, V, pp. 399–400 (Albertino's argument) and 415–416 (reply by Philotheus).

36. '*Gli tifi han ritrovato il modo di perturbar la pace altrui, violar i patrii genii de le reggioni, di confondere quel che la provida natura distinse, per il commerzi radoppiar i diffetti, e gionger vizii a vizii de l'una e l'altra generazione, con violenza propagar nove follie, e piantar l'inaudite pazzie ove non sono, conchiudendosi al fin più saggio quel che è più forte: mostrar novi studi, instrumenti, ed arte de tirannizar, e sassinar l'un l'altro.*' *La cena*, I, p. 96.

37. This was also Campanella's dream, for whom unity signifies in the first place unification. See Tommaso Campanella, *La prima e la seconda Resurrezione, Inediti theologicorum libri XXVII–XXVIII*, Rome, 1955.

38. See *Eroici furori*, Introduction, p. 31.

39. *Docta ignorantia*, II, 12.

40. *De immenso*, II, ix (*Opera*, I, i, pp. 290–291).

41. *De l'infinito*, III, p. 341; *De immenso*, IV, xiii, *Quod plures sint planetae quam quot apparent* (*Opera*, I, ii, p. 65):

'*Constent igitur media atria solis*
Quem circum non duntaxat septena planetae
Discurrat soboles, verum quoque turba latentum.'
(*Ibid.*, pp. 66–67).

42. *De immenso*, I, iii (*Opera*, I, i, pp. 209–210); *De l'infinito*, III, p. 341.
43. '*Siccine distante in sylva male sane notabis*
Ut circa hanc laurum varias errare volucres?'
De immenso, I, iii, (*Opera*, I, i, p. 210).
44. '*. . . unam ad normam venit abstans atque propinquum.*' *Ibid.*, and see III, iv (*Opera*, I, i, p. 345): '*De quo aeque rationabiliter dubitare quispiam posset, atque qui non alias per aerem discurrere volucres existimet, quam quas per sibi unicam patentem fenestram ipse videat pertransire.*'
45. *La cena*, III, p. 160.
46. *Ibid.* and *De immenso*, V, v (*Opera*, I, ii, pp. 132–133).
47. '*. . . continente universale . . . eterea regione per la quale tutto discorre e si muove.*' *De l'infinito*, III, p. 338.
48. '*Num iscut tellus in medio aere vel aethere consistit, ita et luna et sol, et omnia astra.*' *De immenso*, I, iii (*Opera*, I, i, p. 212).
49. *La cena*, III, pp. 172–173.
50. *De l'infinito*, V, p. 412.
51. '*Aether vero idem est quod coelum, inane, spacium absolutum, qui insitus est corporibus, et qui omnia corpora circumplectitur infinitus.*' *De immenso*, IV, xiv (*Opera*, I, ii, p. 78).
52. *Ibid.*, pp. 79–80.
53. *Zodiacus vitae*, XII, line 80.
54. *De immenso*, VIII, ii (*Opera*, I, ii, p. 292). Sub-title.
55. '*. . . Intimius cunctis, quam sint sibi quaeque, vigens est,*
Entis principium, cunctarum fons specierum
Mens, Deus . . .' etc.
De immenso, VIII, x (*Opera*, I, ii, p. 314).
56. '*Primum adverte, minus lucem nos dicere posse,*
Praeterquam venientem obiectum sensibus actu.
Quid lux, quam ponit sermonis certa figura,
Et similis quaedam ratio, atque proportio tali
Nomine concelebrat, cum lucem dicere legem,
Iustitiam, sophiam, virtutem, numina suemus?
Divinam hinc lucem, solis lucem exuperantem,
Cuius clarescant vestigia corpore solis
Igniferi, haud poteris physice signare loquendo.'
De immenso, VIII, vi (*Opera*, I, ii, p. 306). In connection with this passage it will be noted:
1) that Bruno makes light a *quality* of luminous bodies;
2) that he aims at Plato through Palingenius, and once again rejects the possibility of the existence of 'ideas' as separate entities.
57. '*Gnostica nempe tuam cepit sententia mentem?*' *De immenso*, VIII, vi (*Opera*, I, ii, p. 302).
58. *De immenso*, VIII, x; see *La causa*; *De minimo*, I, iv; *De monade*, II.
59. '*Voi mi scuoprite qualche modo verisimile con il quale si potrebbe mantener l'opinion d'Anaxagora; che voleva ogni cosa essere in ogni cosa, perchè, essendo il spirito o anima o forma universale in tutte le cose, da tutto si può produr tutto.*' *La causa*, II, p. 188.
60. Anaxagoras, fragment 11. See *Sigillus sigillorum* (*Opera*, II, ii, p. 196): '*Unde cum anima ubique praesens existat, illaque tota, ideo pro conditione materiae in quacumque re etiam exigua et adscisa mundum nedum mundi simulacrum, valeas intueri, ut non temere omnia in omnibus dicere cum Anaxagora possimus.*'
61. *Summa theologica*, I, 8, 2, ad tertium.
62. '   *Nam si infinita potestas*
Uni est principio, alterius quoque condecet esse.
Nemo enim statuet, finita vi potuisse
Hunc unum statuisse sibi solum exiguumque,

Quem par est contra infinitum obsistere semper.'
De immenso, VIII, vi (*Opera*, I, ii, p. 303). These lines form the conclusion of a paragraph which is entitled: '*Si hic mundus esset malus, a malo esset principio; et sive finitum sive infinitum ex alia parte esset bonum, nihilominus duo essent principia contraria, aequalis virtutis, et principium malum heic posuit hunc mundum, et infinitos alibi alios posuisse potest.'* (*Ibid.*, p. 302.)

63. G. Gentile, '*Poesia e genio'* in *Giornale critico della filosofia italiana*, 1934, p. 6.

64. *La causa, Proemiale epistola*, p. 143.

65. *Docta ignorantia*, II, 12 and 11 (translation by L. Moulinier, pp. 155 and 150).

66. *La causa, Proemiale epistola*, p. 143.

67. '. . . *tutto quel che veggiamo di diversità e differenza, non è altro che diverso e differente volto di medesima sustanza.'* *La causa, Proemiale epistola*, p. 144.

IX

The living universe

Countless universes move in an infinite and homogeneous space, and the motions with which they are endowed depend on a unique and omnipresent force, which is known by various names: nature, universal soul, formal principle or more simply—life. In the same way that one single light illuminates the universe, so one single life animates it: *una lux illuminat, una vita vivificat omnia.*[1]

Consideration of this cosmic life is going to bring us back to the problem already dealt with in chapter IV, The Soul of the universe, but our attention will henceforth de devoted to the effects of this fresh point of view rather than to the causes; we shall no longer be considering the life-giving principle, but the animated object: the universe in its living aspect, as a whole and in its parts. Consequently, we shall not revert to the distinction between the two principles, formal and material, in which Bruno recognized sometimes two substances, and sometimes two aspects or two attributes of the same substance, without ever ceasing (from *De umbris idearum* to *De minimo*) to assert, with Aristotle, that they are indissoluble in fact; and, against Aristotle, the inward action of the former as the life-giving principle; and so, neglecting the substantiality or the non-substantiality of form and of matter, we can consider here only this inner element of the sources of life and motion, and we can abide by the statement in *De immenso*: 'Nature is more than present, it is within things like their germ, it is remote from nothing.'[2] The duality of substances is a question of metaphysics and 'the highest contemplation', but compared with reason and 'natural contemplation' it matters only that there should be no *distance* between the animated object and the force that animates it. That the motions of tangible being result from an internal energy and not from an external impulse or the attraction of a stationary prime mover does not imply that matter and nature are but one, but simply makes them inseparable for any observer.

Negation of inertia. Before Galileo had defined inertial motion, inertia could only be imagined in connection with rest. A body is moved either from within or from without, and if its motion be prolonged or seem to be prolonged indefinitely, we must assume that the cause of this motion is prolonged: *cessante causa cessat effectus.* When he asserts the inner character of the cause, Bruno is only following a tradition that goes back to Antiquity, seeing that Philoponos, abandoning the hypothesis of action by the ambiant air, ascribed the continued motion of a projectile to an internal impulse. This doctrine was resumed by the Nominalists of Paris in the fourteenth century and became known as the doctrine of *impetus* on which the mechanics of Jean Buridan is based. It is only necessary to link *impetus* with the action of the formal principle to arrive, as does Bruno, at the concept of indefinite motion which will ensure the organization and revolution of 'countless universes', starting from the ultimate elements. Bruno's cosmology assumes a nature that carries its vital principle within itself, and, as the infiniteness of the principle involves that of its effect, it follows that cosmic repose becomes inconceivable.

The universe a living body. The inertia of matter being resolutely denied, we must beware of considering the universe as a chaos put in order, as did the pre-Socratics, or Leo, the Hebrew. Creation is not a more or less total victory over the formless, a conquest by the νοῦς of the ἄπειρον. Rather than being comparable with an edifice made of materials abstracted from obscure depths before being assembled on the stocks, the universe is preferably compared with a living being sprung from a germ, from a 'substance in which forms, shapes and members exist, though indistinct and agglomerated, as it were, exactly as in the seed the arm is not distinct from the hand, the bust from the head, the nerve from the bone'.[3]

The universe such as it appears results from a vital impulse, so that tangible being is not separated at any moment from the principle whose powers it develops, and which it is permissible for us to trace back to 'physical universality, the subject of knowledge for philosophers, to the elevation of the archetype, the object of faith for the theologians'.[4]

The prime principle, that is to say, God, can in effect only be an object of faith, the soul of the universe remaining for natural contemplation the final limit beyond which the divinity is entrenched in an unfathomable darkness. As for the soul of the universe, Bruno acknowledges with Plotinus and Marsilio Ficino that 'it governs the universe with greater facility than our soul governs our body'.[5] However, this neo-Platonic reference should not delude us. The same question arises in connection with the universe and the soul of the universe as in the case of angelic powers and celestial spheres: namely, to know if this soul be immanent in the body that it animates, or if it be a separate spiritual substance making use of the body as though it were an instrument. Now, Ficino wavers before this dilemma. Led astray, if not obsessed by the idea of a living heaven, 'he introduces this pagan theme into his christian edifice with lyricism mingled with prudence';[6] and when he declares in his commentary to Plato's *Banquet* that 'the whole body of the universe lives'—*vivit igitur totum mundi corpus*,[7] he endeavours several lines later to reconcile Plato with Denysios and to show that, for the one as well as for the other, the souls of the spheres are angels that the Lord God has endowed with the power of governing the celestial bodies and imparting motion to them. Needless to say, Bruno ignores these scruples and reflections. The immanence of the soul leaves him in no doubt.

Symbiosis. It is not enough for the universe as a whole to be a living body; each of its parts must in addition be animated by its own life, so that the soul of the universe seems to be fragmented therein and proliferated as a multiplicity of souls. Before approaching the problem that such an increase presents to the philosopher who has erected unity of the spiritual principle into a dogma, let us once more read the essential chapter from the treatise *De causa* in which this blossoming of life in innumerable organisms is stated without reservation or ambiguity. The debate takes place between Theophilus, who is always entrusted with setting forth the correct teaching; Dicson, a sympathetic listener who is more than half convinced; and two supernumeraries, Gervasio and Polihimnio, whose sallies enliven the dialogue with a comic note.

'Dicson. That seems to me something quite novel. Do you claim that not only the form of the universe but that all forms of natural objects are life and soul?

Theophilus. Certainly.

Dics. All things are therefore animated?

Theo. Yes.

... Dics. The general opinion is that all things are not living.

Theo. The most general opinion is not the true one. ... Are not there philosophers who say that the universe is animated?

Dics. To be sure, there are many, and some of the greatest.

Theo. And why should not these same philosophers say all parts of the universe are animated?

Dics. They certainly say so, but in respect of the principal parts, those that are the true parts of the universe, for they are no less justified in wanting the soul to be completely in the entire universe and completely in any one of its parts, than they are in wanting the soul of animals that are visible to us to be completely everywhere [in them; that is to say, in each of their parts].

Theo. But what are the parts of the universe that you think are not true ones?

Dics. Those that are not the prime bodies ..., the Earth, the Moon, the Sun and other similar bodies. Besides these principal creatures, there are those that are not prime parts of the universe and of which it is said that some have a vegetative soul, others a sentient soul, and yet others an intellective soul.

Theo. But if the soul, because it is in the whole, is also in the parts, why do you not want it to be in parts of the parts?

Dics. I certainly want it, but in parts of the parts of animated things.

Theo. But what are the things that are not animated or not parts of animated things?

Dics. ... All things that do not have life.

Theo. And what are the things that do not have life, or at least the vital principle?

Dics. To come to a conclusion, there is nothing, according to you, that is not endowed with a soul and the vital principle?

Theo. In the long run, that is exactly what I do mean.

Poliinnio. Then a dead body has a soul? And my boot-trees,[8] my slippers, my riding boots, my spurs, my ring and my gloves[9] are animated? My gown and cloak are animated?

Gervasio. Yes, sir, yes, master Poliinnio, and why not? I certainly think that your gown and cloak are animated when I see an animal like you in them. . . . That's what you mean, isn't it, Theophilus? . . .

Pol. *Maledicat te Deus in secula seculorum.*

Dics. Don't get angry: leave us to arrange the questions.

Pol. *Prosequatur ergo sua dogmata Theophilus.*

Theo. I shall do so. Well, I say that a table, *qua* table, is not animated; nor the gown, any more than leather, *qua* leather, or glass, *qua* glass; but in so far as they are natural and compounded things, they have matter and form in them. A thing, however small or trivial, encloses within itself a portion of spiritual substance, which, if it finds a favourable surrounding, develops into a plant, or into an animal, and acquires the members of no matter what body usually called animated; for the spirit is found in everything and there is no corpuscle, however tiny it be, that does not contain its portion and is animated by it.

Pol. *Ergo, quidquid est, animal est.*

Theo. All things possessing a soul are not said to be animated.

Dics. But at least the things that have life?

Theo. I concede that every thing has a soul and life in itself according to the substance, but not according to the act and working which are the signs of life in the view of the Peripatetics and those who base their definition of life and the soul on far too crude reasons.

Dics. You make me glimpse a credible argument thanks to which we could support the opinion of Anaxagoras, who required that every thing should be in every thing because the spirit, or the soul, or the universal form being in all things, all can be produced from all.'[10]

With regard to this last sentence, we have already had occasion to note that nothing is more unexpected, nor more arbitrary, than the appeal which is made to the authority of Anaxagoras. The 'all in all' of Anaxagoras means, that in each part, however small it be, of matter endowed with qualities and indefinitely divisible, all possible qualities are contained; bodies are not distinguishable from each other except in so far as certain elements predominate; finally, the *voῦs* whose organizing influence leads gradually to these predominances and distinctions acts on the primitive mixture from without.[11] One has only to take the opposite view of these propositions to arrive at Bruno's doctrine, according to which matter fragmented into atoms and deprived of qualities is organized by an omnipresent spiritual principle, thanks to the internal influence.

The soul is able to produce all from all, because it is completely present in each part of the universe, in the same way that the soul of a living being is completely present in each of its members: this symbiotic theme gave inspiration to seventeenth century rationalism, which, without waiting for Leibniz and Spinoza, is fully stated, for example, in the *Philosophiae primae seminarium* of Bisterfeld: 'No being is lonesome in the universe, but every being is symbiotic. . . . Order and pan-harmony confirm this bond in universal nature.'[12]

In Bruno's view, to assimilate the universe to a living body is barely more than giving in to the evidence. On the other hand, difficulties immediately arise when it is a question of defining the way of life suitable to each of the parts of this great body taken singly. The question that then arises for the philosopher is to know by what kind of life the following are animated:

1. The ultimate elements of matter, those that have just been given the name of *minimi corpuscoli.*

2. The objects usually held to be inanimated.

3. The organisms that have life 'according to the act and working', and to which the quality of *living* is generally given.

4. Finally, the 'principal creatures' or celestial bodies.

We shall now consider these various problems in turn.

a) *The atom, the centre of energy.* The source of motion not being motion but the development of a living substance, it follows that the phenomena produced in the universe result from an internal force. Consequently, tangible being for whomever observes the appearances from without is but one with that which we call its laws; and for whomever considers the real from the point of view of possible influence, everything is matter. It seems that 'We could say that matter itself determines its form, and if we regard the universe, in so far as it is a formed body, to be matter, we are allowed to call it matter. . . .' To this flash of wit on the part of Dicson, Theophilus straightway replies: 'No-one can stop you from using the word matter in your way . . . but if that way suits the mechanic or the physician who is satisfied with it in the practice of his art', it is not suitable for a philosopher whose rôle is to 'distinguish principles'.[13]

On the other hand, we have accepted that the universal body is composed of atoms, that is to say, of separate corpuscles; but then, where and how is the energy of the animating principle going to exert itself? According to the *Timaeus*, the soul intervenes at the periphery of the universe in the path of the celestial bodies; whereas according to the *Laws* it controls on the level of the polyhedra, even to changes of state.[14] In both cases its influence is exerted from without; and that is incompatible with Brunonian doctrine, seeing that the formation of simple bodies (endowed, as we shall see, with a 'spirit') should operate by aggregates of inert atoms, subjected to an external constraint.

The soul manifests itself everywhere: if it be not absent from the 'empty continuum', from the ambient aether,[15] how should it be absent from matter properly so-called and from the 'full continuum' which is the atom? If the atom, like everything that exists, is 'governed by the spirit', it can be so only from 'within', seeing that that is the universal law. Consequently, it appears to the 'physicist' definitely as a centre of energy.

Atomism and animism are two corner-stones of Brunonian philosophy, and Bruno cares so little about sacrificing one to the other, that he parts company with Democritos and Epicuros, for whom, however, he does not fail to express admiration, when he finds them relating the birth of universes to the chances of indetermined motions.[16] 'The intention of reconciling the mechanism of the atomists with Platonic and neo-Platonic teleology has been attributed to him.'[17] However, he was far from bothering about such a matter: his borrowings from the atomists, from the Platonists and even on occasion from Aristotle are merely bestowed praise; in such cases the references intended only to point out the fortunate encounters those philosophers had with the truth which he is convinced he possesses. He states that the death of celestial bodies and their recomposition starting from the ultimate elements (an eminently

Democritean theme) is possible, but he immediately adds; 'I do not adhere so much to the concepts of Democritos, I do not accept his impious elements. On the other hand, I recognize the existence of a higher fatherly spirit through which all these elements are governed.'[18]

b) *Spiritus elementorum.* It is not surprising that Bruno criticized Paracelsus for not having raised his chemical principles to the formal principle, the soul of the universe.[19] Was not it his own desire to carry the limit of the knowable beyond the tangible, to the point where his efforts to reach that objective give a pathetic character to his system by depriving it of a great part of its efficacy in the field of positive knowledge? Lasswitz says, that animism prevented Bruno from making any useful application of atomism to mechanics.[20] We could say with just as much justification that he turned chemistry towards alchemy.

On the atomic level, the universal soul is comparable to an energy which we can say exists but which we find it impossible to qualify; on the level of simple or compound bodies it manifests itself as a kind of elementary 'spirit'. This theory is described in *De monade* (prose commentary in chapter V). On the author's own admission, the *De monade*, which is a long musing on the numbers in the decade, gives only conjectural opinions about the genesis of forms. All the same, we may direct our attention to the paragraph entitled *Natura quatuor elementorum in mundo spirituali*, where we find an application of the animistic hypothesis in one definite instance. The elements are four in number, namely, aether (and not fire), air, water and earth. No material body is able to take shape without intervention by the soul, which acts on it through the intermediary of a *spiritus*, of which the following definition is given: 'Intermediate substance through which the soul becomes present in the body and gives to the organized body its proper life.'[21] Minerals, vegetables and animals are similarly subject to this law. For the moment, we shall consider only the first.

Each element has its 'spirit', and metals divide themselves into four classes according as they are more particularly animated by this or that of these elementary spirits. Thus, 'in iron and copper the spirit of earth predominates, in tin and lead the spirit of water, in bronze and silver the spirit of air, in gold only the spirit of aether'.[22] Naturally, all that is said without prejudice to the unicity of the principles, material just as much as formal: in the same way that one same trunk of a tree puts forth four branches, so nature gives rise to four kinds of bodies from one same body and the spirit of these four bodies from one same spirit.[23]

This basic unity would allow us to hope for transubstantiation if art knew how to imitate nature; the dream of the alchemists was not, in itself, therefore, absurd and their set-backs were the result of insufficient knowledge of the conditions of matter and of the order of generation.[24]

Between the soul and tangible bodies, the spirit, already matter though a subtle one, eludes the grasp of our far too coarse organs; but the philosopher discloses its virtue and fecundity in all things. He recognizes in it the 'seed', thanks to which minerals themselves proliferate in the bowels of the earth in the same way that animals and plants multiply on its surface. Thus, the soul, which is only the principle of motion in the atom, intervenes as an organizing and generating force on the mineral level.[25]

c) *Living beings*. If we now pass from minerals to beings that are usually called 'living' because they have life 'according to the act and working', the presence in them of a soul seems so obvious that it is almost superfluous to call attention to the fact. It is appropriate merely to recall that the vital principle in these superior realms remains unique and unigenous; and to describe its action with respect to the complex organisms that it engenders, governs and abandons, when the time comes.

The *internal artificer* (that is one of the numerous names given to the soul of the universe) causes the vegetable to come forth from the seed; and 'in the same way, in the case of animals, by extending its activity from the seed in the first instance, then from the centre of the heart to the external members, and then finally withdrawing the faculties so developed towards the heart, it acts as though it were rewinding the threads that it had pulled tight'.[26] The description of this twofold movement, from the core of the heart to the periphery and then from the periphery to the core of the heart, is resumed in another form in a passage in *De minimo*, where the organization of atoms about a psychic centre is discussed and where the phenomena of birth, life and death are explained in accordance with this theory: 'We are what we are through the indivisible substance of the soul around which, as though about a centre, *exglomeration* and agglomeration of atoms takes place.' Through birth and during growth, the spirit spreads itself from the heart into the mass that constitutes our body; then, as if it were drawing back to itself the threads of this fabric, it returns to the portal through which it entered and through which it withdraws. 'Birth, therefore, is expansion from the centre, life is plenitude of the sphere, and death is contraction back to the centre.' The author then adds, that is 'a very sound argument in favour of our immortality'. In fact, this 'entrance' and 'exit' of the soul has no bearing whatever on its participation in the eternity of the formal principle.[27]

However, when we come to the highest levels in the scale of existence passing from vegetative life to sentient life, then to the intellective, we note that the living organism becomes more independent, more autonomous, and that its own soul seems to become less closely sub-jected to the action of its principle, with the result that death becomes a fearsome trial for the soul, in spite of the everlastingness of the universal soul.

Such is the condition of man; but once again, art can become the 'rival of nature', in the sense that by himself and by an 'heroic' effort man can set the gateway of death apart before the final hour. A judicious practice of introversion, inseparable from the 'frenzy of love', will enable him to perform this withdrawal to the centre, whereby we close our life, and to lead the soul back again to its source, or sufficiently near to its source, for it to be able to realize the ghostly abyss then yawning in front of it and beyond which it hopes for rebirth in the divine light, but no longer through its own effort.[28]

d) *The celestial bodies*. Seeing that all the products of nature, from the atom to the human being, passing from the elements, simple or compound bodies, metals, plants and beasts, are animated, then the celestial bodies must be also in accordance with the logic of the system; and the universal soul must act in them and at the centre of their sphere; and their motions must result from an internal impulse and not from some constraint acting on them from the outside.

Elsewhere we have seen that the complexity of organisms went hand in hand with their autonomy, and that the higher we ascend in the scale of living beings, the more numerous and evident do signs of their freedom become. Consequently, if the celestial bodies occupy the pinnacle of this hierarchy of living beings, then we must ascribe to them a proper soul which is more independent of its principle than in the case of man.

Bruno happened to compare the celestial bodies with atoms because they float, weightless, like grains of dust in the infinite; but that is only a figure of speech having no other purpose than to show to what extent their size is minute having regard to the immensity of the space in which they evolve. Their complexity is not involved: it is obvious and obliges us to compare them with beings endowed with sentient life, at least, namely with animals. This comparison, a quite familiar one during the Renaissance, was one of the most regular themes in Bruno's cosmology from *La cena de le ceneri* to *De immenso*.[29]

First of all, we shall consider the pages he devotes to the life of Earth. Memories of Leonardo or even of Marsilio Ficino[30] will be called to mind by them and will make them seem of little originality at first sight. All the same, neglecting the fresh elements introduced by the descriptions given by them, we are impressed during our reading by the most obvious care taken to establish the truth of a system and to give to any fact the persuasive value of an argument. Thus, the presence of a source of heat in the interior of the terrestrial globe becomes a proof of its vitality. Every animal is warm as a result of a twofold heat, its own and that which it receives from the outside. Now, in the case of the Earth—*Tellus animal magnum*—if it receive its share of the solar rays and in general fire from heaven, it has also an innate heat, inseparable from animal heat. How could the Sun warm the depths from which burning waters spring; how could its heat be propagated to the centre of the Earth when the tiles on our roofs are sufficient to protect our houses?[31]

The possession of life by the planet is furthermore attested by the diversity and multiplicity of its component parts: each of which nourishes the others, proliferates and grows in profusion, and all are interdependent like the limbs of one same body.[32]

Life being accorded to the Earth, it will then not be refused to the Sun, the fertile source of light:

Sol vero et Tellus sunt prima animantia ...

It stands to reason that it will not be denied either to the countless universes, worlds or suns which populate space, seeing that in everyone of them, were we able to explore them, we should find 'rocks, pools, rivers, springs, seas, sands, metals, caverns, mountains, plains and other species, which in the case of animals are the so-called heterogeneous parts ... bones, intestines, veins, arteries, flesh, nerves, lungs, limbs of all kinds. ...'[33]

Fracastoro of Verona speaks in such terms in the third dialogue of *De l'infinito*, and then in his double capacity of astronomer and physician compares terrestrial mishaps with illnesses of the human organism: 'Catarrh, erysipelas, calculus, vertigo and fevers and, numberless other affections or dispositions corresponding to fog, rain, snow, eruptions, fire, lightning, thunder, wind . . . and tempest.'[34] Consequently, like all beings endowed with sentient life, the Earth is subject to 'passions'; it can suffer. The remark of Prudenzio in *La cena de le ceneri* comes to mind: 'If the Earth be alive, it cannot derive pleasure from having grottoes and caverns dug in its back.'[35]

Without attaching more importance than is necessary to this witticism of a pedant who plays the part of common-sense man in order to embarrass the philosopher (although Theophilus takes the trouble to reply), we shall retain the use of the word *dorso* to designate the surface of the Earth. This term, which is commonly used by Bruno, and which does not seem to him to be out of place in the most serious discussions, inevitably calls to mind those humans of the earliest ages mentioned by Aristophanes in Plato's *Banquet*, and whose sphericity is evidence of astral origin. The celestial bodies are not only animals or creatures, but are perfect ones. They move through celestial spaces with supreme ease, *facillimo appulsu*.

They have no more need of wings, than they have of arms, legs or feet. What would be the use to them of those limbs, those means of locomotion and prehension, when they have everything in themselves and move about with their whole body without encountering obstacles that need to be overcome in order to attain the sole objects of their desire: warmth or coolness, light or shade.[35b]

The spherical humans in the fable of Aristophanes were descended from the Sun, the Earth or the Moon; the descendants of the Sun were male, those of the Earth were female, those of the Moon were of both sexes (*Banquet*, 190 *b*). Bruno recognizes two kinds of celestial bodies only: the Suns, which are male; and the Earths, which are female. Moons and Earths are of the same kind and these two words are used indiscriminately when it is a question of comparing fiery celestial bodies with cold ones, at least as regards their surfaces.

We have seen how the celestial bodies belonging to these two kinds —henceforth, we can refer to them as two genera of two sexes— make a beneficial exchange of their warmth and coldness.[36] Now, this exchange must not be seen solely as a physical phenomenon, but also as a biological one and, in short, a union through which they live and thanks to which they propagate life. It is a union of divine beings, the characteristics of which are far superior to those of our experience; a union which involves no loss of substance on the one hand, nor the absorption of a foreign substance on the other; action and passion in the union are reduced to changes that are determined by heat and cold.[37]

So far, we have considered only the sentient life of the celestial bodies, but we must go further. When Doctor Nundinio, in the course of a conversation which is related by Theophilus to his audience in *La cena*, asks Bruno, not without some irony: 'Do you believe that the celestial bodies have a sensitive soul?', he receives the answer: 'Not only sensitive, but intellective; and not only intellective like our own, but possibly more than our own.' Suddenly, being brought face to face with one of the most serious problems, namely, that of astral intelligence, 'Nundinio became silent and stopped laughing'.[38]

If the celestial bodies are endowed with intelligence just as much as we are, possibly more so (and the context shows pretty clearly that this 'possibly' is a purely formal concession), then their soul must have, like our own and like the soul of the universe itself, the dual function of governing their body and attaching itself to divine things. Turning one of these two aspects towards the Supreme Intellect from which it emanates, it contemplates, adores, and bears witness. *Ambasciatori nuncii della magnificenza dell'unico altissimo*—'ambassadors and messengers of the magnificence of the most high unique', the celestial bodies proclaim the excellency of the glory and majesty of God through their bodies of flame.[39] Therefore, it is not in the 'mysteries of necromancers' that we must seek to recognize the divinity, but 'in the splendour of the Sun', in the aspect 'of those countless animated bodies, beings of light, endowed with sense and intelligence, which applaud the supreme unity, good and majesty'.[40]

During his trial at Rome, Bruno resumed these cosmic themes; in his defence he quoted the verse from *Psalm* xviii: *Caeli enarrant gloriam Dei* and he compared the celestial bodies to angels: 'they praise the Lord, they proclaim his majesty and his power through these luminaries and these inscriptions graven in the firmament'. Angels are 'the messengers and interpreters of the divine voice and of nature'; some are 'invisible and hidden from our senses', but others are visible, and they are the celestial bodies.[41]

If one of the aspects of the astral soul be turned towards God, the other is turned towards the body that it animates and which it has the duty to govern. We now glimpse the secret springs of a celestial mechanics just as strange as that of Copernicus or of Ptolemy or of Aristotle. The celestial bodies are moved by a ceaseless motion, and all of them are moved; the stars complete their revolutions as do the planets, and if we say they are 'fixed', it is simply because we do not perceive their displacement on account of the very great distance separating us from the regions in which they take place.[42] We know that the celestial bodies do not receive from the outside the impulse for their eternal motion, which justifies their name of *aethera*:[43] they find it in themselves.[44] Being free in space and not hitched to the spheres, they move *ab anima propria*.[45] However, the weight of the celestial bodies, assuming them to be formed from the same elements as the Earth, and their inevitable fall, if the support of the crystalline spheres were removed, were still quoted in the sixteenth century by supporters of the ancient systems as reasons for not abandoning them. Without reverting to this point, which has already been discussed, we shall now try to describe the freedom of celestial bodies as pictured by Giordano Bruno, and for that purpose we must recall some of the fundamental theorems of his physics:

1. Earth, in so far as it is one of the four elements, is not essentially the heavy element, in spite of what the Aristotelians claim. The fact is proved by experience, seeing that we see earth in the form of dust suspended in the air.[46]

2. Infinite space in which suns and planets evolve is not absolutely empty, but is the receptacle for a substance which is beyond influence of the physical conditions of matter (discontinuity and impenetrability): namely, the aether, a subtle medium suitable for supporting bodies, and all the more because it envelops them in a much larger field in such a manner that the celestial bodies and the Earth itself in the immense depths of the firmament are merely minute points and are able to float like specks of dust in air.[47]

3. The fall of a heavy body, that is to say, its return towards the organism of which it forms part, is a natural motion, though it is

weakened and finally reduced to zero at a very great distance. Thus, an object launched sufficiently far from the Earth would escape from terrestrial attraction. Bruno perceives the possibility of this phenomenon without discerning the physical causes of it, and accounts for it simply by the thickness of the interposed layers of air (or aether). As for the celestial bodies, the distances separating them are such that there cannot be attraction between them and they are never in danger of 'falling' on each other.[48]

If we accept the above, we must then conclude that the only heavy bodies are 'the portions separated from the principal bodies', subject to the condition that they are not too far away from them, and that the celestial bodies are 'weightless'.

Without being subjected to any constraint, and without meeting any obstacle, they then enjoy the same freedom of inertness as the specks of dust that we see floating in a sunbeam;[49] so that the regularity of their motions would become unexplainable if it were not related to transphysical causes.

By introducing *impetus* or internal impulse, Buridan had made the action of motive intelligences unnecessary; but it seemed that that theory, like any other purely physical theory, could have accounted for the revolutions of celestial bodies only if those revolutions had been perfectly regular. Now, in this connection, abandonment of the system of eccentrics and epicycles brought the whole matter up anew. One page of Campanella's *Theologica* will help us to understand what new and embarrassing problems could arise from the ruins of classical astronomy. Campanella distinguishes, on the one hand, the regular motions of celestial bodies which can be ascribed to physical causes (namely, the laws of nature instituted by God but no longer requiring His permanent intervention); and, on the other hand, their aberrations resulting from changes produced throughout the ages in the obliquity of the planets, the displacement of apogees, the anticipation of equinoxes and solstices, necessary corrections but ones in which we must recognize the direct and constant action of the divinity and which give evidence that God governs the firmament as and when He wishes: *Deus temperat coelum terramque sicuti et quando vult.*[50]

Bruno's biocosmology has the following particular feature, and we must admit that it is rather baffling for a positive mind: it claims to reconcile the concept of transphysical motive force with the theory of internal impulse. The soul alone is the origin of celestial revolutions seeing that it is the principle of motion in everything;[51] but the celestial bodies in their capacity of living organisms have this privilege of having *their own soul* for the motive principle.

Any attempt to impose rigorous regularity on celestial revolutions, in other words, to reduce them to uniform, circular motion, free from saving the appearances by multiplying and entangling the spheres, could only be stubbornly combated by a doctrine that set forth the freedom and intelligence of celestial bodies as a fact, and for which a faultless regularity became the sign of blind obedience to imposed laws, to a passivity without glory.

Would the fortunate removal of the firmament from this bondage give rise to anarchy, a cosmic disorder? Certainly not! because the astral intelligence would be sufficient to foresee the eventuality of such a catastrophe; but we must recognize that the course of the celestial bodies, their motion like their respose, are a function of their nature and not of the position they occupy.[52]

Such are the 'reasons' to which it is appropriate to relate not only the arrangement of their revolutions but also their irregularities, complexities, errors—useful corrections, which are evidence of an enlightened will and an active intelligence. It is quite useless to claim to state the laws with mathematical strictness. If the motions of the Earth, or of any other planet, are sometimes faster and then sometimes slower, it is because these worlds require to expose themselves for a shorter or longer time to warmth and light in order better to maintain life in them. Celestial bodies, being endowed with sentient faculties, are capable of understanding, and desire results from the understanding peculiar to their kind. That is the reason why they move with a motion whose end is conservation of their existence and whose motive force is the soul.[53]

NOTES

1. *Sigillus sigillorum* (*Opera*, II, ii, p. 179).
2. '*Plusquam praesens, natura est insita rebus, a nihilo distans.*' *De immenso*, X, viii (*Opera*, I, ii, p. 314).
3. *De causa*, V, p. 254.
4. *Ibid.*
5. *Ibid.*, II, p. 183.
6. A. Chastel, *Marsile Ficin et l'art*, p. 42.
7. Marsile Ficin, *Commentaire sur le Banquet de Platon* (ed. Raymond Marcel), *Oratio sexta*, p. 202.
8. '*i miei calopodii. . . .*' According to Gentile this word comes from the Greek χαλοπόδιον, a diminutive of χαλόπους, wooden leg. E. Namer translates it as '*mes embauchoirs*'.

9. From the Latin *chirotheca*, transcription of the Greek χειροθήχη.

10. *De causa*, II, pp. 185–188. See Aristotle, *Physica*, II, i, 192 *b*: 'Among things that exist, some do so by nature, and others from other causes; animals and their parts, plants and simple bodies such as earth, fire, water and air exist by nature; indeed, concerning these things and other of a like kind, we say that they exist by nature. Now, all the things which we have mentioned manifestly differ from those that do not exist by nature; each natural being has, in effect, within itself a principle of motion and of fixity, some in respect of place, others in respect of increase or decrease, and others in respect of alteration. On the other hand, a bed, a mantle or any object of that kind, in so far as they are entitled to that designation, that is to say, in so far as they are products of art, have no natural tendency to change; but only in so far as they have the quality of being of stone or of wood or of some mixture do they have that tendency and to that extent; for nature is a principle and a cause of motion and of rest for the thing in which it dwells directly, by essence and not by accident.'

11. See above, chapter VIII, p. 243 and note 60.

12. '*Nullum ens in universa rerum natura est solitarium, sed omne ens est symbioticum. . . . Idque universae naturae nexus, ordo et pan-harmonia confirmat.*' Amsterdam edition, 1657, p. 35.

13. 'Dics.—*. . . Appare che potremo dire, che la materia vien figurata da se stessa, se noi vogliamo considerare l'universo corpo formato esser materia, chiamarlo materia* . . . Teo.—*Nessuno vi può impedire che non vi serviate del nome di materia scondo il vostro modo, come a molte sette ha medesimamente raggione di molte significazioni. Ma questo modo di considerare che voi dite, so che no' potrà star bene se non a un mecanico o medico che sta su la prattica, come a colui che divide l'universo corpo in mercurio, sale e solfro* [an allusion to Paracelsus]: *il che dire non tanto viene a mostrar un divino ingegno di medico quanto potrebbe mostrare un stoltissimo che volesse chiamarsi filosofo; il cui fine non e de venir solo a quella distinzion di principii, che fisicamente si fa per la separazione che procede dalla virtù del fuoco, ma anco a quella distinzion de principii, alla quale non arriva efficiente alcuno materiale, perchè l'anima, inseparabile dal solfro, dal mercurio e dal sale, è principio formale; quale non è soggetto a qualità materiali, ma e al tutto signor della materia, non è tocco dall'opra di chimici la cui divisione si termina alle tre dette cose, e che conoscono un'altra specie d'anima che questa del mondo, e che noi doviamo diffinire.*' *La causa*, III, pp. 204–205.

14. Ch. Mugler, '*Sur quelques particularités de l'atomisme ancien,*' in *Revue de philologie, de littérature et d'histoire ancienne*, 1953, p. 174 and note 2.

15. '*Quadruplex est spiritus. Primus* absolutus *scilicet in aetherea amphytrite. . .*' *De monade*, V (*Opera*, I, ii, p. 396); and see above: *Atoms and the void*, p. 137.

16. See above, chapter V.

17. F. Tocco, *Le opere di Giordano Bruno*, p. 270, note 2.

18. '*Sed non propterea rationis carpo elementa*
     Impia, Democriti adstipulatus sensibus, atqui haec
     Mentem alta[m] *agnosco moderantem cuncta paternam.*'
De immenso, V, iii (*Opera*, I, ii, p. 216). These lines are quoted twice by Tocco in *Le opere latine . . .*, once on page 271, where they agree with the text of Fiorentino: *Mentem alta . . .*, and once on page 356 with the addition of *m* to the word *alta*, which addition we think is sensible.

19. See above, note 13.

20. K. Lasswitz, *Geschichte der Atomistik*, I, pp. 391–392.

21. '*Substantia media quaedam, qua anima tum corpori adest, cum corpori propriam per se ipsam organizato vitam elargitur.*' *De monade*, V (*Opera*, I, ii, p. 396).

22. '*Anima metallorum spiritum terreum in cupro et ferro, maiori ex parte, praedominantem habet, aqueum in stanno atque plumbo, aereum in aere et in argento, aethereum in unico auro.*' *Ibid.*, pp. 396–397.

23. '*Natura ex uno stipite, tanquam ramos quatuor, tum ex uno corpore quatuor haec generum corpora, tum ex uno spiritu quatuor horum corporum spiritus educit.*' *Ibid.*, p. 397.

24. *Ibid.*, On the same page, Bruno charges the 'Arabian astrologers' with having sought the spiritual principle that exists in all bodies, using gold as the starting material.

25. '. . . *efficiens, nectens, integrans atque propagans quidquid compostum.*' *De minimo*, I, ii, lines 20–21 (*Opera*, I, iii, p. 139).

26. '*Similmente negli animali spiegando il suo lavore dal seme prima, e dal centro del cuore a li membri esterni, e da quelli al fine complicando verso il cuore l'esplicate facultadi, fa come già nevesse a ringlomerare le già distese fila.*' *De la causa*, II, p. 180. This psycho-physiology clearly derives from Aristotelianism. We know that, according to Aristotle, the heart is the first of all our organs to be born and the last to die. See Louis Bourgey, *Observation et expérience chez Aristote*, Paris, 1955, pp. 91, 94, 121.

27. *De minimo*, I, iii (*Opera*, II, iii, p. 143).

28. The return of the soul to its divine source taking the path through the depths is one of the main themes of *Eorici furori*. See, in particular, the fourth dialogue of the first part (mythological accounts of Actaeon and the solitary sparrow).

29. See *La cena de le ceneri*, III, pp. 169–173; *De l'infinito*, II, pp. 335–336; *De immenso*, IV, xv; V, ix; VI, xv.

30. See A. Chastel, *Marsile Ficin et l'art*, pp. 94–95

31. '*Sicut omnia animalia duplici constamus calore, proprio scilicet nativoque, et externo quod est vel a corpore spirituque Telluris, atque a sole, vel igne in general ita et Tellus animal magnum atque primi ordinis habet sibi cum animali spiritu innatum calorem, quo praecipue ipsa vivit, et alia in suo corpore viventia contemperat, atque vivificat. Quod si non animal hoc divino calore, humoreque (quem spiritum dicimus partim, partimque lucem) particeps, solis virtus nequaquam eo se usque in centrum ingereret telluris, quam imbricibus tectorum nostrorum retundimus.*' *De immenso*, *VI*, xv, chapter heading (*Opera*, I, ii, p. 201).

32. *De immenso*, V, ix (*Opera*, I, ii, pp. 146–149).

33. *Ibid.*, p. 146 and *De l'infinito*, III, pp. 352–353.

34. *Ibid.*, p. 353 and see *De immenso*, V, ix.

35. *La cena*, III, p. 170.

35b. *De immenso*, IV, xv and xvi (*Opera*, I, ii, pp. 80–92).

36. See above, chapter VII note 84.

37. '*Conjugium hoc divum meliori conditione est
    Quam nostrum . . .*'
'. . . *non est ex effluxu propriae substantiae extra suum corpus, vel alienae influxu. . .*'
'*Actio vere et passio consistit in alteratione per calidum et frigidum.*' *De immenso*, VI, v (*Opera*, I, ii, p. 179).

38. *La cena*, III, p. 170.

39. *Ibid.*, V, p. 208 and III, p. 100.

40. '. . . *sed in inviolabili, intermerabilique naturae lege, in bene ad eandem legem instituti animi religione, in splendore solis, in specie rerum, quae de huius nostrae parentis visceribus educuntur, in imagine illius vera corporeo modo explicata de vultu innumerabilium animantum, quae in immensa unius caeli fimbria lucent, vivunt, sentiunt, intelligunt, optimoque uni applaudunt maximo*'. *De immenso*, VIII, x (*Opera*, I, ii, p. 316).

41. Angelo Mercati, *Il Sommario del processo di Giordano Bruno*, Vatican City, 1942, p. 117, note 257.

42. See above, chapter VIII, p. 247 and note 3.

43. *La cena*, *Proemiale epistola*, p. 75 and V, pp. 207–208. The etymology accepted by Bruno is to be found in Plato, *Cratylos*, 410 *b*, and in Aristotle, *De coelo*, I, 3, 270 *b*. Note that Bruno does not apply the term *aethera* to the aether nor to the ultimate firmament, but to the celestial bodies.

44. '*Questi corridori hanno il principio di moti intrinseco la propria natura, la propria anima, la propria intelligenza.*' *La cena*, V, p. 208.

45. '*Sphaerae per aetheream regionem ab anima propria moventur. . . .*' *De immenso*, IV, xv (*Opera*, I, ii, p. 151).

46. *Ibid.*, V, xi, lines 13–14 (*Opera*, I, ii, p. 151).

47. '*Nec Tellus plus immenso gravis aethere habenda est,*
Quam quae sic vacuo corpuscula in aere pendent . . .'
De immenso, VI, ix (*Opera*, I, ii, p. 188).

48. '. . . *Manifestum est* . . . *de gravitate et levitate quod nulla sit in corporibus universi et maximis mundi membris.*' *De immenso*, V, i (*Opera*, I, ii, p. 119); *La cena*, V, p. 211. On gravity, see also *De immenso*, II, iii and ix; IV, ii; VI, ix.

49. '*Ex parte spacii nullum est resistens, nullum impedimentum.*' *De immenso*, IV, ix (*Opera*, I, ii, p. 84).

50. Tommaso Campanella, *Theologica*, xxvii, pp. 90–92 of reference given in chapter VIII, note 37.

51. '*Meminisse debemus animam esse in omnibus motus principium.*' *De immenso*, V, i (*Opera*, I, ii, p. 121).

52. '*Causa motus et quietus non erit a loco et spacio* . . . *capere, sed ab aliis, quas compositionis eorum natura dictat, rationibus.*' *De immenso*, I, v (*Opera*, I, i, p. 220).

53. '*Principium illius motus est sensus, et secundum genus cognitio, et appetitus qui cognitionem secundum genus consequitur: finis est conservatio sui, motor est anima*. . . .' *De immenso*, IV, xv (*Opera*, I, ii, p. 84); see *De immenso*, V, ii (*Opera*, I, ii, pp. 121 ff); *De l'infinito*, III, pp. 341–342. The principle and the laws of movement which had been one of the chief preoccupations of physicists from the fourteenth century (as is proved by the innumerable treatises entitled *De motu*) had never been the subject of deep study on the part of Giordano Bruno. The flagrant inadequacies of his doctrine in this respect are to be explained by his animism. The 'internal impulse', which he relates to the *anima*, remains a prime fact and is enveloped in a mystery which he considers to be impenetrable, because, on his own admission, it is impossible to rise higher than the soul of the universe in considering causes.

X

Time and eternity

Bruno alludes on three occasions in the vernacular dialogues to the 'great year', a cycle at the end of which all the planets will return to their initial positions. In *La cena de le ceneri* it is still only a question of an astronomical phenomenon requiring a very long time, but similar in nature to any other: through the action of the third terrestrial motion 'the eighth sphere seems to move on the poles of the zodiac contrary to the diurnal motion though the signs in order, and so slowly that it is not displaced more than one degree twenty-eight minutes in two hundred years, with the result that 49,000 years are needed to complete the circle'.[1] This calculation is taken from the *Alfonsine Tables*. In the first dialogue of *Spaccio*, Sofia, when disclosing to her surprised listeners the age of Jupiter, implies that the imminent completion of this 'great revolution' (here reduced to 36,000 years) could mark the beginning of a fresh era under the reign of a new firmament.[2] Finally, in *Eroici furori*, at the beginning of the second part, the dialogue opens with an evocation of this great cycle, though no precise duration is assigned to it; but on this occasion, the promise of new times and a reformed universe is replaced by the announcement of a revival, a recommencement: 'The revolution or great year of the universe will be in that space of time during which we return to a certain state of things after passing through other infinitely varied and contrasted states, as we note in connection with particular years, amongst others, the solar year in which the principle of one arrangement of things coincides with the close of a contrary arrangement, and the principle of the latter with the close of the former.'[3] On the other hand, it is said that 'the most excellent things are brought about when the planets are in the sign of the Ram', whereas 'the worst occur when the contrary arrangement and order prevail'. Now, Bruno was not unaware that this conjunction of planets *in Ariete* should occur in the very year in which he was writing those lines, namely, in 1584, as had been predicted by the

269

Bohemian astrologer Cyprian Leowicz.[4] It is not easy to understand why Bruno adds that 'we are nowadays in the dregs of science . . . and morals', and that 'we have every reason to expect a return of better times'. These irrelevancies are of little importance. From the passages in question we need only reserve the fact that the reality of the cosmic cycles is asserted there as a law of nature dominating both the firmament and our destiny.

In the final pages of his analysis of *De immenso*, Felice Tocco, after having shown that Bruno's cosmological doctrine has altered little in those great lines, then lists the discrepancies which he has noted, or believes he has noted, between the vernacular dialogues and the Latin poems. One of them, and not the least important, bears on the great year which was taken into account in the treatises written at London, and which was later to become a subject of derision for our author.[5] Two whole chapters of *De immenso*, the sixth and seventh in Book III, are devoted to refuting the theory of cycles and eternal returns, which are inconceivable in a universe where everything moves and changes without ceasing and where nothing is exactly reproduced throughout the ages. The seventh chapter is entitled: *Prosequitur propositum de vanitate circulorum et anni illius mundani phantasie platonica et aliorum*; and the criticism so explicitly stated in this title assumes, first of all, as it so often does with Bruno, a burlesque form. A flea and a bug discuss their destiny. The flea bemoans his miserable fate; the bug comforts him with the assurance that he will live again and that some thousands of years hence the same conversation between them will be resumed: 'You will see me again, I shall meet you again.'

Tu me iterum repetes, iterum teque ipse revisam.[6]

Nevertheless, whatever he may say, the texts that Tocco compares do not exhibit the essential differences that he would wish to find in them. Quite fairly, however, he suggests an objection to his own thesis when he recalls that the passage from the *Spaccio* cited by him (and quoted above), if it really takes account of the cosmic cycles, implies that they do not involve an eternal recommencement of everything; on the contrary, seeing that Jupiter, regarding the approaching end of the great year with some apprehension, wonders if the succeeding one will be similar to the one that is ending, or if Destiny, higher than the gods, will decide otherwise. To that we may add that Bruno *no-where* admits the possibility of a sequence of facts repeated eternally and exactly. The cosmic—or historical—cycles, in which he so readily takes pleasure in conjuring up order and majesty both in the Latin works and the vernacular dialogues, are only ever compared with our solar years, which never bring back the same events, as we know from experience. The 'great seasons' rule over our climates and fortunes, but they differ from our summers and winters only in the slowness of their development[7]. In that sense, we can say that life starts afresh, that empires succeed empires, that recent history sometimes offers an echo of the most ancient and of its heroic ups and downs: Pepin appropriated the effects of Aeneas, Roland those of Achilles, but each time, fresh attire was cut from the old material: *exit de panno antiquo nova vestis.* . . .[8]

To summarize, the 'cycles' whose existence we can accept form the temporal framework of similar vicissitudes, though they are not similar in all respects; and furthermore they only ever put rhythm into the destinies of a closed domain: the planetary system, the history of the human race. As for the 'eternal return', Bruno mentions it in *De immenso* only to discard it amongst the 'fantastic' dreams of philosophers; a criticism which is only too well deserved in his opinion in a work dealing with the infinite universe.

Indeed, whether it be a question of cosmic cycles, of eternity, of tangible being or of any other problem relating to the development of the universe, it is absolutely necessary to distinguish two orders of time in order to understand Bruno's thought: the time of finite *worlds*, which will be properly the 'cosmic' time, a rhythmic time divided into periods, and multiform in the sense that it adapts itself everywhere to the planetary system whose revolutions it measures; and the time, unimaginable and without end, of the 'infinite and unimaginable' universe. For the sake of clarity, these two aspects of time will be considered separately.

I. COSMIC TIME

Although Bruno gives the most complete description of his views on time[9] in *Acrotismus camoeracensis*, that is to say, within the framework of a polemic against Aristotle, his starting points are strictly Aristotelian. According to Aristotle, time is not directly measurable, but the correspondence that exists in local motion between the time elapsed and the distance travelled allows one of them to be measured when the other is measured. On the other hand, time is in the first place a psychological reality: *Dicit Philosophus quod si non esset anima non esset tempus.*[10] So that 'objectively based in the reality of motion, time has its completed existence only in the soul by which it is perceived.'[11]

As regards the parallelism between, or better the interdependence of, time and motion, Bruno hardly departs from the doctrine of the Schoolmen, and whatever the impetuous vivacity of the discussion contained in article xxxix of *Acrotismus*, it reduces to a dispute of words. Still, on reading we should be tempted, in spite of Aristotle and contrary to what he asserts, to believe that time is not the measure of motion; rather, it is motion that is the measure of time.[11b]

Any measure of time would be impossible without motion; in a universe in a state of perfect rest, all consciousness of time would be abolished; but we must note that it would be the notion of time and not time itself that would disappear with motion.[11c] We could even complete this particular without falsifying the reasoning thus set in train and say that the awareness we have of the one is linked with the experience we derive from the other—neglecting time and motion in themselves.

When Bruno takes objection to Aristotle and his School on account of the famous formula: 'Time is the number of motion', he forgets that the number in question is the 'numbered number' (*numerus numeratus*) and not the 'numbering number' (*numerus numerans*), the concrete number and not the abstract number. Experience of motion precedes and conditions the notion of time, but when we wish subsequently to measure the motion, we divide it into successive 'times'. In practice, then, time is certainly the measure of motion.[12]

As for the psychological reality of time, *i.e.*, the time of actual experience and which has been perceived through motion, Bruno does not disregard it. There we have the pulsations of life, the rhythms of the organism which impose the notion of time on the mind in the first place. Experience of the external world merely corroborates internal experience; it amplifies it, perfects it, and in its turn influences the mind of the man who is curious of his own destiny. The circular motions of celestial bodies suggest to anyone who meditates on the history of individuals, families, institutions and empires, the picture of a revolving wheel, the familiar allegory in which the poet of *Eroici furori* so frequently takes delight.[13]

Nevertheless, if the problem of time be presented in the same terms by Bruno and Aristotle (the use of a certain vocabulary being explained by Bruno's early philosophical up-bringing), the disagreement between their solutions is insuperable.

Bruno thinks as follows: time inseparable from motion—no matter if it be measured by itself or if it serve to measure something—is the time of which we are conscious; perceived time and not absolute time which it would be convenient to call by another name, as we shall see later. Absolute time is pre-existent to motion, and would exist in a supposedly stationary and unchangeable universe: 'Most certainly, if there were no motion or change, nothing could be called temporal; there would be only one single and same time in all things, one single and same duration, called eternity (*una eademque duratio quae aeternitas dicitur*), whilst time that is the age of each particular thing would be abolished (*tempus quoddest cujusque rei aetas nummum esset*).'[14] The development which starts in this fashion is a continuation of article xi in *Acrotismus*; it explains the meaning and defines the scope of the sentence: 'That is why Aristotle had to link motion not with time, but with the notion of time.' Furthermore, duration *which is called eternity* is one, whereas time *which is the age of things* is multiple; there is not one time but many times, each world having its own proper time. Whether we measure time in years or in great cycles, our years are never anything but those of *our* world; our cycles, those of *our* firmament: those longer or shorter periods would in no way be able to give rhythm to the life of the universe. In the letter of dedication to Sir Philip Sidney which prefaces the dialogues of *Eroici furori*, Bruno evokes the words in the *Apocalypse* 'according to which the dragon will be kept in chains for a thousand years, and at the end of a thousand years will be set free'; but we could speak of a 'year', a 'season', a 'night' just as well as of a thousand years, this expression being employed here figuratively in order to designate a fatal cycle of 'ascent and descent'. 'Furthermore,' he adds, 'it is quite certain that this period of a thousand years was not calculated according to the revolution that defines our solar year, but definitely according to the proportions of various orders and measures to which the diversity of the firmament is subjected; for the years of the celestial bodies differ amongst themselves just as much as particular species differ.'[15]

The Aristotelian point of view is quite the reverse. Perceived time is linked with motion, and there is no other. There is no time apart from motion which it measures, and apart from the soul which perceives it. This same time is, moreover, unique for the reason that the universe is one, that it is organized about a centre and animated by eternal motion. No doubt time can measure the most diverse motions, and it would seem that we have there a root of plurality; nevertheless, it is unique because there exists a privileged motion on which everything depends and which allows it to be the measure of all that moves in the body of the universe, namely, the motion of the first firmament (or the last if we start from the Earth), 'which by its regularity and perpetuity, is perfectly adapted to this function of supreme and universal mensuration'.[16]

Consequently, the disagreement between the two doctrines as to the concept of time results in their disagreement as to the concept of the universe. Aristotle's time is that of a finite universe, of a body, of an organism. For Bruno, the universe is infinite and composed of an infinity of worlds; so that the motion from which it is inseparable cannot be that motion of the *firmament*—this expression no longer has any meaning when we discard the hypothesis of the 'spheres'— but the motion of the *celestial bodies*: *Tempus quod est mensura motus non est in coelo, sed in astris.* Its lack of unity results therefrom: 'In the universe, the times are equal to the number of celestial bodies.'[17]

The positions seem to be reversed here: Bruno seems to deny, and Aristotle to accept, the existence of absolute time; but for Aristotle, time is only apparently absolute, because of the privileged celestial motion of which it is the measure; on the other hand, for Bruno, cosmic times are relative to various motions of the celestial bodies, but there is a universal and truly absolute time that transcends them, *duratio una quae dicitur aeternitas.* A cosmic timepiece exists in the Aristotelian universe: the motion of the eighth sphere, the most regular of them all, is called the *primum mobile* or prime mover; it regulates and measure the duration of everything.[18] In the Brunonian universe, countless timepieces measure countless times, amongst which the one that is our own and which it is given to us to know is closely linked with the revolution of our planet and the nearest celestial bodies.

On the other hand, if we remember that, in this universe, matter is substantially one; that the ultimate elements are identical, unchangeable, beyond reach of every vicissitude and, so to speak, not subject to time; that every change depends on a local motion and that this local motion is possible only because a space exists between the material bodies and between the elements comprising them, namely, the mysterious aether 'that we may call the void'; if we remember all that, then we come to the conclusion that in such a system, time (cosmic time, temporality) necessarily implies the void. Without the void, no motion; without motion, no cognizable time, no possibility of developing. So that cosmic development results from an insufficiency in existence, in the same way that an insufficiency in existence resulted, as we have seen, from the diversity of particular souls and the chances of their immortality.

Having accepted the indestructibility of matter and having excluded all notion of periodic cycles in the course of which the same events should reappear without end, we are led to think that the universe passes ceaselessly in the course of time from a definitely completed past to an absolutely fresh future. Would the question of the eternity of the universes and of their destinies be resolved in that manner?

Aristotle asserts the eternity of the universe by distinguishing two eternities: the stationary eternity of the prime motive force and the eternal, regular motion of the *primum mobile*. Time, a stranger to the former, measures the latter.

Bruno parts company with Aristotle in that he does not distinguish two eternities, but two times: that of the universe, which is eternity, and that of the worlds. Now, the eternity of *the worlds*—the only one that we have to consider for the moment—is not guaranteed by the indestructibility of matter, as in the case of the universe. It remains in question. By 'worlds' we have to understand the celestial bodies, the countless earths and suns that are strewn throughout infinite space. Is each of these worlds, like the universe as a whole, co-eternal with God? It must be admitted that our texts reveal some hesitation of thought on this matter. Certain texts would let us assume that Bruno believes in the perennial state of the Earth, which, thanks to the renewal of its various organs, would prolong its existence indefinitely: 'Death and dissolution not being suitable to the entirety of that mass which constitutes our globe, and the annihilation of all nature being impossible, it follows that in the course of time and in a certain order [the Earth] renews itself through the alteration and change of all its parts.'[19] If it were otherwise, the celestial bodies would be destined to die, as do the lesser creatures such as we. We must, therefore, abide by what is taught in Plato's *Timaeus*, where the Prime Principle that has engendered everything addresses the gods (*i.e.*, the celestial bodies), saying: 'You are not indissoluble, but you will not be dissolved.'[20]

Theophilus uses these words in the fifth dialogue of *La cena* when he freely summarizes the passage from *Timaeus* (41 *b*): 'You are neither immortal nor incorruptible. However, you shall never be dissolved . . . because my will constitutes a stronger bond for you . . . than those which joined you at birth.' 'That is what Plato believes, and that is what we believe, too,' says Theophilus. The same idea, with the same reference to Plato, occurs in the second dialogue of *De la causa*: 'Those magnificent celestial bodies, those great creatures, those excellent gods are compounded and dissoluble . . . even though they are not worthy on that account to be dissolved, as has been well said in *Timaeus*.'[21] Bruno reverts to this subject for a third time in the second dialogue of *De l'infinito*, where he defines what should be, in his opinion, the 'nutrition' of the celestial bodies: this Earth is not eternal because its parts are eternal, but because they modify themselves: particles of matter suspended in the immense aether come and nourish it, so to speak, whereas others are ejected, as is the case with animals.[22]

As the eternity of the Earth (eternal though corruptible) is a fundamental Aristotelian idea, Gentile thought it necessary to point out with regard to the passage from *La cena* quoted above that it was an 'Aristotelian relic', of which no trace remained in *De immenso*; it was a rather risky comment seeing that the sentence to which it applies occurs immediately before the quotation from Plato and states that '*these bodies* that are corruptible sometimes run the risk of being dissolved'. On the other hand the plural *questi corpi* shows quite clearly that it is not a question of the Earth alone, but also of all the celestial bodies that share with it in fact an immortality from which they profit through the will of God, but does not in the least result from their nature; the celestial bodies, like all bodies with the exception of the ultimate elements of matter, being compounded and therefore corruptible.[23]

The Latin works subsequent to the dialogues in the vernacular do not express any different idea. In *De immenso* (II, v and V, iii) and in *De rerum principiis*, the death of the celestial bodies is not stated as being inescapable, but is regarded as merely possible. Bruno retracts so little that he invokes the same Platonic text in *De immenso* as in *La cena* and *De la causa*. Celestial bodies are living together, they are therefore liable to die. Is their death comparable with our own? We know nothing for sure about that (*hoc certe nescimus*); what we definitely know is that being compounded they are capable of being dissolved. This possibility of the death of worlds is stated twice in *De immenso* and again in *De rerum principiis*.[24] However, was not the possibility already recognized in the dialogues written at London, even though it were in the hypothesis of an immortality assured to the celestial bodies through divine favour? In the Latin works only the *probability* of this death of worlds is differently appraised. In considering it to be greater—or even infinite in the open field of a limitless future—Bruno, far from denying his doctrine, draws therefrom the expected consequences.

II. UNIVERSAL TIME

The indestructibility of matter and the perennial state of the soul of the universe assures an endless duration to the universe. In the letter of dedication of *De l'infinito*, Bruno praises the Ancient atomists, Democritos and Epicuros, for having, both of them, taught that everything renews itself and reconstitutes itself indefinitely, 'the same number always succeeding the same number', and for having saved thereby 'the constancy of the universe'.[25] If *the worlds* live and die— or are capable of dying—it is in the depths of a universe whose eternity, based on atomistic physics and postulated by a cosmology that sees an aspect of God in nature, is not in doubt.

Creation, chaos and end of the world. We have seen how Brunonian cosmology excluded any idea of creation, creation *a nihilo* (a universe rising into being at the behest of the unchangeable and through the power of divine will), just as much as by putting a pre-existing chaos into order (sudden or progressive conquest of the $\overset{,}{\alpha}\pi\epsilon\iota\rho\text{o}\nu$ by the $\nu\text{o}\widehat{\upsilon}\varsigma$).[26] We shall now see how the hypothesis of an end of the world must be similarly discarded.

The destruction, the end of *a world* is possible, and so is the creation of a world, if by that we understand the appearance of some new star. It would perhaps be likewise permitted to call chaos the state of dispersion that would follow the death of a celestial body and preceding the birth of a fresh one; but these terms would only designate partial destructions, voids and creations, simple 'vicissitudes' happening in cosmic time, and in no instance would they be applicable to the universe, for even the simultaneous end of *all the worlds* would not be the end of the universe; it would not have the character of a Heraclitean conflagration, it would be only the sum of an infinite number of distinct events, whose simultaneity would remain fortuitous. In several lines in *De immenso*, this vision of the death of all the worlds, presented moreover expressly as a limiting case of zero probability, is accompanied by the calm certitude that even then universal life would resume its course through the influence of an organizing principle, and not through some happy combination born of chance, as Democritos would have it.[27]

The idea of a chaos raises a problem whose solution is less obvious. Whilst discarding the hypothesis of a primordial chaos from which the universe might have arisen, and that of a final chaos, the abyss into which it would fall again after the consummation of the ages, it seems that we can assume, that in certain circumstances and in some fixed region of space, a chaotic universe will follow for a time the condition of a destroyed universe. Such an eventuality would not be incompatible with the cosmology of *De immenso*. However, it is clear that Bruno is reluctant to imagine the presence in his universe of a chaos even limited in time and in space. He prefers to assume that the death of a world must be immediately followed by the recomposition of its dispersed elements, without the interregnum of a disorder that the omnipresence of the formal principle and the constancy of its directing influence would not permit. 'Now, Nature is either nothing, or it is a divine power working on matter, *a perpetual order* imposed on everything.'[28] A partial disorder is only an illusion of our partial view of things. Being just as foreign to nature as to birth and death, it is unable to find a place in a universe that is perfect at every instant.

If *worlds* can die, the age of the *universe* is limitless, for beyond all that endures there exists duration, whose absolute nature and infinitude the author of *De minimo* does not hesitate to declare, even though he cautiously makes a reservation in respect of the eternity 'of this world'.[29] This 'duration', independent of any measure—that is to say of any motion—is, however, only a view of the mind, on the same level as matter without form or as form without matter. In reality, duration and its content are inseparable; and consequently the question of development as regards the universe arises afresh.

How can this development be pictured? For most of the Greek cosmologers, the infinity of time linked to periodic cycles finds its most suitable expression in circular motion. Undoubtedly, for Anaximander, the ἀπείρων is just as much a temporal as a spatial receptacle, and thus we have the outline of the concept of an eternity that includes time and transcends it;[30] but for Heraclitos and Empedocles this idea of a receptacle becomes indistinct and the periodic cycle becomes the sole form of temporal infinity. Plato accepts the cosmic cycles, but not the everlasting return (whatever Bruno may say on the matter), and Democritos imagined the successive, but not cyclic, destruction and recomposition of worlds: would a regular periodicity never be the result of chance? Bruno, as we have seen, discards all these theories without distinction, his conception of the universe being just as incompatible with the hypothesis of 'included' cycles (seeing that no ἀπείρων is able to envelop a universe which is itself infinite), as with that of cycles taking in the entire universe, seeing that they would constitute a blasphemous limitation of the divine power: any periodic representation of development would reduce the real to a very small portion of the possible. Without even considering the eternal return, would a succession of 'universal' years and seasons comparable with our seasons and years by conceivable? On one page of *De immenso*, Bruno ridicules the Arab philosopher who believed he could declare, against the eternity of the universe, that the infinity of years should be equal to twelve times that of the months, the infinity of months to thirty times that of the days, etc.[30b] Such an argument would be valid also against the immensity of the universe and the 'uncountability' of the universes, seeing that the suns are infinite in number and that there exist more worlds than suns. However, all that is childish, and Bruno adds, 'we have already refuted that absurdity at greater length in our books on "the existence and contemplation of the minimum"'.[31]

What is an 'absurdity' in Bruno's view, is to divide time and the infinite universe into periods only suitable for giving life to restricted, or at least perishable, universes.

Must we, therefore, substitute the straight line for the symbol of the circle, and having abandoned all idea of cycles, accept that of indefinite progress? What sense would there be in a progress that was able to tend only towards an end already attained? If the first hypothesis, that of cycles and returns, confesses itself to be incompatible with the infiniteness of the divine powers whose influence it would limit;[32] the second, that of progress, cannot agree with the simultaneity, laid down as a principle, of the divine power and the divine act. Not only is it impossible to produce anything better, but also anything new, in a universe where everything has been completed from all eternity.

The stationary universe. There remains a third symbol: the broken or wavy line, a sinuous path, without beginning or end, without principle and without purpose, never returning on itself and wending its way towards nothing. Would this representation satisfy the philosopher any more? Definitely no! No figure evoking the idea of a path and a trudging along (even ordered, and *a fortiori* disordered) would be an adequate symbol of eternity.

The eternal is essentially unchangeable: if the universe be eternal, then it is stationary, as was asserted by Parmenides and Xenophanes, the first of whom is quoted in *De la causa*, and the second in *De minimo*.[33] Bruno several times compares immobility to an infinitely rapid motion, though admittedly in rather obscure terms. So, to the various motions into which he divides that of the Earth, or any other celestial body, he adds another mysterious one, which is unknown to astronomers and beyond the reach of experience; it consists in a kind of instantaneous rotation as a result of which every point on a circumference is present, and is always present, on the entire circumference. In *Eroici furori*, the picture of a wheel turning on its axis and accompanied by the motto *Manens moveor* is given as the emblem for the conjunction of the mobile and the immobile. Elsewhere, a sun is shown between two circles, one interior, the other exterior, with the motto *Circuit*: 'This double circle drawn both in and around it' means that its motion 'is ended and continues'; 'so that the Sun always finds itself in all points of the cycle it covers, for it moves in an instant . . . it is similarly present in all points of the circumference; motion and rest are conjoined and united in it'. Those are the words of Tansillo, and the person with whom he is speaking replies that he has already understood the meaning of the discourse; that he learned 'from the dialogues in *De l'infinito*, where it is stated that the Divine Wisdom is mobile to the highest degree, as was said by Solomon, and that it is at the same time very stable, as anyone endowed with reason will think and understand'.[34]

However, this theme is developed most clearly and fully in the fourth chapter of the first book of *De minimo*; first of all in the poetical text; then in the prose commentary, where the identity of absolute motion and rest with the simultaneous position of a point everywhere on the circumference is stated, and where allusion is again made to the 'divine wisdom', *mobilissima et immobilissima*.[35]

Bruno's emphasis on the image of the wheel would lead us to assume, if not adherence, to the theory of cycles, which is definitely rejected, then at least a very unlikely concession to that theory. Nothing could be more erroneous. The *wheel* is only a symbolic figure destined, like every true symbol, to express the inexpressible, and to let us attain this incomprehensible truth that beyond all motions that affect material objects, and amongst others the celestial bodies, there exists a 'universal' motion which is necessarily rest, for the universe, in its infinitude, is unchangeable. It contains everything, so that nothing can be added to it, and nothing can be taken away from it. Its unchangeableness, a consequence of its co-eternity with God, deprives it of development. For the universe, motion is rest and time is abolished.

Simultaneity of all the possibles. In the above passages we have noticed several topics that occur in the writings of Nicholas of Cusa: the coincidence of motion and rest in the infinite; the coincidence of opposites; and the identification in God of existence and ability to exist, which is frequently asserted. Bruno, however, draws more daring conclusions from these premises than the theologian from the Rhine had done; for, if Nicholas of Cusa admits that he does not understand how creation could have taken place in time, seeing that the cause is eternal, he accepts this mystery, whereas Bruno, having less respect for dogma, logically concludes in favour of the eternity of a universe which, being the reflection of God and the 'explication' of the prime principle, participates in its attributes.

If, on the other hand, development is looked at in the Aristotelian manner as the blossoming of a form which imposes itself on matter and replaces 'privation', we shall accept that motion—the measure of time and physical sign of all development—is definitely the act of that which is in potentiality, according to the classical definition. The being which is in course of development, or in motion, is as though it were half-way between potentiality and act.[36] Thus, motion associates the two concepts of potentiality and act and 'finally appears as an imperfect act, as potentiality not yet excited to action'.[37]

However, if, as does Bruno, we accept these facts subject to making time the measure of motion and not making motion the measure of time, it will be permissible for us to deduce that motion is 'a non-instantaneous passage from potentiality to the act', *motus est exitus de potentia in actu non subito*—a definition that was held to be erroneous by St Thomas Aquinas and not in agreement with the teaching of the Master.[38] Now, to accept this definition of motion is to declare both the divine immobility and the co-existence of all the possibles, seeing that all the potentialities of God are actuated and that their excitation requires no time at all: '. . . The Prime Principle is all that it can be and itself would not be all if it could not be all; therefore, act and potentiality are but one in it. Such is not the case with other things, which, if they are what they are able to be, are able also not to be, or to be different from, what they are, for not one of them is all that it can be. Man is not all that he can be; stone is not all that it can be . . .', etc.[39] Therefore, only the Prime Principle exhausts its possibilities; as these possibilities are infinite, they are exhausted only in the infinite, and as their excitation to action is immediate, they are exhausted in an instant.

The idea of total actuation, outside of the temporal field, of the divine possibilities had been familiar to Christian thought for a long while, but this actuation was placed on the level of the intelligibles. The possibilities were realized in the mind of God before being so in the course of time in the created universe. 'God could not gainsay himself', wrote St Bernard, 'nor fail to accomplish that which *He has already accomplished* in reality. In fact, the Scriptures say that *He has accomplished* everything that will supervene in the future.'[40] Bruno, however, having joined the universe and his principle together, no longer distinguishes these two methods of accomplishment. He replaces a fatal and inescapable development by an effective instantaneity; so that he arrives at this unnatural conception, again in his grandiose manner, of a universe where all the possibles are contained in the present hour, from the beginning and for ever. The succession of time affects only worlds and not the universe; it is an illusion of our partial experience. Form, which destroys itself here by the *effluence*[41] of the elements of matter through which it was realized, is found again elsewhere in another region of infinite space as a result of their confluence; so that, what is past for us is present elsewhere, and what is future for us is already present elsewhere.

Eternity is not an indefinite time, a succession of hours or centuries, but a unique instant: 'Past, present and future in the eyes of God are but one present, one single eternal present.'[42]

Unity, perennity, unchangeable presence are therefore the attributes of the universe. If the universe as a whole cannot undergo any alteration, it is equally true, and experience confirms the fact, that it contains number in its unity, and all development in a single instant: its unchangeability is not death, but life possessed in its plenitude. Such is the divine (and universal) life, which is very different from that of the objects and beings that come within our ken, it is even very different from cosmic life, if by that term we mean the life of *worlds*.[43]

Cycles, rectilinear progress of irreversible duration, eternal present, such are the three possible forms of a time that we assume to be endless. The first two reduce, or seem to reduce, to the reality of celestial revolutions and the development of history but they only affect partial objects. On the other hand, the third is not allowed in our experience, though it alone is adequate for the dimensions of the infinite universe.

Every soul being conscious of itself would wish to escape from time, from worlds, and from their cycles and progress in order to attain intellectual light in an instant through total vision of Nature as suggested by the fable of Actaeon. Still, it is that of the philosopher whose doctrine was developed round a thought, or rather an obsession, of absolute unity, and who, rightly regarded as one of the founders of modern rationalism, none the less dreamed of escaping from the bondage of discourse, of eliminating every sign and any language that would imply duration in order to bring all understanding to the ineffable simplicity of direct comprehension.

Unity is not conceived on the human scale as the result of *unification* (political, religious or anything else), or as the fortunate crowning of an organization of the universe and of the Earth first of all.[44] The return to the Unity does not demand and does not even involve external activity; it is not motion, but a folding back on itself, 'towards the centre', to the point where our soul reattaches itself to the universal soul—a purely spiritual exercise whose ultimate term coincides with what we call death.

An exploration of space, however far we could be carried, or of time however long we could continue, would not bring us closer to— nor would it take us further away from—an objective both inaccessible and very near, 'nearer to us than we are ourselves'. In all places, at every instant, we are at the limit of the divine, on the horizon of eternity.

NOTES

1. '*Il terzo moto si prende da quel che par che l'ottava sfera secondo l'ordine di segni, a l'incontro del moto diurno, sopra i poli del zodiaco, si muove si tardi, che in decento anni non si muove più ch'un grado, e 28 minuti: di modo che in quaranta nove milia anni vien a compir il circolo.*' *La cena*, pp. 226–227. According to Copernican data the precession would last only 23,000 years.
2. *Spaccio*, I, pp. 28–29; and see *De rerum principiis* (1590) (*Opera*, III, p. 538).
3. *Eroici furori*, II, i, p. 300.
4. In his treatise *De conjunctionibus magnis insignioribus superiorum planetarum*, published at Leuingen (Bavaria) in 1564 and reprinted by Thomas Vautrollier at London, 1573.
5. F. Tocco, *Le opere latine di Giordano Bruno*, pp. 324–325.
6. *De immenso*, III, vii (*Opera*, I, i, pp. 367–368).
7. '*Ad vicissitudinem tempestatum et fortunarum quibus haec inferiora non annuis, sed saecularibus vicissitudinibus permutantur atque disponuntur.*' *De rerum principiis* (*Opera*, III, p. 538).
8. '*Quondam*
   Ut Minos fuerat cristata casside pulcher,
   Ut sumpsit clypeum torsitque hastile venuste,
   Sic habet Arcturus iunctam cum viribus artem,
   Gottifridum vestit Turnus, gaudetque Pipinus
   Aeneae numeris, spoliisque Rolandus Achillis.
   Exit de panno antiquo nova vestis, et hic sunt
   Syndonem in alterius femoralia Caesaris acta.'
De minimo, I, i (*Opera*, I, iii, p. 136).
9. *Acrotismus. Ubi de tempore*, end of the discussion of the fourth book of *Physica* (*Opera*, I, i, pp. 143–150).
10. St Thomas Aquinas, *Physica*, IV, lectio 17; see Aristotle, *Physica*, IV, xiv, 26.
11. H. D. Gardeil, *Introduction à la philosophie de saint Thomas d'Aquin*, p. 76.
11*b*. '*Potius motus est mensura temporis, quam tempus mensura motus.*' *Acrotismus*, art. xxxix.
11*c*. '*Nihilominus tempus esse dicimus, si omnia quieverint. Propterea non tempus sed temporis cognitionem motui alligare debuit Aristoteles.*' *Ibid.*, art. xl (*Opera*, I, i, p. 148).
12. The adjectives (slow, rapid, accelerated, uniform, rhythmic, etc.) applied to motion nearly always imply the idea of time.
13. See, for example, *Eroici furori*, II, i, 5, pp. 322–324 (Emblem of the wheel accompanied by the motto *Manens moveor*).
14. *Acrotismus* (*Opera*, I, i, p. 148).
15. '*Questo (dicono alcuni) è significato dove' è detto in rivelatizone che il drago sarà avvinto ne le catene per mille anni, e passati quelli sarà disciolto. A cotal significazione voglion che mirino molti altri luoghi dove il millenario ora è espresso, ora è significato per un anno, ora per una etade, ora per un cubito, ora per una ed un'altra maniera. Oltre che certo il millenario istesso non si prende secondo le rivoluzioni definite da gli anni del sole, ma secondo le diverse ragioni de le diverse misure ed ordini con li quali son dispensate diverse cose: per che così son differenti gl anni de gl astri, come le specie de particolari non son medesime.*' *Eroici furori*, *Argomento*, p. 113.
16. H. D. Gardeil, *Initiation à la philosophie de saint Thomas d'Aquin*, II, *Cosmologie*, p. 77.
17. '. . . *tot sane erunt in universo tempora, quot sunt in astra.*' *Acrotismus*, art. xxxviii (*Opera*, I, i, pp. 143–144) and the continuation: '*Neque enim potest esse tale unum in universo, ut omnium motuum mensura existat: quandoquidem si nos essemus in alio astro, apertissime constaret brevissimum motum omnium esse ab isto, sicut in luna cinstat alium esse motum diurnum, ubi octo et vigenti dierum spatio in sua superficie recipit, quod hoc astrum, tellus, spatio vigenti quatuor horarum.*'
18. '*Quia primus motus Aristoteli habeatur omnium regulatissimus, utpote qui*

motus octavae sphaerae hic singularis esset primus, ideao ex ipso capta est ratio temporis et mensurae durationis omnium.' Ibid., p. 145.

19. '*Però a questa massa intierna della qual consta questo globo, questo astro, non essendo conveniente la morte, et la dissoluzione; ed essendo a tutta natura impossibile l'annihilazione: a tempi a tempi, con certo ordine, viene a rinovarsi, alterando, cangiando, mutando le sue parti tutte.*' *La cena*, V, p. 216.

20. '*Voi siete dissolubili ma non vi dissolverete.*' *La cena, ibid.; Timaeus*, 41 a–b.

21. *De la causa*, II, p. 177 (trans. Namer, p. 86).

22. '*Come appare anco ne gli animali, li quali non si continuano altrimente se non gli nutrimenti che riceveno, ed escrementi che sempre mandano.*' *De l'infinito*, II, p. 321.

23. *La cena*, V (ed. Gentile, 1925, p. 118, note 1). Gentile refers to *De immenso*, II, v and V, iii (*Opera*, I, i, p. 272 and I, ii, pp. 125–127). The title of the first of these two chapters reads as follows: ' *Digressio quaedam, quod si veluti dissolubiles, ex natura compositionis, sunt mundi, dissolvantur partibus a toto corpore diffluentibus, non inconvenit universali agitatione atomos (seu quomodocunque appelles prima corpora) infinite vagari.*'

24. '*Certe scimus (illa anaimalia) composita esse et consequenter dissolubilia.*' *De immenso*, II, v (*Opera*, I, i, p. 274); and see *ibid.*, V, iii; *De rerum principiis* (*Opera*, III, p. 52).

25. *De l'infinito, Proemiale epistola*, p. 282.

26. See above, chapter II.

27. '*Ergo si quae sors destruat unum*
    E mundis, plureisve simul, vel si lubet omneis
    (Quod sane haud rerum patitur sine fine potestas . . .)
    Vita recursabit, naturaque materiei,
    Hoc ipso instaurata, suo dat cuncta recessu.'
De immenso, V, iii (*Opera*, I, ii, p. 126).

28. '*Vel nihil est natura, vel est divina potestas*
    Materiam exagitans, impressusque omnibus ordo
    Perpetuus.'
De immenso, VI, x (*Opera*, I, ii, p. 193).

29. '*Duratio absolute est infinita; de mundi hujus aeternitate vel tempore non definio.*' *De minimo*, I, vi (*Opera*, I, iii, p. 153).

30. See, R. Mondolfo, *L'infinito nel pensiero dei Greci*, Florence, 1934, pp. 39 ff.

30b. '*Alchazeles . . . mahumetanus theologus . . . in libro destructionum contra aeternitarios adducit argumentum ex eo quod opporteret infinitos duodecies plures fuisse annos quam menses, trigesies circiter plures quam dies. . . .*' *De immenso*, I, iv (*Opera*, I, i, p. 217).

31. *Ibid.*, pp. 217–218. Allusion to the chapter from *De minimo* quoted above (note 29).

32. '*Infinita causa injuriose finiti dicitur effectus causa.*' *De immenso*, I, ix (*Opera*, I, i, p. 235).

33. *De la causa*, V, p. 254; *De minimo*, I, iv, line 33 ff (*Opera*, I, iii, p. 145). See, Aristotle, *Metaphysica*, I, 5, 986 *b*, 9–35.

34. *Eroici furori*, I, v, p. 260 (corrected translation); *Spaccio*, VII, 24; see, *De l'infinito*, I, p. 305; *De minimo*, I, iv (*Opera*, I, iii, p. 148). If Bruno is referring to the last mentioned text by the words *e dove si dechiara come la divina sapienza è mobilissima*, etc., we must believe that some fragments of *De minimo* are written at London.

35. *De minimo*, I, iv (*Opera*, I, iii, p. 148). The poetic text ends with the lines:
    '*Ergo quies motusque simul sunt maxime in illo*
    Uno, quod minime motum, quod maxime idemque est
    A fine ad finem gradiens; immobile prorsus
    Et simul in cunctis totum manet et super ipsa. . . .'
(*Ibid.*, p. 146).

36. '*Neque est potentia existentis in potentia, neque est actus existentis in actu, sed est actus existentis in potentia.*' St Thomas Aquinas, *Physica*, III, *lectio* 2.

37. H. D. Gardeil, *Initiation à la philosophie de saint Thomas d'Aquin, Cosmologie*, p. 59.

38. St Thomas Aquina, *Physica*, III, *lectio* 2.

39. *De la causa*, III, pp. 218–219.

40. *Sermons sur le Cantique des Cantiques*, LXVIII, 6 (trans. Albert Béguin, Paris, 1953, p. 705).

41. The nouns *effluxus, influxus* (and the corresponding verbs) form part of Bruno's philosophical vocabulary. See, for example, *De immenso*, II, v (*Opera*, I, i, p. 272).

42. '*Praeteritum, praesens . . . atque futurum
      Ante Deum praesens unum est unumque perenne.*'
De immenso, I, xii (*Opera*, I, i, p. 244).

43. On the two meanings of the word *instant*, which may mean either an 'atom of time' (*atomo di tempo*) or 'the whole time' (*tutto il tempo*), see *Eroici furori*,I, v, 14, motto: *Amor instat ut instans*, pp. 288 ff.

44. As Tommaso Campanella does to the contrary. See P. H. Michel, '*Cosmologies de la Renaissance*, II, *Le règne de l'unité*,' in *Diogène*, April -1957, pp. 114 ff.

The Subsequent History of Brunonian Philosophy

The preceding account of the main themes in Brunonian cosmology may have tempted many a reader to ask impatiently: What is the use of it all? Why rescue from oblivion a doctrine that is contradicted by facts and one from which nobody at the present time imagines any profit can be derived? The question is no doubt justifiable; it could, however, be asked in respect of any other system of the universe, but it merely tells us that Bruno's system, like any other, belongs to history and must be placed in an historical perspective where its presence may justify itself.

Now, it will be justified only in a future perspective. Indeed, it is not enough for a cosmology or a physics to add something to the sum total of previous doctrines: it must enrich them with permanent, fruitful ideas. Fruitful, in that they arouse curiosity, give rise to doubt, instigate the development of fresh hypotheses; permanent, in that they are consistent, be it one point only, with some truth secure for the future and that the subsequent progress of knowledge is no longer in danger of being disturbed. Those are the more or less conscious, clear demands of posterity. The fortune of a system will depend, therefore, on the satisfaction that it will provide or that we feel will be provided in respect of those demands: the fortune changes with the passage of time, because it is linked on the one hand with the most recent state of scientific knowledge, and on the other hand with the greater or less historical inclination of successive generations.

The classical age (XVII–XVIII centuries). The seventeenth century saw the rapid decline of the traditional disciplines derived from medieval Aristotelianism; incapable of fresh progress, they survived, or rather they refused to die, as they were always taught in the Schools under the protection of the highest authorities; but modern

287

science has gradually supplanted them: the best minds support heliocentric astronomy; the new physics no longer accepts a distinction between the sublunary world and the celestial world.

These two contrary movements were to exert an equally unfavourable influence initially and for a long while on Bruno's posthumous reputation.

For the supporters of a continually threatened, but still powerful, tradition, the author of *De immenso* remained the enemy, the ungodly one who was rightly condemned to the flames. His opinions—especially those relating to astronomy—were subject to severe strictures throughout the whole of the seventeenth century and down to the middle of the eighteenth. In 1700, a French cleric, Marc Antoine Guigues, referred to the hypothesis according to which the stars would be 'as many suns illuminating other worlds'; this was in a work which was published at Rome under the title *La sphère géographico-céleste*. He adds, 'To believe that, it would be necessary to have the mind of Giordano Bruno who was burnt by the judgment of the Holy Inquisition for having maintained such an impertinence.' Later still (we purposely choose late examples as evidence of endless opposition), an Italian, Giovanni Crivelli, in his *Elementi di fisica* (Venice, 1731), writes about the 'extravagant' doctrines of Giordano Bruno—infinitude of the universe, plurality of worlds, etc.

On the subject of the plurality of worlds, as well as on some others, agreement between his ideas and theories in fashion at any time were to give Bruno some recompense. He had at least a share in the applause lavished on Fontenelle by an enlightened public. Indeed, he happened to receive justice. An historian of science, Noël Regnault, S.J., in a work on *L'origine ancienne de la physique nouvelle* (Paris, 1734), expressed the opinion that the revival of Platonism in the fifteenth and sixteenth centuries did not carry knowledge beyond the point where submission to Aristotle had left it; but *Bruno and then Descartes have shaken off the yoke*. The author means the yoke of the science of antiquity, whether it be Aristotelian or Platonic; modern minds must acknowledge their debt to it, but must no longer be slaves to it.

We must not be deceived by this tribute to Bruno: it is not unique, but it is exceptional. In fact, the new knowledge did not accept the dangerous heritage from Bruno; it did not try to rescue his memory; it even pretended to ignore him, at first, undoubtedly through prudence, though there were other reasons too. If fear of anathema from

Rome partly explains the silence of a Galileo or a Descartes, it cannot be the sole cause of disaffectedness or forgetfulness that have persisted long after any such fear ceased to be justified.

The reticent and frequently contemptuous attitude of the best minds with regard to Bruno depends, in our view, to a great extent on a more justifiable scruple: the new knowledge, which was being built up, was based on principles no less foreign to those of 'Brunonian philosophy' than to those of Aristotelian scolasticism; its methods, too, were different, and in so far as it consented to recognize sources, it found them elsewhere. For Galileo, Descartes and Leonardo da Vinci, knowledge of nature is nothing if not mathematical. 'No doctrine merits the name of science if it does not survive mathematical proof' said Leonardo; from the very first page of the *Dialogo sopra i due massimi sistemi del mondo*, Galileo proclaims his wish to base physics on mathematics: 'That the Phythagoreans held the science of numbers in high esteem, and that Plato himself admired the human understanding and believed it to partake of divinity simply because it understood the nature of numbers, I know very very well; *nor am I far from being of the same opinion*'; and Descartes (*Les Principes de la philosophie*, II, 64): 'I do not accept principles in physics unless they are also accepted in mathematics.' So much for the principles. As for the methods, not only is more importance being continually given to observation, but also problems are no longer presented in the same terms, nor are they resolved with the help of the same logical instruments; the path of knowledge goes from the observed fact to its immediate causes, then from there to the first causes—assuming that such a step is permissible, that is to say, if a more rigorous discipline of thought does not require that we confine ourselves to establishing the sequence of phenomena. That is how Galileo reasons, whereas Bruno constructs his universe at one fell swoop on the basis of intuitions which appear to him as evidence, and, starting from henceforth uncontroverted premises, returns to tangible facts along a descending path.

Differences of this kind might not have been sufficient to keep Bruno as an exile, on the side-line, away from the field of the new knowledge, at least when that knowledge started to build up, for at that time its uncertainties, enthusiasms, the very multiplicity of its attempts could have created favourable conditions for a more liberal reception. However, the period was one in which a 'prudent silence' was imposed; and when certain fears had disappeared, a veering of learned opinion was no longer possible, the gap was too wide between the statements of an overbold cosmology and those of a positive science which was more and more careful to check the results of its observations or calculations.

Some examples will serve to make the position described above easier to understand.

Contrary to the Aristotelians, Bruno professes the infinite universe, the infinitely great realized, and necessarily realized, from the fact that the universe is an aspect of God, Himself infinite. Such a concept, though based on theological data and expressed in form unacceptable to positive science, obviously coincides with the tendency of modern astronomy continually to enlarge its domain and to push the limits of the sky further and further away, after having broken the framework of a confined, closed cosmos. If we merely consider the estimates of the Earth's distance from the Sun throughout the ages, we shall find that they changed to a very small, even insignificant, extent from Antiquity to the end of the seventeenth century. Ptolemy put the solar orbit at a distance of 1210 terrestrial radii; Copernicus, using the same unit, lowered the figure to 1179, Tycho Brahe to 1150; Galileo raised it to 1208 and Gaultier de La Valette (c. 1564–1647) to 1218. Then, suddenly, the perspective changed: at the end of the seventeenth century, Cassini, making the calculation by different methods, found a nearly correct result, and put the Sun at a distance of 23,000 terrestrial radii, a figure which would have been unthinkable by astronomers fifty years earlier.

The assessment of interstellar space held many other surprises in store; there was a reluctance to acknowledge the existence of such abysses, and the absence of parallax in respect of the fixed stars was long considered to be a sound argument in favour of geocentrism. However, what frightened the geocentrists and troubled the heliocentrists themselves to the point of making them undecided in the face of the consequences of their own theory tallied on the other hand with the vision of a limitless firmament, populated and strewn with countless universes. Modern astronomy would probably have paid tribute to Giordano Bruno on this matter and recognized him as one of its forerunners. However, it has not done so, for one of the rules of positive science is to accept nothing that it has not observed or calculated. Now, that is the case with infinity. Bruno states the infinite as a fact, which is contradictory and, to many minds, absurd. The more and more distant worlds discovered or assumed by astronomers remain at measurable distances with respect to the eye of the observer: to express these distances, it is sufficient to change the unit of measurement, to go from the radius of the Earth to the radius of its orbit, then to the light-year and to the parsec; but we shall never see the term infinite distance introduced into a technical vocabulary, because infinity is properly *that which is not given*. As Galileo says on one admirable page of his *Discorsi*, any attempt to reach an infinite does not bring us closer, but takes us away from it: thus, progression in a series of numbers takes us away from unity. Thinking as a cosmologist rather than as a physicist, Bruno excludes himself from positive science and puts himself doubly in disagreement with it, seeing that by accepting the infinite he destroys the cosmos, that is to say, the ordered universe, to which seventeenth-century astronomy was still faithful to the extent, for example, that it refused (as did Galileo) to grant any non-circular motion the character of natural motion.

When he professes the infinitely great, Bruno contradicts Aristotle and—without the help of the least optical instrument—announces the discovery of worlds far remote from the Earth, but he is not in tune with the spirit of the new knowledge. Will he be content when he denies the infinitely small? Here, too, he opposed the teaching of Aristotelianism, and assigning a limit to the divisibility of matter, he seems to come close to Galileo, who also accepted *indivisibles*. However, that is only an illusion suggested by the use of similar terms coloured by different meanings. Bruno's atoms are the smallest bodies existing in nature, but they are, nevertheless, bodies having a certain form (that of a sphere) and a certain size. Bruno, like Pierre de la Ramée before him, draws an impassable frontier between mathematics and physics. Pierre de la Ramée wrote: 'Let the mathematicians have infinitely divisible magnitudes as their province, but let the physicists have nothing but what is finite and divisible in a finite manner.' Gassendi was close to this opinion. Nevertheless, in the case of these writers, the trouble taken to define two domains does not imply that one of them must be regarded as inferior, whereas in the case of Bruno, for whom mathematics is but useless dreaming, he reveals an atitude that is far more openly hostile to all mathematization of natural sciences.

In order to make the contradiction between the physics of Bruno and of Galileo more evident, we cannot choose a better example than their relative ideas concerning the ultimate elements of matter and the void by which they are necessarily surrounded. Galileo's 'indivisibles', the constituents of all material bodies, are *without magnitude*; they resemble geometrical points and like them are infinitely small, they merge together when in contact and consequently any conceivable number may be accumulated without ever occupying a measurable space; conversely, when they separate, the material body which they then constitute will not only have magnitude but also will occupy a measurable space, and will be able to dilate and distend itself as much as possible without ever reaching the limit of its possible distension. In this theory, the void is a necessary condition for magnitude. The ultimate elements as imagined by Bruno have, quite to the contrary, an inherent magnitude. It is obvious, therefore, that a fixed space will not be able to hold an infinite number of these elements. However close we assume them to be, *i.e.*, in contact, they will be extremely numerous on account of their extremely small size, but they will not be infinitely numerous. Consequently, if dilation of this compact mass takes place, its constituent elements will leave voids between them; at first, they will be very small, then they will become larger and larger as the dilation progresses. In this way the 'great voids' of interstellar space will appear, in which moreover, according to this hypothesis, there is always a rarefied air.

To account for the phenomena of contraction and expansion, both theories invoke the atom and the void, but, as we see, in a totally different manner. In fact, one depends on the science of Antiquity (definitely not Aristotelian, but Pythagorean), linked with rational quantities and discrete numbers; whereas the other states a new science which does not fear to represent physical phenomena by concepts of virtual infinity, of limits, and of the irrational.

Another essential feature of Brunonian atomism is that it lays down the substantial identity of matter as a principle: the ultimate elements of all bodies are identical in substance. This Democritean concept from Antiquity is one that was not retained in classical chemistry, which, as all historians of science since Lasswitz and Mabilleau have pointed out, owes nothing to the atomism of Bruno. Classical chemistry ignores it, or resolutely discards it, so as to link up with medieval alchemy and, more remotely, with Empedocles. It assumes that there is not one unique substance at the root of all compounds, but a plurality of *simple bodies*, more or less considerable in number. If, then, a property of compounds results from order and control, it resists any possible analysis in simple bodies: it appears on the atomic level. Gassendi went so far as to assume that qualitatively different atoms were the sub-strata of cold and heat, of the colours we see, of the odours we breathe, etc. Imbued with similar doctrines, Molière's learned ladies spoke of bourgeois atoms. Voltaire, in his *Dictionnaire philosophique* (article: *atome*), says that atomism makes water remain always water, meaning thereby that the smallest portion, the ultimate element of water, possesses the same properties. Voltaire did not doubt—and nobody did then—that water was a simple body; he deceived himself; but what is of importance here is the property of the ultimate element; furthermore, the time was near when Lavoisier would correct a common error by establishing a valid list of simple bodies besides a nomenclature which is still in use today. The fact that classical chemistry arrived at this nomenclature clearly shows the Bruno's rigorously Monist atomism did not exercise the least influence on its development.

A final example of the difference between Bruno's physics and the new knowledge will allow us to appreciate even better what separates them on the level of their principles and presuppositions. As we have seen, Bruno considers that the influence of the 'formal principle' is constantly exerted everywhere on 'passive' matter, in other words, that the soul is the source of all motion, whether it be in connection with living beings, atoms or celestial bodies. Nothing is farther from positive science and classical mechanics in particular. The latter, as Newton proclaimed, does not make hypotheses; it accepts motion as a fact, studies phenomena, establishes their regular succession, and deduces laws therefrom without attempting to go back to a 'first cause'; it abandons as far as possible problems whose solution would imply previous answers from a cosmology or a metaphysics. When Galileo, in the second dialogue of *Dialogo sopra i due massimi sistemi del mondo*, tackles the problem of falling bodies, Salviati (spokesman for the author) puts the question—to him insoluble—as to the cause of the movement of heavy bodies 'downwards', that is to say, towards the centre of the Earth. Simplicio, the naive and confirmed Aristotelian, who replies, expresses surprise that anyone could find any shadow of difficulty there. He considers that the matter is clear and the solution obvious: he says, 'Everybody knows that the cause of downward motion is gravity.' Salviati immediate replies: 'You are mistaken; you ought to have said that everyone knows *that it is called gravity.*' There is, then, a point where the explanation of the phenomenon fails, where it stops (at least provisionally) and in full consciousness is satisfied with a word. It is quite another matter if we speak of the 'formal principle' or of 'the soul of the universe', for these expressions do not refer, like the word 'gravity', to the pure and simple statement of the phenomenon; they introduce a fresh idea, they depend on a theory that claims to take account of the universe as a whole, from its origin to its end merged in God.

The nineteenth century. The industrial age appears: a new civilization comes into being in a fresh climate and its sudden triumph imposes a revision of all the earlier values.

At the beginning of this book we noted that Bruno's fortune—we called it 'his legend'—underwent notable changes during the nineteenth century, and in the long run, they were favourable. However, the question that we now put forward is whether 'Brunonian philosophy' will finally find some justification in present-day science, and some enlightened sympathy from the learned world.

Science, by which we mean the whole body of natural sciences, remained during the nineteenth century what it had become during the previous two centuries: it remained what we hesitate more and more to call 'modern' and what we would rather describe as 'classical', in contradistinction to the science of Antiquity and the Middle Ages on the one hand, and present-day science on the other. It remained unchanged without modifying its principles, and accomplished remarkable progress; its methods were more certain, its equipment was perfected, and in its practical applications it found a brilliant proof—which it justifiably believed to be decisive—of the truth of the fundamental axioms to which it faithfully adhered. Total abandonment of the science of Antiquity and termination of its final resistance crowned its conquests. The Church, finally following Galileo's good advice, ceased to take part in the disputes of astronomers; the condemnations were forgotten, some were expressly revoked: the *De revolutionibus orbium coelestium* of Copernicus, which had been on the *Index librorum prohibitorum* since 1616, was removed in 1822.

Did Bruno benefit from these tardy rehabilitations? In one sense, yes! as the emblem of liberty, the heroic defender of the rights of reason, he takes his place as one of the forerunners of modern thought. Nevertheless, most of them who praise him in this manner know little of his doctrines and do not properly understand in what way they are incompatible with the principles of the sciences as they were sub-sequently taught in schools, whereas educated man and historians of science are, on the other hand, struck by these incompatibilities, which have been recognized for a long while and which seem to have become greater and more irreducible with every fresh advance of knowledge. A follower of Galileo could still be grateful to the writer of *De immenso* for the attitude he adopted and stoutly defended against the supporters of geocentrism; but the twentieth century astronomer will hardly be interested in dead controversies; some problems have received a definitive solution; others no longer arise: they have ceased to be problems and now belong only to history, for which a rebellious, heterodox schoolman is still a schoolman in spite of all. Lasswitz, in an article on Bruno and atomism, gives a list of the latter's mistakes, and is very close to considering Bruno's inter-pretation of natural phenomena as the product of an imagination steeped in fable.[1]

The present time. Once again the scene changes, and work like that of Bruno's appears in a new perspective to contemporary eyes. This shift in the point of view operates on two distinct planes which are conveniently considered separately: they are that of the history of science and that of science itself.

Like the history of belles-lettres, art, philosophy and other branches of culture, the history of science started to lose at the beginning of the century (and it has now completely lost) the standardized character for which it had till then been almost con-strained to show a preference. The historian refrains more and more and as much as possible from judging old works: in particular he does not require them to conform to such rules as are prevalent in his own time and which he himself would be disposed to regard as being the best. Resolutely putting aside a preference that he knows to be a function of the period and place in which he lives, he betakes himself to the region in which the subject of his study is located and approaches this subject with favourable confidence. That is why we find ourselves taking part in unexpected rehabilitations whose benefit extends moreover to the Aristotelians just as much as to their opponents. We do not ask more from the *savant* or philosopher of former times than that which provided the interest and novelty of his work in his period, and paradoxically it is there that we seek proofs of its permanent worth. If, on certain matters, his opinions coincide with what later discoveries now allow us to regard as acquired truths, so much the better, but this very agreement is far from being the major pre-occupation of the most recent historians of doctrines. For example, not one of them would dream of comparing Bruno's physics or his description of the planetary system with the data of present-day physics or astronomy in order to point out his 'errors', as was still being done in the last century by a Lasswitz and even a Felice Tocco. In other words, the historian now keeps to the historical plane. This is the case, amongst others, with Vincenzo Magnano in his study on *Scotus Erigena and Giordano Bruno* (1907).[2] or Antonio Aliotta on the *Problem of the Infinite* (1911).[3] In addition, we may mention at random the following, for the choice increases with the passage of years; *La tradition de Buridan et la science italienne au XVIe siècle* by Pierre Duhem (1911),[4] *La pensée italienne et le courant libertin* by J. Roger Charbonnel (1919),[5] etc. These various works have this is common; they give evidence of the same abandonment of standardized criticism in favour of an examination of historical situations. They enable us to take part in the evolution of a problem without claiming to relate its successive solutions to a solution which is assumed to be correct and thereby established out of period.

This salutary respect for the contingencies of history must not, however, exclude all possibility for the historian of a scientific doctrine from comparing that doctrine with the most recent data of science and, let us not shrink from the word, with its most recent truths: for, without flattering ourselves, as was sometimes the case in a former over vain-glorious century, of putting the finishing touch to an edifice on unshakeable foundations, we are permitted to believe that we have just got over a stage on the path of knowledge, which like all the earlier ones has enabled us to acquire fresh concepts and more or less bold, general hypotheses, as well as some definite ideas, henceforth beyond dispute.

Now, one of the benefits of historical research is to have revealed amongst those thoughtful men, who remained on the fringe of science and were unknown to its normal progress, the long misunderstood talent for prophetic intuition. Because their theories did not take sufficient account of the best facts of their period, or because they were not capable of being incorporated in the great syntheses that immediately followed, they were soon regarded as aberrant and fell into a disfavour that could have been permanent. However, it happened that some of them came to light at a much later date, because they were strangely and unforeseeably located in a field of research, which had remained unnoticed but was suddenly explored: for example, figured numbers, polygons or polyhedra of the early Pythagoreans, which had been discarded by Euclid because they were unsuitable for accurate geometrical application, reappeared after two thousand years in the combinative analysis of Leibniz.

We can now resume a consideration from this point of view of some themes from Bruno's cosmology which we have compared with theorems in classical science.

As regards the infinitude of the universe, Bruno's position in respect of present-day astronomy remains the same as it was formerly. Seeing that the infinite cannot be subject to sentient perception (as Bruno himself was obliged to acknowledge) it remains excluded from the realm of experience, and the notion of infinity, given or realized, implies a contradiction that a rigorous mind always refuses to accept. That is a question of principle; but if we consider the results of observation of the skies and compare them with the intuitions in *De immenso*, we shall find that the differences between those dreams and results are of a quite different order in our century from what they were in the time of Galileo, when he discovered the satellites of Jupiter by means of his first telescope. In so far as it rejects the cosmic scheme of the Aristotelians, the new astronomy (that of the seventeenth-century) agrees in many particulars with Bruno's theses and brilliantly confirms what he devined or glimpsed.[6]

The crystalline spheres having been broken and a breach made in the ultimate firmament, there was no longer any obstacle to the distribution of the fixed stars throughout endless space, that is to say, indefinite, *virtually infinite* space. On the other hand, since the introduction of a fourth dimension into calculations, and seeing that the observable phenomena can no longer be explained without assuming a curvature of the rays of light in the space-time *continuum*, the universe is, as it were, closed upon itself; and here we seem to be further removed from Bruno's concepts than was classical astronomy. On the other hand, however, classical astronomy was still exploring only a relatively restricted zone of the depths of sidereal space, whereas the dimensions of the finite (though expanding) cosmos of present-day astrophysics are such that they seem to agree better, in their enormous field, with the 'unimaginable' abysses of the Brunonian universe.

If we pass from the largest to the smallest dimensions, we shall find that the latest advances in microphysics support Bruno, who rejects infinite divisibility, against classical physics, which was disposed to accept it, either because it assumed (with Descartes) matter to be continuous, or because it imagined (with Galileo) indivisibles 'without magnitude'. The peremptory demands of discontinuity, rationality and discrete numbers—a questionable survival of Pythagorism—could but seem antiquated and anti-scientific to any physicist making any pretensions of giving a mathematical interpretation to natural facts. A refusal to put any limit (at least theoretical) on divisibility was obligatory in classical science. This very firm position has, nevertheless, been upset: the limit that was but lately refused is now accepted; better still, it has been reached, and with the ultimate element of matter, not on the level of the atom but on the level of its constituent particles. That which for Bruno was only a mental view, a cosmic hypothesis comparable with those of the atomists in Greco-Latin Antiquity, has become the subject of calculation and experiment. It is not one of the least surprises for the historian of science to find the charge of inaccuracy rebound on the supporters of the infinitely divisible, a charge which the latter had so often hurled at their opponents. The whole number ceases to be the approximation of some irrational datum, it becomes the expression of a reality ignored by the classical physicist, and which, moreover, it is excusable to ignore. Physics, said Louis de Broglie, has worked for a long while as though matter were continuous, for *it is satisfied with approximate calculations*, and in a certain sense it has a perfect right to be indifferent to the question. Sciences such as hydrodynamics, the study of fluids, acoustics, the theory of elasticity 'reason as if matter were continuous, isolating in this continuum the elements of volume whose interaction with neighbouring elements of volume are calculated and to which the laws of mechanics are applied. Nevertheless, nothing prevents these methods from being reconciled with the hypothesis of an atomic structure of matter by assuming that the elements of volume under consideration, although they are very small, are already sufficiently large to contain an enormous number of molecules, and to possess the properties of matter taken in mass.'[7] In practice, we work on phenomena only of macroscopical dimensions and we may believe that everything happens as if the material realm on which we are working were continuous,[8] but in truth the laws drawn from our experiments 'are valid only for phenomena on a large scale';[9] and if we approach microphysics we must acknowledge the granular structure of matter. Arithmetic then has its revenge on geometry, that science of perfect forms but not of natural realities, which Bruno classes as chimeras or at least amongst the tricks of the imagination when he states, for example, that the boundary of the circle is traced only in our mind (*definit cyclum tantum mens*).

As for the substantial unity of matter, we have seen above that Bruno's theory according to which this unity is absolute—the ultimate elements being rigorously identical, not only of the same substance, but of the same size and shape—was in disagreement with classical chemistry, based on the distinction between a plurality of simple bodies. Now, on this matter also, the new physics (that of the present-day) has come close to the intuitions of Brunonian philosophy: it does not verify them exactly because it dissociates the atoms into a certain number of different particles, but it does admit they are right to a certain extent seeing that these particles are the same for all atoms and that the latter, in the last analysis, are defined by the number, arrangement and interaction of their constituents.

We come now to the final theme: the soul of the universe, panpsychism, the formal (or spiritual) principle, the prime cause of all motion. From the point of view of classical science, we have there the great scandal, as well as one of the main reasons why Bruno, excluded from the jealously upheld realms of technical astronomy and experimental physics, did not have, even on the morrow of his death, the distinction of being discussed before being classed until the close of the nineteenth century amongst useless dreamers.[10] The time has come to confront an animism, not long since rejected, by present-day science. We shall consider three aspects in turn: *a*) the influence of the spiritual principle on the ultimate elements; *b*) the characteristic of living beings ascribed to celestial bodies; *c*) the internal animation of all natural objects, summarised in the formula: nature operates from the centre (*la natura opra dal centro*).

a) The internal energy of the atom (a direct consequence of the soul's omnipresence) is incompatible with the law of inertia as stated by Galilean physics and which remained unshaken for three centuries. 'The dynamics of the material point starts from the principle of inertia according to which a material point that is not subjected to any external influence maintains the same state of motion (or of rest) throughout time.'[11] Those are the words of Louis de Broglie who then shows how the first thought of the physicist, after he has recognized the complexity of the atoms, must be to ascribe to their constituent elements the inertia of the classical atom. 'Electrons and protons have an extremely small mass, but nevertheless their mass is not zero, and an enormous number of protons and electrons would constitute a notable mass as a whole. It is, therefore, tempting to assume that all material bodies, essentially characterized by the fact that they are heavy and have inertia, *i.e.*, by their mass, are formed uniquely, in the last analysis, from an enormous number of protons and electrons.'[12] The downward path may be guessed; but the danger was avoided through the rapid advances of the new physics since the end of the nineteenth century. The first theory of electrons (up to about 1910) was inadequate to account for the properties of matter on the atomic scale, and considerable modifications were made, which made it necessary to accept the existence of radiation, the emission of energy, and to abandon at the same time, the stability of the atom. Subsequently, phenomena could no longer be explained, and experimental facts could no longer be understood, except by appealing to concepts very different from those of classical physics. The principle of inertia was valid only for phenomena on our scale, and matter, from the point of view of its ultimate elements, was reduced to energy, and matter was recognized as a storehouse of energy.[13] Certainly, Bruno could not go so far. It is none the less remarkable that he was so firmly committed in that direction, seeing that he was guided only by his intuition without the support of the least experiment.

b) In Bruno's mind, the life of celestial bodies is not a legend, a symbol or a metaphor, but one of the theorems of his physics and the fundamental axiom of his astrobiology.[14] The Earth, like the other celestial bodies, for it is one of them, lives and moves 'according to its own soul'. No doubt, the idea was not new, but in making it his very own, Bruno provided it with exact details whose obvious purpose is to show up its scientific character. That was enough to arouse suspicions. In the age of enlightenment, a page of poetry evoking the slumbers of the Earth, its rage and weariness might have been accepted and possibly admired, but how could anyone read without a smile an author who seriously compared earthly mishaps with the mishaps to our organism, to catarrh, and erysipelas? Yet now, since the work of Eugène Suess, we hear talk of the biosphere in terms that are strangely reminiscent of what we should but lately have taken for mythological fantasy. Everything living on the planet forms mass, definitely not like the parts of an articulated organism, but like a physical reality of an order apart, characterized by well defined specific properties. Pierre de Saint-Seine has said: 'The most positive science has recognized the necessity of resorting to this idea that Life and its major mutations are a function of physico-chemical conditions which control the evolution of the planet, that is to say, they can be defined only as properties of the Earth considered as a whole';[15] and Theilhard de Chardin says: 'Deep within itself, the living world is constituted by consciousness clothed in flesh and bone. From the Biosphere to the Species everything is only . . . an immense ramification of psychism seeking itself through forms.'[16]

c) ' *Deep within itself.* . . .' For a writer who says nothing without due consideration, these simple words must mean that the 'psychism which seeks itself' is not breathed into from without as was the spirit of the first man in old paintings representing the creation of Adam. Teilhard de Chardin designates it as *the Within*, an expression which he uses frequently and is related to certain expressions that we have met in Bruno's writings, and which seems to explain them. In specifying the modes of action of this *Within* on the object which it animates, Teilhard de Chardin writes: 'Essentially . . . *all energy is of a psychic nature*. But in each particular element . . . this fundamental energy is divided into two distinct components: a tangential energy which makes the element dependent on elements of the same order . . . as itself in the universe; and a radial energy which draws it in the direction of a state that is always more complex and centred, towards the front.'[17] We are earnestly told that this 'radial' energy (*i.e.*, coming from the centre) is the more essential of the two: 'What would . . . the mechanical energies themselves be without some Within to nourish them? . . . Beneath the *tangential*, the *radial*. The *impetus* of the universe, revealed by the great pressure of consciousness, can have its ultimate source . . . only in the existence of some principle within motion.'[18]

It would be easy to find several passages in *De la causa* which would convey remarkably the same effect as the sentences quoted above. The reader may find pleasure in seeking them for himself. It is enough that we have indicated some agreements between certain of Bruno's intuitions and certain results or reasoned hypothese of present-day science. Will those agreements be maintained with the science of tomorrow? We do not know. History pursues its course, and everyone of the facts which we regard as being most certainly established runs the risk of being contradicted at some time in the future.

NOTES

1. '*Giordano Bruno und die Atomistik*' in *Vierteljahrschrift für wissenschaftlicher Philosophie*. Leipzig, 1884.

2. *Scoto Erigene e Giordano Bruno*.

3. *Il problema dell'infinito*. This study of infinity in mathematics is preceded by a history of the problem.

4. Chapter VII: *Des progrès accomplis en la dynamique parisienne par les Italiens: Giordano Bruno*.

5. This work deals particularly with moral and religious problems. Nevertheless, Bruno's work is approached with cosmological bias in the chapter entitled: *Le nouveau système du monde et l'orientation immanentiste*.

6. See, for example, what is said about the lunar surface and its 'accidents' which should become visible when close to; Bruno in *De immenso*, IV, iii; and Galileo in *Dialogo sopra i due massimi sistemi del mondo*, First day.

7. Louis de Broglie, *La Physique nouvelle et les quanta*, Paris, 1937, p. 41.

8. *Ibid.*, p. 287.

9. *Ibid.*, p. 244.

10. We have mentioned that L. Mabilleau refused to give Bruno the character of atomic philosopher on account of his 'animism'. See above, p. 137.

11. L. de Broglie, *op. cit.*, p. 20.

12. *Ibid.*, p. 71.

13. *Ibid.*, p. 80.

14. See above, chapter IX.

15. '*La biosphère*', in *Études*, November 1948, p. 160.

16. *Le phénomène humain*, Paris, 1956, p. 165

17. *Ibid.*, p. 62.

18. *Ibid.*, p. 162.

Index of Names

Printed in Great Britain by
William Clowes & Sons, Limited
London, Beccles and Colchester